D0914111

The Letters

SPINOZA

The Letters

Translated by

SAMUEL SHIRLEY

Introduction and Notes by

Steven Barbone, Lee Rice, and Jacob Adler

Hackett Publishing Company, Inc.

Indianapolis/Cambridge

Baruch Spinoza: 1632 – 1677

Copyright © 1995 by Hackett Publishing Company, Inc.

00 99 98 97 96 95   1 2 3 4 5 6

For further information, please address

    Hackett Publishing Company, Inc.
    P.O. Box 44937
    Indianapolis, Indiana 46244-0937

Library of Congress Cataloguing-in-Publication Data
Spinoza, Benedictus de, 1632-1677.
    [Correspondence. English]
    The letters/translated by Samuel Shirley; introduction and
notes by Steven Barbone, Lee Rice, and Jacob Adler.
      p.   cm.
    Includes bibliographical references and indexes.
    ISBN 0-87220-275-5 (cloth)
    1. Spinoza, Benedictus de, 1632-1677 – Correspondence.
2. Philosophers – Netherlands – Correspondence. I. Shirley, Samuel,
1912- . II. Barbone, Steven. III. Rice, Lee, 1941- . IV. Adler,
Jacob. V. Title.
B3958.S45 1995
199´.492 – dc20   95-23700
                                                                                    CIP

Publication of this work was made possible in part by a grant from the
Division of Research Programs of the National Endowment for the
Humanities, an independent federal agency.

The paper used in this publication meets the minimum
requirements of American National Standard for Information Sciences – Permanence of Paper for Printed Library
Materials, ANSI Z39.48 – 1984.

CONTENTS

THE LETTERS OF SPINOZA

[Dates in braces are conjectural]

Translator's Preface

The text adopted for this translation is that of Gebhardt (1925), any deviation being signified in footnotes. In cases where the letters were originally written in Dutch, I have given primacy to the Dutch over the Latin, except where the original Dutch has been lost. My paragraphing is intended to ease the task of the reader.

No translator of the Letters can disregard the outstanding work of Wolf (1928), but I hope to have furnished a translation that stands on its own feet. Adhering as closely to the Latin or Dutch as is compatible with reasonable English idiom, I leave room for different glosses which scholars may put on the text. Footnotes to the text have been provided by Steven Barbone and Lee Rice.

I have followed for technical terms of Spinoza's philosophy the same translation practices as were utilized in my earlier translation of Spinoza's *Ethics* (2nd edition, Indianapolis: Hackett, 1992). A list of these terms, together with my reasons for selecting their English equivalents, is also given in this edition (pp. 21-29).

My chief debt is to Steven Barbone and Lee Rice, without whose encouragement and active help I could not have undertaken this work. Others who have kindly allowed me to consult them on various points are Father Roland Teske, S.J., Alan Gabbey, Wim Klever, Douglas Den Uyl, Pierre-François Moreau, and Jacob Adler.

Samuel Shirley
    Cornwall, England

Editors' Preface

The introduction which follows is intended to give the reader a basic picture of the topics covered in Spinoza's letters, the correspondents, and the historical context in which they were written. We have tried as much as possible, both in the text of the introduction and in the notes to it and to the individual letters, to avoid a particular interpretation of Spinoza's philosophical meaning where there remains controversy among scholars themselves. It is a particular strength of Shirley's translation that it remains neutral with respect to the interpretation of those passages which are crucial to one of a variety of different readings of Spinoza. Where a passage is controversial in its interpretation, where an historical reference is questionable, or where a variety of interpretations figure heavily in contemporary Spinoza research, we have made every effort to provide the reader with information on these in the footnotes and further references in the bibliography which follows the letters. In doing so we hope to have kept our introduction as brief as possible, in order to allow Spinoza and his correspondents to speak for themselves in the letters following.

Much the same strategy has been implemented for footnotes both to the introduction and to the individual letters. On matters of purely historical interest, we have followed the French edition of Meinsma unless otherwise indicated by explicit reference within a footnote. The more recent study of Piet Steenbakkers (1994) has also been most valuable in corrected and emending the notes to Meinsma. On matters of philosophical interpretation, in all cases we have tried to indicate central differences among interpretations and principal sources for these interpretations themselves.

The great strength of the forthcoming French edition of Spinoza (Latin with facing French) is the collective efforts of the many scholars making up the various teams devoted to different works and different problems. Even with the letters themselves, problems of text, interpretation, background, and reference are likely to exceed the working knowledge of any single scholar or translator. While the present translation has been the primary work of four persons, many others have contributed along the way. Accordingly, the number of persons to whom thanks are owed is extensive. The preliminary version of Shirley's translation was available to Barbone and Rice in 1992. Notes and preliminary versions of the introduction were prepared in 1993 and continued with Professor Adler through 1994 and 1995, while a complete review of the translation was under way. The collectivity of our effort is further reflected by its Anglo-American form: while retaining Shirley's English spelling and typographical conventions in the letters and in our notes to them, the co-editors have used American forms in the introductory material following. Comparisons to the excellent translations and commentaries of Domínguez (Spanish) and Appuhn (French) were also made. Steven Barbone contributed many insights from consultations with those working on the French edition, and a meeting in La Briantais in the spring of 1995 produced additional information and sources. For critique and suggestions relating to specific passages and sections of the introduction and the translation of the letters, we are also deeply indebted to Douglas Den Uyl (Louisville), Marjorie Grene (Blacksburg, Virginia), Wim Klever (Rotterdam), Pierre-François Moreau (Paris), Francis Pastijn (Milwaukee), Fr. Roland Teske, S.J. (Milwaukee), and Michael Wreen (Milwaukee). Deborah Wilkes (Hackett Publishing Company) contributed extensive editorial suggestions and patience. A research grant from Marquette University enabled extensive work by Lee Rice; and Fr. Thaddeus Burch, S.J., Dean of Marquette's Graduate School, supported a research grant which enabled us to have the valuable assistance of William Innis in completing the manuscript.

Steven Barbone
    Ecole Normale Supérieure de Fontenay-St Cloud
Lee Rice
    Marquette University
Jacob Adler
    University of Arkansas

Introduction
Spinoza's Correspondence and Spinoza's Correspondents

Steven Barbone
Jacob Adler
Lee Rice

1. The Correspondence and Its History

Benedict Spinoza died in the Hague on Sunday, 21 February 1677, at the home of his landlord and friend, Henryk Van der Spyck, at approximately three o'clock in the afternoon, while Van der Spyck and his wife were at church. Spinoza's close friend, Dr. Lodewijk Meyer,[1] was alone in attending him,[2] though his death, probably from tuberculosis, had been expected for some time. Meyer returned the following day to

---

1. Meyer (1630-1681), or Meijer, was born in Amsterdam and moved in Collegiant circles. He obtained his degrees (medicine and philosophy) at the University of Leiden in 1660 and probably also studied with Spinoza's friend and Latin teacher Franciscus Van den Enden. Meyer's doctoral thesis in philosophy was entitled *De materia, ejusque affectionibus motu, et quiete* ["On Matter, and its Affections Motion and Rest"] (Amsterdam: Francisci Hackii), reproduced in Latin, with French translation, in Renée Bouveresse, *Spinoza et Leibniz: l'idée d'animisme universel* (Paris: Vrin, 1992), 295-312. The medical thesis was *De calido nativo ejusque morbis* ["On Innate Heat and its Diseases"]: a copy exists in the Leiden University Library. He also published, anonymously in 1666, a treatise, *Philosophia interpres scripturae sanctae*, available also in French translation: *La philosophie l'interprète de l'écriture sainte*, tr. J. Lagrée et P.-F. Moreau (Paris: Intertextes Editeur, 1988). For information on Van den Enden, see Meinsma (1984), 252-253, 384-389; Wim Klever, "Proto-Spinoza Franciscus Van den Enden," *Studia Spinozana* 6 (1990), 281-290; and Wim Klever, "Spinoza and Van den Enden in Borch's Diary in 1661 and 1662," *Studia Spinozana* 5 (1989), 311-326. Meyer was also the editor of an influential dictionary, *Nederlandtsches Woorden-schat*, by Johan Hofman. This work went through many editions. In the 1669 and subsequent editions, it is called *L. Meijers Woordenschat* (Amsterdam: by de Wed. van Jan Hendriksz. Boom, 1969). The last edition is the twelfth (Dordrecht: Bluees, 1805).
2. Some scholars, notably Errol Harris, argue that it was Georg Schuller rather than Meyer who was present at Spinoza's death. We are following Meinsma here.

Amsterdam, leaving Spinoza's many friends in the Hague to attend to the funeral and the modest estate. The burial was held on Thursday, 25 February, at the Nieuwe Kirk. By the following Tuesday (2 March), Van der Spyck and several of Spinoza's friends had completed the inventory of his estate, except for the written works. The night before his death, Spinoza had given a box containing all of his writings and letters to Van der Spyck with instructions that, in the event of his death, they were to be sent to Jan Rieuwertsz, a bookseller and close friend of Spinoza in Amsterdam.[3]

During his lifetime, Spinoza published only two works: the *Principles of Cartesian Philosophy*, an unfinished commentary on Descartes's philosophy published under his own name, and the *Theologico-Political Treatise*, published anonymously.[4] Although Spinoza did explore the possibility of publishing his major philosophical work, the *Ethics*, in his lifetime, like many revolutionary thinkers of his time he decided to avoid both controversy and ecclesiastical censure by arranging posthumous publication of his principal works, and by circulating these same works privately among friends during his lifetime.

Rieuwertsz, having found himself so easily in possession of Spinoza's manuscripts, appears at first not to have known what to do with them. Gottfried Leibniz had visited Spinoza at an earlier date, and expressed interest in securing his *Ethics* in final form, and Rieuwertsz wrote to him at Hannover (where he was the librarian) to offer this manuscript for sale. On 29 March he again wrote to Leibniz and withdrew the offer. The inventory of works which he listed in that letter included:

1. The *Ethics*.
2. The *Treatise on the Reform of the Understanding*.
3. A manuscript on saltpeter (Letter VI).
4. The unfinished *Political Treatise*.
5. A variety of signed letters.

---

3. Details of their friendship are summarized in Wim Klever, "Letters to and from Neercassel about Spinoza and Rieuwertsz," *Studia Spinozana* 4 (1988), 329-340.
4. In what follows we use standard abbreviations for Spinoza's works: 'CM' for *Cogitata metaphysica*, 'E' for *Ethica*, 'KV' for *Korte Verhandeling*, 'PPC' for *Principia philosophiae cartesianae*, 'DIE' for *Tractatus de intellectus emendatione*, 'Ep' for the letters, 'TP' for *Tractatus politicus*, and 'TTP' for *Tractatus theologico-politicus*. References to E and PPC are internal: Def(inition), P(roposition), Dem(onstration), Schol(ium), Ax(iom), Cor(ollary), etc.

Spinoza's friends had in fact decided both to edit and to publish all of these works together. It is probable that Meyer was charged with the manuscript of the *Ethics*, Georg Schuller the remaining four manuscripts, and Johan Bouwmeester the text of another treatise, *The Compendium of Hebrew Grammar*. These works appeared later in the same year, 1677, in a volume simply entitled *Opera Posthuma*. In this edition, the correspondence included seventy-four letters (with an additional letter provided as an introduction to the *Political Treatise*).

There is no means of knowing the total number of letters which were originally in Rieuwertsz's possession, but we do know that there were many more than were printed. The omitted letters were destroyed for a variety of reasons. One of these was fear by the editors themselves of the Dutch authorities and Calvinist clergy (which explains also the omission of all the names of Spinoza's Dutch correspondents from the published letters). The separate title page of the *Correspondence* in the *Opera Posthuma* emphasizes the contribution which the letters are to make to the understanding of Spinoza's philosophy. It appears clear that the editors were uninterested in Spinoza's personal history or the biographical details thereof. Letters of purely personal interest were discarded as "of no importance,"[5] and the editors are also known to have deleted from those letters which were published passages which they deemed of only personal importance (e.g., the concluding paragraphs of Ep6). It was probably for the same reason that they did not include the *Apologia* or defense which Spinoza had written following his excommunication in 1656, nor the *Short Treatise* (*Korte Verhandeling*), probably written between 1656 and 1660,[6] both of which they regarded as only of personal interest, insofar as they had been superseded by the later works. Since the publication of the *Opera Posthuma*, other letters have been found; and it is reasonable to assume that still others may be found in the future. Of Spinoza's own letters, twelve are extant in autograph or in facsimile (Ep6, Ep9, Ep15, Ep23, Ep27, Ep28, Ep32, Ep43, Ep46, Ep49, Ep69, and Ep82).[7]

---

5. This is the phrase used by Rieuwertsz's son: see Freudenthal (1899), 267.
6. For information on these early writings and their probable history, see *Les premiers écrits de Spinoza*, Actes du colloque organisé par le Groupe de recherches spinozistes, *Revue des sciences philosophiques et théologiques* 71 (1987), reprinted in *Archives de philosophie* 51 (1988).
7. For further details on the *Opera Posthuma*, see F. Akkerman and H. G. Hubbeling, "The Preface to Spinoza's Posthumous Works," *Lias* 6 (1979), 103-173; F. Akkerman, *Studies in the Posthumous Works of Spinoza* (Groningen: Krisp Repro

The editors of the *Opera Posthuma* arranged the letters first by correspondent, then by chronology for each correspondent, and then they were numbered from I to LXXIV. When the editors Van Vloten and Land published their new edition of the *Opera Omnia* in 1882,[8] they rearranged the letters in chronological sequence and added nine additional letters which had been discovered after the printing of the *Opera Posthuma*. They also added the letter which had been used as a preface to the *Tractatus Politicus* which brought the number in their edition to eighty-four. The Van Vloten and Land numbering has been accepted as definitive in all subsequent editions. When Gebhardt prepared his critical edition,[9] two additional letters had been discovered; and these were numbered XLVIIA and LXVIIA, and subsequently discovered letters have been likewise intercalated into the Van Vloten and Land numbering sequence.

The *Opera Posthuma* was entirely in Latin. Since some of the letters had been originally written in Dutch, these were translated into Latin, sometimes by Spinoza, often by his friends or the editors; but, where a translation appeared, it was described as a *versio*. Later in 1677, however, a Dutch version of the *Opera Posthuma* (not including the *Compendium of Hebrew Grammar*) also appeared.[10] In this edition, all letters were in Dutch. Letters originally in Dutch were printed, and those written in Latin were translated. Also in some cases there are two Latin versions of the same letter: the original and an amended copy or first draft retained by Spinoza. Volume IV of the Heidelberg Academy edition contains all extant versions and information on the history of each version.

The Gebhardt (or Heidelberg Academy) edition, recognized as critical when published, has since been criticized for a variety of

---

Meppel, 1980); J. H. Leopold, *Ad Spinoza Opera Posthuma* (The Hague: Martinus Nijhoff, 1902); and Piet Steenbakkers, *Spinoza's Ethica from manuscript to print* (Assen: Van Gorcum, 1994).

8. J. Van Vloten and J. P. N. Land, ed. *Benedicti de Spinoza Opera Quotquot Reperta Sunt*, 4 vols. (The Hague: Nijhoff, 1882). This edition was reissued in 2 volumes in 1914. An earlier edition by Carolus Bruder was published in 1844 (Leipzig: Bernhardt Tauchnitz).

9. Carl Gebhardt, ed., *Opera, im Auftrag der Heidelberger Akademie der Wissenschaften*, 4 vols. (Heidelberg: Carl Winters Verlag, 1925). Gebhardt also translated the letters: *Spinozas Briefwechsel* (Leipzig: Felix Meiner, 1914).

10. *De Nagelate Schriften van B.d. S. Als Zedekunst, Staatkunde, Verbetering van't Verstant*, Amsterdam, [Jan Rieuwertsz], 1677.

reasons, and it is no longer regarded as definitive by the majority of scholars.[11] In 1985 the *Groupe de recherches spinozistes*, domiciled in St.-Cloud but with an international membership, began a new edition of all Spinoza's works, with facing French translations, taking advantage of the wealth of historical and textual research which has been done since Gebhardt.[12] This forthcoming edition may eliminate many of the editorial changes made by Gebhardt, since current research often favors the versions of the letters contained in the *Opera Posthuma* and often the versions of other works contained in the Van Vloten and Land edition.

A standard source of information on Spinoza's life and friends, and the historical circumstances under which his works (including the letters) were written, is K. O. Meinsma's *Spinoza en zijn Kring* ("Spinoza and His Circle").[13] A German translation appeared in 1904 and a French edition in 1983 (see citations in the bibliography). The latter contains very extensive and updated notes and appendices, which take into account the large body of research done since 1896. The page citations which follow are to this French edition, as are historical points not otherwise referenced. Other sources, especially the valuable work of Steenbakkers, are also listed in the bibliography, and are cited in notes where they correct or amplify the French edition of Meinsma. We follow Shirley's conventions for those Dutch names which are anglicized.

The letters of Spinoza were slow to reach anglophone readers, and the first complete translation appeared only in 1928.[14] The earlier Elwes edition of Spinoza's works contained only a selection of abridged

---

11. Its limitations and problems are summarized (with additional references) by F. Akkerman in "L'édition de Gebhardt de l'*Ethique* de Spinoza et ses sources," *Raison présente* 43 (1977), 37-51.
12. Piet Steenbakkers is currently active in the editorial project. See his "La nouvelle édition critique du texte latin de l'*Ethique*," in *Travaux et documents 2: Méthode et métaphysique*, ed. Groupe de recherches spinozistes (Paris: Presses Universitaires de France, 1989; 105-120); *Opera minora van Spinoza: Een bespreking an aantekeningen* (Amsterdam: Richard Tummers Boekverkoper, 1988); "Lodewijk Meyer's Catalogue of Passions (1670): Between Descartes and Spinoza," in Volume 3 of "Spinoza by 2000, The Jerusalem Conferences" (Leiden: E. J. Brill, 1996); and *Spinoza's Ethica from manuscript to print* (Assen: Van Gorcum, 1994).
13. The Hague: Marinus Nijhoff, 1896.
14. A. Wolf, tr. and ed. *The Correspondence of Spinoza* (London: Frank Cass, 1928). A reprint of this edition appeared in 1966.

letters in translation.[15] A complete French edition had appeared much earlier.[16] Of contemporary translations into other languages, two are particularly reliable, and have been utilized by us in the final stages of editorial work on the present translation: the French edition of *La Pléiade*[17] and the Spanish edition by Atilano Domínguez.[18]

A new critical edition of the letters, including those discovered since the Gebhardt edition and perhaps additional letters which may turn up in the future, will doubtless appear as part of the ongoing French project of re-editing the complete corpus of Spinoza's writings, but it is likely to be among the last works produced in this project.[19] The present translation is based largely on Gebhardt, but takes into account the more recently discovered letters and additional critical work published through 1995. Shirley's translation is both readable and accurate. Readers undertaking research on Spinoza's philosophy or philosophical development will want to consult both the Latin (and/or Dutch) texts and variants as well as the developing literature, much of which is cited in our introduction (and, to a more limited extent, in footnotes to the letters themselves). For readers seeking a general understanding of the *Ethics* or political writings through the letters, or an understanding of the historical context in which Spinoza's thought developed, we believe that the present translation and edition are optimal. In the following sections of our introduction, we undertake a thematic approach to the letters in order to provide necessary background on the correspondents themselves and their philosophical interests.

Introductions written by philosophers to the works of a philosopher, despite their historical and critical goals, are inevitably philosophical themselves, and there are many elements of Spinoza's philosophy about which competing interpretations are still being argued and researched. The authors of this introduction, being both philosophers and

---

15. R. H. M. Elwes, ed. and tr. *Spinoza's Chief Works*, 2 vols. (London: Bohn, 1883-84).

16. Emile Saisset, ed. and tr. *Oeuvres de Spinoza*, 3 vols. (Paris: Charpentier, 1872).

17. Benoît Spinoza, *Oeuvres complètes*, texte traduit, présenté, et annoté par R. Caillois, M. Francès, et R. Misrahi (Paris: Gallimard, 1954). The translation and notes for the letters (pp. 1048-1525) are by Robert Misrahi.

18. *Correspondancia* (Madrid: Allianza Editorial, 1988).

19. See F. Akkerman, "Vers une meilleure édition de la correspondance de Spinoza," *Revue internationale de philosophie* 31 (1977), 4-26.

Spinozists, have their own reading and assessment of these interpretations, which will naturally color the weighting and order of what follows, but which, like any interpretation, is open to challenge and improvement. In what follows, where a particular issue about which there remains extensive philosophical disagreement is raised, we have made every effort to provide the reader (usually in footnotes) with a perspective on other and different interpretations and their central loci in the secondary literature.

2. Philosophy and Nature:
The Oldenburg Correspondence

Henry (Heinrich) Oldenburg was born about 1620 in Bremen, where his father, also Henry Oldenburg, had been a professor of philosophy since 1610. His father died in 1634, and the younger Oldenburg remained in Bremen where he pursued studies in theology. On 2 November 1639 he received the degree of Master in Theology after successfully defending a thesis entitled *De ministerio ecclesiastico et magistratu politico*. Shortly thereafter he left his native country for England where he remained until 1648. In 1648 he appears to have undertaken extensive travel in Europe, returning to Bremen about 1652. The following year the Council of Bremen sent Oldenburg to negotiate with Cromwell for the neutrality of Bremen during the war between England and Holland. He remained in England and engaged in both diplomatic work and teaching. His political activities put him into contact with the poet John Milton (then Cromwell's Latin Secretary); the details of their continued friendship are documented in a series of extant letters between them.

During the mid-1650s Oldenburg also became an acquaintance of Thomas Hobbes. Oldenburg was registered in 1656 as a student at Oxford, where he made the acquaintance of Richard Jones, the nephew of Robert Boyle. In 1657 he and Jones undertook an extended voyage through Europe, spending time in France, Italy, Germany, and the Netherlands. The letters from Oldenburg to Boyle from this period indicate that he had acquired a lively interest in physics, and during his travels he came into contact also with Christiaan Huygens. Correspondence with Milton in 1659 indicates that Oldenburg was fearful that the monarchy would be restored in England.

In 1661 Oldenburg was in Leiden visiting with his friend, Johannes Coccejus, professor of theology, and it was apparently through him that he became aware of the young philosopher Spinoza, who was living then at nearby Rijnsburg. The details of his travels in Holland are obscure, but he did spend some time with Spinoza and also visited Huygens at least once. His first letter to Spinoza (Ep1) was sent in August of 1661 from London and indicates that the young philosopher had made a strong impression upon him. It was during this period also that he became involved with the group of philosophers and scientists which was to form the nucleus of the Royal Society. When this Society was incorporated in 1662, Oldenburg was appointed joint-secretary, and he at once set about to establish correspondents for it throughout Europe.

The period from 1661 to 1665 includes an extended correspondence with Spinoza and marks a continued effort on Oldenburg's part to obtain a full understanding of Spinoza's philosophy. Spinoza's reply to Oldenburg's offer to initiate an exchange of letters (Ep2, dated September of 1661 and sent from Rijnsburg) reveals both the enthusiasm generated by their earlier meeting and his respect and affection for his correspondent. Hampered in part by his theological inclinations and also by his lack of formal training in philosophy, Oldenburg was never to achieve this goal of a deep understanding of Spinoza's philosophy. Spinoza's patient and detailed replies to his queries, often elaborated with examples, make this block of correspondence extremely valuable for understanding the more complex sections of the *Ethics*. Meinsma's remark on this count is worth quoting:

> What he lacked in understanding was made up for by Oldenburg with friendship and moderation. At no time did he forget the respect which the mind and character of his friend had inspired, never did he become sidetracked on the false routes pursued by the vociferous and the fanatics who hatefully assaulted the philosopher, whom they in no way understood, treating him as an anti-christ and as an apostle of disbelief. [Meinsma 465, translation ours]

Despite their continual disagreements and misunderstandings in matters of philosophy and of physics, the two thinkers retained both respect and deep friendship for one another throughout their many exchanges. The first four letters (Ep1-4), dated 1661, deal with general questions of philosophical method, and probably relate directly to the conversations between them during Oldenburg's visit.

In October of 1661 Oldenburg sent Spinoza Boyle's treatise on nitre,[20] with a request, made on behalf of Boyle, for comments and criticism. Spinoza's reply (Ep6, dated 1662) is one of the longest in his entire correspondence and was preserved in its entirety in the archives of the Royal Society. It provides detailed annotations on particular aspects of Boyle's experiments, as well as a general critique of Boyle's corpuscular philosophy.

In his experiment on the reconstitution ('redintegration') of nitre, Boyle added live coals to a crucible of nitre to kindle it. He then heated the mixture to eliminate the 'volatile parts', and divided the remaining 'fixed nitre' into two parts. Having dissolved the first part in water, he added 'spirit of nitre', which was added to the second part without first dissolving it in water. Both solutions were set near a window to evaporate, and both eventually yielded nitre crystals. Boyle's objective here was twofold. First, he wanted to disconfirm the scholastic theory of substantial forms, and secondly he wanted to demonstrate that secondary qualities are caused by primary qualities. Boyle's nitre was probably potassium nitrate, his fixed nitre potassium carbonate, and the spirit of nitre may have been citric acid, though it is unlikely that he (or Spinoza) were dealing with pure substances which we can now identify. Neither Spinoza nor Boyle realized the significance of the carbon in the chemical reaction.

In his experiment dealing with fluidity Boyle is opposing the Epicureans, for whom smoothness was determined by roundness of atoms. He offered instead three hypotheses to account for smoothness: (1) the small size of particles, (2) empty space or 'vacuum' between them, or (3) the movement of component particles. He argues that both shape and size may hinder the fluidity of a body, and expresses doubt about the Cartesian 'first matter'. The critique of Epicurean atomism was continued in a section, "On Solidity," with a series of experiments wherein Boyle took two pieces of marble moistened with wine to prevent air from separating them, and attached one to a scale. The intent was to suggest that air pressure may account for the cohesiveness of smooth bodies.

Spinoza's detailed critique is aimed both at Boyle's methodology and at specific aspects of the experiments. Oldenburg offered a brief

---

20. *De nitro, fluiditate et firmitate* ["On Nitre, Fluidity, and Firmness"]. This work was not among the works catalogued in Spinoza's library after his death.

reply in Ep7 and sent more detailed comments on Boyle's behalf in 1663 (Ep11). Ep13, Spinoza's reply, continues the debate on the homogeneity versus heterogeneity of nitre (Boyle defending the latter, Spinoza arguing against the decisiveness of his evidence) and the place of experimentation in the scientific method.[21] In Ep13 Spinoza mentions also the origin of his unfinished *Principles of Descartes' Philosophy* (PPC), dictated to a student (probably Caesarius) and sent to press by a group of friends. One of these friends was Lodewijk Meyer, who wrote the preface to the published work.[22]

Ep14 and Ep16 continue the dialogue on scientific method and take up also the question of the void or the existence of a vacuum in nature, topics to which both men returned (Ep25-26) in 1665 after a break of two years. Oldenburg's interest (Ep 29) has now extended to optics, recent works of Huygens on motion, comets and the nature of sound (Ep31). Spinoza also indicates (Ep30) that he is beginning work on the *Tractatus theologico-politicus* (TTP).

The closing exchange between the two men in 1665 (Ep32-33) follows on a remark which Spinoza made earlier (Ep30) on the status of human beings as parts of nature which accord with the whole. In reply to a request for elaboration, Spinoza provides in Ep32 an extensive discussion of the individuation of particular bodies in nature with the celebrated example of the "worm in the bloodstream."[23] This letter

---

21. For a detailed analysis of Spinoza's disagreement with Boyle on the nature of the experimental method, see Richard McKeon, *The Philosophy of Spinoza* (New York: Longmans, Green, & Co., 1928), ch. 6, "Spinoza and Experimental Science," 130-157. See also D. Parrochia, "Les modèles scientifiques de la pensée de Spinoza," in *Travaux et documents 2: Méthode et métaphysique*, ed. Groupe de Recherches Spinozistes (Paris: Presses Universitaires de France, 1989). 47-66; and Christopher E. Lewis, "Baruch Spinoza, A Critic of Robert Boyle: On Matter," *Dialogue* (PST) 27 (1984), 11-22.

22. A readable translation is that of Halbert H. Britan: Benedictus De Spinoza, *The Principles of Descartes' Philosophy* (La Salle: Open Court, 1905). A more recent translation appears in the first volume of Curley's edition. The most extensive commentary on this work is that of André Lécrivain, "Spinoza et la physique cartésienne," *Cahiers Spinoza* 1 (1977), 235-266; 2 (1978), 93-206. A more recent anthology contains articles dealing not only with the Boyle correspondence and the PPC, but also Spinoza's subsequent development, including the correspondence with Tschirnhaus. See Marjorie Grene and Debra Nails, ed., *Spinoza and the Sciences* (Dordrecht: Reidel, 1986).

23. For a detailed analysis of Ep32 and its relation to parallel discussions in the *Ethics*, see Lee Rice, "Spinoza on Individuation," *The Monist* 55 (1971), 640-659 [reprinted in *Spinoza: Essays in Interpretation*, ed. M. Mandelbaum and E. Freeman (La Salle: Open Court, 1975)]; William Sacksteder, "Spinoza on Part and Whole: The Worm's Eye View," *Southwestern Journal of Philosophy* 8 (1977), 139-159; and François Zourabichvili, "L'identité individuelle chez Spinoza," in

provides invaluable commentary on the axioms and lemmata following Proposition 13 of *Ethics* Part 2, and the direction in which Spinoza is moving, not just in physical theory, but in the development of a psychology of the individual person.[24] Ep33 is the last letter before a break of thirteen years in the correspondence with Oldenburg. The year 1665 marked the onset of the plague in London, and also the beginning of the war (1665-1667) with Holland, with the great fire occurring the following year. In such times of social and political upheaval, Oldenburg's extensive foreign correspondence inevitably incurred distrust among politicians, including the king himself, who was too involved in political intrigues to be able to avoid distrusting others. In June of 1667, Oldenburg was imprisoned in the Tower of London where his two-month stay was ended by the close of the war. He emerged a more cautious, and perhaps somewhat embittered, man. During the ensuing years, he also became theologically and politically more conservative, perhaps under the influence of Robert Boyle's particular species of religious conservativism. His correspondence with Spinoza resumed (Ep61) in 1675, and will be taken up in part VI in connection with Spinoza's political writings.

Spinoza: Puissance et ontologie, ed. Myriam Revault d'Allonnes and Hadi Rizk (Paris: Editions Kimé, 1994), 85-107.

24. See Hans Jonas, "Spinoza and the Theory of Organism," *Journal of the History of Philosophy* 3 (1973), 259-278. Vol. 8 (1992) of *Studia Spinozana* is also devoted to Spinoza's psychology and contains several articles dealing with individuation.

3. Spinoza to Friends and Students

[Simon de Vries, Lodewijk Meyer, Pieter Balling, Johan Bouwmeester, Jarig Jelles]

After his excommunication from the Jewish community in Amsterdam in July of 1656,[25] it was only natural that Spinoza should begin to move in ever wider Christian circles to maintain ties with intellectual society. Though he is believed to have been already proficient in Dutch, Hebrew, Spanish, and Portuguese, he was not yet expert in Latin or Greek. Franciscus Van den Enden, an ex-Jesuit, met and apparently was impressed by the learning of the young man, for he offered to take him into his school where Spinoza would improve his Latin in return for teaching some classes. It was at Van den Enden's school that a small circle of friends, bonded together by common philosophical interests, formed and became centered around Spinoza. Spinoza probably took a regular part in these friendly gatherings which continued until he left the school and moved to Rijnsburg in 1662 or 1663.[26] The distance did not keep the friends entirely separated, for a group of

---

25. Much remains uncertain about the circumstances of the excommunication, and even the motives. For an historical summary and commentary, see Gabriel Albiac, *La synagogue vide: Les sources marranes du spinozisme,* tr. Marie-Lucie Copete and Jean-Frédéric Schaub (Paris: Presses Universitaires de France, 1994), 13-44.

26. For Van den Enden and his circle in general, see four studies by Marc Bedjai: *Le docteur Franciscus van den Enden, son cercle et l'alchimie dans les Provinces-Unies au XVIIe siècle* (Paris: République des Lettres, 1991; Vol. 2 of *Nouvelles de la République des Lettres*); "Franciscus van den Enden, maître spirituel de Spinoza," *Revue de l'Histoire des Religions* 207 (1990), 289-311; "Métaphysique, éthique et politiques dans l'oeuvre du docteur Franciscus van den Enden (1602-1674)," *Studia Spinozana* 6 (1990), 291-302; and "Métaphysique, éthique et politique dans l'oeuvre du Dr Franciscus van den Enden," *Aries* 12-13 (1991), 116-120. Wim Klever has written three studies on the relation between Spinoza's philosophical development and Van den Enden: "Spinoza and Van den Enden in Borch's Diary in 1661 and 1662," *Studia Spinozana* 5 (1989), 311-326; "Proto-Spinoza Franciscus van den Enden," *Studia Spinozana* 6 (1990), 281-290; and "A New Source of Spinozism: Franciscus van den Enden," *Journal of the History of Philosophy* 29 (1991), 613-631. See also Omero Proietti, "Le Philedonius de Franciscus van den Enden et la formation rhétorico-littéraire de Spinoza (1656-1658)," *Cahiers Spinoza* 6 (1991), 9-82.

Collegiants were known to travel to and from Amsterdam and Rijnsburg, and presumably Spinoza met with some of them in that village. His absence from Amsterdam still did not end the meetings there; instead, the friends continued meeting and discussing Spinoza's philosophy (see Ep8). His closest connections were apparently with members of the Christian group known as Collegiants (see Section 8 below). When questions arose, one member of the group would write to ask for clarification on a specific point. Because of this, the correspondence is invaluable since it often can be used for the understanding of the more difficult passages of the PPC and the first parts of the *Ethics*. Also, just as the correspondence between Spinoza and Oldenburg shows Spinoza's patience and gentleness, so too the correspondence between Spinoza and this circle of friends reveals to us a very human man who loved and was loved by his friends (see especially Ep28).

We turn now to those friends and the particular concerns which interested them. Simon Joosten de Vries[27] (1633/4-1667) was an Amsterdam merchant and is believed to have belonged to the Mennonite sect. Colerus relates that de Vries had once offered Spinoza two thousand florins so that the philosopher might live more comfortably, but he politely declined, claiming that he preferred a more simple and modest lifestyle. We also believe that de Vries had wanted to name Spinoza as his sole heir, but that Spinoza was able to convince him that it would be both unnatural and unethical for de Vries to do so as he did have a brother (Simon de Vries was unmarried and without children); instead Spinoza agreed to accept a small annuity from the de Vries estate, but later had the amount reduced from five hundred to three hundred florins.

Lodewijk Meyer[28] was also among this group of friends. He was very interested in the theater and served as director for the Municipal

---

27. For more information on de Vries, see A. M. Vaz Dias and W. G. van der Tak, *Spinoza and Simon Joosten de Vries. Jelles' Origins, Life, and Business* (Leiden: Brill, 1989).

28. See the opening section for more details on Meyer, and also C. L. Thijssen-Schoute, *Lodewijk Meyer en diens verhouding tot Descartes en Spinoza* (Leiden: Brill, 1954); and Piet Steenbakkers, *Spinoza's Ethica from manuscript to print* (Assen: Van Gorcum, 1994), 17-35. Steenbakkers provides the most extensive and accurate summary of our knowledge to date of Meyer's editorial contributions to the O.P.

Theater of Amsterdam. He also had somewhat of a flair as a poet. Other than Spinoza, he counted among his best friends Johan Bouwmeester (1630-1680), who also was a member of the philosophical discussion group formed at Van den Enden's school. Like Meyer, Bouwmeester had many interests. He pursued medicine, language, physics, alchemy, chemistry, geology, geography, and, also like Meyer, theater and poetry. Again like Meyer, he was a medical doctor, having completed his thesis in 1658 at Leiden, and he too at one time directed the Municipal Theater. These two friends have made lasting contributions to Spinoza's corpus of writings: Meyer wrote the preface and oversaw the publication of the PPC for Spinoza in 1663, and Bouwmeester is thought to be the author of the short poem which precedes it.[29] Spinoza's remarks to Bouwmeester concerning method in Ep37 have also been connected in theme and content to Spinoza's early and unfinished work, the *Treatise on the Improvement of the Intellect*.[30]

Pieter Balling (?-1669), though a member of this group of friends, was not thought to have been a Collegiant, though he did belong to the Mennonite sect and was heavily influenced by Spinoza in his theology.[31] Because of his work as a mercantile agent, he had business associations with several Spanish companies; that he was able to converse with Spinoza in that language is thought to be one reason for their close friendship. He is usually given credit for writing and publishing the first Spinozistic work, *Het Licht op den Kandelaar* ["The Light of the Candlestick"] in 1662, a treatise not so much on light as it is a philosophical text reflecting Spinoza's ideas.[32] The second edition (1684) was published under his name by Rieuwertsz. In 1664 he translated the PPC into Dutch. It was the untimely death of his son in that same year that

---

29. The authorship of that poem has been contested. Many attribute it to Jan Bresser, but both Meinsma (276) and Wolf (1928, 51) give reasons for giving Bouwmeester credit.
30. See Theo Zweerman, *L'introduction à la philosophie selon Spinoza: Une analyse structurelle de l'Introduction du Traité de la Réforme de l'Entendement suivie d'un commentaire de ce texte* (Assen: Van Gorcum, 1993), 22-33.
31. See two studies by Wim Klever: "De spinozstische prediking van Peter Balling," *Doopsgezinde Bijdragen* 14 (1988), 55-85; and "Spinoza's *Hebrew Grammar* praised by Petrus van Balen," *Studia Spinozana* 5 (1989), 365-368.
32. The work was taken by some for a Quaker work, and an English translation was published as an appendix to Willem Sewel's *History of the Rise, Increase, and Progress of the Quakers*. The Dutch original, edited by Carl Gebhardt, was reprinted in *Chronicon Spinozanum* IV (1924-1926).

occasioned his correspondence with Spinoza (see Ep17), and this letter, discussed more fully below, reveals what might be termed as a "paternal" concern Spinoza shows for his friends as he demonstrates an emotional side which does not contradict his philosophical nature and consoles while yet instructing and bringing his friend to greater understanding.

The last friend represented in this group is Jarig Jelles[33] (1619/20?-1683), who like Balling is not thought to have been a Collegiant, though he too was a member of the Mennonite sect. He was a very successful merchant of spices, but in 1653 he decided to devote himself to philosophical studies. Jelles helped persuade Spinoza to write and to publish the PPC, and he helped to finance in its publication. After the TTP appeared, Wolf reports that it was he who instigated its translation into Dutch by Jan H. Glazemaker.[34] It was also he to whom Spinoza wrote in 1671 (Ep44) to ask for his help in repressing the publication of that translation. Spinoza thought that once the book was read by the public at large, both it and the Latin original would be banned. Jelles was able to honor the request, and the Dutch version did not appear until after Spinoza's (and Jelles's) death in 1693. Along with Meyer and some others, Jelles was responsible for the publication of the *Opera posthuma*, and he is believed to have written the preface for this work. His *Confession of Faith*,[35] which was written either to stave off accusations of heresy or to request reactions from friends, was reviewed by Spinoza (see Ep48a, Ep48b), who found it either wanting or adequate (depending on which fragment one reads). It was published a year after his (Jelles's) death.[36] That he was well advanced in his love for God and men is evidenced, some believe, because in his preface to the *Opera posthuma*, he never once alludes to Spinoza's Jewish origin.[37]

---

33. Jelles was also the author of the preface to the *Opera Posthuma*. See F. Akkerman and H. G. Hubbeling, "The Preface to Spinoza's Posthumous Works 1677, and its Author Jarig Jelles (c. 1619/20-1683)," *Lias* 6 (1979), 103-173.
34. See Wolf (1928), 52. The sources and history of these and other editions and translations is studied in detail by F. Akkerman in *Studies in the Posthumous Works of Spinoza* (Groningen: Groningen University Press, 1980).
35. See our notes and bibliographical references to Ep48a and Ep48b.
36. Jarig Jelles, *Belydenisse der algemeenen en Christelyken geloofs, vervaltet in een brief aan N. N., door Jarig Jelles* (Amsterdam: Jan Rieuwertsz, 1684).
37. Wolf (1928), 53. Although a philosopher's ethnic or religious background may seem unimportant to us in this century, it is noteworthy that Jelles does omit this information about Spinoza. Was it that Jelles purposely left out this fact so as not to prejudice his readers, or was it that it never occurred to him to include it, since he presumably cared for Spinoza the man/philosopher and not Spinoza the Jew?

Overall, with the exception of the Jelles correspondence, most of the correspondence within this grouping occur rather early on and then seem to drop off. While it is true that many of the letters were destroyed by the editors of the *Opera posthuma* because the editors thought that they contained little of philosophic interest or that the letters could possibly bring troubles from the ecclesiastical or public authorities, we assume the frequency of exchanges included in the *Opera* to be an accurate gauge of Spinoza's philosophical correspondence. Rather than an indication that Spinoza's friends forgot or were forgotten by him, we prefer to understand that the group, for various reasons, began to drift apart from the former philosophical interests which previously bound them together. Certainly Spinoza's departure and then the early deaths of de Vries and Balling may account for some of the waning interest.[38] Meyer and Bouwmeester's lively attentions to theater and poetry also left these two with less time for philosophical studies. Jelles, though he continued to attend to philosophy, seemed to grow more interested in religion, and so he, too, might have found less occasion to correspond with Spinoza. We maintain, nevertheless, that this circle of friends was a major source of joy for Spinoza, and that their correspondence provides invaluable and reliable insights into Spinoza the man and his philosophy. It is these philosophical points to which we now turn.

As the letters themselves are often a mixture of varied concerns and topics, we will not treat them here in their numeric order, but instead we will deal with them in topical groups each of which sheds some light upon an important but relatively distinct cluster of issues. We begin with the first question raised by the first letter – definition (see Ep8, Ep9) – and note that problems with definition are a common theme running through much of this correspondence. What Spinoza attempts to clarify for his friends is the difference between stipulative and explicative definitions.[39] This latter type of definition points

---

38. Wolf (1928) lists additional reasons for the small amount of correspondence between the years 1667-1670 (see 435).
39. The nature of definition in Spinoza and its relation to the geometrical method as he conceived it has roots in Hobbes. Gueroult's monumental two-volume commentary on the first two parts of the *Ethics* deals with this issue most extensively. See Martial Gueroult, *Spinoza: Dieu (Ethique, 1)* (Paris: Aubier, 1968), 19-84. See also, by the same author, *Spinoza: L'âme (Ethique, 2)* (Hildesheim: Georg Olms Verlag, 1974).

to an object and concerns the essence of that object; thus this type of definition must be true in order for it to be a good definition. Stipulative definitions, on the other hand, need not be true since they explain a thing only as it is conceived by the imagination. Thus, to use one of Spinoza's examples, a "good" (explicative) definition of Solomon's Temple would be an accurate description of it while a "bad" definition might be a description of how something I might build and call "Solomon's Temple" might be achieved. Likewise, a "good" stipulative definition is one which, as Lewis Carroll's Humpty Dumpty would say, "means just what I choose it to mean – neither more nor less"; and so, to return to Spinoza, Borelli's "figural" could be a good definition depending upon what is stipulated by "straight line". Spinoza suggests that it is because people are not always rigorous enough in distinguishing the type of definition used that they often run into trouble with their concepts. In fact, regarding the idea of infinity, Spinoza writes, "I repeat, if men had paid careful attention to these distinctions, they never would have found themselves overwhelmed by such a throng of difficulties" (Ep12).

The subject of infinity naturally leads to another concern for Spinoza's friends: What is substance? On this question, the correspondence helps clarify many points in the *Ethics* which confused Spinoza's readers. Ep12 tells us again that "existence pertains to its [substance's] existence" (see E1P7) and that "no Substance can be conceived as other than infinite" (see E1P8). Thus the explicative (and stipulative, for Spinoza) definition of substance involves infinite existence.[40] The definition of modes, on the other hand, does not include necessary nor infinite existence; modes are those particular things which we sense and experience. It is in this way that substance as an infinite whole is grasped by the intellect and cannot be known by experience while individual modes must be known through experience since their definitions do not entail existence (see Ep10).[41] A major point of Ep9 and Ep12 is that while infinite substance contains all the modes that there are, substance is *not* divisible into parts; that is, no mode is a "part" of substance – a mode is merely a particular affection of substance. Thus,

---

40. Or 'eternal existence', the phrase most often employed by Spinoza.
41. For more detailed analysis of the de Vries correspondence in general, see Lydia Trompeter, "Spinoza: A Response to de Vries," *Canadian Journal of Philosophy* 11 (1981), 525-538.

that which is infinite in its essence (i.e., substance) is non-divisible, eternal, and conceived only though the intellect; finite modes, however, are perceived through the imagination, have duration, and may be divided (by imagination) into parts. Measure, time, and number, therefore, are particular modes of the imagination and so are finite.[42]

This should help to elucidate de Vries' question concerning thought and idea in Ep8 and Spinoza's response in Ep9. De Vries and his companions have confused the whole and the sum of its supposed parts and the attribute of thought with its modes. They wonder how it is that they may conceive of infinite intellect under the attribute of thought and also conceive it as made up of ideas. What they have done, Spinoza explains, is to have imagined that the infinite whole, thought, to be composed of finite parts, ideas. Here the particular ideas are modes of the attribute thought which truly is infinite as conceived in itself by the intellect. So though the infinite intellect consists of all these ideas, it consists of all the ideas *together*, not of all the ideas imagined separately. Spinoza reminds de Vries that intellect, "although infinite, belongs to Natura naturata, not to Natura naturans."[43]

The difference, too, between the intellect and the imagination is stressed in several of these letters. Ep37 to Bouwmeester suggests that all clear and distinct ideas arise only from other clear and distinct ideas, and not from any other cause. Thus the intellect, if it should have any true and adequate idea, must get this idea through its own powers and not from any external source. The imagination, however, often has faulty or inadequate conceptions of things. The intellect, therefore,

---

42. Ep12, the so-called "Letter on the Infinite," has generated a wealth of commentary. The most extensive treatment is in Gueroult (1968), 500-528. Gueroult's interpretation of the distinctions made by Spinoza for kinds of infinity in this letter is that of different *objects*. In his *Qualité et quantité dans la philosophie de Spinoza* (Paris: Presses Universitaires de France, 1995), Charles Ramond offers an extended critique of Gueroult and offers a new interpretation. For a summary of the literature and problems, see Lee C. Rice, "Spinoza's Infinite Extension," *History of European Ideas*, 1995.

43. *Natura naturans* and *Natura naturata* (literally "naturing nature" and "natured nature") are mediaeval scholastic terms adapted by Spinoza to reflect his two ways of conceiving nature. One way ("*naturans*") is to conceive nature as active and productive: this is the infinite whole, nature as it is and is conceived in itself. The second way is to imagine nature ("*naturata*") as it is expressed as modes: this is the sum of all the individual "parts" taken together as one, nature as it necessarily follows from an attribute. See E1P29Schol for Spinoza's definitions and explanations.

inasmuch as it understands the true causes of things, is not subject to the vagaries of fate while the imagination, not knowing the true causes of things, is liable to be swayed and confused by external circumstances.

Ep17 also addresses the imagination. Specifically in this letter, Spinoza writes about omens.[44] All thoughts which occur in the imagination must have a cause, and this cause must be, of course, either physical or mental. If the cause is physical, then the imagination, not understanding the necessary order of things, cannot sense, even in a confused way, the future. If, however, the cause of an imagined thought is received under the attribute of thought, then it is possible that the mind could have some confused knowledge about related ideas, some of which may come to pass: this qualifies those images produced by the imagination as omens.[45]

There are several other topics addressed in these letters. For example, Spinoza also makes some additional comments on infinity. In Ep12 he alludes to the now commonly accepted notion that there may be unequal infinities: "For it does not follow that things which cannot be adequately expressed by any number must necessarily be equal. . . ." He also touches upon the difference between indefinite and infinite – a problem which seemed to plague Descartes and many of his predecessors. Other letters included in this grouping include instructions and requests (Ep12a, Ep15, Ep28, Ep44) or touch upon miscellaneous experiments or explanations. Ep39 discusses optics; Ep40 concerns a famous report of an alchemist's experience; Ep41 reports on an experiment on water pressure; Ep50 remarks on some of Spinoza's perceived differences between himself and Hobbes.[46] Ep44 relates Spinoza's

---

44. This letter, and its implications for Spinoza's general account of imagination (*imaginatio*, the first kind of knowledge) is studied in detail by Michèle Bertrand, *Spinoza et l'imaginaire* (Paris: Presses Universitaires de France, 1983).

45. Martial Gueroult understands this letter to show "*vestiges de la pensée pure*" of Descartes in Spinoza. Gueroult also argues that this letter has more to do with freedom of the will than is apparent at first glance. See Gueroult, *Spinoza*, II (New York: Georg Olms Verlag Hildesheim, 1974), 572-577. For further study, see also Juan D. Sanchez-Estop, "Des présages à l'entendement; Notes sur les présages, l'imagination et l'amour dans la lettre à P. Balling," *Studia Spinozana* 4 (1988), 57-74.

46. Though Spinoza is rather clear and to the point concerning the difference between him and the English philosopher, generations of commentators continue to confuse and to identify the two. For a detailed account of their differences, see Alexandre Matheron *Individu et communauté chez Spinoza* (Paris; Editions de Minuit, 1988), 151-179; Steven Barbone and Lee Rice, "La naissance d'une nouvelle politique," in a forthcoming (1995) anthology edited by Pierre François

criticism of a contemporary political tract – *Homo politicus* – which is thought to have been modeled after Machiavelli's *Prince*. Since Spinoza so highly regarded Machiavelli[47] it seems strange, however, that he should so harshly criticize this tract; some have thought that Spinoza wrote the TP in response to this treatise.[48] Finally, a brief comment on Ep48a. Though both Blyenbergh (see Ep20) and Jelles confess to the authority of Scripture, note that it is the former who explicitly places the testimony of Scripture over that of reason. While Jelles suffers no censure for his belief in scriptural authority, Blyenbergh earns only Spinoza's disapproval.[49]

Moreau (Paris: Presses Universitaires de France).
47. See TP5 and TP10.
48. Or at least this seems to be suggested by Wolf (1928) 439.
49. See TTP, Preface: "Sed cum in iis, quae Scriptura expresse docet, nihil reperissem, quod cum Intellectu non conveniret, nec quod eidem repugnaret, et praeterea viderem, . . . omnino mihi persuasi, Scripturam Rationem absolute liberam relinquere; et nihil cum Philosophia commune habere, sed tam hanc quam illam proprio suo talo niti."

4. Faith and Theology:
The Blyenbergh Correspondence

On 26 December 1665, while he was staying at Long Orchard, Spinoza received a letter (Ep18) written by William Blyenbergh, who was then a grain merchant at Dordrecht. He was probably born in Amsterdam, but details of his early life are little known.[50] His theological interests were sufficiently clear from a book which he published in 1663 and whose title was as long as the book was short.[51] Perhaps, if Spinoza had known of this work, he may have declined to initiate any correspondence with Blyenbergh at the outset, but he clearly did not. After a brief introduction expressing his desire to undertake correspondence with Spinoza and his familiarity with the *Principles of Cartesian Philosophy*, Blyenbergh asked him to address the question whether divine concursus is a cause of evil. Spinoza sent him (5 January 1665, Ep19), a courteous reply, offering to continue their correspondence, and providing an exposition of his claim that evil is nothing positive, that it arises only with respect to ideas which are confused beings of reason (and therefore inadequate), and that it represents nothing at all in the divine intellect. Given that Spinoza did not understand the character and preoccupations of his correspondent, there is no reason to see this letter as more than an expanded development of the overly brief treatment of evil in the *Ethics* (E4P64-E4P65).

Realizing that Spinoza's account threatened what Spinoza calls the vulgar concept of God (of which Blyenbergh's own notion is a primordial example), Blyenbergh sent an enormously verbose reply on 16

---

50. See Meinsma 286 and 306 (ff. 12) for what details are certain.
51. *De kennisse Godts en Godts-Dienst, beweert tegen d'Uytvluchten der Athëisten: In welcke met klare un naturrlijcke reden getoont wert dat Godt een Godts-dienst in geschapen en geopenbaert heeft, dat Godt volgens deselve oock wil gedient wesen, en dat de Christelycke Godts-dienst neit alleen met Godts geopenbaerde Godts-dienst over-een komt, maer oock met in-geschapen reden.* "The knowledge of God and his service affirmed against the outrages of atheists, in which it is demonstrated with clear and natural reasons that God has created and revealed a religion, that God also wishes to be served in accordance with this religion, and that the Christian religion corresponds not only to the religion revealed by God, but also to our innate reason." Reprints of the booklet were made in 1671 and 1700.

January (Ep20). It begins with a statement of what Blyenbergh conceives to be the "rules" of Christian philosophy and the limits of human reason. Blyenbergh insisted that, whenever reason comes into apparent conflict with the dictates of his faith, it is reason which must be regarded as defective. The letter proceeds to accuse Spinoza of making human behavior too dependent upon God, lack of fidelity to revelation, and a disbelief in afterlife which, since it contradicts Scripture, must be obviously false. It ends with a closing incantation to God. Polite to a fault but realizing that he had nothing whatever to say to his prospective correspondent, Spinoza replied (Ep21) that the two should terminate their correspondence, and that, if Blyenbergh found Scripture superior to reason, he should not expend his energies upon philosophy. Noting that "I had intended to end this letter here," Spinoza was unable to refrain from embarking on a more technical presentation of his position before closing.

While providing a brief summary of his objections to anthropomorphism, Spinoza's statements of his position in Ep21 and in the balance of their correspondence should probably be more carefully interpreted in the context of his stated desire to end their exchange, his knowledge that Blyenbergh is not a philosophical thinker, and Spinoza's own proclivity to avoid discussing his own philosophical positions with those whom he judged unable to understand them. He had scarcely returned to Voorburg when he received another missive from Blyenbergh (Ep22) announcing his impending trip to Leiden and intention to visit the philosopher in person. The letter went on to accuse Spinoza of being unfriendly in his original reply and to underline the questions of dependence upon God and of human freedom. Spinoza's reply was once again polite, expressing his willingness to meet with Blyenbergh. Ep23 also provides a restatement of Spinoza's earlier remarks on evil, this time using the example of Nero and restating earlier objections to anthropomorphism (the notions that God 'approves' of some actions, and that our actions can cause pleasure or pain to God).

The threatened meeting apparently did take place in March, since on 27 March 1665 (Ep24) Blyenbergh mentioned it and raised again the issues of sin and error which, he claimed, Spinoza did not resolve during their meeting. By this stage, and perhaps in light of their meeting, Spinoza had come to realize that the only manner in which he could terminate their correspondence was to stop writing. His last letter to Blyenbergh, dated more than two months later (Ep27), underlined his insistence that ethical issues relate to physics and metaphysics rather than theology and ended by curtly stating that time is lacking to respond in a more extended fashion.

Samuel Shirley suggests that Spinoza is not entirely without blame for some of the confusion which pervades the Blyenbergh correspondence. Spinoza had no reason to assume, when Blyenbergh first wrote to him, any greater familiarity on the part of his correspondent with Spinoza's own teaching than the little one could glean from Meyer's few remarks at the beginning of the PPC. Even in Ep21 Spinoza sometimes argues from his own positions and sometimes from those of Descartes, so that Blyenbergh's request in Ep24 for Spinoza to distinguish his own positions from those of Descartes is assuredly a reasonable one. While Blyenbergh's remarks are often little more than religious homily, he also does reveal an ability to argue more incisively.[52] One instance of this is his insistence in Ep24 that Spinoza's position implies that the individual human personality does not survive death, an implication which is, we believe, correct.[53] One, but perhaps not the only reason, why Blyenbergh has gotten such bad press is Spinoza's impatience with him.

Nine years later, following the publication of Spinoza's *Tractatus Theologico-Politicus*, Blyenbergh published a volume of more than five hundred pages entitled, *The Truth of the Christian Religion and the Authority of Holy Scripture Affirmed Against the Arguments of the Impious, or a Refutation of the Blasphemous Book Entitled Tractatus Theologico-Politicus*.[54] Following Spinoza's death in 1677 and the publication of the *Ethics*, he also published a "Christian" refutation of it in 1682 and was duly elected in 1695 Burgomaster of Dordrecht as a defender of the faith.

---

52. Another, and also sympathetic, view of Blyenbergh is given by Gabriel Albiac, *La synagogue vide*, tr. Marie-Luce Copete and Jean-Frédéric Schaub (Paris: Presses Universitaires de France, 1994), 428-434.

53. See Lee Rice, "Mind Eternity in Spinoza," *Iyyun* 41 (1992), 319-334. Rice and Blyenbergh are not without their critics, however. For an opposing interpretation, see Alexandre Matheron, *Le Christ et le salut des ignorants chez Spinoza* (Paris: Aubier, 1971), esp. 205-208. A critique of Rice's position by one of Matheron's disciples is also offered in *Archives de philosophie* 56 (1993), 32-33.

54. *De Wearheyt van de Chr. Godtsdienst en de Authoriteyt der H. Schriften beweert tegen de Argumenten der Ongodsdienstige of een Wederlegginge van dat Godtlasterlycke Boeck, genoemt Tractatus Theologico-Politicus*, Leiden, 8 September 1674.

The extent to which Spinoza's replies to Blyenbergh should be construed as revelatory of his own position has been raised above. Clearly his first letter may be construed as less questionable than his subsequent replies. Wim Klever has also suggested[55] that Blyenbergh's remarks in Ep24 provide an accurate, albeit brief, account of their meeting and discussion, and that some of Spinoza's later remarks concerning both religious faith and anthropomorphism in the TTP (especially in its preface) may be directed to just those points which he raised in his brief correspondence with Blyenbergh. Given the brevity also of Spinoza's treatment of the problem of evil in the *Ethics*, it is impossible to avoid seeking some clarification and expansion of his thought in this block of correspondence, though considerable care should be taken in so doing.[56]

---

55. See his "Spinoza Interviewed by Willem van Blyenbergh," *Studia Spinozana* 4 (1988), 317-320.
56. On this problem see Wim Klever, "Blijenbergh's Tussing with Evil and Spinoza's Response," *Tijdschrift voor Filosofie* 55 (1993), 307-329; and Manfred Walther, "Discours sur la réalité du mal ou l'irritation d'une conscience quotidienne," in *La Etica de Spinoza: Fundamentos y significado* Ed. Atilano Domínguez (Castilla-La Mancha: Ediciones de la Universidad, 1992), 213-216. On Spinoza's general account of evil and our knowledge thereof in the *Ethics*, see William Frankena, "Spinoza on the Knowledge of Good and Evil," *Philosophia* 7 (1977), 15-44.

5. Freedom and Philosophical Method
[Georg Hermann Schuller and Walther von Tschirnhaus]

Spinoza's correspondents had many and varied interests, and several writers' concerns overlap the questions of other correspondents. Thus, although care was taken when the correspondence was divided into the six sections we present, the reader should not be too surprised that some issues should reappear. In this section, we look at the Schuller/Tschirnhaus correspondence as a block, but we shall broach concerns presented in sections 3, 4, and 6. It is natural that these two writers be grouped together since they seemed to be good friends, and Tschirnhaus often corresponded with Spinoza through their mutual friend Schuller. Many of Schuller's interests, then, are presumed to be those of Tschirnhaus.

Georg Hermann Schuller (1651-1679)[57] was one of Spinoza's many physician friends. As noted earlier, some believe that it was he rather than Meyer who was with Spinoza at his death.[58] Though he settled in Amsterdam, where he no doubt met Spinoza, he was from the town of Wezel in the Cleves district. He was not one of Spinoza's most educated friends, but he did have a lively interest in alchemy which Spinoza thought frivolous. His extant letters reveal too that he was a master of neither Latin nor German (he was a regular correspondent with Gottfried Leibniz).[59] We believe that Spinoza had given him a copy of the yet unpublished *Ethics* which he shared with Tschirnhaus and also possibly Leibniz. The day following Spinoza's burial, he wrote a letter to Leibniz offering to sell him several of Spinoza's works which he now had. (It may be that these were works which he previously possessed prior to Spinoza's death since among the works were letters to Meyer which had been passed around [see Ep80 where he refers to the "letter on the Infinite"].) However, before Leibniz could reply, Schuller wrote again to him (March 29, 1677) saying that the manuscripts were no

---

57. For more biographical information, see Wim Klever, "La clé du nom: Petrus van Gent (et Schuller) à partie d'une correspondance," *Cahiers Spinoza* 6 (1991), 169-202.
58. See Wolf (1928) 53.
59. See Meinsma 432. For more on Leibniz, see our section 7.

longer for sale since they were being collected by Spinoza's other friends to create the *Opera posthuma*.

Ehrenfried Walther von Tschirnhaus (1651-1708),[60] by comparison, was a brilliant thinker and closer to being Spinoza's equal. A German count, he studied at the University of Leiden, and as a volunteer soldier, he distinguished himself at the siege of Wezel. His actions did not escape notice, and he was offered promotion to captain, but he refused it and returned to Leiden. In 1674, he met Schuller in Amsterdam, and it was through Schuller that he came into contact with Spinoza. In 1675, he traveled to London where he met Oldenburg, Boyle, and many leading scientists: Hooke, Newton, Flamsteed, Malpighi, Huygens, and van Leeuwenhoek. In 1683, he published *Medicina mentis* ["The Mind's Medicine"] which seems to be fashioned after Spinoza's DIE. He discovered the method for measuring curves by the means of tangents (see Ep59) and is given credit for the invention of porcelain making.[61] He seems to have promised Spinoza not to share Spinoza's thoughts nor to talk to others about him; however, one can only wonder how successful he was in keeping his word (see Ep63, Ep70).[62] He was a correspondent intellectually worthy of Spinoza, and his letters add a great deal to our understanding of Spinoza's philosophy.

The issue of personal freedom is one of the major topics in their exchange. Note that much of their discussion is clarified by heeding Spinoza's definition: "I say that that thing is free which exists and acts solely from its own nature, and I say that that thing is constrained (*coactus*) which is determined by something else to exist and to act in a fixed and determinate way" (Ep58).[63] According to Spinoza, then, nothing but the whole of nature is free since all individual modes found in nature are caused or determined by either nature directly or indirectly by nature through some other mode found there. Human freedom, except in a very especial sense (see Ep58; E4P67Dem,

---

60. For detailed biographical information, refer to E. Winter, *E. W. von Tschirnhaus (1651-1708). Ein Leben im Dienste Akademiegedankens* (Berlin: Walther de Gruyter, 1959) or Tschirnhaus, *Médecine de l'Esprit ou principes généraux de l'art de découvrir*, introduction, translation, notes, and appendices by Jean-Paul Wurtz (Strasbourg: Université de Strasbourg, 1980).

61. See Wolf (1928) 48.

62. Meinsma 466 does not believe that he was successful at all.

63. Cf. also E1Def7.

E4P68Dem), is a product of the imagination and has no real meaning. Spinoza illustrates this point with the famous example of the rolling stone which, as it rolls, imagines to itself that it freely rolls from its own volition even though we understand that the stone moves from certain external forces and continues to do so in light of those forces. In the same way, Spinoza contends that people act from external, albeit unknown to them, forces which determine and affect all their actions despite their belief, like that of the stone, that they act freely (see Ep58; cf. E3P2Schol). Spinoza goes further than applying mechanistic principles solely to the physical universe; he holds also that just as in extension all things are caused by another thing, so too in thought. Therefore, Spinoza does not even grant that a person may freely think as he chooses, but that even one's thoughts are determined by external causes which often remain unknown to the thinker.

The sense of freedom which Spinoza is attacking is what has come since to be called the incompatibilist theory, and had been strongly defended by Descartes, and was later to be developed by both Kant[64] and Sartre.[65] Under an incompatibilist account, human freedom makes human behavior exempt from scientific laws and explanation. This is just the "kingdom within a kingdom" account of human nature upon which Spinoza heaps scorn in the Preface to *Ethics* 3, and whose existence he rightly denies. Yet the fifth part of the *Ethics* is subtitled, "On Human Freedom"; so Spinoza shares with contemporary compatibilist philosophers the belief that human actions (certainly not all, and assuredly not always) are free in a sense which is consistent with a scientific world view. He also argues strongly for another (or possibly an extension of this first kind of) freedom at the level of civil society in his political writings. The details of the sense in which, for Spinoza, human behavior may achieve freedom, are complicated and the subject of a great deal of philosophical commentary.[66]

---

64. See Steven Barbone, "Kant and Compatibilism," *Idealistic Studies* 24 (1994), 111-123, for an analysis of the relation between Kant and Descartes on the issue of freedom.
65. See Steven Barbone, "Nothingness and Sartre's Fundamental Project," *Philosophy Today*, Summer 1994, 191-204.
66. The best contemporary treatments of the problem, we believe, are in J. I. Friedman, "Spinoza's Denial of Free Will in Man and God," in *Spinoza's Philosophy of Man*, ed. Jon Wetlesen (Oslo: Universitetsforlaget, 1978), 51-84; Don Garrett, "Freedom and the Good in Spinoza's *Ethics*," in *Spinoza: Issues and Directions*, ed. Edwin Curley and Pierre-François Moreau (Leiden: E. J. Brill, 1990), 221-238; Stuart Hampshire, "Spinoza's Theory of Human Freedom," *Monist* 55 (1971), 554-566; S. Paul Kashap, *Spinoza and Moral Freedom* (New York: State

It was Spinoza's doctrine on freedom, and denial of incompatibilism, which got him into much trouble with the religious authorities and thinkers of his time. In a sense, the heat of the debate is something which the modern reader may be hard put to understand. The doctrine of freedom which Spinoza denies is one held only by theologians and some philosophers, whereas the freedom of which he claims that human beings are sometimes capable is the ordinary notion of "freedom from aversive control," as he explicitly makes clear at the beginning of E5. The psychologist B. F. Skinner once noted that men have never gone to war or fought for Cartesian or Sartrean freedom (whose existence is denied by Spinoza), but rather for freedom *from* economic, political, and environmental oppression (whose possibility Spinoza strongly affirms).

We should remember, however, that to his contemporaries Spinoza's attack looked like (and indeed was) an attack on the anthropomorphic god-judge of popular religion. For this reason his notions concerning freedom give not just a little consternation to his correspondents who mention that if people were not free, it would not make sense to blame or to praise them, to punish or to reward them (temporally as well as eternally) or to practice virtue or to avoid vice (see Ep57 as well as Ep22, Ep77, Ep79). Spinoza's response to Tschirnhaus, quite consistent with his other writings, is that a virtuous or a wicked act has the same outcome whether it is performed freely or from necessity. Spinoza raises an issue which plagued Descartes as well as virtually all theists who believe in some special sense of human freedom: if God knows that a person will perform a virtuous action, then it is necessary that that person perform that act, and so the question of freedom is, in *this* sense, really moot.

This group of letters is also important since it helps to clarify some issues and problems concerning the attributes. Spinoza is very clear on one point here: there are only two attributes *knowable* to the human mind – thought and extension (Ep64). Some commentators have been led by this to conclude that, when Spinoza writes that there are an

---

University of New York Press, 1987); George L. Kline, "Absolute and Relative Senses of *Liberum* and *Libertas* in Spinoza," in *Spinoza nel 350o anniversario della nascita*, ed. Emilia Giancotti (Urbino: Bibliopolis, 1982), 259-80; G. H. R. Parkinson, "Spinoza on the Power and Freedom of Man," *Monist* 55 (1971), 527-553; and Jean Préposiet, *Spinoza et la liberté des hommes* (Paris: Gallimard, 1967).

infinity of attributes, he means by "infinity" "all that there are," but really only two.[67] That there are other attributes besides these two is, however, stated in E2P7Schol, to which Spinoza refers the reader in Ep64; the other attributes express essences of nature unknown or unknowable to us. These Tschirnhaus calls the "other worlds," but these "other worlds" are really our own world just comprehended by God or other minds which perceive those attributes in a manner differently than we do. Does this mean, then, that the attribute of thought is "bigger" than the other attributes since it takes in the ideas of the infinite modes as they exist under all the other attributes (see Ep70)? This problem bothered Tschirnhaus, and it is the bane of the extensive literature which has attempted to provide a complete and consistent account of the theory of attributes.[68] Unfortunately, Spinoza does not reply directly to Tschirnhaus' query but writes rather that perhaps the misunderstanding is due more to a slip of the pen rather than a real philosophical misinterpretation (Ep72). We suspect that it was not, and that Tschirnhaus' concerns were both legitimate and well-founded. The core of the problem lies in saying in what manner two infinities may be *different* (since the attribute of thought comprehends the attribute of extension, there is a many-one mapping, as we would now put it) but also have the same cardinality. If it is something like this which Spinoza may have had in mind, little wonder that he should have been evasive. The theory of infinities in the seventeenth century had just succeeded in breaking away from theological muddles, but was light years away

---

67. See, for example, Jonathan Bennett, *A Study of Spinoza's Ethics* (Indianapolis: Hackett Publishing Company, 1984), 75-79; Wolf (1928) 462-463.

68. We mention only some recent and useful treatments, most of which provide further bibliography on the extensive literature. See Jacob Adler, "Divine Attributes in Spinoza: Intrinsic and Relational," *Philosophy & Theology* 4 (1989), 33-52; Bernard Balan, "Spinoza et la théorie de l'identité dans las philosophie de l'esprit," in *Spinoza au XXe siècle*, ed. Olivier Bloch (Paris: Presses Universitaires de France, 1993), 307-26; Victor Delbos, "La doctrine spinoziste des attributs de Dieu," *L'Année Philosophique* 23 (1913), 1-17; Atilano Domínguez, "Modos infinitos y entendimiento divino en la metafísica de Spinoza," *Sefarad* 38 (1978), 107-141; Don Garrett, "Ethics 1P5: Shared Attributes and the Basis of Spinoza's Monism," in *Central Themes in Early Modern Philosophy*, ed. A. J. Cover and Mark Kulstad (Indianapolis: Hackett, 1990), 69-107; F. S. Haserot, "Spinoza's Definition of Attribute," *Philosophical Review* 62 (1953), 499-513; Thomas C. Mark, "The Spinozistic Attributes," *Philosophia* 7 (1977), 55-82; and Margaret D. Wilson, "Notes on Modes and Attributes," *Journal of Philosophy* 78 (1981), 584-586.

from the logically coherent formulation which was to be provided by Cantor, Dedekind, and others.[69]

Another issue which Tschirnhaus raises is the difference between true and adequate ideas (Ep59). Included in this discussion are the question whether it is possible that some adequate ideas are "more" adequate than other adequate ideas and how error is possible if one possesses an adequate idea. In replying Spinoza notes that there is really no difference between true and adequate ideas except that while a true idea merely is one which agrees with its object, the adequate idea agrees with its object in that the nature of the object (and hence all its properties and its cause – see E1Ax4, E1P8Schol2) is known (Ep60). What this means is simply that an adequate idea is one which includes not just the thing in all its essential properties, but also its cause; for a deductivist such as Spinoza, such an idea is necessarily true. This reply also short-circuits the suggestions made in Ep57 by Tschirnhaus that truth is relative.

Spinoza insists that no adequate idea is "more" adequate than another adequate idea, and that the confusion comes in where it *seems* that some ideas are adequate, but in fact turn out not to be so. This is the source of error – that we assent to an idea which we believe to be adequate but in reality is not. There are still problems here, though, since while Spinoza customarily uses 'adequate' in a sense in which it is all-or-nothing, his definitions (see E2Def4 and E3Def2) clearly suggest, as does his usage at other times, that adequacy may be properly described in degrees. The connection between adequacy of ideas and adequacy of causes, while paramount in the *Ethics*, seems strangely absent in these letters. Once again the interested reader is advised to consult the rather extensive literature on the problem.[70]

This block of letters ends with comments on refraction and on Descartes' physics. Here are some of Spinoza's strongest criticisms on

---

69. The suggestion which we here adopt as to resolution of Tschirnhaus's difficulties would not be accepted by all scholars. It is defended, for example, by H. F. Hallett in *Benedict de Spinoza: The Elements of His Philosophy* (London: Athlone Press, 1957), and more recently with explicit reference to the Tschirnhaus correspondence by Alexandre Matheron, "Physique et ontologie chez Spinoza: l'énigmatique réponse à Tschirnhaus," *Cahiers Spinoza* 6 (1991), 83-110.

70. One attempt at resolution, together with a review of others and the related literature, is made by Lee Rice, "La causalité adéquate chez Spinoza," *Philosophiques* 19 (1992), 45-60.

Descartes' physics: "Descartes' principles of natural things are of no service, not to say quite wrong" (Ep81; cf. Ep83). Spinoza ends by promising to elaborate more on this topic should his health hold out, but we are deprived of any further comments. The question of the direction of Spinoza's physical thought, and its general role in his philosophy, must be answered from hints and remarks made elsewhere in the letters and in the *Ethics*.[71]

---

71. In his extensive writings on Spinoza, Wim Klever (among others) holds that Spinoza's philosophy is essentially the development of Spinozistic physics. For a critique of this view, and a summary of alternative interpretations, see Pierre-François Moreau, *Spinoza: L'Expérience et l'éternité* (Paris: Presses Universitaires de France, 1994), esp. 262-287. Moreau deals explicitly with the Tschirnhaus correspondence.

6. The Tractatus Theologico-Politicus

In 1670 Spinoza moved from Voorburg to the Hague, where he was to live until his death in 1677. The *Tractatus Theologico-Politicus*, which he had begun sometime in the mid-1660s, appeared early in 1670 in a printing which did not bear its author's name but which did bear a false city of origin, "Hamburgi, apud Henricum Künraht."[72] Meinsma believes that the greater part of the printing had in fact been distributed outside Holland prior to its appearance at the bookstore of Spinoza's friend, Jan Rieuwertsz,[73] for fear of censure by the religious authorities.

These fears were subsequently proven to be well-founded. In May of 1670 a German professor, Jacobius Thomasius, published a long essay "against an anonymous author, on the freedom to philosophize," which was followed one month later by an inaugural dissertation by one of his colleagues (Friedrich Rappolt) "against the naturalists."[74] In June the consistory of Amsterdam published a warning, "that one should not lose sight of the boldness of the papists, the Socinians, or the excessive liberties taken by printers, especially the pernicious book

---

72. Details on the probable development of the problematic of the TTP by Spinoza, and of its sources and relationship to the *Ethics*, may be found in F. Akkerman, "Etablissement du texte du *Tractatus Theologico-Politicus*," in *L'Ecriture sainte au temps de Spinoza et dans le système spinoziste*, ed. Groupe de Recherches Spinozistes (Paris: Presses de l'Université de Paris-Sorbonne, 1992), 91-108; Edwin Curley, "Notes on a Neglected Masterpiece, II: Theologico-Political Treatise as a Prolegomenon to the Ethics," in *Central Themes in Early Modern Philosophy*, ed. A. J. Cover and Mark Kulstad (Indianapolis: Hackett, 1990), 109-159; and Richard Popkin, "The First Published Discussion of a Central Theme in Spinoza's *Tractatus*," *Philosophia* 17 (1987), 101-109.
73. See Meinsma, 378-388. Rieuwertsz was born in Amsterdam in 1617, and opened his bookstore, which quickly became known as the most liberal in Amsterdam, sometime during 1640. It was also a central clearing house for pamphlets circulated by Anabaptists and Collegiants. It was during Spinoza's stay in Amsterdam (1654 or early in 1655) that he met and befriended a number of people active among the Collegiants, some of whom were to become correspondents. These included not just Rieuwertsz, but also Simon de Vries, Jarig Jelles, and Pieter Balling.
74. The complete titles are in A. Van der Linde, *Benedictus Spinoza: Bibliografie* (Nieuwkoop: B. de Graaf, 1965), 358.

entitled *Tractatus Theologico-Politicus*."[75] The book became an instantaneous and notorious *cause célèbre* in Amsterdam, and demands for a translation into the vernacular inevitably followed. The Latin edition was sent, probably by Rieuwertsz himself, to Jan Hendriksz Glazemaker, already well-known for his translations of Latin texts (notably Seneca and Descartes), with the request for a translation. The translation was scheduled for publication in early 1671 when Spinoza, first learning of its existence, wrote to his friend Jarig Jelles (Ep44), requesting that he attempt to suppress it. Jelles was apparently successful in his efforts, since Glazemaker's translation did not see light of day until 1693, and then it appeared under the singularly inappropriate title, *The Orthodox Theologian*.[76]

The 1670s were a period fraught with problems and pain for Spinoza. In August of 1672 a mob murdered and desecrated the corpses of Cornelius and Johan de Witt following the outbreak of the war with France. The latter had resigned his position as Councillor Pensionary of Holland because of popular support for the restoration of the monarchy under the Prince of Orange, William III; Cornelius had been imprisoned for allegedly conspiring against the Prince. Spinoza was sufficiently angry to propose posting a placard denouncing the *vulgus* who had committed the crime as *ultimi barbarorum*, but was dissuaded from doing so by his landlord, who feared that Spinoza would thereby meet a similar fate. A year later Spinoza was to confront a similar mob outside his own residence, following an abortive effort to visit the Prince of Condé in French-occupied Utrecht. In February of the following year Spinoza received a letter from J. Louis (or Ludwig) Fabritius, Councillor to the Elector Palatine Karl Ludwig, offering him a chair of philosophy at the University of Heidelberg on condition that he not disturb the officially recognized religion. That letter (Ep47) received a brief and polite refusal from Spinoza in March of 1673 (Ep48). Three years following the publication of the TTP, Spinoza remained painfully aware of the necessary conflict between the new philosophy and science and virtually any established religion.[77]

---

75. See Meinsma, 378-382, for additional details.
76. See F. Akkerman, "J. H. Glazemaker, An Early Translator of Spinoza," in *Spinoza's Political and Theological Thought*, ed. C. de Deugd (Amsterdam: North Holland Publishing Co., 1984), 23-29.
77. For a more detailed account of the historical impact of the appearance of the TTP, see Myriam Revault d'Allonnes, "Spinoza et la 'crise' du théologico-politique," in *Le Religieux dans le Politique: Le Genre Humain* (Paris: Seuil, 1991), esp. 69-80.

Lambert van Velthuysen was born in Utrecht in 1622 and studied medicine, philosophy, and theology at the University of Utrecht beginning in 1643. After establishing himself in Utrecht as a physician, he became an enthusiastic supporter of Descartes' philosophy and was also publicly known as a Collegiant sympathizer. In 1655 he published a short treatise in support of the Copernican system against the condemnations of religious authorities.[78] An abbreviated version of the treatise appeared in Utrecht in 1657 and contained a spirited defence of the Cartesian method. His liberalism continued to bring him in conflict with the Calvinist clergy until his death in 1685 and probably stimulated his initial interest in the TTP, of which he sent a review to his friend and colleague Jacob Ostens early in 1671.[79]

Ostens immediately forwarded the review to Spinoza (Ep42, 24 January 1671). While Velthuysen was sympathetic, Spinoza's doctrine was too radical even for this self-proclaimed liberal, who argues that Spinoza's doctrine in the TTP undermines all revelational religion and that it reduces to a form of atheism. The significant doctrines which Velthuysen underlines in support of his charges are universal necessitarianism, Spinoza's view of the prophets, the impossibility of miracles, the claim that God could have created no world other than this, and Spinoza's insistence that the ceremonial worship of God should be controlled by civil authorities. Ep43 contains Spinoza's reply to Velthuysen

---

78. *Bewys, dat het gevooelen van die genen, die leeren der Sonne Stilstandt en des Aertrycks Beweging niet strydich is met Godts-Woort* ("A proof that the opinion of those who teach that the sun is immobile and that the earth moves is not in contradiction with the word of God"). For a list of van Velthuysen's other writings, see W. N. A. Klever, *Verba et Sententia Spinozae, or Lambertus van Velthuysen (1662-1685) on Benedictus de Spinoza* (Amsterdam: APA – North Holland, 1991). Van Velthuysen's *Opera Omnia* were published in Rotterdam (1680), and a copy of this edition exists in the Amsterdam Library.

79. Ostens, born in 1625 in Utrecht, established a practice as surgeon in 1651 in Rotterdam, where he was widely known as a promoter of anabaptism. Spinoza probably made his acquaintance in the early 1650s. Ostens is cited as the author of *Notes on the Confession of G. Aldendorp [et al.] concerning the principle articles of the Christian faith* (Amsterdam, 1665): see Christophorus Sandius, *Bibliotheca Antitrinitariorum* (Freistadii [i.e., Amsterdam]: Apud Johannem Aconium, 1684; reprinted, Warsaw: Panstwowe Wydawnnictswo Naukowe, 1967), p. 168. No copy of Ostens' work seems to have survived. Sandius indicates that he died in 1679 and was pastor of a Mennonite Church in Rotterdam. Little else is known of him, and his importance for us is solely that of an intermediary between Velthuysen and Spinoza. See Meinsma, 286-287.

via Ostens. While it is a brief letter (compared to the letter to which it is a reply), it is interesting to compare it to Spinoza's interchanges with Blyenbergh. While there is some annoyance in Spinoza to the charge of atheism,[80] his reply indicates his belief in Velthuysen's sincerity and intelligence (two qualities which he appears to have found lacking in Blyenbergh).[81] Most of this letter is a response to the charges that he wished to undermine religion and that universal necessity is contrary to revealed religion. Four years later (Ep59, 1675) Spinoza wrote directly to Velthuysen, and suggested that he send detailed arguments against the claims which he found objectionable in the TTP; but, so far as we know, this last interchange received no reply.

The other block of letters of major importance for understanding the TTP and the development of Spinoza's political thought is the second part of his correspondence with Oldenburg, resumed with a letter (Ep61, dated 8 June 1675) from the latter acknowledging receipt of the TTP. This was followed a few weeks later by a second letter (Ep62) in which Oldenburg discusses Spinoza's plans for the publication of the *Ethics* in five parts. Spinoza's reply (Ep68) indicated that the theologians and Cartesians had already begun raising objections to the as-yet-unseen *Ethics*, and that he had therefore postponed its publication. In closing he asked Oldenburg to send him a list of passages which had caused uneasiness about the TTP. In his brief reply to this request (Ep71), Oldenburg mentions the identification of God with nature, Spinoza's denial of the authority of miracles, and the fact that his view concerning Christ is unclear in the TTP.

---

80. The charge, which survived in Bayle's Dictionary, was often applied in the seventeenth century to anyone who did not accept the speaker's (or the current orthodox) account of the divinity. In 1667 a celebrated trial was held by the Reformed Church of Amsterdam against the heresy and atheism of Johannes Koerbagh. For details see Meinsma, 355-385. For Spinoza's relationship with Koerbagh see Gerrit H. Jongeneelen, "An Unknown Pamphlet of Adriaan Koerbagh," *Studia Spinozana* 3 (1987), 405-418. See also Errol E. Harris, *Atheism and Theism* (New Orleans: Tulane University Press, 1977).

81. The care and attention which Spinoza expended on the claims of Velthuysen to which he did reply in Ep43 have suggested to some commentators that Velthuysen's writings provide clear and correct interpretations of the TTP on many points. See Hans W. Blom, "Lambert van Velthuysen et le naturalisme," *Cahiers Spinoza* 6 (1991), 203-212; and Wim Klever, *Verba et sententiae Spinozae or Lambert van Velthuysen (1662-1685)* (Amsterdam: APA, 1991).

Spinoza's reply (Ep73) to Oldenburg's brief list indicates the extent to which Spinoza was concerned with the practice of religion as a *practical* matter rather than the defence of the philosophical underpinnings of the TTP. He defends his view of the identity of God and nature by appeal to the early Hebrews,[82] reasserts his claim that the belief in miracles is based on ignorance, and attempts to provide some clarification of his attitude toward Christ. Spinoza appears to have gotten his point concerning the practicality of his concerns across to Oldenburg at last, since Oldenburg re-expresses his reservations (Ep74, dated December 1675) on miracles and necessity in the TTP in terms of their purported consequences for religious behavior: the destruction of punishment, virtue, and divine ordination, and the elevation of the human mind beyond its capacities. Spinoza's reply (Ep75) is a carefully worded restatement of themes expounded at greater length in the TTP itself: that necessity obviates neither divine nor human law, that God should not be conceived as a judge, and that Christ's resurrection should be interpreted only as allegory.

In his letter of 7 February 1676 (Ep78) Oldenburg reiterates his opinion that, if God is the cause of evil, then God becomes blameworthy. He further suggests that Spinoza's own allegorical interpretation of Christ's passion and resurrection is not in accordance with Spinoza's own stated method of scriptural interpretation – a claim on which some contemporary commentators have indeed followed him.[83] Spinoza once again reiterates (Ep78) his account of virtue and vice in terms of his account of individual essences given in the *Ethics*,[84] and restates his position on the allegorical interpretation of Christ's resurrection. Oldenburg's brief retort (Ep79, 11 February 1676) – that God is cruel if he makes humans imperfect and then punishes them, that Spinoza's examples are not convincing, and that

---

82. Spinoza's understanding of the relationship between the early Hebrew notions of divinity and its relationship to the Hebrew state is summarized by Sylvain Zac, "Spinoza et l'état des Hébreux," *Speculum Spinozanum: 1677-1977*, ed. S. Hessing (London: Routledge & Kegan Paul, 1977), 543-571.

83. See Sylvain Zac, *Spinoza et l'interprétation de l'Ecriture* (Paris: Presses Universitaires de France, 1965).

84. See Steven Barbone, "Virtue and Sociality in Spinoza," *Iyyun* 42 (1993), 383-395; Lee Rice, "Tanquam Naturae Humanae Exemplar: Spinoza on Human Nature," *Modern Schoolman* 68 (1991), 291-304; and Lee Rice, "Le nominalisme de Spinoza," *Canadian Journal of Philosophy* 24 (1994), 19-32.

Spinoza is still inconsistent in taking all scriptural claims about Christ except the resurrection as literal – closes their correspondence. It would be hazardous to guess why it closes at this point, as Oldenburg's questions are neither pointless nor without merit. Perhaps Spinoza's own illness reduced his ability to carry on with all of his correspondence; perhaps he realized that the Oldenburg who renewed correspondence in 1675 was a much-changed man from the earlier correspondent; or perhaps he was convinced that the political theory associated with the TTP should be divorced from the problems (and turmoil caused by them) of scriptural exegesis. This latter possibility is suggested in part by the last letter we have from Spinoza (Ep84), dated the same year, and announcing that he had begun work on the (never to be completed) *Tractatus Politicus*.

There are three major interpretive problems which arise in connection with the program of scriptural analysis and interpretation which Spinoza advances in the TTP, and we can only mention them here. The first is that of a providing a complete and unambiguous statement of how scriptural interpretation is to proceed according to Spinoza.[85] The second, but related, problem is that of providing an interpretation of the TTP (and, indeed, of Spinoza's political theory as a whole) in accordance with the metaphysics, epistemology, and moral theory found in the *Ethics*. That many of Spinoza's philosophical statements in the TTP seem to be at variance with the positions offered in the *Ethics* is the basis of the claim by Leo Strauss that the TTP contains a "hidden doctrine" beneath the surface of a more popular presentation.[86] Yet a third problem is that raised by Oldenburg: an

---

85. On which see especially Sylvain Zac, *op. cit.*; René Bouveresse, ed., *Spinoza: Science et Religion* (Paris: Vrin, 1988); Miguel Benitez, "Du bon usage du *Tractatus Theologico-Politicus*: La religion du Chrétien," in *Spinoza au XVIIIe siècle*, ed. O. Bloch, "Actes des Journées d'Etudes à la Sorbonne (1987)" (Paris: Méridiens Klincksieck, 1990), 75-84.; Pierre-François Moreau, "Les principes de la lecture de l'Ecriture sainte dans le T.T.P.," in *L'Ecriture sainte au temps de Spinoza et dans le système spinoziste*, ed. Groupe de Recherches Spinozistes (Paris: Presses de l'Université de Paris-Sorbonne, 1992), 119-32; and Winfried Schroder, "Das *Symbolum Sapientiae/Cymbalum Mundi* und der *Tractatus Theologico-politicus*," *Studia Spinozana* 7 (1991), 227-239.

86. See his *Die Religionskritik Spinozas als Grundlage seiner Bibelwissenschaft: Untersuchungen zu Spinozas Theologisch-Politischen Traktat* (Berlin: Akademie-Verlag, 1930), and also "How to Study Spinoza's *Theologico-Political Treatise*" in *Persecution and the Art of Writing*, ed. J. Wilson (Glencoe, Ill.: Free Press, 1952), 142-201. Strauss' theory of an esoteric doctrine has come under extensive criticism in more recent years. For a detailed examination and critique, see Errol E. Harris, *Is There an Esoteric Doctrine in the Tractatus Theologico-Politicus?* (Leiden: E. J. Brill, 1978); and Jacques Moutaux, "Exotérisme et philosophie: Léo Strauss et

unambiguous statement of Spinoza's position on the status of Christ.[87] All of these problems arise in the correspondence itself, which can provide some illumination on how the works of Spinoza are to be interpreted and integrated.

The importance of Spinoza's political philosophy as an early statement of political liberalism cannot be underestimated. In the anglophone tradition Spinoza has too often been confusedly identified with Hobbes, only to be refuted or ignored in the history of political thought and of free-market economics. The appearance of Alexandre Matheron's *Individu et communauté chez Spinoza* in 1969 (Paris: Editions de Minuit) signaled a growing interest in Spinoza among francophone researchers, one which has begun to make its way into anglophone analysis,[88] which succeeded in providing a critical rejection of much which had been published earlier in English.[89] At the same time, additional commentaries concerning both the TTP and the TP have been undertaken in Europe.[90] The role of the correspondence in the development of a fuller understanding of Spinoza's politics and his legacy to later thinkers will doubtless be substantial, but must await assessment by future historians and philosophers.

---

l'interprétation du *Traité théologico-politique*," *Spinoza au XXe Siècle*, ed. Olivier Bloch (Paris: Presses Universitaires de France, 1993), 421-44.

87. See Alexandre Matheron, *Le Christ et le salut des ignorants* (Paris: Aubier, 1971).

88. To date the best and most thorough analysis of this new understanding in English to date is that of Douglas Den Uyl, *Power, State, and Freedom* (Assen: Van Gorcum, 1983).

89. For an historical summary of the earlier anglophone traditions in interpreting Spinoza's political philosophy, see Steven Barbone and Lee Rice, "La naissance d'une nouvelle politique," in a forthcoming (1995) anthology edited by Pierre-François Moreau (Paris: Presses Universitaires de France).

90. See especially Etienne Balibar, *Spinoza et la politique* (Paris: Presses Universitaires de France, 1985); Gilles Deleuze, *Spinoza et le problème de l'expression* (Paris: Editions de Minuit, 1968); Pierre Macherey, *Hegel ou Spinoza* (Paris: Editions la Découverte, 1990); Antonio Negri, *L'anomalia selvaggia: Saggio su petere e potenza in Baruch Spinoza* (Rome: Feltrinelli, 1981); and André Tosel, *Spinoza ou le crépuscule de la servitude: essai sur le Traité théologico-politique* (Paris: Aubier, 1984); Three volumes of the annual *Studia Spinozana* are also of particular interest in this respect: I (1985), devoted to Spinoza's social philosophy; III (1987), devoted to Hobbes and Spinoza; and VIII (1992), devoted to Spinoza's psychology and social psychology.

7. Miscellaneous Correspondents and Topics

[John Hudde, Johan van der Meer, Gottfried Leibniz, J. Louis Fabritius, John George Graevius, Hugo Boxel, Alfred Burgh, and Nicholas Steno]

Nelson Goodman notes that a filing or classification system is always adequate and complete if it has one folder marked "miscellaneous," and in this final grouping of letters we follow his wisdom and have assigned various and sundry authors to the "miscellaneous" folder. This is not to suggest, however, that the topics treated here are unimportant, since many reinforce what is discussed in letters which fall more naturally under other headings. As the correspondents and their concerns are varied, we treat them here in chronological order rather than order of importance or philosophical interest.

John Hudde (1628-1704) was a native of Amsterdam and took a lively political interest in his city. In 1667 he became a member of that town's governing body, and in 1672 he was elected burgomaster for the first of at least eighteen times.[91] Besides politics, he had a keen interest in optics (so it is believed that he came to know Spinoza through Christiaan Huygens) and the theories of chance and probability. He is supposed to have been quite adept in mathematics; and when he forsook mathematical research in favor of politics, no less a luminary than Newton bemoaned the loss.[92] He also knew Leibniz (see below) personally, and it was through his relationship with Leibniz that we believe that these letters (Ep34-Ep36) were written to him.[93] The Spinoza/Hudde correspondence is concerned primarily with the existence of God and proofs for God's necessary existence and other divine properties. Spinoza (as he often does with his correspondents)

---

91. Wolf conjectures that perhaps Spinoza purposely developed his friendship with the burgomaster, as well as the de Witt brothers, in an attempt to gain some political protection. See Wolf (1928) 45. If Wolf is correct, one might add Conrad Burgh, father of Alfred Burgh (see below), to this list.
92. Meinsma 324.
93. Van Vloten reports that the letters were addressed to Christiaan Huygens, but notes made by Leibniz on copies of them show them to be in fact Hudde's. See Meinsma 323.

calls his attention to the nature of definition (Ep34), and that from certain definitions he is able to derive the necessary and unique existence of God. Note a definition does not, Spinoza underlines, include number in the definiens, since number is a product of the imagination (see Ep12) and not essential to the nature of an object.[94] From necessary existence, other properties are derived (Ep35) which are also unique to God. Ep36 is meant to clarify difficulties in the previous letter: if something is infinite, it admits no negation, and if it admits no negation, there is nothing to prevent its existing; therefore an infinite being must necessarily exist. This is in fact an extended version of the second of the three proofs given by Spinoza in E1P11.

Concerning Johan van der Meer, almost nothing is known. The single letter addressed to him is interesting only insofar as it informs us of the then current interest in the developing science of probability, and provides evidence of Spinoza's wide range of interest and knowledge. In addition to this one letter on probability, it is possible that Spinoza did write more on this subject. In 1687 *Reeckening van Kanssen* ["Calculation of Chances"] was published along with the *Treatise on the Rainbow*, but there is little evidence on which to base his authorship of it.

Gottfried Leibniz (1646-1716) is probably Spinoza's most famous correspondent.[95] The abilities of this philosopher, who co-invented the differential calculus – independently but simultaneously with Newton – cannot be doubted. He had varied interests in physics, language, mathematics, law, philosophy, and theology, and his many works include: "Discourse on Metaphysics," "Preface to a Universal

---

94. Cf. E1P8Schol2.
95. For more information on the Leibniz-Spinoza relationship, see: W. Bartuschat, "Spinoza in der Philosophie von Leibniz," in *Spinozas Ethik und ihre frühe Wirkung*, ed. K. Cramer, W. G. Jacobs, and W. Schmidt-Biggeman (Wolfenbuttel: Herzog August Bibliotek, 1981) 51-66; Yvon Belaval, "Le *Leibniz et Spinoza* de M. Georges Friedmann," *Revue de Métaphysique et de Morale* 53 (1948), 307-321; Y. Belaval, "Leibniz lecteur de Spinoza," *Archives de Philosophie* 1983, 531-552; Renée Bouveresse, *Spinoza et Leibniz: l'idée d'animisme universel* (Paris: Vrin, 1992); Léon Brunschvicq, *Spinoza et ses contemporains*, 4th ed. (Paris: Presses Universitaires de France, 1951), esp. 237-270; Georges Friedmann, *Leibniz et Spinoza*, 2nd ed. (Paris: Gallimard, 1962). Friedmann's work is considered central in tracking relationships between the philosophical doctrines of the two thinkers. *Studia Spinozana* 6 (1990) has "Spinoza and Leibniz" as its theme and offers information on more recent research and commentary on some of Friedmann's proposals.

Characteristic," "Principles of Nature and Grace," "Monadology," and the *Theodicy*. Despite his academic interests, he turned to politics and entered the service of the Elector of Mainz. In 1672 he was sent to Paris on the diplomatic mission of trying to convince Louis XIV to turn his aggression toward Egypt and away from the German provinces. In Paris, he met both Huygens and Tschirnhaus and probably learned something of Spinoza's philosophy. Before returning to his work at the court of Hanover in 1676, Leibniz made trips to England and to Holland where he visited Spinoza. In his lifetime, Leibniz was not a popular man; perhaps this was due to his quarrels with the Royal Society over the discovery of the calculus; perhaps it was because his personal diplomatic style caused him to appear two-faced and untrustworthy; perhaps he just was not a pleasant person. Though many of his contemporaries did not appreciate him, much of his work, especially in the field of mathematics, has vindicated him (especially in his battles with Newton) in our time.[96] His extant correspondence with Spinoza (Ep45-Ep46) is of little interest to us philosophically since it deals primarily with questions on optics. It has been argued, however, by many commentators, that many elements of Leibniz's continually evolving philosophy arose as attempts to avoid Spinoza's naturalism and determinism.

The correspondence with J. Louis Fabritius (1632-1697), though it has little philosophical to say, shows us a very personal side of Spinoza (Ep47-Ep48). Fabritius, a professor of philosophy and theology at the University of Heidelberg, had been requested by the Prince Palatine (whose son he tutored), brother of Queen Christina of Sweden, to bring to that university some of the best minds of Europe.[97] Spinoza is extremely polite in his rejection of Fabritius' offer, basing his refusal on his love for peace and tranquillity which his solitude better afforded him than would a professorship. In retrospect, we know Spinoza made a wise decision; in 1674, the French army occupied Heidelberg, closed the university, and banished all professors.

---

96. For a brief comparison between the contemporary appreciations of Leibniz and of Spinoza, see Meinsma 499.

97. For possible political motives behind the plan, see Wolf (1928) 441-441; and P. Clair, "Spinoza à travers les journaux en langue française à la fin du XVIIe siècle," *Cahiers Spinoza* 2 (1978), 207-240.

Ep48 is addressed to John George Graevius (1632-?), who was a professor of rhetoric at the University of Utrecht. The brief letter, only three lines long in the original Latin, is merely a request that Graevius return a borrowed work. There is not much either philosophically or personally interesting about this man except that he had a passionate dislike for the TTP and may have been involved in some of the intrigues against Spinoza.[98]

About Hugo Boxel (dates unknown), very little is known. He is believed to have been a member of the governing class in Holland and is thought to have favored forging a political understanding with France (for which he was probably removed from office). What is interesting about the Boxel-Spinoza correspondence (Ep51-Ep56) is the fact that Boxel exemplifies a certain kind of intellectual prevalent in Spinoza's time: he accepts much of the new science and philosophy, but still holds on to certain superstitious beliefs because they cannot be demonstrated to be false (that they have not been demonstrated to be true has no bearing on the matter – Scripture or Church authority suffices). Thus, the exchange between him and Spinoza is off and running: Do you believe in ghosts? (Ep51); No – there is no evidence for them and much to suggest that they are products of the imagination (EP52); Yes, but, . . . and Boxel plays his hand showing him not to be so enlightened after all (Ep53, Ep55). The letters are important, nevertheless, not because we learn that ghosts are not female (Ep53), but because they touch on several important philosophical topics: aesthetics (Ep53-Ep55),[99] God's necessity and the necessity of the world (Ep53-Ep56),[100] human freedom (Ep55-Ep56),[101] the difference between intellect and imagination (Ep 56), and the number of attributes (Ep56).[102] In the end, however, Spinoza ends their correspondence by noting that the two are working from different first principles, so that there is little hope for consensus between them (Ep56).

Alfred Burgh (1651-?) and Nicholas Steno (1638-1686)[103] both

---

98. For more information, see Wolf (1928) 56; Meinsma 391: "Il peut avoir été un grand savant: sur le plan de l'amitié il semble avoir manqué singulièrement de caractère."
99. Cf. the preface to E4; PPC1P7.
100. Cf. Ep75; E1P11.
101. Cf. Ep57-Ep58; E4App1-2 and cf. E4P68Dem.
102. Cf. Ep63-Ep66.
103. For more information on Steno, see Leo S. Olschki, ed. *Niccolo Stenone, 1638-1686* (Florence: Leo S. Olschki, 1988).

wrote to Spinoza from Florence at about the same time in 1675,[104] each with the same purpose: to convert Spinoza to Roman Catholicism. The former was a student of Van den Enden and quite possibly of Spinoza; his father, Conrad Burgh, was the General Treasurer of the United Provinces. His conversion to Catholicism was a blow to his parents, who asked Spinoza to help them regain their son.[105] His letter to Spinoza (Ep67) has a mocking tone, and, in the words of Wolf, is quite "ill-mannered" and "stupid";[106] his arguments are hardly philosophical and not even substantive from a rhetorical standpoint, and he ends by threatening Spinoza with eternal damnation. Spinoza's reply (Ep76) is a bit more civil and philosophical, although he is guilty of throwing many of Burgh's arguments back at him. Spinoza rightly accuses his former friend of acting "not so much through the love of God as fear of Hell, which is the single cause of superstition" (Ep75), and closes with the wish that the young man soon recover his senses.

Steno, on the other hand, probably got to know Spinoza while stationed at the University of Leiden. He was a bit more learned than Burgh, and his geological tractate, *De solido intra solidum naturaliter contendo dissertationis prodromus* (1669) ["The Forerunner of a Dissertation concerning a Solid naturally contained within a Solid"] was among the books in Spinoza's library. Note that he greets Spinoza as the "Reformer of the New Philosophy" (Ep67a), which could hardly have been a flattering title since it was addressed by a convert from one of the reformed religions. Also noteworthy is that Steno, unlike Burgh, is both philosophical and friendly. He confronts Spinoza's ideas as presented in the TTP and attempts to appeal to reason rather than to his own passions or fears. No reply is known to have been sent by Spinoza, and perhaps the only reason why the Burgh letter was answered was because his parents had pleaded with Spinoza on his behalf.

Finally, Ep84 is included because it gives the reader an idea of the final form and intended structure of the incomplete TP. We are unable to identify to whom the letter had been addressed, but the editors of the *Opera posthuma* included it as a preface to the incomplete TP.

---

104. Perhaps not a coincidence. See Wolf (1928) 465.
105. Burgh apparently took extra pains to demonstrate his newly found faith. He is reported to have frequently run long distances bare-footed as a form of penance and openly rejoiced at his parents' displeasure with his conversion. See Meinsma 454.
106. Wolf (1928) 465.

8. The Sects and Religious Movements

Even prior to his excommunication and banishment from the Jewish community in 1656, Spinoza moved within the circles of many of the religious sects and movements in seventeenth-century Holland. The number probably increased after his banishment. Many of his closest friends and correspondents were also active in one or another of these movements, and these are mentioned at various points throughout the letters.

The importance of the religious movements in the interpretation of Spinoza's political treatises cannot be overestimated. As in England, political problems centered on the conceptual problem of the relation of church to state, which led to both a proliferation of sects and many inextricable mixtures of religious and political partisanship. Spinoza had a great deal to say about such problems in the TTP, especially with reference to the Dutch experience. For the same reasons, Hobbes had a great deal to say with reference to the English experience in both *Leviathan* and *De cive*. A *collegium* was an independent discussion group, typically devoted to an unconventional religious view. Collegiant (as dissident religious movements were often called) meetings began in Amsterdam in the early seventeenth century, were interrupted to some extent in 1648, but drew the attention of the Consistory in 1650. Cornelius Moorman, Daniel van Breen, and Adam Boreel (1603-1666) were among the leaders of these small discussion groups, which met regularly to discuss and interpret scriptural passages.[107] The *Borelists*, followers of Boreel, founded a group of Collegiants and were opposed to religious authority and to confessions of faith. Boreel was once regarded (wrongly) as the author of one of the movement's principal manifestos, *Light on the Candlestick*, which was in fact written by Spinoza's friend, Pieter Balling.[108]

---

107. See Meinsma 147-153, and Andrew C. Fix, *Prophecy and Reason: the Dutch Collegiants in the Early Enlightenment* (Princeton: Princeton University Press, 1991).
108. A Latin translation of *Light on the Candlestick* is included among Boreel's *Works*, and was consequently attributed to him, though he was probably only the translator.

In 1653, six pastors delegated by their Synods wrote to the Dutch Assembly to complain about the proliferation of heresy and the publication of heretical books. An edict issued by the Assembly in September of that year prohibited both the sale and possession of heretical books. The effects of this and other edicts which followed are difficult to assess, beyond the fact that there was a cessation, but only a brief one, of Collegiant meetings in Amsterdam. In general the civil authorities were reluctant to take any genuinely effective actions in response to the Consistory's repeated complaints until they were goaded into lashing out against Adriaan Koerbagh, for whose works a formal trial of heresy was begun in 1668.[109]

It is not known how long Spinoza remained in close contact with the Collegiant circles, but he did have contact with them through at least 1663 and probably a good deal longer. It was through them that he came into contact, in 1656, with the circle of friends of Franciscus Van den Enden. This circle included Simon de Vries, Pieter Balling, Jarig Jelles, Lodewijk Meyer, Johan Bouwmeester, Adriaan Koerbagh, Jan Rieuwertsz, and Jan Pietersz.

A full account of the history and development of the movements and sects at this period can be found in Meinsma's study,[110] but we offer a brief reference summary of the principal ones here.

---

109. Adriaan Koerbagh died in prison in 1669, Jan Koerbagh survived until 1672. See Hubert Vandenbossche, *Spinozisme en Kritiek bij Koerbagh* (Brussels: Vrije Universiteit Brussel, Centrum voor de Studie van der Verlichting, 1974). For details concerning their writings and the trial, see Meinsma 355-385. Meinsma is certainly correct in believing that the details and notoriety of the trial made their effects known in the pages of the TTP itself. See Jan and Adriaan Koerbagh, *Een ligt schijende in duystere plaatsen* (Brussels: Vrije Universiteit Brussel, Centrum voor de Studie van der Verlichting, 1974). This is the first edition, based on two manuscripts in the Rijksmuseum Meermanno-Westreenianum, Den Haag. Vandenbossche has an excessive estimate of the similarities between the thought of Spinoza and the Koerbaghs, but provides extensive biographical and bibliographical information.

110. For more detailed studies of the religious movements in seventeenth-century Holland, see also Pierre Clair, *Libertinage et incrédules* (Paris: CNRS, 1983); Karlfried Grunder and Wilhelm Schmidt-Biggeman, ed., *Spinoza in der Frühzeit seiner religiösen Wirkung* (Heidelberg: Lambert Schneider, 1984); H. G. Heimbrock, *Vom Heil der Seele: Studien zum Verhältnis von Religion und Psychologie bei Baruch Spinoza* (Frankfurt am Main: Peter Lang, 1981); and H. J. Siebrand, *Spinoza and the Netherlanders* (Assen: Van Gorcum, 1988).

The *Anabaptist* movement was born in Zurich in 1525, when Konrad Grebel underwent a second baptism. What distinguished the movement from orthodox baptist teaching was its refusal to recognize the baptism of children. Anabaptists were opposed to institutionalized religion, private property, and institutionalized political authority. Following a period of efforts to overthrow regional governments by force, the movement came under the more moderate governance of Menno Simons (1496-1561), and by Spinoza's time its members were also known as *Mennonites* because of their adherence to the Simons' teaching. Among Spinoza's Mennonite friends should be mentioned Jarig Jelles, Simon de Vries, and Pieter Balling. It should be noted that members of the *Baptist* movement, while they distinguished themselves from the Anabaptists, also refused baptism to children: this movement was also active in Spinoza's time.

The *Antitrinitarian* movement underwent a resurgence during the sixteenth century, partly under the the influence of *Resurgents* and *Anabaptists*. The *Socinians* (*quod vide*) were also Antitrinitarians.

Arians followed the teaching of Arius (death, 336) in denying the divinity of Christ. The term 'Arian' was most used in Spinoza's time as a means of insulting Antitrinitarians.

The *Arminians* followed the teaching of Jacobus Arminius (1560-1609). The year 1603 marked a debate between Arminius and Gomar on the questions of freedom of the will and religious tolerance, both strongly supported by Arminius and his followers. Arminians were also called *Remonstrants* in Spinoza's time. The movement attained political prominence through the support of the Grand Pensioner Johan Van Oldenbarneveldt. In 1610, Uytenbogaert, a disciple of Arminius and teacher of Oldenbarneveldt, published the *Remonstrant Manifesto*. The movement soon split into factions, the *Counter-Remonstrant* element of which was the more biblical and humanistic, but opposed religious tolerance. At the Synod of Dordrecht (1618-1619) this faction gained temporary dominance, but its political and religious intolerance was held in check by Johan de Witt (prior to his murder) during Spinoza's time. In 1619 the Synod of Dordrecht condemned Arminianism and put Oldenbarneveldt to death.

The *Brownists* (Robert Browne, 1549-1636) supported full independence of church and state, as well as the independence of local religious communities. One of their leading members, John Robinson (1576-1625), emigrated to the Colonies with a group of Brownists aboard the *Mayflower*.

The official religion of the Dutch state was *Calvinism* (John Calvin, 1509-1564) and believed in salvation through faith rather than through works. Officially the movement supported separation of church and state. Unofficially many of the Calvinist clergy in Spinoza's time supported the overthrow of the Dutch Republic, restoration of the Prince of Orange, and a greater role for their church in the wielding of political power.

The *Collegiants* were less a definite religious sect than a general movement, and the term was often used in Spinoza's time as an umbrella for dissidents of many kinds. The Collegiant movement was formed just as the Thirty Year War began.[111] The Collegiant group at Rijnsburg was born when the Remonstrant community found itself without a pastor and established a new movement under the direction of Van der Kodde. They denied all ceremonial and ecclesiastical authority and recognized only scripture. Spinoza appears to have had some Collegiant friends during his residence in Rijnsburg,[112] and some have suggested that he may have settled there because it was their headquarters.

Lucianism was not a movement or sect so much as a poetic term applied in Spinoza's time to freethinkers. The name is derived from Lucian (120-180), who derided the Greek gods. The term was applied often in Spinoza's day to his friend and teacher Franciscus Van den Enden.[113] Nor were the *Curious* as such a sect or movement. They supported communication with divinity through observation of and meditation about the world about them and proposed travel expeditions to further such understanding. Many of them were present in the French army during the war with Holland. The *Enthusiasts*, also called *Schwärmer* or *Spiritualists*, opposed all dogma, confessions of faith, and ecclesiastical authority. Their members were often found in *Anabaptist* communities. The *Independents*, also known as *Congregationalists*, were also opposed to all forms of religious authority.

The *Quaker* movement was founded by George Fox (1624-1691) and had many supporters in Holland. They opposed all ritual and

---

111. For the development of the movement and Spinoza's many contacts with it through friends and correspondents, see Meinsma 147-180.
112. See Louis Van Bunge, *Johannes Bredenburg (1643-1691): Een Roterdamse Collegiant in de ban van Spinoza* (Rotterdam: Universiteits Erasmus Drukkerij, 1990).
113. See Meinsma 181-214.

emphasized a personal religious experience based upon the 'inner light'. They were also pacifists. Some researchers believe that what is probably Spinoza's earliest work, the *Korte Verhandeling*, may have been written at the request of Quaker friends, and perhaps may have been used as a discussion topic at informal Quaker meetings.[114] During Spinoza's time there was an influx of English Quaker leaders into the Netherlands.

The *Lutheran* movement was founded by Martin Luther (1483-1546) and had few adherents in Holland. The two principal factions in the seventeenth century were centered in Wittenberg and Helmstadt. Colerus, Spinoza's first biographer, was a member of the more rigorous Wittenberg faction.

The *Millenarians* believed in the proximity of the return of Christ, and their followers were often members of Anabaptist communities.

The *Socinians* were disciples of the two cousins Laelius (1526-1562) and Faustus (1539-1605) Socinus. The *De Jesu Christo Servatore*, a principal document of the movement, was published in 1594.[115] Banished from Poland in 1656, they were very numerous in the Holland of Spinoza's time,[116] and their members exercised considerable influence among Arminian and Mennonite communities as well. They placed great emphasis on freedom of the will; and, contrary to Spinoza, they argued that scripture could always be reconciled with reason.

---

114. Two articles by Richard H. Popkin explore these and other possible relationships. See "Spinoza, the Quakers, and the Millenarians," *Manuscrito* 6 (1982), 113-133; and "Spinoza's Relations with the Quakers in Amsterdam," *Quaker History* 73 (1984), 14-28.

115. The work was actually written by Faustus Socinus (Rakow, Poland: Typis Alexii Rodecii, 1594).

116. Amsterdam was the place of publication of the *Bibliotheca Fratrum Polonorum* (ed. A. Wiszowaty and F. Kuyper. Irenopoli [i.e., Amsterdam]: 1660), a massive ten-volume compilation of the works of Faustus Socinus and his followers.

9. Philosophical Importance of the Letters

When Wolf published the first complete English translation of Spinoza's letters in 1928,[117] he noted in his introduction that a close reading and study of them would necessitate radical changes in the then-prevalent interpretation of Spinoza's philosophy. Between 1928 and the present writing of this introduction (1994), the number and extent of those changes which have taken place would probably have even surprised even Wolf. Certainly not all of them have arisen from scholarly work on the letters. As mentioned earlier, the separation of Spinoza's political thought from that of Hobbes (especially among anglophone authors) has been a contributing factor, as has been the waning of the Hegelian and idealist misinterpretations of Spinoza.[118] The wealth of textual work which has been done on Spinoza's writings is also a major factor in our new understanding of him and the current and ongoing repositioning of him in the history of philosophy. Many of these factors are now only beginning to have further effects. The future will bring additional textual insight and philosophical reflection. Interest in Spinoza's political theory, epistemology, psychology, and physics continues to grow in the contemporary philosophical literature. This interest is not purely historical. In many cases a careful reading of Spinoza will bring to light substantial contributions to systematic debates on issues of importance in a twentieth-century philosophy, especially issues which are in an important sense ahistorical in their scope.[119]

---

117. A. Wolf, *The Correspondence of Spinoza* (London: Frank Cass), reprinted in 1966.
118. While much of the work on Spinoza in the earlier part of this century has been by French and German scholars, the importance of the writings of H. F. Hallett in arguing against the nineteenth-century idealistic readings among anglophone authors should be emphasized. See his *Aeternitas: A Spinozistic Study* (Oxford: Clarendon Press, 1930); *Benedict de Spinoza: The Elements of His Philosophy* (London: Athlone Press, 1957); and *Creation, Emanation, and Salvation* (The Hague: Martinus Nijhoff, 1962).
119. One of the finest recent examples is Charles Ramond, *Qualité et quantité dans la philosophie de Spinoza* (Paris: Presses Universitaires de France, 1995). A good example in English is Jonathan Bennett, *A Study of Spinoza's Ethics* (Indianapolis: Hackett, 1984). Bennett makes liberal use of the letters. While he often misses a major point for want of a more studied historical approach, and while we also find some of his assessments questionable, his work is solid evidence for Spinoza's ability to speak to contemporary issues. In French, the earlier commen-

The role of the letters will doubtless continue to be a major one in subsequent interpretations and reassessments of Spinoza. The *Ethics* and the two political treatises are and should be the final statements of Spinoza's mature philosophical positions. But the geometrical style of the *Ethics* is difficult for the reader and certainly imposed constraints on Spinoza himself. The letters frequently provide a more informal and less technical presentation of themes developed more formally in it, and no less frequently do they also provide further (often technical) elaborations of points which are pursued only in passing in the *Ethics*.

While Spinoza's own philosophical thought was expressed in the terminology of Descartes, who is rightly regarded as the father of modern philosophy, both in his method and in his conclusions Spinoza is not a Cartesian. Much of what Spinoza writes, both in his works and in his letters, is offered as a critique, sometimes explicit, of his great predecessor. To the very great extent whereby philosophy after Descartes has developed in response to the problems and paradoxes which Descartes bequeathed to his successors, Spinoza's philosophy has much to teach us today as it did his many correspondents.

---

taries of Martial Gueroult on the first two parts of the *Ethics* make extensive use of the letters to clarify and to expand points developed too briefly in Spinoza's other writings.

Appendix: Chronology

1536	Calvin publishes the *Institution of the Christian Religion.*
1565	Beginning of the war of independence of the Spanish-Dutch region against Spain.
1579	The "Union of Utrecht" establishes the United Provinces.
1594	Publication of Socinus' *De Christo Servatore.*
1600?	The Espinosa family emigrates from Portugal to Nantes, and thence to Amsterdam.
1602	Foundation of the East India Company.
1603	Arminius and Gomar debate at Leiden on the questions of tolerance and freedom of the will.
1609	Foundation of the Bank of Amsterdam.
1610	Uytenbogaert, a disciple of Arminius and teacher of Oldenbarneveldt, publishes the *Remonstrant Manifesto.*
1614	H. de Groot begins work on the *De Imperio Summarum Potestarum* (published in 1647).
1618	The Thirty Years' War begins.
1619	The Synod of Dordrecht condemns Arminianism and puts Oldenbarneveldt to death. The Collegiant sect is formed. Descartes is a soldier in the army of Maurice of Nassau.
1628	Descartes is living in Holland.
1632	Birth of Baruch d'Espinosa at Amsterdam.
1633	Papal condemnation of Galileo, who is placed under house arrest. Descartes decides not to publish *Le Monde.*
1636	Carried clandestinely to Amsterdam, Galileo's *Discourse Concerning Two New Sciences* is published by Elzevier.
1638	The founding of the great Portuguese Synagogue of Amsterdam. Spinoza is registered as a student in the Hebrew school.
1639	Naudé, a "libertine" philosopher, publishes his *Considerations Politiques sur les Coups d'Etat*, a work inspired by Machiavelli.
1640	Beginning of the English civil war.
1641	Descartes publishes his *Meditationes de Prima Philosophia.* Jansenius publishes *Augustinus.*

1642	Hobbes publishes *De Cive*.
1645	Milton publishes the *Areopagitica*, a manifesto for freedom of the press.
	Herbert of Cherbury publishes his *De Religione Gentilium*.
1647	Descartes' *Méditations Metaphysiques* published in French translation.
1648	The Peace of Munster. Definitive establishment of the United Provinces.
1649	Charles I of England is executed.
1650	A failed coup d'état by William II of Orange. Jan de Witt becomes the Grand Pensioner of the Netherlands.
1651	Cromwell institutes the Act of Navigation.
	Hobbes publishes the *Leviathan*.
1656	Spinoza is banished from the Jewish community in Amsterdam. He studies humanities, Latin, philosophy, and theatre at the school of the ex-Jesuit, Van den Enden.
1660	Restoration of the Stuarts in England. Spinoza leaves Amsterdam and moves to Rijnsburg, where he is a familiar visitor among Collegiant circles. He begins work on the unfinished DIE (published in 1677).
1661	Beginning of the reign of Louis XIV.
1662	Founding of the Royal Society. Oldenburg is its joint-secretary, and Boyle and Newton are charter members.
1663	Spinoza is installed at Voorburg. He there publishes the PPC, with an appendix (CM).
1665	Beginning of the second Anglo-Dutch war.
1668	Ecclesiastical condemnation of Adriaan Koerbagh, one of Spinoza's students.
1670	Spinoza publishes (anonymously and in Latin) the TTP.
	Posthumous publication of the *Pensées* of Pascal.
1671	Spinoza is installed in the Hague, where he prevents (possibly at the suggestion of Jan de Witt) the appearance of the vernacular edition of the TTP (see Ep44).
1672	Louis XIV invades Holland.
	Jan de Witt and his brother are massacred by a mob, probably inspired by Calvinist clergy.
	William II of Orange becomes *stadthouder*.
1673	Spinoza declines the chair of philosophy at Heidelberg.
	Spinoza visits the military camp of the Prince de Condé.
	Huygens publishes the *Horologium Oscillatorium*.

1674	The States of Holland publish a formal condemnation of the TTP and "other heretical and atheistic writings." Malebranche publishes the *Recherche de la Vérité*, which is accused of being of Spinozist inspiration.
1675	Spinoza completes and circulates *Ethica* I, but declines to publish it. He begins work on the TP.
1676	Spinoza receives Leibniz as his visitor (and distrusts him). The Synod of The Hague orders an inquiry into the authorship of the TTP.
1677	Death of Spinoza. His friends edit and publish the *Opera Posthuma* and *Nagelate Schriften*, all of whose contents are condemned by the political authorities and Calvinists the following year.
1681	Bossuet writes the *Politique Tirée de l'Ecriture Sainte* and also his *Discours sur l'Histoire Universelle*, and succeeds in preventing the publication of Richard Simon's *Critical History of the Old Testament* (which draws its inspiration from the TTP).
1685	Louis XIV revokes the Edict of Nantes.
1687	Newton publishes the first edition of the *Mathematical Principles of Natural Philosophy*.
1688	The "Glorious Revolution": William III becomes King of England.
1689	Locke publishes his *Letter on Tolerance* and his *Essay on Civil Government*.
1697	In his *Dictionnaire Historique et Critique*, Bayle characterizes Spinoza as "un athée de système, étrangement vertueux."
1710	Leibniz publishes his *Theodicy*.

The Letters

of certain learned men
to B.d.S.
and the Author's replies
contributing not a little to the
elucidation of his other works.

LETTER 1
To the most esteemed B.d.S., from Henry Oldenburg.

[Known only from the O.P. The original is lost.]

Most illustrious Sir, esteemed friend,

With such reluctance did I recently tear myself away from your side when visiting you at your retreat in Rijnsburg, that no sooner am I back in England than I am endeavouring to join you again, as far as possible, at least by exchange of letters. Substantial learning, combined with humanity and courtesy – all of which nature and diligence have so amply bestowed on you – hold such an allurement as to gain the affection of any men of quality and of liberal education. Come then, most excellent Sir, let us join hands in unfeigned friendship, and let us assiduously cultivate that friendship with devotion and service of every kind. Whatever my poor resources can furnish, consider as yours. As to the gifts of mind that you possess, let me claim a share in them, as this cannot impoverish you.

At Rijnsburg we conversed about God, about infinite Extension and Thought, about the difference and agreement of these attributes, and about the nature of the union of the human soul with the body; and also about the principles of the Cartesian and Baconian philosophy. But since we then spoke about such important topics as through a lattice-window and only in a cursory way, and in the meantime all these things continue to torment me, let me now, by the right of the friendship entered upon between us, engage in a discussion with you and cordially beg you to set forth at somewhat greater length your views on the above-mentioned subjects. In particular, please be good enough to enlighten me on these two points: first, wherein you place the true distinction between Extension and Thought, and second, what defects you find in the philosophy of Descartes and Bacon, and how you consider that these can be removed and replaced by sounder views. The more frankly you write to me on these and similar subjects, the more closely you will bind me to you and place me under a strong obligation to make an equal return, if only I can.

Here there are already in the press *Certain Physiological Essays*,[1] written by an English nobleman, a man of extraordinary learning. These treat of the nature of air and its elastic property, as proved by forty-three experiments; and also of fluidity and firmness and the like. As soon as they are printed, I shall see to it that they are delivered to you through a friend who happens to be crossing the sea. Meanwhile, farewell, and remember your friend, who is,

> Yours in all affection and devotion,
> Henry Oldenburg.

London, 16/26 August 1661.

---

1. Robert Boyle's essays were published in 1661, with a Latin version published in London (1665) and Amsterdam (1667). The term 'physiological' is the same in sense as 'physical' – that which concerns nature. See *The Works of the Honourable Robert Boyle* (London, 1772, Vol. I, p. 359), *A physico-chymical Essay, with some Considerations touching the differing parts and redintegration of Salt-Petre*. Sections 3-11 (pp. 377seq) deal with the experiments: *The history of fluidity and firmness*.

LETTER 2
To the most noble and learned H. Oldenburg
from B.d.S.

[Known only from the O.P. The original is lost.
No date is given, but a conjectural date is September 1661.]

Esteemed Sir,

You yourself will be able to judge what pleasure your friendship affords me, if only your modesty will allow you to consider the estimable qualities with which you are richly endowed. And although, with these qualities in mind, I feel myself not a little presumptuous in venturing upon this relationship, especially when I reflect that between friends all things, and particularly things of the spirit, should be shared, nevertheless this step is to be accredited not so much to me as to your courtesy, and also your kindness. From your great courtesy you have been pleased to belittle yourself, and from your abundant kindness so to enlarge me, that I do not hesitate to enter upon the friendship which you firmly extend to me and deign to ask of me in return, a friendship which it shall be my earnest endeavour diligently to foster.

As for my mental endowments, such as they are, I would most willingly have you make claim on them even if I knew that this would be greatly to my detriment. But lest I seem in this way to want to refuse you what you ask by right of friendship, I shall attempt to explain my views on the subjects we spoke of – although I do not think that this will be the means of binding you more closely to me unless I have your kind indulgence.

I shall begin therefore with a brief discussion of God, whom I define as a Being consisting of infinite attributes, each of which is infinite or supremely perfect in its own kind.[2] Here it should be observed that by attribute I mean every thing that is conceived in itself and through itself, so that its conception does not involve the conception of any other thing. For example, extension is conceived through

---

2. See E1Def6. The phrasing, 'infinite attributes, . . . each infinite', clearly suggests that the first occurrence of 'infinite' refers to number in our modern sense (whereas Spinoza uses *numerus* only in a finitary sense). So there is an infinity of attributes, each of which is itself infinite.

itself and in itself, but not so motion; for the latter is conceived in something else, and its conception involves extension.[3]

That this is a true definition of God is evident from the fact that by God we understand a supremely perfect and absolutely infinite Being. The existence of such a Being is easily proved from this definition; but as this is not the place for such a proof,[4] I shall pass it over. The points I need to prove here in order to satisfy your first enquiry, esteemed Sir, are as follows: first, that in Nature there cannot exist two substances without their differing entirely in essence; secondly, that a substance cannot be produced, but that it is of its essence to exist; third, every substance must be infinite, or supremely perfect in its kind.[5]

With these points established, esteemed Sir, provided that at the same time you attend to the definition of God, you will readily perceive the direction of my thoughts, so that I need not be more explicit on this subject. However, in order to provide a clear and concise proof, I can think of no better expedient than to arrange them in geometrical style and to submit them to the bar of your judgment. I therefore enclose them separately herewith,[6] and await your verdict on them.

Secondly, you ask me what errors I see in the philosophy of Descartes and Bacon. In this request, too, I shall try to oblige you, although it is not my custom to expose the errors of others. The first and most important error is this, that they have gone far astray from knowledge of the first cause and origin of all things. Secondly, they have failed to understand the true nature of the human mind. Thirdly, they have never grasped the true cause of error. Only those who are completely destitute of all learning and scholarship can fail to see the critical importance of true knowledge of these three points.

That they have gone far astray from true knowledge of the first cause and of the human mind can readily be gathered from the truth of the three propositions to which I have already referred; so I confine myself to point out the third error. Of Bacon I shall say little; he speaks very confusedly on this subject, and simply makes assertions while proving hardly anything. In the first place he takes for granted that the

---

3. These definitions are essentially the same as given in the *Ethics*: see E1Def3 and E1Def4.
4. Spinoza in fact gives three proofs in E1P11.
5. See E1P5, E1P6, E1P8.
6. See *Ethics* Part 1, from the beginning to Prop. 4. [Footnote in the O.P.]

human intellect, besides the fallibility of the senses, is by its very nature liable to error, and fashions everything after the analogy of its own nature, and not after the analogy of the universe, so that it is like a mirror presenting an irregular surface to the rays it receives, mingling its own nature with the nature of reality, and so forth.[7] Secondly, he holds that the human intellect, by reason of its peculiar nature, is prone to abstractions,[8] and imagines as stable things that are in flux, and so on. Thirdly, he holds that the human intellect is in constant activity, and cannot come to a halt or rest.[9] Whatever other causes he assigns can all be readily reduced to the one Cartesian principle, that the human will is free and more extensive than the intellect, or, as Verulam more confusedly puts it, the intellect is not characterised as a dry light, but receives infusion from the will.[10] (We should here observe that Verulam often takes intellect for mind, therein differing from Descartes.) This cause, then, disregarding the others as being of little importance, I shall show to be false. Indeed, they would easily have seen this for themselves, had they but given consideration to the fact that the will differs from this or that volition in the same way as whiteness differs from this or that white object, or as humanity differs from this or that human being. So to conceive the will to be the cause of this or that volition is as impossible as to conceive humanity to be the cause of Peter and Paul.[11]

Since, then, the will is nothing more than a mental construction (*ens rationis*), it can in no way be said to be the cause of this or that volition. Particular volitions, since they need a cause to exist, cannot be said to be free; rather, they are necessarily determined to be such as they are by their own causes. Finally, according to Descartes, errors are themselves particular volitions, from which it necessarily follows that errors – that is, particular volitions – are not free, but are determined by external causes and in no way by the will. This is what I undertook to demonstrate. Etc.

---

7. The reference is probably to *Novum Organum* I, 41, which deals with the "Idols of the Tribe."
8. See *Novum Organum* I, 51.
9. See *Novum Organum* I, 48.
10. See Verulam's *Novum Organum*, Book 1, Aphorism 49. [Footnote in the O.P.]
11. On the relation between 'humanity' and individual persons, see E1P8Schol2. Spinoza's claim that will is merely one mode of thought is developed in E1P32.

LETTER 3
To the esteemed B.d.S., from Henry Oldenburg

[Known only from the O.P. The original is lost.]

Excellent Sir and dear Friend,

Your very learned letter has been delivered to me and read with great pleasure. I warmly approve your geometrical style of proof, but at the same time I blame my obtuseness for not so readily grasping what you with such exactitude teach. So I beg you to allow me to present the evidence of this sluggishness of mine by putting the following questions and seeking from you their solutions.

The first is, do you understand clearly and indubitably that, solely from the definition of God which you give, it is demonstrated that such a Being exists? For my part, when I reflect that definitions contain no more than conceptions of our mind, and that our mind conceives many things that do not exist and is most prolific in multiplying and augmenting things once conceived, I do not yet see how I can infer the existence of God from the conception I have of him. Indeed, from a mental accumulation of all the perfections I discover in men, animals, vegetables, minerals and so on, I can conceive and form one single substance which possesses in full all those qualities; even more, my mind is capable of multiplying and augmenting them to infinity, and so of fashioning for itself a most perfect and excellent Being. Yet the existence of such a Being can by no means be inferred from this.

My second question is, are you quite certain that Body is not limited by Thought, nor Thought by Body? For it is still a matter of controversy as to what Thought is, whether it is a corporeal motion or a spiritual activity quite distinct from what is corporeal.

My third question is, do you regard those axioms you have imparted to me as being indemonstrable principles, known by the light of Nature and standing in no need of proof? It may be that the first axiom is that of kind, but I do not see how the other three can be accounted as such. For the second axiom supposes that there exists in Nature nothing but substance and accidents, whereas many maintain that time and place are in neither category. Your third axiom, that 'things having different attributes have nothing in common' is so far from being clearly conceived by me that the entire Universe seems rather to prove the contrary. All things known to us both differ from one another in some respects and agree in other respects. Finally, your fourth axiom, namely, 'things which have nothing in common with one another cannot be the cause one of the other', is not so clear to my befogged intellect as not to require some light to be shed on it. For God has nothing formally in common with created things; yet we almost all hold him to be their cause.

Since, then, these axioms do not seem to me to be placed beyond all hazard of doubt, you may readily conjecture that your propositions based on them are bound to be shaky. And the more I consider them, the more I am overwhelmed with doubt concerning them. Against the first I hold that two men are two substances and of the same attribute, since they are both capable of reasoning; and thence I conclude that there are two substances of the same attribute. With regard to the second I consider that, since nothing can be the cause of itself, we can scarcely understand how it can be true that 'Substance cannot be produced, nor can it be produced by any other substance.' For this proposition asserts that all substances are causes of themselves, that they are each and all independent of one another, and it makes them so many Gods, in this way denying the first cause of all things.

This I willingly confess I cannot grasp, unless you do me the kindness of disclosing to me somewhat more simply and more fully your opinion regarding this high matter, explaining what is the origin and production of substances, the interdependence of things and their subordinate relationships. I entreat you, by the friendship on which we have embarked, to deal with me frankly and confidently in this, and I urge you most earnestly to be fully convinced that all these things which you see fit to impart to me will be inviolate and secure, and that I shall in no way permit any of them to become public to your detriment or injury.

In our Philosophical Society we are engaged in making experiments and observations as energetically as our abilities allow, and we are occupied in composing a History of the Mechanical Arts, being convinced that the forms and qualities of things can best be explained by the principles of mechanics, that all Nature's effects are produced by motion, figure, texture and their various combinations, and that there is no need to have recourse to inexplicable forms and occult qualities, the refuge of ignorance.[12]

I shall send you the book I promised as soon as your Dutch ambassadors stationed here dispatch a messenger to the Hague (as they often do), or as soon as some other friend, to whom I can safely entrust it, goes your way.

Please excuse my prolixity and frankness, and I particularly urge you to take in good part, as friends do, what I have said frankly and without any disguise or courtly refinement, in replying to your letter. And believe me to be, sincerely and simply,

Your most devoted,
Henry Oldenburg.

London, 27 September 1661.

---

12. This paragraph summarises the basic principles of the 'mechanical philosophy'.

LETTER 4
To the noble and learned Henry Oldenburg, from B.d.S.

[Known only from the O.P. The original is lost.
No date is given, but a conjectural date is October 1661.]

Most esteemed Sir,

While preparing to go to Amsterdam to spend a week or two there, I received your very welcome letter and read your objections to the three propositions which I sent you. On these alone I shall try to satisfy you, omitting the other matters for want of time.

To your first objection, then, I say that it is not from the definition of any thing whatsoever that the existence of the defined thing follows, but only (as I demonstrated in the Scholium which I attached to the three propositions) from the definition or idea of some attribute; that is (as I explained clearly in the case of the definition of God), from the definition of a thing which is conceived through itself and in itself. The ground for this distinction I have also stated in the afore-mentioned Scholium with sufficient clarity, I think, especially for a philosopher. A philosopher is supposed to know what is the difference between fiction and a clear and distinct conception, and also to know the truth of this axiom, to wit, that every definition, or clear and distinct idea, is true. Once these points are noted, I do not see what more is required in answer to the first question.

I therefore pass on to the solution of the second question. Here you seem to grant that, if Thought does not pertain to the nature of Extension, then Extension will not be limited by Thought; for surely it is only the example which causes you some doubt. But I beg you to note, if someone says that Extension is not limited by Extension, but by Thought, will he not also be saying that Extension is not infinite in an absolute sense, but only in so far as it is Extension? That is, does he not grant me that Extension is infinite not in an absolute sense, but only in so far as it is Extension, that is, infinite in its own kind?[13]

---

13. The distinction between the two types of infinity is given in E1Def2. The proofs of the absolute infinity of extension and of thought are given in E2P1-P2.

But, you say, perhaps Thought is a corporeal activity. Let it be so, although I do not concede it; but this one thing you will not deny, that Extension, in so far as it is Extension, is not Thought; and this suffices to explain my definition and to demonstrate the third proposition.

The third objection which you proceed to raise against what I have set down is this, that the axioms should not be accounted as 'common notions' (*notiones communes*).[14] This is not the point I am urging; but you also doubt their truth, and you even appear to seek to prove that their contrary is more probably. But please attend to my definition of substance and accident,[15] from which all these conclusions follow. For by substance I understand that which is conceived through itself and in itself, that is, that whose conception does not involve the conception of another thing; and by modification or accident I understand that which is in something else and is conceived through that in which it is. Hence it is clearly established, first, that substance is prior in nature to its accidents; for without it these can neither exist nor be conceived. Secondly, besides substance and accidents nothing exists in reality, or externally to the intellect; for whatever there is, is conceived either through itself or through something else, and its conception either does or does not involve the conception of another thing. Thirdly, things which have different attributes have nothing in common with one another;[16] for I have explained an attribute as that whose conception does not involve the conception of another thing. Fourth and last, of things which have nothing in common with one another, one cannot be the cause of another; for since in the effect there would be nothing in common with the cause, all it would have, it would have from nothing.

As for your contention that God has nothing formally in common with created things, etc., I have maintained the exact opposite in my definition. For I said that God is a Being consisting of infinite attributes, each of which is infinite,[17] or supremely perfect, in its kind.

---

14. These are what Oldenburg had called 'indemonstrable principles' in the previous letter. Spinoza's casting of them as 'common notions' is in accordance with his discussion of them in E2P37-P40.
15. Spinoza rarely uses the term 'accident', which is scholastic in origin. His preferred term is 'mode', which differs significantly in sense. He links the usage to 'modification or accident' in the next sentence.
16. See E1P2-P3.
17. See our note to the phrase 'infinite attributes' in Ep2.

As to your objection to my first proposition, I beg you, my friend, to consider that men are not created, but only begotten, and that their bodies already existed, but in a different form.[18] However, the conclusion is this, as I am quite willing to admit, that if one part of matter were to be annihilated, the whole of Extension would also vanish at the same time.[19]

The second proposition does not make many gods, but one only, to wit, a God consisting of infinite attributes, etc.

---

18. See E1P8Schol2.
19. This passage adumbrates what Jonathan Bennett calls 'Spinoza's field metaphysics.' See his *A Study of Spinoza's Ethics* (Indianapolis: Hackett, 1984), 97-110.

LETTER 5
To the esteemed B.d.S., from Henry Oldenburg.

[Known only from the O.P. The original is lost.]

My very dear friend,

Receive herewith the little book[20] I promised, and send me in return your opinion of it, especially with regard to the experiments he concludes concerning nitre, fluidity and solidity.[21] I am most grateful to you for your learned second letter, which I received yesterday. Still, I very much regret that your journey to Amsterdam prevented you from answering all my doubts. I beg you to send me, as soon as your leisure permits, what was then omitted. Your last letter did indeed shed a great deal of light for me, but not so much as to dispel all the darkness. This will, I hope, be the happy outcome when you will have clearly and distinctly furnished me with your views on the true and primary origin of things. For as long as it is not quite clear to me from what cause and in what manner things began to be, and by what connection they depend on the first cause, if there be such a thing, then all that I hear and all that I read seems to me quite incoherent. I therefore most earnestly beg you, most learned Sir, to light my way in this matter, and not to doubt my good faith and gratitude. I am,

      Your very devoted,
      Henry Oldenburg.

London 11/21 October 1661.

---

20. This is Boyle's *Certain Physiological Essays* mentioned in Ep1. Oldenburg has apparently procured an advance copy of the Latin translation.
21. *De nitro, fluiditate et firmitate*: see section 2 of our introduction for an account of this work and of the secondary literature relating to the discussion in the following letters.

LETTER 6
To the most noble and learned Henry Oldenburg, from B.d.S. Containing comments on the book of the most noble Robert Boyle, on Nitre, Fluidity and Solidity.

[Printed in the O.P. The original is extant. The last two
paragraphs of this translation appear only in the original.
The letter is undated, but a conjectural date is early 1662.]

Esteemed Sir,

I have received the very talented Mr. Boyle's book, and read it through,
as far as time permitted. I thank you very much for this gift. I see that I
was not wrong in conjecturing, when you first promised me this book,
that you would not concern yourself with anything less than a matter of
great importance. Meanwhile, learned Sir, you wish me to send you my
humble opinion on what he has written. This I shall do, as far as my
slender ability allows, noting those points which seem to me obscure or
insufficiently demonstrated; but I have not as yet been able to peruse it
all, far less examine it, because of my other commitments. Here, then,
is that I find worthy of comment regarding Nitre, etc.[22]

Of Nitre.

First, he gathers from his experiment on the redintegration of Nitre
that Nitre is a heterogeneous thing, consisting of fixed and volatile
parts. Its nature, however, (at least as shown by its behaviour) is quite
different from the nature of its component parts, although it arises
from nothing but a mixture of these parts. For this conclusion to be
regarded as valid, I suggest that a further experiment seems to be
required to show that Spirit of Nitre is not really Nitre, and cannot be
reduced to solid state or crystallised without the help of salt of lye. Or
at least one ought to have enquired whether the quantity of fixed salt

---

22. For a summary of the experiments on which Spinoza is commenting in what follows, see part 2 of our introduction.

remaining in the crucible is always found to be the same from the same quantity of Nitre, and to vary proportionately with the quantity of Nitre.[23] And as to what the esteemed author says (section 9) he discovered with the aid of scales, and the fact that the observed behaviour of Spirit of Nitre is so different from, and even sometimes contrary to, that of Nitre itself, in my view this does nothing to confirm his conclusion.

To make this clear, I shall briefly set forth what occurs to me as the simplest explanation of this redintegration of Nitre, and at the same time I shall add two or three quite easy experiments by which this explanation is to some extent confirmed. To explain what takes place as simply as possible, I shall posit no difference between Spirit of Nitre and Nitre itself other than that which is sufficiently obvious; to wit, that the particles of the latter are at rest whereas those of the former, when stirred, are in a state of considerable commotion. With regard to the fixed salt, I shall suppose that this in no way contributes to constituting the essence of Nitre. I shall consider it as the dregs of Nitre, from which the Spirit of Nitre (as I find) is itself not free; for they float in it in some abundance, although in a very powdery form. This salt, or these dregs, have pores or passages hollowed out to the size of the particles of Nitre. But when the Nitre particles were driven out of them by the action of fire, some of the passages became narrower and consequently others were forced to dilate, and the substance or walls of these passages became stiff and at the same time very brittle. So when Spirit of Nitre was dropped thereon, some of its particles began to force their way through those narrower passages; and since the particles are of unequal thickness (as Descartes has aptly demonstrated),[24] they first bent the rigid walls of the passages like a bow, and then broke them. When they broke them, they forced those fragments to recoil, and, retaining the motion they already had, they remained as equally incapable as before of solidifying and crystallising. The parts of Nitre which made their way through the wider passages, since they did not touch the walls of those passages, were necessarily surrounded by some very fine matter and by this were driven upwards, in the same way as bits of wood by flame or heat, and were given off as smoke. But if they

---

23. Spinoza is suggesting that the 'fixed nitre' (probably potassium carbonate) is an impurity in the nitre.

24. See Descartes' *Principles of Philosophy* IV, 110.

were sufficiently numerous, or if they united with fragments of the walls and with particles making their way through the narrower passages, they formed droplets flying upwards. But if the fixed salt is loosened by means of water[25] or air and is rendered less active, then it becomes sufficiently capable of stemming the onrush of the particles of Nitre and of compelling them to lose the motion they possessed and to come again to a halt, just as does a cannonball when it strikes sand or mud. The redintegration of Nitre consists solely in this coagulation of the particles of Spirit of Nitre, and to bring this about the fixed salt acts as an instrument, as is clear from this explanation. So much for the redintegration.

Now, if you please, let us see first of all why Spirit of Nitre and Nitre itself differ so much in taste; secondly, why Nitre is inflammable, while spirit of Nitre is by no means so. To understand the first question, it should be noted that bodies in motion never come into contact with other bodies along their broadest surfaces, whereas bodies at rest lie on other bodies along their broadest surfaces. So particles of Nitre, if placed on the tongue while they are at rest, will lie on it along their broadest surfaces and will thus obstruct its pores, which is the cause of the cold sensation. Furthermore, the Nitre cannot be dissolved by saliva into such very minute particles. But if the particles are placed on the tongue while they are in active motion, they will come into contact with it by their more pointed surfaces and will make their way through its pores. And the more active their motion, the more sharply they will prick the tongue, just as a needle, as it either strikes the tongue with its point or lies lengthwise along the tongue, will cause different sensations to arise.

The reason why Nitre is inflammable and the Spirit of Nitre not so is this, that when particles of Nitre are at rest, they cannot so readily be borne upwards by fire as when they have their own motion in all directions. So when they are at rest, they resist the fire until such time as the fire separates them from one another and encompasses them from all sides. When it does encompass them, it carries them with it this way and that until they acquire a motion of their own and go up in smoke. But the particles of the Spirit of Nitre, being already in motion and separate from one another, are dilated in every direction in increased

---

25. If you ask why an effervescence takes place when Spirit of Nitre is poured onto the dissolved fixed salt, read the note on section 25 [Spinoza's note].

volume by a little heat of the fire; and thus some go up in smoke while others penetrate the matter supplying the fire before they can be completely encompassed by flame, and so they extinguish the fire rather than feed it.

I shall now pass on to experiments which seem to confirm this explanation. First, I found that the particles of Nitre which go up in smoke with a crackling noise are pure Nitre. For when I melted the Nitre again and again until the crucible became white-hot, and I kindled it with a live coal,[26] I collected its smoke in a cold glass flask until the flask was moistened thereby, and after that I moistened the flask yet further by breathing on it, and finally set it out to dry in the cold air.[27] Thereupon little icicles[28] of Nitre appeared here and there in the flask. Now it might be thought that this did not result solely from the volatile particles, but that the flame could be carrying with it whole particles of Nitre (to adopt the view of the esteemed author) and was driving out the fixed particles, along with the volatile, before they were dissolved. To remove such a possibility, I caused the smoke to ascend through a tube (A) over a foot long, as through a chimney, so that the heavier particles adhered to the tube, and I collected only the more volatile parts as they passed through the narrower aperture (B). The result was as I have said.

Even so, I did not stop at this point, but, as a further test, I took a larger quantity of Nitre, melted it, ignited it with a live coal and, as

---

26. Neither Spinoza nor Boyle appreciated the chemical contribution made by the coal to the reaction.

27. When I did this, the air was very clear. [Spinoza's note]

28. The term *stiriolae* is here used in the sense of 'crystalline'.

before, placed the tube (A) over the crucible; and as long as the flame lasted, I held a piece of mirror close to the aperture (B). To this some matter adhered which, on being exposed to air, became liquid. Although I waited some days, I could not observe any sign of Nitre; but when I added Spirit of Nitre to it, it turned into Nitre.

From this I think I can infer, first, that in the process of melting the fixed parts are separated from the volatile and that the flame drives them upwards separately from one another; secondly, that after the fixed parts are separated from the volatile with a crackling noise, they can never be reunited. From this we can infer, thirdly, that the parts which adhered to the flask and coalesced into little icicles were not the fixed parts, but only the volatile.

The second experiment, and one which seems to prove that the fixed parts are nothing but the dregs of Nitre, is as follows. I find that the more the Nitre is purified of its dregs, the more volatile it is, and the more apt to crystallise. For when I put crystals of purified or filtered Nitre in a glass goblet, such as A, and poured in a little cold water, it partly evaporated along with the cold water, and the particles escaping upwards stuck to the rim of the glass and coalesced into little icicles.

The third experiment, which seems to show that when the particles of Nitre lose their motion they become inflammable, is as follows. I trickled droplets of Spirit of Nitre into a damp paper bag and then added sand, between whose grains the Spirit of Nitre kept penetrating; and when the sand had absorbed all, or nearly all, the Spirit of Nitre, I dried it thoroughly in the same bag over a fire. Thereupon I removed the sand and set the paper against a live coal. As soon as it caught fire it gave off sparks, just as it usually does when it has absorbed Nitre itself.[29]

---

29. For information on the chemical reactions, see Pierre-François Moreau, *Spinoza: L'expérience et l'éternité* (Paris: Presses Universitaires de France, 1994), 270-283.

If I had had time for further experimentation, I might have added other experiments which would perhaps make the matter quite clear. But as I am very much occupied with other matters, you will forgive me if I defer it for another time and proceed to other comments.

Section 5. When the esteemed author discusses incidentally the shape of particles of Nitre, he criticises modern writers as having wrongly represented it. I am not sure whether he includes Descartes; if so, he is perhaps criticising Descartes from what others have said. For Descartes is not speaking of particles visible to the eye. And I do not think that the esteemed author means that if icicles of Nitre were to be rubbed down until they became parallelepipeds or some other shape, they would cease to be Nitre. But perhaps he is referring to some chemists who admit nothing but what they can see with their eyes and touch with their hands.

Section 9. If this experiment could be carried out rigorously, it would completely confirm the conclusion I sought to draw from the first experiment mentioned above.

From section 13 to 18 the esteemed author tries to prove that all tangible qualities depend solely on motion, shape and other mechanical states. Since these demonstrations are not advanced by the esteemed author as being of a mathematical kind, there is no need to consider whether they carry complete conviction. Still, I do not know why the esteemed author strives so earnestly to draw this conclusion from this experiment of his, since it has already been abundantly proved by Verulam, and later by Descartes. Nor do I see that this experiment provides us with clearer evidence than other experiments readily available. For as far as heat is concerned, is not the same conclusion equally clear from the fact that if two pieces of wood, however cold they are, are rubbed against each other, they produce a flame simply as a result of that motion? Or that lime, sprinkled with water, becomes hot? As far as sound is concerned, I do not see what is to be found in this experiment more remarkable than is found in the boiling of ordinary water, and in many other instances. As to colour, to confine myself to the obvious, I need say no more than that we see green vegetation assuming so many and such varied colours. Again, bodies that give forth a foul smell emit even a fouler smell when agitated, and especially if they become somewhat warm. Finally sweet wine turns sour, and so with many other things. All these things, therefore, I would consider superfluous, if I may use the frankness of a philosopher. This I say because I fear that others, whose regard for the esteemed author is not as great as it should be, may misjudge him.[30]

Section 24. I have already spoken of the cause of this phenomenon. Here I will merely add that I, too, have found by experience that particles of the fixed salt float in those saline drops. For when they flew upwards, they met a plate of glass which I had ready for the purpose. This I warmed somewhat so that any volatile matter should fly off, whereupon I observed some thick whitish matter adhering to the glass in places.

Section 25. In this section the esteemed author seems to intend to prove that the alkaline parts are driven hither and thither by the impact of the salt particles, whereas the salt particles ascend into the air by their own force. In explaining the phenomenon I too have said that the particles of Spirit of Nitre acquire a more lively motion because, on entering the wider passages, they must necessarily be encompassed by some very fine matter, and are thereby driven upwards as are particles of wood by fire, whereas the alkaline particles received their motion from the impact of particles of Spirit of Nitre penetrating through the narrower passages. Here I would add that pure water cannot so readily dissolve and soften the fixed parts. So it is not surprising that when Spirit of Nitre is poured onto the solution of the said fixed salt dissolved in water, an effervescence should take place such as the esteemed author describes in section 24. Indeed, I think this effervescence will be more violent than if Spirit of Nitre were to be added to the fixed salt while it is still intact. For in water it is dissolved into very minute molecules which can be more readily separated and more freely moved than when all the parts of the salt lie on one another and are firmly attached.

Section 26. Of the taste of the acidic Spirit I have already spoken, and so it remains only to speak of the alkali. When I placed this on the tongue, I felt a sensation of heat, followed by a prickling. This indicates to me that it is some kind of lime; for in just the same way that lime becomes heated with the aid of water, so does this salt with the aid of saliva, perspiration, Spirit of Nitre, and perhaps even moist air.[31]

---

30. In the letter I sent I deliberately omitted these words. [Spinoza's note]
31. Spinoza did not understand the nature of the alkali. Boyle was the first chemist to establish our modern classification of substances into acid, alkaline, and neutral. See A. R. and M. B. Hall, ed., *The Correspondence of Henry Oldenburg*, 11 vols. (Madison: University of Wisconsin Press, 1965-67), 1, 467-470.

Section 27. It does not immediately follow that a particle of matter acquires a new shape by being joined to another; it only follows that it becomes larger, and this suffices to bring about the effect which is the object of the esteemed author's inquiry in this section.

Section 33. What I think of the esteemed author's method of philosophising I shall say when I have seen the Dissertation which is mentioned here and in the Introductory Essay, page 33.[32]

On Fluidity.

Section 1. "It is quite manifest that they are to be reckoned among the most general states. . . etc." In my view, notions which derive from popular usage, or which explicate Nature not as it is in itself but as it is related to human senses, should certainly not be regarded as concepts of the highest generality, nor should they be mixed (not to say confused) with notions that are pure and which explicate Nature as it is in itself. Of the latter kind are motion, rest, and their laws; of the former kind are visible, invisible, hot, cold, and, to say it at once, also fluid, solid, etc.[33]

Section 5. "The first is the littleness of the bodies that compose it, for in the larger bodies. . . etc." Even though bodies are small, they have (or can have) surfaces that are uneven and rough. So if large bodies move in such a way that the ratio of their motion to their mass is that of minute bodies to their particular mass, then they too would have to be termed fluid, if the word 'fluid' did not signify something extrinsic and were not merely adapted from common usage to mean those moving bodies whose minuteness and intervening spaces escape detection by human senses. So to divide bodies into fluid and solid would be the same as to divide them into visible and invisible.

The same section. "If we were not able to confirm it by chemical experiments." One can never confirm it by chemical or any other

---

32. In the Latin edition Boyle had written: "We shall never be able to investigate so completely the subtle workings of nature that there would not remain many natural phenomena which cannot be explained by the principles of the atomical philosophy." The English version, which Spinoza did not see, was more cautious, claiming only that perhaps men would never be able to fully explain all things.

33. Spinoza is largely following Descartes here. See PPC2P1.

experiments, but only by demonstration and by calculating. For it is by reason and calculation that we divide bodies to infinity, and consequently also the forces required to move them. We can never confirm this by experiments.[34]

Section 6. ". . . great bodies are not well adapted to forming fluid bodies. . . etc." Whether or not one understands by 'fluid' what I have just said, the thing is self-evident. But I do not see how the esteemed author confirms this by the experiments quoted in this section. For (since we want to doubt what is certain)[35] although bones may be unsuitable for forming chyle and similar fluids, perhaps they will be quite well adapted for forming some new kind of fluid.

Section 10. ". . . and this by making them less pliant than formerly. . . etc." They could have coagulated into another body more solid than oil without any change in the parts, but merely because the parts driven into the receiver were separated from the rest. For bodies are lighter or heavier according to the kinds of fluids in which they are immersed. Thus particles of butter, when floating in milk, form part of the liquid; but when the milk is stirred and so acquires a new motion to which all the parts composing the milk cannot equally accommodate themselves, this in itself brings it about that some parts become heavier and force the lighter parts to the surface. But because these lighter parts are heavier than air so that they cannot compose a liquid with it, they are forced downwards by it; and because they are ill adapted for motion, they also cannot compose a liquid by themselves, but lie on one another and stick together. Vapours, too, when they are separated from the air, turn into water, which, in relation to air, may be termed a solid.

Section 13. "And I take as an example a bladder distended with water rather than one full of air. . . etc." Since particles of water are always moving ceaselessly in all directions, it is clear that, if they are not restrained by surrounding bodies, the water will spread in all directions. Moreover, I am as yet unable to see how the distention of a bladder full of water helps to confirm his view about the small spaces.

---

34. Spinoza's view is that the infinite divisibility of matter is not subject to experimental confirmation, and consequently that Boyle's claim that effective forces can be indefinitely small is not experimentally confirmable either. He is *not* denying that the particulate structure of matter is confirmable, nor is he claiming, contrary to some of his commentators (such as the Halls), that experiments can have no demonstrative force.

35. Here we read 'certa' for Gebhardt's *incerta*.

The reason why the particles of water do not yield when the sides of the bladder are pressed with a finger – as they otherwise would do if they were free – is this, that there is no equilibrium or circulation as there is when some body, say our finger, is surrounded by a fluid or water. But however much the water is pressed by the bladder, yet its particles will yield to a stone also enclosed in the bladder, in the same way as they usually do outside the bladder.

Same section. "whether there is any portion of matter. . . ." We must maintain the affirmative, unless we prefer to look for a progression to infinity, or to grant that there is a vacuum, than which nothing can be more absurd.

Section 19. ". . . that the particles of the liquid find admittance into those pores and are held there (by which means. . . etc.)" This is not to be affirmed absolutely of all liquids which find admittance into the pores of other bodies. If the particles of Spirit of Nitre enter the pores of white paper, they make it stiff and friable. This may be seen if one pours a few drops into a small iron receptacle (A) which is at white heat and the smoke is channelled through a paper covering (B). Moreover, Spirit of Nitre softens leather, but does not make it moist; on the contrary, it shrinks it, as also does fire.

Same section. "Since Nature has designed them both for flying and for swimming. . . ." He seeks the cause from purpose.[36]

Section 23. ". . . though their motion is rarely perceived by us. Take then. . . etc." Without this experiment and without going to any trouble, the thing is sufficiently evident from the fact that our breath, which in winter is obviously seen to be in motion, nevertheless cannot be seen so in summer, or in a heated room. Furthermore, if in summer the breeze suddenly cools, the vapours rising from water, since by reason of the change in the density of the air they cannot disperse through it as readily as they did before it cooled, gather again over the surface of the water in such quantity that they can easily be seen by us. Again, movement is often too gradual to be observed by us, as we can gather in the case of a sundial and the shadow cast by the sun; and it is frequently too swift to be observed by us, as can be seen in the case of an ignited piece of tinder when it is moved in a circle at some speed; for then we imagine the ignited part to be at rest at all points of the circle which it describes in its motion. I would here give the reasons for this, did I not judge it superfluous. Finally, let me say in passing that, to understand the nature of fluid in general, it is sufficient to know that we can move our hand in any direction without any resistance, the motion being proportionate to the fluid.[37] This is quite obvious to those who give sufficient attention to those notions that explain Nature as it is in itself, not as it is related to human senses. Not that I therefore dismiss this piece of research as pointless. On the contrary, if in the case of every liquid such research were done with the greatest possible accuracy and reliability, I would consider it most useful for understanding their individual differences, a result much to be desired by all philosophers as being very necessary.

---

36. Spinoza is here accusing Boyle of appealing to 'final causes' or purposes in nature. A summary of Spinoza's rejection of teleology is offered in the appendix to the first part of the *Ethics*. "But I will make this additional point, that this doctrine of Final Causes turns Nature completely upside down, for it regards as an effect that which is in fact a cause, and vice versa." Boyle was one of the few scientists of his day who did not reject final causality.
37. For the Cartesian analysis of fluidity, see PPC2P9-P11.

On Solidity.

Section 7. "...(it seems consonant) to the universal laws of Nature...." This is Descartes' demonstration, and I do not see that the esteemed author produces any original demonstration deriving from his experiments or observations.

I had made many notes here and in what follows, but later I saw that the esteemed author had corrected himself.

Section 15. "... and once four hundred and thirty-two (ounces) ..."[38] If one compares it with the weight of quicksilver enclosed in the tube, it comes very near to the true weight. But I would consider it worthwhile to examine this, so as to obtain, as far as possible, the ratio between the lateral or horizontal pressure of air and the perpendicular pressure.[39] I think it can be done in this way:

Let CD in figure 1 be a flat mirror thoroughly smoothed, and AB two pieces of marble directly touching each other. Let the marble piece A be attached to a hook E, and B to a cord N. T is a pulley, and G a weight which will show the force required to pull marble B away from marble A in a horizontal direction.

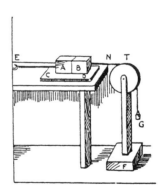

---

38. This figure is in fact an error introduced by Boyle's Latin translator.
39. Pascal had proven that vertical and horizontal pressures are identical, though Spinoza seems not to be aware of this here.

In figure 2, let F be a sufficiently strong silk thread by which marble B is attached to the floor, D a pulley, G a weight which will show the force required to pull marble A from marble B in a perpendicular direction.[40] It is not necessary to go into this at greater length.

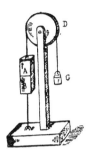

Here you have, my good friend, what I have so far found worthy of note in regard to Mr. Boyle's experiments. As to your first queries, when I look through my replies to them I do not see that I have omitted anything. And if perchance I have put something obscurely (as I often do through lack of vocabulary), please be good enough to point it out to me. I shall take pains to explain it more clearly.

As to the new question you raise, to wit, how things began to be and by what bond they depend on the first cause, I have written a complete short work on this subject, and also on the emendation of the intellect,[41] and I am engaged in transcribing and correcting it. But sometimes I put the work aside, because I do not as yet have any definite plan for its publication. I am naturally afraid that the theologians of our time may take offence, and, with their customary spleen, may attack me, who utterly dread brawling. I shall look for your advice in this matter, and, to let you know the contents of this work of mine which may ruffle the preachers, I tell you that many attributes which are attributed to God by them and by all whom I know of, I regard as belonging to creation. Conversely, other attributes which they, because of their prejudices, consider to belong to creation, I contend are attributes of

---

40. At this point the *Opera Posthuma* letter breaks off with the remark, "The rest is lacking." The rest of the letter is translated from the original.
41. This is the *Tractatus de intellectus emendation* (never completed).

God which they have failed to understand. Again, I do not differentiate between God and Nature in the way all those known to me have done. I therefore look to your advice, for I regard you as a most loyal friend whose good faith it would be wrong to doubt. Meanwhile, farewell, and, as you have begun, so continue to love me, who am,

       Yours entirely,
       Benedict Spinoza.

LETTER 7
To the esteemed B.d.S., from Henry Oldenburg.

[Known only from the O.P. The original is lost.
The letter is undated, but a conjectural date is late in July 1662.]

It is many weeks ago, esteemed Sir, that I received your very welcome letter with its learned comments on Boyle's book. The author himself joins with me in thanking you most warmly for the thoughts you have shared with us, and would have indicated this more quickly had he not entertained the hope that he might soon be relieved of the quantity of business with which he is burdened so that he could have sent you his reply along with his thanks at the same time. However, so far he finds himself disappointed of this hope, being so pressed by both public and private business that at present he can do no more than convey his gratitude to you, and is compelled to defer to another time his opinion on your comments. Furthermore, two opponents have attacked him in print, and he thinks himself bound to reply to them at the first opportunity. These writings are directed not against his *Essay on Nitre* but against another book of his containing his Pneumatic Experiments,[42] proving the elasticity of air. As soon as he has extricated himself from these labours he will also disclose to you his thoughts on your objections. Meanwhile he asks you not to take amiss this delay.

The College of Philosophers of which I spoke to you has now, by our King's grace, been converted into a Royal Society and presented with the public charter[43] whereby it is granted special privileges, and there is a very good prospect that it will be endowed with the necessary funds.

I would by all means urge you not to begrudge scholars the learned fruits of your acute understanding both in philosophy and theology, but

---

42. Boyle's *New Experiments Physico-Mechanical touching the Spring of the Air and its Effects, made for the most part in a new Pneumatical Engine*. The air-pump was also called the *machina boyleana*, and was created by Robert Hooke and Boyle in 1659 after they read about the pump constructed by Guericke. This treatise contains an extended critique of Thomas Hobbes and of the Jesuit thinker Franciscus Linus, both of whom (like Spinoza) argued against the claim that there was any true vacuum in nature.
43. The public charter for "The Royal Society" was granted on 15 July 1662.

to let them be published despite the growlings of pseudo-theologians. Your republic is quite free, and in it philosophy should be pursued quite freely; but your own prudence will suggest to you that you express your ideas and opinions as moderately as you can, and for the rest leave the outcome to fate.

Come, then, excellent Sir, away with all fear of stirring up the pygmies of our time. Long enough have we propitiated ignorance and nonsense. Let us spread the sails of true knowledge and search more deeply than ever before into Nature's mysteries. Your reflections, I imagine, can be printed in your country with impunity, and there is no need to fear that they will give any offence to the wise. If you find such to be your patrons and supporters (as I am quite sure that you will find them), why should you dread an ignorant Momus? I will not let you go, honoured friend, until I have prevailed on you, and never will I permit, as far as in me lies, that your thoughts, which are of such importance, should be buried in eternal silence. I urgently request you to be good enough to let me know, as soon as you conveniently can, what are your intentions in this matter.

Perhaps things will be happening here not unworthy of your notice. The afore-mentioned Society will now more vigorously pursue its purpose, and maybe, provided that peace lasts in these shores, it will grace the Republic of Letters with distinction. Farewell, distinguished Sir, and believe me to be,

Your very devoted and dear friend,
Henry Oldenburg.

LETTER 8
To the esteemed B.d.S., from Simon de Vries.

[Printed in the O.P. The original is extant.
There are certain omissions in the O.P. text.]

Most upright friend,

I have long wished to pay you a visit, but the weather and the hard winter have not favoured me. Sometimes I bewail my lot, in that the distance between us keeps us so far apart from one another. Fortunate, yes, most fortunate is your companion Casuarius[44] who dwells beneath the same roof, and can converse with you on the highest matters at breakfast, at dinner, and on your walks. But although we are physically so far apart, you have frequently been present in my thoughts, especially when I am immersed in your writings and hold them in my hand.

---

44. For Simon de Vries see the third section of our introduction. Casuarius [*sic*]: Johannes Caesarius, whose name is incorrectly spelled by De Vries (see Spinoza's spelling in Ep9), was probably born in Amsterdam in 1642 and is believed to have been a student of Franciscus Van den Enden through whom he may have become acquainted with Spinoza. Though the reasons as to why he may have been living with Spinoza are unclear, he is thought to have been part of a group of Collegiants who were known to frequent Rijnsburg while Spinoza resided there. Spinoza's judgment of the young man may have proven itself to be correct (again, see Ep9). In 1665 he was able to meet ecclesiastical approval and was ordained by the Reformed Church; it was not until much later (1668) that he was successful at finding a post, and this was a position in the Dutch colony of Malabar. His skills in Latin were very useful there to the governor of the colony who had a tremendous interest in botany and wished to catalogue the flora. Despite the fact that his contemporaries noted his incompetence in the science of plants, he was able to put together a quite celebrated tome on the plant life of Malabar. He was given permission to return to Europe late in 1676 and was freed from his official duties in 1677, but he died of fever and dysentary before he could return. We also note that the Van Vloten and Land edition cites "Casuarius" as "casuarius" (Ep8) and "Caesario" as "caesario" (Ep9). In this instance, the difference between upper and lower case marks a decided difference between the two texts. "Casuarius," though not commonly used, is a late mediaeval Italian latinism meaning a "miserable fellow," and so it could be possible that De Vries was referring to someone else, of whom he (De Vries) was envious, by that term. This explanation, however, would fail to account for Spinoza's later referring to the same person as "caesario." Perhaps for 'Caesarius', 'Casearius' was intended; and later on, for 'Caesario' and 'caesario', 'Caseario' and 'casesario'.

But since not everything is quite clear to the members of our group (which is why we have resumed our meetings), and in order that you may not think that I have forgotten you, I have set myself to write this letter.

As for our group, our procedure is as follows. One member (each has his turn) does the reading, explains how he understands it, and goes on to a complete demonstration, following the sequence and order of your propositions. Then if it should happen that we cannot satisfy one another, we have deemed it worthwhile to make a note of it and to write to you so that, if possible, it should be made clearer to us and we may, under your guidance, uphold truth against those who are religious and Christian in a superstitious way, and may stand firm against the onslaught of the whole world.

So, when the definitions did not all seem clear to us on our first reading and explaining them, we were not in agreement as to the nature of definition. In this situation, in your absence, we consulted a certain author, a mathematician named Borelli.[45] In his discussion of the nature of definition, axiom, and postulate, he also cites the opinions of others on this subject. His own opinion goes as follows: "Definitions are employed in a proof as premises. So they must be quite clearly known; otherwise knowledge that is scientific or absolutely certain cannot be acquired from them." In another place he writes: "In the case of any subject, the principle of its structure, or its prime and best known essential feature, must be chosen not at random but with the greatest care. For if the construction and feature named is impossible, then the result will not be a scientific definition. For instance, if one were to say, 'Let two straight lines enclosing a space be called figurals', the definitions would be of non-entities, and would be impossible. Therefore from these it is ignorance, not knowledge, that would be deduced. Again, if the construction or feature named is indeed possible and true, but unknown to us or doubtful, then the definition will not be sound.

---

45. Giovanni Alfonso Borelli (1608-1679) was a mathematician with many other interests: astronomy, physics, biology. As well as publishing an edition of Euclid (*Euclides restitutus*), he also published several other mathematical treatises. Like Descartes, he too finished his days under the protection of Queen Christiana of Sweden.

For conclusions that derive from what is unknown and doubtful are also uncertain and doubtful, and therefore afford us mere conjecture or opinion, and not sure knowledge."

Tacquet[46] seems to disagree with this view; he asserts, as you know, that it is possible to proceed directly from a false proposition to a true conclusion. Clavius,[47] whose view he (Borelli) also introduces, thinks as follows: "Definitions are arbitrary terms, and there is no need to give the grounds for choosing that a thing should be defined in this way or that. It is sufficient that the thing defined should never be asserted to agree with anything unless it is first proved that the given definition agrees with that same thing." So Borelli maintains that the definition of any subject must consist of a feature or structure which is prime, essential, best known to us, and true, whereas Clavius holds that it matters not whether it be prime, or best known, or true or not, as long as it is not asserted that the definition we have given agrees with some thing unless it is first provided that the given definition agrees with that same thing. We are inclined to favour Borelli's view, but we are not sure whether you, Sir, agree with either or neither. Therefore, with such various conflicting views being advanced on the nature of definition – which is accounted as one of the principles of demonstration – and since the mind, if not freed from difficulties surrounding definition, will be in like difficulty regarding deductions made from it, we would very much like you, Sir, to write to us (if we are not giving you too much trouble and your time allows) giving your opinion on the matter, and also on the difference between axioms and definitions. Borelli admits no real distinction other than the name; you, I believe, maintain that there is another difference.

Next, the third Definition[48] is not sufficiently clear to us. I brought forward as an example what you, Sir, said to me at the Hague, to wit, that a thing can be considered in two ways: either as it is in itself, or in relation to another thing. For instance, the intellect; for it can be considered either under Thought or as consisting of ideas. But we do not quite see what difference could be here. For we consider that, if we

---

46. Andreas Tacquet published *Elements of Plane and Solid Geometry* in 1654.
47. Christopher Clavius (1537-1612) was another well known mathematician of the era. He helped to revise the Gregorian calendar, and in 1574 he published an edition of Euclid with commentary to which de Vries refers in this letter.
48. See E1Def3-4.

rightly conceive Thought, we ought to comprehend it under ideas, because with the removal of all ideas we would destroy Thought. So the example not being sufficiently clear to us, the matter still remains somewhat obscure, and we stand in need of further explanation.

Finally, at the beginning of the third Scholium to Proposition 8,[49] we read: "Hence it is clear that, although two attributes may be conceived as really distinct (that is, the one without the aid of the other), it does not follow that they constitute two entities or two different substances. The reason is that it is of the nature of substance that all its attributes – each one individually – are conceived through themselves, since they have been in it simultaneously." In this way you seem, Sir, to suppose that the nature of substance is so constituted that it can have several attributes, which you have not yet proved, unless you are referring to the fifth definition[50] of absolutely infinite substance or God. Otherwise, if I were to say that each substance has only one attribute, I could rightly conclude that where there are two different attributes there are two different substances. We would ask you for a clearer explanation of this.

Next, I am most grateful for your writings which were conveyed to me by P. Balling[51] and gave me great pleasure, particularly the Scholium to Proposition 19.[52] If I can here serve you, too, in any way which is within my power, I am yours to command. You need only let me know. I have begun a course of anatomy, and am about half way through. When it is completed, I shall begin chemistry, and thus following your advice I shall go through the whole medical course. I must stop now, and await your reply. Accept my greetings, who am,

> Your very devoted,
> S.J.D'Vries.

1663. Given at the Hague, 24 February
       To Mr. Benedict Spinoza, at Rijnsburg.

---

49. Probably E1P10Schol in the finished version of the *Ethics*.
50. See E1Def6.
51. See the third section of our introduction.
52. We are not able to determine about which proposition in the final version of the *Ethics* de Vries writes.

LETTER 9
To the learned young man Simon de Vries, from B.d.S.

[Printed in the O.P. The original is extant. The O.P. text
is an abridged version of the original, and the last
paragraph appears only in the Dutch edition of the O.P.
The letter is undated. A conjectural date is February 1663.]

My worthy friend,

I have received your letter, long looked for, for which, and for your cordial feelings towards me, accept my warmest thanks. Your long absence has been no less regretted by me than by you, but at any rate I am glad that my late-night studies[53] are of use to you and our friends, for in this way I talk with you while we are apart. There is no reason for you to envy Casearius.[54] Indeed, there is no one who is more of a trouble to me, and no one with whom I have had to be more on my guard. So I should like you and all our acquaintances not to communicate my opinions to him until he will have reached a more mature age. As yet he is too boyish, unstable, and eager for novelty rather than for truth. Still, I am hopeful that he will correct these youthful faults in a few years time. Indeed, as far as I can judge from his character, I am reasonably sure of this; and so his nature wins my affection.

As to the questions raised in your group (which is sensibly organised), I see that your difficulties result from your failure to distinguish between the kinds of definition. There is the definition that serves to explicate a thing whose essence alone is in question and the subject of doubt, and there is the definition which is put forward simply for examination. The former, since it has a determinate object, must be a true definition, while this need not be so in the latter case. For example, if someone were to ask me for a description of Solomon's temple, I ought to give him a true description, unless I propose to talk nonsense with him. But if I have in my own mind formed the design of a temple that I

---

53. Because Spinoza earned his living grinding and making lenses, night time was the only free time he had in which to pursue philosophy.
54. See note to 'Casuarius', Ep8.

want to build, and from its description I conclude that I will have to purchase such-and-such a site and so many thousands of stones and other materials, will any sane person tell me that I have reached a wrong conclusion because my definition may be incorrect? Or will anyone demand that I prove my definition? Such a person would simply be telling me that I had not conceived that which in fact I had conceived, or he would be requiring me to prove that I had conceived that which I had conceived, which is utter nonsense. Therefore a definition either explicates a thing as it exists outside the intellect – and then it should be a true definition, differing from a proposition or axiom only in that the former is concerned only with the essences of things or the essences of the affections of things, whereas the latter has a wider scope, extending also to eternal truths – or it explicates a thing as it is conceived by us, or can be conceived. And in that case it also differs from an axiom and proposition in requiring merely that it be conceived, not conceived as true, as in the case of an axiom. So then a bad definition is one which is not conceived.

To make this clearer, I shall take Borelli's example of a man who says that two straight lines enclosing an area are to be called figurals. If he means by a straight line what everybody else means by a curved line, his definition is quite sound (for the figure intended by the definition would be

or some such figure), provided that he does not at a later stage mean a square or any other such figure. But if by a straight line he means what we all mean, the thing is plainly inconceivable, and so there is no definition. All these considerations are confused by Borelli, whose view you are too much inclined to embrace.

Here is another example, the one which you adduce towards the end of your letter. If I say that each substance has only one attribute, this is mere assertion unsupported by proof. But if I say that by substance I mean that which consists of only one attribute, this is a sound definition, provided that entities consisting of more than one attribute are thereafter given a name other than substance.

In saying that I do not prove that a substance (or an entity) can have more than one attribute, it may be that you have not given sufficient attention to the proofs. I advanced two proofs, the first of which is as follows: It is clear beyond all doubt that every entity is conceived by us under some attribute, and the more reality or being an entity has, the more attributes are to be attributed to it. Hence an absolutely infinite entity must be defined. . . and so on. A second proof – and this proof I take to be decisive – states that the more attributes I attribute to any entity, the more existence I am bound to attribute to it; that is, the more I conceive it as truly existent. The exact contrary would be the case if I had imagined a chimera or something of the sort.

As to your saying that you do not conceive thought otherwise than under ideas because thought vanishes with the removal of ideas, I believe that you experience this because when you, as a thinking thing, do as you say, you are banishing all your thoughts and conceptions. So it is not surprising that when you have banished all your thoughts, there is nothing left for you to think. But as to the point at issue, I think I have demonstrated with sufficient clarity and certainty that the intellect, even though infinite, belongs to *Natura naturata*, not to *Natura naturans*.[55]

Furthermore, I fail to see what this has to do with understanding the Third Definition,[56] or why this definition causes you difficulty. The definition as I gave it to you runs, if I am not mistaken, "By substance I understand that which is in itself and is conceived through itself; that is, that whose conception does not involve the conception of another thing. I understand the same by attribute, except that attribute is so called in respect to the intellect, which attributes to substance a certain specific kind of nature." This definition, I repeat, explains clearly what I mean by substance or attribute. However, you want me to explain by example – though it is not at all necessary – how one and the same thing can be signified by two names. Not to appear ungenerous, I will give you two examples. First, by 'Israel' I mean the third patriarch: by 'Jacob' I mean that same person, the latter name being given to him because he seized his brother's heel.[57] Secondly, by a 'plane surface'[58] I

---

55. For the distinction, see E1P29Schol. Spinoza is here revising and reviving a medi-aeval distinction. For information on the (debated) significance of the distinction within Spinoza's own philosophy, see James Collins, *Spinoza on Nature* (Carbon-dale: Southern Illinois University Press, 1984), 26-49; H. Siebeck, "Ueber die Entstehung der Termini *natura naturans* und *natura naturata*," *Archiv für Geschichte der Philosophie* 3 (1890), 370-378; and Harry M. Tiebout, "Deus, sive Natura," *Philosophy and Phenomenological Research* 16 (1955-56), 512-521. The phrases occur more frequently in KV than in Spinoza's later writings.
56. E1Def3-4.
57. See Genesis 25:26 for an account of Jacob's name and 35:10 for an account of the change of this name to Israel.
58. Aristotle reports Democritus' account that a smooth surface or plane is one which reflects back all rays of light, and thus it has a white appearance. By con-trast, a rough surface would reflect only a few rays, and so it would seem black.

mean one that reflects all rays of light without any change. I mean the same by 'white surface', except that it is called white in respect of a man looking at it.

With this I think that I have fully answered your questions. Meanwhile I shall wait to hear your judgment. And if there is anything else which you consider to be not well or clearly enough explained, do not hesitate to point it out to me, etc.

This theory was still considered valid even in Spinoza's time, and modifications of it can be found in Boyle's (1664) *Experiments and Considerations touching Colours*.

LETTER 10
To the learned young man Simon de Vries, from B.d.S.

[Known only from the O.P. The original is lost.
Undated. A conjectural date is March 1663.]

My worthy friend,

You ask me whether we need experience to know whether the definition of some attribute be true. To this I reply that we need experience only in the case of those things that cannot be deduced from the definition of a thing, as, for instance, the existence of modes; for this cannot be deduced from a thing's definition. We do not need experience in the case of those things whose existence is not distinguished from their essence and is therefore deduced from their definition. Indeed, no experience will ever be able to tell us this, for experience does not teach us the essences of things. The most it can do is to determine our minds to think only about the certain essences of things. So since the existence of attributes does not differ from their essence, we shall not be able to apprehend it by any experience.

As to your further question as to whether things or the affections of things are also eternal truths, I say, most certainly. If you go on to ask why I do not call them eternal truths, I reply, in order to mark a distinction, universally accepted, between these and the truths which do not explicate a thing or the affection of a thing, as, for instance, 'nothing comes from nothing'. This and similar propositions, I say, are called eternal truths in an absolute sense, by which title is meant simply that they do not have any place outside the mind,[59] etc.

---

59. Spinoza here again is trading on there being plural types of definition. "Eternal truth" has more than one kind of definition. Any truth, if it is true once, is always and forever true, so that "I had eggs for breakfast on January 1, 1995" is an eternal truth, but this is not what we usually mean by "eternal truth." What we normally mean by this name is a proposition which we cannot conceive as false such as "Nothing comes from nothing" (to use Spinoza's example) or "2 + 2 = 4" (to use another example). These truths, however, have no existence outside the mind, and so it may be that here Spinoza makes a not so subtle attack on Platonism in all its forms.

LETTER 11
To the esteemed B.d.S., from Henry Oldenburg.

[Known only from the O.P. The original is lost.]

Excellent Sir and Dear Friend,

I could produce many excuses for my long silence, but I shall reduce my reasons to two: the illness of the illustrious Mr. Boyle and the pressures of my own business. The former has prevented Boyle from replying to your Observations on Nitre at an earlier date; the latter have kept me so busy over several months that I have scarcely been my own master, and so I have been unable to discharge the duty which I declare I owe you. I rejoice that, for the time at least, both obstacles are removed, so that I can resume my correspondence with so close a friend. This I now do with the greatest pleasure, and I am resolved, with Heaven's help, to do everything to ensure that our epistolary intercourse shall never in future suffer so long an interruption.

Before I deal with matters what concern just you and me alone, let me deliver what is due to you on Mr. Boyle's account. The observations which you composed on his short Chemical-Physical Treatise he has received with his customary good nature, and sends you his warmest thanks for your criticism. But first he wants you to know that it was not his intention to demonstrate that this is a truly philosophical and complete analysis of Nitre, but rather to make the point that the common doctrine of Substantial Forms and Qualities accepted in the Schools rests on a weak foundation, and that what they call the specific differences of things can be reduced to the magnitude, motion, rest and position of the parts.

With this preliminary remark, our Author goes on to say that his experiment with Nitre shows quite clearly that through chemical analysis the whole body of Nitre was resolved into parts which differed from one another and from the original whole, and that afterwards it was so reconstituted and redintegrated from these same parts that it lacked little of its original weight. He adds that he has shown this to be a fact, but he has not been concerned with the way in which it comes about, which seems to be the subject of your conjectures, and that he has reached no conclusion on that matter, since that went beyond his purpose. However, as to what you suppose to be the way in which it comes about, and your view that the fixed salt of Nitre is its dregs and other such theories, he considers that these are merely unproved speculations. And as to your idea that these dregs, or this fixed salt, has openings hollowed out to the size of the particles of Nitre, on this subject our Author points out that salt of potash combined with Spirit of Nitre constitutes Nitre just as well as Spirit of Nitre combined with its own fixed salt. Hence he thinks it clear that similar pores are to be found in bodies of that kind, from which nitrous spirits are not given off. Nor does the Author see that the necessity for the very fine matter, which you allege, is proved from any of the phenomena, but he says it is assumed simply from the hypothesis of the impossibility of a vacuum.

The Author says that your remarks on the causes of the difference of taste between Spirit of Nitre and Nitre do not affect him; and as to what you say about the inflammability of Nitre and the non-inflammability of Spirit of Nitre, he says that this presupposes Descartes' theory of fire,[60] with which he declares he is not yet satisfied.

With regard to the experiments which you think confirm your explanation of the phenomenon, the Author replies that (1) Spirit of Nitre is indeed Nitre in respect of its matter, but not in respect of its form, since they are vastly different in their qualities and properties, viz. in taste, smell, volatility, power of dissolving metals, changing the colours of vegetables, etc. (2) When you say that some particles carried upwards coalesce into crystals of Nitre, he maintains that this happens because the nitrous parts are driven off through the fire along with Spirit of Nitre, as is the case with soot. (3) As to your point about the effect of purification, the Author replies that through that purification the Nitre is for the most part freed from a certain salt which resembles common salt, and that its ascending to form icicles is something it has in common with other salts, and depends on air pressure and other causes which must be discussed elsewhere and have no bearing on the present question. (4) With regard to your remarks on your third experiment, the Author says that the same thing occurs with certain other

---

60. See Descartes, *Principles of Philosophy* IV, 80-119. For Descartes the physical universe is composed of three primordial elements. The first, which forms the sun, stars, and core of the earth, is swiftly moving. The second is transparent and fills the space of the heavens. The third is the most dense and forms the crust of the earth. Particles of terrestrial bodies become fire when they are separated and carried along by the motion of the first element.

salts. He asserts that when the paper is actually alight, it sets in motion the rigid and solid particles composing the salt and in this way causes them to sparkle.

Next, when you think that in the fifth section the noble Author is criticising Descartes, he believes that you yourself are here at fault. He says that he was in no way referring to Descartes, but to Gassendi and others who attribute to Nitre a cylindrical shape when it is in fact prismatic, and that he is speaking only of visible shapes.

To your comments on sections 13-18, he merely replies that he wrote these sections with this main object, to demonstrate and assert the usefulness of chemistry in confirming the mechanical principles of philosophy, and that he has not found these matters so clearly conveyed and treated by others. Our Boyle belongs to the class of those who do not have so much trust in their reason as not to want phenomena to agree with reason. Moreover, he says that there is a considerable difference between superficial experiments where we do not know what Nature contributes and what other factors intervene, and those experiments where it is established with certainty what are the factors concerned. Pieces of wood are much more composite bodies than the subject dealt with by the Author. And in the case of ordinary boiling water fire is an additional external factor, which is not so in the production of our sound. Again, the reason why green vegetation changes into so many different colours is still being sought, but that this is due to the change of the parts is established by this experiment, which shows that the change of colour was due to the addition of Spirit of Nitre. Finally, he says that Nitre has neither a foul nor a sweet smell; it acquires a foul smell simply as a result of its decomposition, and loses it when it is recompounded.

With regard to your comments on section 25 (the rest, he says, does not touch him) he replies that he has made use of the Epicurean principles[61] which hold that there is an innate motion in particles; for he needed to make use of some hypothesis to explain the phenomenon. Still, he does not on that account adopt it as his own, but he uses it to support his view against the chemists and the Schools, demonstrating merely that the facts can be well explained on the basis of the said hypothesis. As to your additional remark at the same place on the

----

61. These principles had been revived by Pierre Gassendi (1592-1655) in defence of the new physics.

inability of pure water to dissolve the fixed parts, our Boyle replies that it is the general opinion of chemists from their observations that pure water dissolves alkaline salts more rapidly than others.

The Author has not yet had time to consider your comments on fluidity and solidity. I am sending you what I here enclose so that I may not any longer be deprived of intercourse and correspondence with you. But I do most earnestly beg you to take in good part what I here pass on to you in such a disjointed and disconnected way, and to ascribe this to my haste rather than to the character of the illustrious Boyle. For I have assembled these comments as a result of informal talk with him on this subject rather than from any deliberate and methodical reply on his part. Consequently, many things which he said have doubtless escaped me, which were perhaps more substantial and better expressed than what I have here set down. All blame, therefore, I take on my own shoulders, and entirely absolve the Author.

Now I shall turn to matters that concern you and me, and here at the outset let me be permitted to ask whether you have completed that little work of such great importance, in which you treat of the origin of things and their dependence on a first cause, and also of the emendation of our intellect. Of a surety, my dear friend, I believe that nothing can be published more agreeable and more welcome to men who are truly learned and wise than a treatise of that kind. That is what a man of your talent and character should look to, rather than what pleases the theologians of our age and fashion. They look not so much to truth as to what suits them. So I urge you by our bond of friendship, by all the duties we have to promote and disseminate truth, not to begrudge or deny us your writings on these subjects. If, however, there is some consideration of greater weight than I can foresee which holds you back from publishing the work, I heartily beg you to be pleased to let me have by letter a summary of it, and for this service you will find me a grateful friend.

There will soon be more publications[62] from the learned Boyle which I shall send you by way of requital, adding an account of the entire constitution of our Royal Society, of whose Council I am a member with twenty others, and joint secretary with one other. At

---

62. These are the *Considerations touching the Usefulness of Experimental Natural Philosophy* and the *Experiments and Considerations touching Colours*, published respectively in 1663 and 1664, with Latin translations published at the same time.

present lack of time prevents me from going on to other matters. To you I pledge all the loyalty that can come from an honest heart, and an entire readiness to do you any service that lies within my slender powers, and I am, sincerely,

      Excellent Sir, yours entirely,
      Henry Oldenburg.

London, 3 April 1663.

LETTER 12
To the learned and wise Lodewijk Meyer,
Doctor of Medicine and Philosophy, from B.d.S.

[Printed in the O.P. The original is lost, but
a copy made by Leibniz has been preserved.]

Dearest Friend,

I have received two letters from you, one dated January 11 and
delivered to me by our friend N.N.,[63] the other dated March 26 and
sent to me by an unknown friend from Leiden. They were both very
welcome, especially as I gathered from them that all is well with you
and that I am often in your thoughts. My most cordial thanks are due
to you for the kindness and esteem you have always seen fit to show
me. At the same time I beg you to believe that I am no less your
devoted friend, and this I shall endeavour to prove whenever the occasion arises, as far as my slender abilities allow. As a first offering, I
shall try to answer the request made to me in your letters, in which you
ask me to let you have my considered views on the question of the
infinite. I am glad to oblige.

The question of the infinite has universally been found to be very
difficult, indeed, insoluble, through failure to distinguish between that
which must be infinite by its very nature or by virtue of its definition,
and that which is unlimited not by virtue of its essence but by virtue of
its cause. Then again, there is the failure to distinguish between that
which is called infinite because it is unlimited, and that whose parts
cannot be equated with or explicated by any number, although we may

---

63. For information on Meyer, see our introduction, footnote 1 and section 3. The
friend "NN" was quite possibly Pieter Balling (see introduction, section 3) who
was known to travel to and from Amsterdam and Rijnsburg and no doubt
delivered letters for and from Spinoza. This letter was apparently circulated
among many of Spinoza's friends, and came to be referenced as the 'Letter on the
Infinite' or the 'Letter on Infinity'. A lengthy commentary on the letter itself is
given by Martial Gueroult, *Spinoza: Dieu (Éthique, 1)* (Paris: Editions Aubier,
1968), 500-528. An extensive commentary and critique of Gueroult's reading of
the letter is given by Charles Ramond, *Qualité et quantité dans la philosophie de
Spinoza* (Paris: Presses Universitaires de France, 1995), 131-170.

know its maximum or minimum. Lastly, there is the failure to distinguish between that which we can apprehend only by the intellect and not by the imagination, and that which can also be apprehended by the imagination. I repeat, if men had paid careful attention to these distinctions, they would never have found themselves overwhelmed by such a throng of difficulties. They would clearly have understood what kind of infinite cannot be divided into, or possess any, parts, and what kind can be so divided without contradiction. Again, they would also have understood what kind of infinite can be conceived, without illogicality, as greater than another infinite, and what kind cannot be so conceived. This will become clear from what I am about to say. However, I shall first briefly explain these four terms: Substance, Mode, Eternity, Duration.

The points to be noted about Substance are as follows. First, existence pertains to its essence; that is, solely from its essence and definition it follows that Substance exists. This point, if my memory does not deceive me, I have proved to you in an earlier conversation without the help of any other propositions. Second, following from the first point, Substance is not manifold; rather there exists only one Substance of the same nature. Thirdly, no Substance can be conceived as other than infinite.[64]

The affections of Substance I call Modes. The definition of Modes, in so far as it is not itself a definition of Substance, cannot involve existence. Therefore, even when they exist, we can conceive them as not existing. From this it further follows that when we have regard only to the essence of Modes and not to the order of Nature as a whole, we cannot deduce from their present existence that they will or will not exist in the future or that they did or did not exist in the past. Hence it is clear that we conceive the existence of Substance as of an entirely different kind from the existence of Modes. This is the source of the difference between Eternity and Duration. It is to the existence of Modes alone that we can apply the term Duration; the corresponding term for the existence of Substance is Eternity, that is, the infinite enjoyment of existence or – pardon the Latin – of being (*essendi*).[65]

---

64. See E1P8.
65. The particles *ens* and gerundive *essendum* were scholastic forms generally associated with the old philosophy. Cicero complained that (classical) Latin, unlike Greek, had few abstract nouns. The mediaeval thinkers freely created them.

What I have said makes it quite clear that when we have regard only to the essence of Modes and not to Nature's order, as is most often the case, we can arbitrarily delimit the existence and duration of Modes without thereby impairing to any extent our conception of them; and we can conceive this duration as greater or less, and divisible into parts. But Eternity and Substance, being conceivable only as infinite, cannot be thus treated without annulling our conception of them. So it is nonsense, bordering on madness, to hold that extended Substance is composed of parts or bodies really distinct from one another. It is as if, by simply adding circle to circle and piling one on top of another, one were to attempt to construct a square or a triangle or any other figure of a completely different nature. Therefore the whole conglomeration of arguments whereby philosophers commonly strive to prove that extended Substance is finite collapses of its own accord. All such arguments assume that corporeal Substance is made up of parts. A parallel case is presented by those who, having convinced themselves that a line is made up of points,[66] have devised many arguments to prove that a line is not infinitely divisible.

However, if you ask why we have such a strong natural tendency to divide extended Substance, I answer that we conceive quantity in two ways: abstractly or superficially, as we have it in the imagination with the help of the senses, or as Substance, apprehended solely by means of the intellect. So if we have regard to quantity as it exists in the imagination (and this is what we most frequently and readily do), it will be found to be divisible, finite, composed of parts, and manifold. But if we have regard to it as it is in the intellect and we apprehend the thing as it is in itself (and this is very difficult), then it is found to be infinite, indivisible, and one alone, as I have already sufficiently proved.

Further, from the fact that we are able to delimit Duration and Quantity as we please, conceiving Quantity in abstraction from Substance and separating the efflux of Duration from things eternal, there arise Time and Measure: Time to delimit Duration and Measure to

---

66. This argument, and its relation to the divisibility of extension, receives an extended treatment by Spinoza in E1P15Schol. While the argument suggests Zeno's paradoxes of motion, in fact Spinoza addresses those paradoxes only in his commentary on Descartes (see PPC2P6Schol). The importance of Spinoza's rejection of the divisibility argument is great, since it threatens his claim that extension is an attribute of substance. See also Jonathan Bennett, "Spinoza's Vacuum Argument," *Midwest Studies in Philosophy* 5 (1980), 391-399.

delimit Quantity in such wise as enables us to imagine them easily, as far as possible. Again, from the fact that we separate the affections of Substance from Substance itself, and arrange them in classes so that we can easily imagine them as far as possible, there arises Number, whereby we delimit them. Hence it can clearly be seen that Measure, Time and Number are nothing other than modes of thinking, or rather, modes of imagining. It is therefore not surprising that all who have attempted to understand the workings of Nature by such concepts, and furthermore without really understanding these concepts, have tied themselves into such extraordinary knots that in the end they have been unable to extricate themselves except by breaking through everything and perpetrating the grossest absurdities. For there are many things that can in no way be apprehended by the imagination but only by the intellect, such as Substance, Eternity, and other things. If anyone tries to explicate such things by notions of this kind which are nothing more than aids to the imagination, he will meet with no more success than if he were deliberately to encourage his imagination to run made. Nor again can the Modes of Substance ever be correctly understood if they are confused with such mental constructs (*entia rationis*) or aids to the imagination. For by so doing we are separating them from Substance and from the manner of their efflux from Eternity, and in such isolation they can never be correctly understood.

To make the matter still clearer, take the following example. If someone conceives Duration in this abstracted way and, confusing it with Time, begins dividing it into parts, he can never understand how an hour, for instance, can pass by. For in order that an hour should pass by, a half-hour must first pass by, and then half of the remainder, and the half of what is left; and if you go on thus subtracting half of the remainder to infinity, you can never reach the end of the hour. Therefore many who are not used to distinguishing mental constructs from real things have ventured to assert that Duration is composed of moments, thus falling into the clutches of Scylla in their eagerness to avoid Charybdis. For to say that Duration is made up of moments is the same as to say that Number is made up simply by adding noughts together.

Further, it is obvious from the above that neither Number, Measure, nor Time, being merely aids to the imagination, can be infinite, for in that case Number would not be number, nor Measure measure, nor Time time. Hence one can easily see why many people, confusing these three concepts with reality because of their ignorance of the true nature of reality, have denied the actual existence of the infinite. But let their deplorable reasoning be judged by mathematicians who, in matters that they clearly and distinctly perceive, are not to be put off by arguments of that sort. For not only have they come upon many things inexpressible by any number (which clearly reveals the inadequacy of number to determine all things) but they also have many instances which cannot be equated with any number, and exceed any possible number. Yet they do not draw the conclusion that it is because of the multitude of parts that such things exceed all number; rather, it is because the nature of the thing is such that number is inapplicable to it without manifest contradiction.

For example, all the inequalities of the space lying between the two circles ABCD in the diagram exceed any number, as do all the variations of the speed of matter moving through that area.

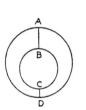

Now this conclusion is not reached because of the excessive magnitude of the intervening space; for however small a portion of it we take, the inequalities of this small portion will still be beyond any numerical expression. Nor again is this conclusion reached, as happens in other cases, because we do not know the maximum and minimum; in our example we know them both, the maximum being AB and the minimum CD. Our conclusion is reached because number is not applicable to the nature of the space between two non-concentric circles. Therefore if anyone sought to express all those inequalities by a definite number, he would also have to bring it about that a circle should not be a circle.[67]

67. Spinoza's geometrical example is ambiguous, and has led to two divergent interpretations of the account of infinity offered here. Gueroult (1966) views the distinctions in senses of infinity as related to distinct types of *objects* (see also Gueroult 1968, 500-528). Charles Ramond (1995, 103-114) criticizes Gueroult's reading, and offers an interpretation in terms of the kinds of knowledge involved (131-152).

Similarly, to return to our theme, if anyone were to attempt to determine all the motions of matter that have ever been, reducing them and their duration to a definite number and time, he would surely be attempting to deprive corporeal Substance, which we cannot conceive as other than existing, of its affections, and to bring it about that Substance should not possess the nature which it does possess. I could here clearly demonstrate this and many other points touched on in this letter, did I not consider it unnecessary.

From all that I have said one can clearly see that certain things are infinite by their own nature and cannot in any way be conceived as finite, while other things are infinite by virtue of the cause in which they inhere; and when the latter are conceived in abstraction, they can be divided into parts and be regarded as finite. Finally, there are things that can be called infinite, or if you prefer, indefinite, because they cannot be accurately expressed by any number, while yet being conceivable as greater or less. For it does not follow that things which cannot be adequately expressed by any number must necessarily be equal, as is sufficiently evident from the given example and from many others.

To sum up, I have here briefly set before you the causes of the errors and confusion that have arisen regarding the question of the infinite, explaining them all, unless I am mistaken, in such a way that I do not believe there remains any question regarding the Infinite on which I have not touched, or which cannot be readily solved from what I have said. Therefore I do not thing there is any point in detaining you longer on this matter.

However, in passing I should like it here to be observed that in my opinion our modern Peripatetics have quite misunderstood the demonstration whereby scholars of old sought to prove the existence of God. For, as I find it in a certain Jew named Rab Chasdai,[68] this proof

---

68. Hasdai (or Ḥasdai, or Chasdai) Crescas was a celebrated Jewish theologian (1340?- 1410). The term 'Rab' (more commonly 'Rav' today) is rather vague, possibly indicating 'Mr.' or 'Dominus' but also possibly a higher level of respect. Today it usually means 'Rabbi'. Crescas opposed the then-fashionable Aristotelean proof for the existence of God as first mover, made even more popular by Maimonides' and Thomas Aquinas' adaptations. Instead, Crescas suggested that it is not conceivable that the world should exist conditionally, and therefore it must be that there exist an uncaused cause which sustains all things. (This argument is thus similar to that of William of Occam whose proof for God is based not on an infinite regress of causes, but that there be something which conserves all that exists; Occam, *Quaestiones in libros physicorum Aristotelis*, qq. cxxxii-cxxxvi). The point is that Spinoza relies on Crescas' reasoning in his own proof for the existence of infinite substance. One cannot prove that substance exists merely by going from effect to cause, to the cause's cause, to the cause of the cause's

runs as follows: "If there is granted an infinite series of causes, all things which are, are also caused. But nothing that is caused can exist necessarily by virtue of its own nature. Therefore there is nothing in Nature to whose essence existence necessarily pertains. But this latter is absurd; therefore also the former."[69] So the force of the argument lies not in the impossibility of an actual infinite or an infinite series of causes, but only in the assumption that things which by their own nature do not necessarily exist are not determined to exist by a thing which necessarily exists by its own nature.

I would now pass on – for I am pressed for time – to your second letter, but I shall be able more conveniently to reply to the points contained therein when you will kindly pay me a visit. So do please try to come as soon as you possibly can. For the time of my moving is rapidly approaching. Enough, farewell, and keep in ever in your thoughts, who am, etc.

Rijnsburg, 20 April 1663.

---

cause, and so on *ad infinitum*. Instead, for Spinoza, substance is the whole in/through/by which all (modes) things exist; this underlying substrate must be if anything is since it is what sustains or allows any mode to be. It is that some imagine substance to be divisible or durational that causes them to misunderstand its nature and essence which is to be eternal, "infinite, indivisible, and one alone" (see also Ep40P). For more details on Crescas' proof see two studies by Harry A. Wolfson: "Spinoza on the Unity of Substance," *Chronicon Spinozanum* 2 (1922), 92-117; and *Crescas' Critique of Aristotle* (Cambridge (Mass.): Harvard University Press, 1929). On Crescas' life, see Yitzhak Baer, *A History of the Jews in Christian Spain*, 2 vols. (Philadelphia: Jewish Publication Society, 1992), esp. 2:466, n. 24, and sources cited there.

69. The argument to which Spinoza refers can be found in Bk. 1, Part 1, Ch. 3, and Bk. 1, Part 2, Ch. 3, of Crescas' major work, *Or Adonai*, also called *Or ha-Shem* (Ferrara: Abraham Usque, 1555). Both mean "The Light of the Lord." The former passage is translated in Wolfson's study, *Crescas' Critique of Aristotle* (Cambridge (Mass.): Harvard University Press, 1929), 220-229. There are various recent reprints and editions of *Or Adonai*, but neither the first edition nor subsequent editions are reliable. The edition prepared by Shelomoh Fisher (Jerusalem: Sifre Ramot, 1988) has the advantage of vocalization marks to assist in deciphering Crescas' cryptic prose. *Or Adonai* appears not to have been fully translated into any language, but extensive excerpts are found in Wolfson's book, as well as in Warren Harvey, *Hasdai Crescas's Critique of the Theory of the Acquired Intellect*, Columbia University dissertation, 1973.

LETTER 12A
To Lodewijk Meyer, from B.d.S.

[Not in the O.P. nor in Gebhardt.
Discovered by Offenberg and published in 1975.]

My very dear friend,

Yesterday I received your very welcome letter[70] in which you ask, first, whether in Chapter 2 of Part I of the Appendix you have correctly indicated all propositions, etc. which are there cited from Part I of the Principia; secondly, whether my assertion in Part II that the Son of God is the Father himself[71] should not be deleted; and finally, whether my statement that I do not know what theologians understand by the term 'personalitas' should not be changed.[72] To this I reply,

1. That everything you have indicated in Chapter 2 of the Appendix has been correctly indicated. But in Chapter 1 of the Appendix, page 1, you have indicated the Scholium to Proposition 4, whereas I would prefer you to have indicated the Scholium to Proposition 15, where my declared purpose is to discuss all modes of thinking. Again, on page 2 of the same chapter, you have written these words in the margin, 'Why negations are not *ideae*,' where the word 'negations' should be replaced by '*entia rationis*', for I am speaking of the '*ens rationis*' in general, and saying that it is not an 'idea.'

2. As to my saying that the Son of God is the Father himself, I think it follows clearly from this axiom, namely, that things which agree with a third thing agree with one another. However, since this is a matter of no importance to me, if you think that it may give offence to some theologians, do as seems best to you.

---

70. For more information on this letter and the recently discovered response, see A. K. Offenberg, "Letter from Spinoza to Lodewijk Meyer, 26 July 1663" in *Speculum Spinozanum: 1677-1977*, ed. Siegfried Hessing (London: Routledge & Kegan Paul, 1977) 426-435.

71. It seems that Meyer did think it better to remove this statement from the *Cogitata metaphysica* since it does not appear in either of the versions which have come down to us.

72. Apparently Meyer followed Spinoza's suggestions here: see CM2, sec. 8.

3. Finally, what theologians mean by the word *'personalitas'* is beyond me, though I know what philologists mean by it. Anyway, since the manuscript is in your hands, you can better decide these things yourself. If you think they ought to be changed, do as you please.

Farewell, my dear friend, and remember me who am,

      Your most devoted,
      B. de Spinoza.

Voorburg, 26 July 1663.

LETTER 13
To the noble and learned Henry Oldenburg, from B.d.S.

[Known only from the O.P. The original is lost.]

Most Noble Sir,

Your letter, which I have long looked for, I have at last received, and am also free to answer it. But before embarking on this task, I shall briefly relate the circumstances which have prevented an earlier reply.

When I moved my furniture here in April, I went to Amsterdam. There some of my friends requested me to provide them with a transcript of a certain treatise containing a short account of the Second Part of Descartes' *Principles* demonstrated in geometric style, and the main topics treated in metaphysics, which I had previously dictated to a young man[73] to whom I did not wish to teach my own opinions openly. Then they asked me to prepare the First Part too by the same method, as soon as I could. Not to disappoint my friends, I immediately set about this work, completed it in two weeks and delivered it to my friends, who finally asked my permission to publish the whole thing. They readily obtained my consent, but on condition that one of them, in my presence, should give it a more elegant style and add a short preface warning readers that I do not acknowledge everything in the treatise as my own views, 'since I have written in quite a few things which are completely opposed to my own opinions', and should illustrate this fact by one or two examples. One of my friends who has undertaken the publication of this little book has promised to do all this,[74] and that is why I was delayed at Amsterdam for some time. And

---

73. This was Caesarius: see Ep8.
74. This was Lodewijk Meyer: see Section I of the introduction. Meyer provided a brief introduction to the PPC, underlining the fact that Spinoza was axiomatising Descartes' thought rather than his own. From this some commentators (e.g., Wolfson) have concluded that the PPC and its appendix (the *Cogitata Metaphysica*) should be completely disregarded in the interpretation of Spinoza's philosophy. But this judgment is clearly too severe. While Meyer mentions especially the Cartesian account of will as being denied by Spinoza, Spinoza is more than an expositor in the PPC. He often provides alternative or reworked proofs for Descartes' own stated positions, and no less often is his exposition of some points a thinly veiled critique of the position defended by Descartes. The present letter also indicates the order in which PPC was written: first the second part, then the first, and presumably the third part added as an afterthought. This third part is

right from the time of my return to this village where I now live, I have scarcely been my own master because of friends who have been kind enough to call on me.

Now at last, my very dear friend, I have time enough to tell you this, and also to give you the reason why I am allowing this treatise to be published. Perhaps as a result there will be some men holding high positions in my country who will want to see other of my writing which I acknowledge as my own, and so will arrange that I can make them available to the public without risk of trouble. Should this come about, I have no doubt that I shall publish some things immediately; if not, I shall keep silent rather than thrust my opinions on men against my Country's wishes and incur their hostility. I therefore beg you, my honoured friend, to be patient until that time; for then you will either have the treatise in print or a summary of it, as you request. And if in the meantime you would like one or two copies of the work which is now in the press, when I am told so and I also find a convenient way of sending it, I shall comply with your wish.

I now turn to your letter. I thank you most warmly, as I should, and also the noble Boyle, for your outstanding kindness towards me and your goodwill. The many affairs in which you are engaged, of such weight and importance, have not made you unmindful of your friend, and indeed you generously promise that you will make every effort in future to avoid so long an interruption in our correspondence. The learned Mr. Boyle, too, I thank very much for being so good as to reply to my observations, in however cursory and preoccupied a way. I do indeed admit that they are not of such importance that the learned gentleman, in replying to them, should spend time which he can devote to reflections of a higher kind. For my part I did not imagine – indeed, I could never have been convinced – that the learned gentleman had no other object in view in his *Treatise on Nitre* than merely to demonstrate that the puerile and frivolous doctrine of Substantial Forms and Qualities rests on a weak foundation. But being convinced that it was

---

incomplete, which can probably be explained by Spinoza's expressed lack of interest. It should also be noted that Balling's Dutch translation of the PPC appeared in 1664, the year following the Latin edition. It was more than a translation, but less than the new edition for which Meyer expressed hope in his preface. A number of new passages are added in the Dutch, and there is little reason to believe that these additions were not either made or approved by Spinoza himself.

the esteemed Boyle's intention to explain to us the nature of Nitre, that it was a heterogeneous body consisting of fixed and volatile parts, I intended in my explanation to show (as I think I have more than adequately shown) that we can quite easily explain all the phenomena of Nitre, such as are known to me at least, while regarding Nitre as a homogeneous body, not heterogeneous. Therefore it was not for me to prove, but merely to hypothesize, that the fixed salt is the dregs of Nitre, so that I might see how the esteemed Mr. Boyle could prove to me that this salt is not the dregs but a very necessary constituent in the essence of Nitre without which it could not be conceived. For this, as I say, I thought to be the object of the esteemed Mr. Boyle's demonstration.

When I said that the fixed salt has passages hollowed out according to the dimensions of the particles of Nitre, I did not need this to explain the redintegration of Nitre. For from my assertion that its redintegration consists merely in the coagulation of the Spirit of Nitre, it is apparent that every calx whose passages are too narrow to contain the particles of Nitre and whose walls are weak is well fitted to halt the motion of the particles of Nitre, and therefore, by my hypothesis, to redintegrate the Nitre itself. So it is not surprising that there are other salts, such as tartar and potash, with whose aid Nitre can be redintegrated. My only purpose in saying that the fixed salt of Nitre has passages hollowed out in accord with the dimensions of the particles of Nitre was to assign a reason why the fixed salt of Nitre is more suited to redintegrate Nitre without much loss of its original weight. Indeed, from the fact that there are other salts from which Nitre can be redintegrated, I thought I might show that the calx of Nitre is not necessary for constituting the essence of Nitre, if the esteemed Mr. Boyle had not said that there is no salt more universal than Nitre; and so it might have lain concealed in tartar and potash.

When I further said that the particles of Nitre in the larger passages are encompassed by finer matter, I inferred this, as the esteemed Mr. Boyle says, from the impossibility of a vacuum. But I do not know why he calls the impossibility of a vacuum a hypothesis, since it clearly follows from the fact that nothing has no properties.[75] And I am surprised

---

75. Spinoza further developed this Cartesian argument for the nonexistence of a vacuum in PPC2P3. It is also mentioned in E1P15Schol, which contains a probable reference to the PPC. For an analysis of the vacuum argument as it is understood by Spinoza (rather than Descartes), see Jonathan Bennett, "Spinoza's Vacuum Argument," *Midwest Studies in Philosophy* 5 (1980), 391-399. A more elaborate presentation of the argument in connection with what Bennett calls

that the esteemed Mr. Boyle doubts this, since he seems to hold that there are no real accidents.[76] Would there not be a real accident, I ask, if Quantity were granted without Substance.

With regard to the causes of the difference of taste between Spirit of Nitre and Nitre itself, I had to suggest these so as to show how I could quite easily explain the phenomena of Nitre merely as a result of the difference I was willing to allow between Spirit of Nitre and Nitre itself, taking no account of the fixed salt.

My remarks as to the inflammability of Nitre and the non-inflammability of Spirit of Nitre do not presuppose anything other than that for kindling of a flame in any body there needs be some matter that can separate and set in motion the parts of the body, both of which facts I think are sufficiently taught us by daily experience and reason.

I pass on to the experiments which I put forward so as to confirm my explanation not in any absolute sense but, as I expressly said, to some degree. Against the first experiment which I adduced, the esteemed Mr. Boyle advances nothing beyond what I myself have most expressly remarked. As for the others which I also attempted so as to free from suspicion that which the esteemed Mr. Boyle joins me in noting, he has nothing whatever to say. As to his remarks on the second experiment, to wit, that through purification Nitre is for the most part freed from a salt resembling common salt, this he only says but does not prove. For, as I have expressly said, I did not put forward these experiments to give complete confirmation to my assertions, but only because they seemed to offer some degree of confirmation to which I had said and had shown to be consistent with reason. As to his remark that rising to form little icicles is common to this and to other salts, I do not know how this is relevant; for I grant that other salts also have dregs and are rendered more volatile if they are freed from them. Against the third experiment, too, I see nothing advanced that touches me. In the fifth section I thought that our noble Author was criticising Descartes, which he has also done elsewhere by virtue of the freedom

---

Spinoza's 'field metaphysics', is given in his *A Study of Spinoza's Ethics* (Indianapolis: Hackett, 1984), 98-103.

76. See Ep4. The scholastics had used the term 'accident' to apply to any nonessential quality whatever, but had called 'real accidents' those qualities which 'inhered' in substances but were distinct from them. Principal among these were colour and others of the qualities called 'secondary' by those adopting Galileo's new science of matter.

to philosophise granted to everyone without hurt to the reputation of either party. Others, too, who have read the writings of the esteemed Mr. Boyle and Descartes' Principles may well think like me unless they are expressly warned. And I still do not see that the esteemed Mr. Boyle makes his meaning quite clear; for he still does not say whether Nitre will cease to be Nitre if its visible icicles, of which alone he says he is speaking, were to be rubbed until they changed into parallelepipeds or some other shape.

But leaving these matters, I pass on to the esteemed Mr. Boyle's assertions in sections 13. . . 18. I say that I willingly admit that this redintegration of Nitre is indeed an excellent experiment for investigating the nature of Nitre – that is, when we already know the mechanical principles of philosophy, and that all variations of bodies come about according to the laws of mechanics; but I deny that these things follow from the said experiment more clearly and evidently than from many other commonplace experiments, which do not, however, provide definite proof. As to the esteemed Mr. Boyle's remark that he has not found these views of his so clearly expounded and discussed by others, perhaps he has something I cannot see against the arguments of Verulam and Descartes whereby he considers he can refute them. I do not cite these arguments here, because I do not imagine that the esteemed Mr. Boyle is unaware of them. But this I will say, that these writers, too, wanted phenomena to accord with their reason; if they nevertheless were mistaken on certain points, they were but men, and I think that nothing human was alien to them.[77]

He says, too, that there is a considerable difference between those experiments (that is, the commonplace and doubtful experiments adduced by me) where we do not know what is contributed by Nature and what by other factors, and those where the contributing factors are clearly established. But I still do not see that the esteemed Mr. Boyle has explained to us the nature of the substances that are present in this affair, namely, the nature of the calx of Nitre and the Spirit of Nitre, so that these two seem no less obscure than those which I adduced, namely, common lime and water. As for wood, I grant that it is a more composite body than Nitre; but as long as I do not know the nature of either, and the way in which heat is produced in either of them, what, I

---

77. A reference to the familiar line from Terence: "*Homo sum, humani nihil a me alienumst.*"

ask, does this matter? Again, I do not know by what reasoning the esteemed Mr. Boyle ventures to assert that he knows what Nature contributes in the matter under our consideration. By what reasoning, pray, can he demonstrate to us that the heat was not produced by some very fine matter? Perhaps because there was little lost from the original weight? Even if nothing had been lost, in my opinion no inference could be drawn; for we see how easily things can be dyed some colour as a result of a very small quantity of matter, without thereby becoming heavier or lighter to the senses. Therefore I am justified in entertaining some doubt as to whether there may not have been a concurrence of certain factors imperceptible to the senses, especially while it is not known how all those variations observed by the esteemed Mr. Boyle during the experiments could have arisen from the said bodies. Indeed, I am sure that the heat and the effervescence recounted by the esteemed Mr. Boyle arose from foreign matter.

Again, that disturbance of air is the cause from which sound originates can, I think, be more easily inferred from the boiling of water (I say nothing here of its agitation) than from this experiment where the nature of the concurrent factors is quite unknown, and where heat is also observed without our knowing in what way or from what causes it has originated. Finally, there are many things that emit no smell at all; yet if their parts are to some degree stirred up and become warm, they at once emit a smell; and if again they are cooled, they again have no smell (at least of human sense – perception) – such as amber, and other things which may also be more composite than Nitre.

My remarks on the twenty-fourth section show that Spirit of Nitre is not pure Spirit, but contains much calx of Nitre and other things. So I doubt whether the esteemed Mr. Boyle could have been sufficiently careful in observing what he says he has detected with the aid of scales, namely, that the weight of Spirit of Nitre which he added was roughly equal to the weight lost during detonation.

Finally, although to our eyes pure water can dissolve alkaline salts more rapidly, yet since it is a more homogeneous body than air, it cannot, like air, have so many kinds of corpuscles which can penetrate through the pores of every kind of calx. So since water is made up mostly of definite particles of a single kind which can dissolve calx up to a certain limit – which is not the case with air – it follows that water will dissolve calx up to that limit far more rapidly than air. But on the other hand, since air is made up of both grosser and far finer particles and all kinds of particles which can in many ways get through much narrower pores than can be penetrated by particles of water, it follows that air can dissolve calx of Nitre if not as rapidly as water (because it cannot be made up of so many particles of a particular kind) yet far more effectively and to a finer degree, and render it less active and so more apt to halt the motion of the particles of the Spirit of Nitre. For as yet the experiments do not make me acknowledge any difference between Spirit of Nitre and Nitre itself other than that the particles of the later are at rest, while those of the former are in very lively motion with one another. So the difference between Nitre and Spirit of Nitre is the same as that between ice and water.

But I do not venture to detain you any longer on these matters; I fear I have been too prolix, although I have sought to be as brief as possible. If I have nevertheless been boring, I beg you to forgive me, and at the same time to take in good part which is said frankly and sincerely by a friend. For I judged it wrong, in replying to you, to keep altogether silent on these matters. Yet to praise to you what I could not agree with would have been sheer flattery, than which I deem nothing to be more destructive and damaging in friendships. I therefore resolved to open my mind quite frankly, and in my opinion nothing is more welcome than this to philosophers. Meanwhile, if it seems more advisable to you to consign these thoughts to the fire than to pass them on the learned Mr. Boyle, they are in your hands. Do as you please, so long as you believe me to be a most devoted and loving friend to you and to the noble Mr. Boyle. I am sorry that my slender resources prevent me from showing this otherwise than in words. Still. . . etc.

17/27 July 1663.

LETTER 14
Henry Oldenburg to the esteemed B.d.S.

[Known only from the O.P. The Latin original is lost.
In the penultimate paragraph, the last sentence
appears only in the Dutch edition of the O.P.]

Esteemed Sir, most honoured friend,

I find much happiness in the renewal of our correspondence. Know therefore how I rejoiced to receive your letter dated 17/27 July, and particularly on two accounts, that it gave evidence of your well-being and that it assured me of the constancy of your friendship. To crown it all, you tell me that you have committed to the press the first and second parts of Descartes' *Principia* demonstrated in the geometric style, while generously offering me one or two copies of it. Most gladly do I accept the gift, and I ask you please to send the treatise now in the press to Mr. Peter Serrarius[78] living at Amsterdam, for delivery to me. I have arranged with him to receive such a package and to send it on to me by a friend who is making the crossing.

But allow me to say that I am by no means content with your continued suppression of the writings which you acknowledge as your own, especially in a republic so free that there you are permitted to think what you please and to say what you think. I wish you would break through those barriers, especially since you can conceal your name and thus place yourself beyond any risk of danger.

The noble Boyle has gone away: as soon as he returns to town, I shall communicate to him that part of your learned letter which

---

78. Peter Serrarius was born in Belgium in 1663, lived in Amsterdam, and was a frequent visitor to London. Few details of his life are known. In 1667 he published, as a reply to Meyer's *Philosophy the Interpreter of Holy Scripture*, a treatise entitled *Responsio ad Exercitationem Paradoxam* (Amsterdam: Typis Cunradi, 1667). For what details we have, see two works by Ernestine G. E. van der Wall: *De mystieke chiliast Petrus Serrarius (1600-1669) en zijn wereld* (University of Leiden dissertation, 1987); and "The Amsterdam Millenarian Petrus Serrarius (1600-1669) and the Anglo-Dutch Circle of Philo-Judaists," in J. van den Berg and E. G. E. van der Wall, eds., *Jewish-Christian Relations in the Seventeenth Century* (Dordrecht: Kluwer, 1988), 73-94.

concerns him, and as soon as I have obtained his opinion on your views, I shall write to you again. I think you have already seen his *Sceptical Chymist* which was published in Latin some time ago and is widely circulated abroad. It contains many Chemico-Physical paradoxes, and subjects the Hypostatical principles of the Spagyrists, as they are called, to a strict examination.[79]

He has recently published another little book which perhaps has not yet reached your booksellers. So I am sending it to you enclosed herewith, and I ask you as a friend to take in good part this little gift. The booklet, as you will see, contains a defence of the power of elasticity of air against a certain Francis Linus, who busies himself to explain the phenomena recounted in Mr. Boyle's *New Physico-Mechanical Experiments* by a thread of argument that eludes the intellect as well as all sense-perception.[80] Read it, weigh it, and let me know what you think of it.

Our Royal Society is earnestly and actively pursuing its purpose, confining itself within the limits of experiment and observation, avoiding all debatable digressions.

Recently an excellent experiment has been performed which greatly perplexes the upholders of a vacuum but is warmly welcomed by those who hold that space is a plenum. It is as follows. Let a glass flask A, filled to the brim with water, be inverted with its mouth in a glass jar B containing water, and let it be placed in the Receiver of Mr. Boyle's New Pneumatic Machine. Then let the air be pumped out of the Receiver. Bubbles will be seen to rise in great quantity from the water into the flask A and to force down all the water from this into the jar B below the surface of the water contained therein. Let the two vessels

---

79. The Spagyrists followed the views of Paracelsus (1490-1541) in rejecting the Aristotelian chemistry of the four elements (earth, fire, air, water) in favour of three ultimate principles: salt, sulphur, and mercury. Like Boyle and most seventeenth-century chemists, they used 'principle' and 'element' interchangeably. Boyle poked fun at the 'hypostatical' theory by pointing out, quite correctly, that it could only account for chemical change by begging the question and stretching the properties of the putative three elements beyond any recognisable meaning. Some chemists of the time adopted both the three Paracelsian elements in conjunction with the four elements of Aristotle (a theory which Aristotle himself adopted rather uncritically from Empedocles).

80. The full title of Boyle's treatise was *Defensio doctrinae de elatere et gravitate aeris, adversus Franc. Lini objectiones*. It was published in 1663, and a copy was in the official inventory of Spinoza's library.

be left in this state for a day or two, the air being repeatedly evacuated from the said Receiver by frequent pumpings.

Then let them be removed from the Receiver, and let the flask A be refilled with this water from which air has been removed and again inverted in the jar B, and let both vessels be once more enclosed in the Receiver. When the Receiver has again been emptied by the requisite amount of pumping, perhaps a little bubble will be seen to rise from the neck of the flask A, which, rising to the top and expanding with the continued pumping, will once again force out all the water from the flask, as before. Then let the flask be again taken from the Receiver, filled to the top with water from which the air has been removed, inverted as before, and placed in the Receiver. Then let the Receiver be thoroughly evacuated of air, and when it has been well and truly evacuated, water will remain in the flask in such a state of suspension that it will not descend at all. In this experiment the cause which, according to Boyle, is believed to sustain the water in the Torricellian experiment (namely, the pressure of the air on the water in the vessel B)[81] seems completely removed, and yet the water in the flask does not descend.[82]

I had intended to add more, but friends and business call me away. I shall only add this: if you would like to send me the things you are having printed, please address your letter and packages in the following way. . . etc.

I cannot conclude this letter without urging you again and again to publish your own thoughts. I shall not cease to exhort you until you satisfy my request. In the meantime, if you should be willing to let me have some of the main points contained therein, oh! how I would love you and with how close a tie I would hold myself bound to you! May all go well with you, and continue to love me, as you do.

> Your most devoted and dear friend,
> Henry Oldenburg.

London, 31 July 1663.

---

81. Torricelli (1608-1647), once a collaborator with Galileo, created the barometer. His celebrated experiment (1643) showed that air pressure can support a column of water to a length inversely proportional to its specific gravity.
82. We know now that it is the tensile strength of the water which must be taken into account to explain the null result of the experiment.

LETTER 15
Cordial greetings to Mr. Lodewijk Meyer, from B. de Spinoza

[Not in the O.P. This letter was discovered by
Victor Cousin, and published in 1847.]

My dear friend,

The Preface which you sent me through our friend de Vries[83] I now
return to you through him. As you will see for yourself, I have made a
few notes in the margin; but there still remain a few things which I
have thought it better to let you have by letter.

First, where on page 4 you inform the reader of the occasion of my
composing the First Part, I should like you also at the same time to
point out, either there or wherever you please, that I composed it
within two weeks. Thus forewarned, no one will imagine that what I
present is so clear that it could not have been expounded more clearly,
and so they will not be put out by a mere word or two which in some
places they may find obscure.

Second, I should like you to mention that many of my demonstrations are arranged in a way different from that of Descartes, not to
correct Descartes, but only the better to preserve my order of exposition and thus to avoid increasing the number of axioms. And it is also
for the same reason that I have had to prove many things which Descartes merely asserts without proof, and to add other things which Descartes omitted.

Finally, my very dear friend, I beg you most earnestly to leave out
what you wrote at the end against that petty man,[84] and to delete it

---

83. For de Vries, see section 3 of the introduction.
84. We cannot determine the passage to which Spinoza refers, since it was apparently
deleted as he requested. Who is that petty man (*illum homunculum*) of whom
Spinoza writes? Perhaps Caesarius (cf. Ep8), but a recent article suggests it may
have been the contemporary Christian and orthodox Cartesian Florentius Schuyl
who had published his Latin translation of Descartes' *Traité de l'homme, De homine*, six months after Spinoza's PPC appeared. Some have suggested that it was
the poet, Joost den Vondel: see, for instance, Th. de Valk, "Spinoza en Vondel,"
De Beiaard 6 (1921), 440-458 (esp. p. 443). For additional information on the passage see Wim Klever, "Qui était l'Homunculus?" *Bulletin de l'association des
amis de Spinoza* 29 (1993) 24-27.

entirely. And although I have many reasons for making this request of you, I shall mention only one. I should like everyone to be able readily to accept that this publication is meant for the benefit of all men, and that in publishing this book you are motivated only by a wish to spread the truth, and so you are chiefly concerned to make this little work welcome to all, that you are inviting men in a spirit of goodwill to take up the study of the true philosophy, and your aim is the good of all. This everyone will readily believe when he sees that no one is attacked, and that nothing is advanced which might be offensive to some person. If, however, in due course that person or some other chooses to display his malicious disposition, then you can portray his life and character, and not without approval. I therefore beg you to be good enough to wait until then, and to allow yourself to be persuaded, and to believe me to be your devoted and zealous friend,

      B. de Spinoza.

Voorburg, 3 August 1663.

    Our friend de Vries had promised to take this with him, but since he does not know when he is going back to you, I am sending it by someone else.

    I am sending along with this a part of the Scholium to Proposition 27 of Part 2, as it begins on page 75, for you to give to the printer to be typeset again.

    What I am here sending you will have to be printed again and 14 or 15 lines must be added, which can easily be inserted.[85]

---

85. The first edition of the PPC (1663) shows clearly that eleven lines of small type had been interpolated on pages 76 and 77 after these pages had been typeset.

LETTER 16
Henry Oldenburg to the esteemed B.d.S.

[Known only from the O.P. The original is lost.]

Distinguished Sir and most honoured Friend,

Scarcely three or four days have passed since I sent you a letter by the ordinary post. In that letter I made mention of a certain booklet written by Mr. Boyle, which has to be sent to you. At that time there appeared no hope of quickly finding a friend to deliver it. Since that time someone has come forward sooner than I expected. So receive now what could not then be sent, together with the dutiful greetings of Mr. Boyle who has now returned to town from the country.

He asks you to consult the preface which he wrote to his Experiments on Nitre, so as to understand the true aim which he set himself in that work: namely, to show that the doctrines of the more firmly grounded philosophy now being revived are elucidated by clear experiments, and that these experiments can very well be explained without the forms, qualities and the futile elements of the Schools.[86] In no way did he undertake to pronounce on the nature of Nitre, nor again to criticize opinions that may be expressed by anyone about the homogeneity of matter and the differences of bodies arising solely from motion, shape, and so on. He says that he meant only to show this, that the various textures of bodies produce their various differences, and that from these proceed very different effects, and that, as long as there has been no reduction to prime matter, some heterogeneity is properly inferred therefrom by philosophers and others. Nor would I think that there is disagreement between you and Mr. Boyle on the fundamental issue.

As to your saying that any calx, whose passages are too narrow to contain the particles of Nitre and whose walls are weak, is apt to halt the motion of the particles of Nitre and therefore to reconstitute the Nitre, Boyle replies that if Spirit of Nitre is mixed with other kinds of calx, it will not, however, combine with them to form true Nitre.

---

86. See the notes to Ep3, Ep6, and Ep14.

As to the argument you employ to deny the possibility of a vacuum, Boyle says that he knows it and has seen it before, but is not by any means satisfied with it. He says there will be an opportunity to discuss the matter on another occasion.

He has requested me to ask you whether you can provide him with an example where two odorous bodies, when combined into one, compose a body that is completely odourless, as Nitre is. Such, he says, are the parts composing Nitre; for Spirit of Nitre gives out a foul smell, while fixed Nitre is not without smell.

He further asks you to consider well whether, in comparing ice and water with Nitre and Spirit of Nitre, you are making a proper comparison. For the whole of the ice is resolved only into water, and when the odourless ice turns again into water it remains odourless, whereas the Spirit of Nitre and its fixed salt are found to have different qualities, as the printed Treatise quite clearly tells us.

These and similar things I gathered from our illustrious author in conversation on this subject. I am sure that, through weakness of memory, my recollection does him grave injustice rather than credit. Since you are both in agreement on the main point, I am not inclined to enlarge any further on these matters. I would rather persuade you both to unite your abilities in striving to advance a genuine and firmly based philosophy. May I urge you especially, with your keen mathematical mind, to continue to establish basic principles, just as I ceaselessly try to entice my noble friend Boyle to confirm and elucidate them by experiments and observations repeatedly and accurately made.

You see, my dear friend, what I am striving for, what I am trying to attain. I know that our native philosophers in our kingdom will in no way fail in their duty to experiment, and I am no less convinced that you in your own land will actively do your part, whatever snarlings or accusations may come from the mob of philosophers or theologians. Having already exhorted you to this in numerous previous letters, I will restrain myself lest I weary you. I shall just make this one further request, that you will please send me with all speed by Mr. Serrarius whatever has already been committed to print, whether it be your commentary on Descartes or something drawn from your own intellectual stores. You will have me that much more closely bound to you, and will understand that, under any circumstance, I am,

Your most devoted,
Henry Oldenburg.
London, 4 August 1663.

LETTER 17
To the learned and sagacious Pieter Balling, from B.d.S.

[Known only from the O.P. The original is lost. It was
written in Dutch, and the Latin version which appears in
the O.P. may have been made by Spinoza. The Dutch edition
has what appears to be a re-translation from the Latin.]

Dear Friend,

Your last letter, written, if I am not mistaken, on the 26th of last
month, has reached me safely. It caused me no little sorrow and anxiety, though that has much diminished when I reflect on the good sense
and strength of character which enable you to scorn the adversities of
fortune, or what is thought of as such, at the very time when they are
assailing you with their strongest weapons. Still, my anxiety increases
day by day, and I therefore beg and beseech you not to regard it as burdensome to write to me without stint.

As for the omens which you mention, namely, that while your child
was still well and strong you heard groans such as he uttered when he
was ill and just before he died, I am inclined to think that these were
not real groans but only your imagination; for you say that when you
sat up and listened intently you did not hear them as clearly as before,
or as later on when you had gone back to sleep. Surely this shows that
these groans were no more than mere imagination which, when it was
free and unfettered, could imagine definite groans more effectively and
vividly than when you sat up to listen in a particular direction.

I can confirm, and at the same time explain, what I am here saying
by something that happened to me in Rijnsburg last winter.[87] When
one morning just at dawn I awoke from a very deep dream,[88] the
images which had come to me in the dream were present before my
eyes as vividly as if they had been real things, in particular the image of
a black, scabby Brazilian whom I had never seen before. This image

---

87. Spinoza moved from Rijnsburg to Voorburg in 1663. Perhaps he visited Rijnsburg
later, or perhaps he refers to the winter of 1662-63.
88. For conjectures concerning Spinoza's dream, see L. Feuer, "The Dream of
Benedict de Spinoza," *American Imago* 14 (1957) 225-242.

disappeared for the most part when, to make a diversion, I fixed my gaze on a book or some other object; but as soon as I again turned my eyes away from such an object while gazing at nothing in particular, the same image of the same Ethiopian kept appearing with the same vividness again and again until it gradually disappeared from sight.

I say that what happened to me in respect of my internal sense of sight happened to you in respect of hearing. But since the cause was quite different, your case was an omen, while mine was not. What I am now going to tell you will make the matter clearly intelligible.

The effects of the imagination arise from the constitution either of body or of mind. To avoid all prolixity, for the present I shall prove this simply from what we experience. We find by experience that fevers and other corporeal changes are the cause of delirium, and that those whose blood is thick imagine nothing but quarrels, troubles, murders and things of that sort. We also see that the imagination can be determined simply by the constitution of the soul, since, as we find, it follows in the wake of the intellect in all things, linking together and interconnecting its images and words just as the intellect does its demonstrations, so that there is almost nothing we can understand without the imagination instantly forming an image.

This being so, I say that none of the effects of the imagination which are due to corporeal causes can ever be omens of things to come, because their causes do not involve any future things. But the effects of imagination, or images, which have their origin in the constitution of the mind can be omens of some future event because the mind can have a confused awareness beforehand of something that is to come. So it can imagine it as firmly and vividly as if such a thing were present to it.

For instance (to take an example like your case), a father so loves his son that he and his beloved son are, as it were, one and the same.[89]

_____

89. This passage in Spinoza has caused more than a few commentators great trouble. While the present translation does much to preserve Spinoza's sense of counterfactuals (the Latin letter makes heavy use of the subjunctive mood (e.g., "*ut is* [*pater*] *et dilectus filius* quasi *unus idemque* sint" [emphasis ours]) it would still be easy for the unwary reader to imagine that Spinoza waxes mystical on the hypostatic union of the Trinity or even on lesser Plotinian-type unions here on Earth. What Spinoza may have exactly meant in writing to console his grieving friend may not always be clear, but what he did not write or did not mean is certain: no two (distinct) essences are the same though it is possible that they might be so related that they affect each other *as if* they *were* the same.

And since (as I have demonstrated on another occasion)[90] there must necessarily exist in Thought an idea of the affections of the essence of the son and what follows therefrom, and the father by reason of his union with his son is a part of the said son, the soul of the father must likewise participate in the ideal essence of his son, and in its affections and in what follows therefrom, as I have elsewhere demonstrated at some length. Further, since the soul of the father participates ideally in the things that follow from the essence of the son, he can, as I have said, sometimes imagine something from what follows on the essence of the son as vividly as if he had it in front of him – that is, if the following conditions are fulfilled: (1) If the event which is to happen in the course of the son's life is one of importance. (2) If it is such as we can quite easily imagine. (3) If the time at which this event will take place is not very remote. (4) Finally, if his body is in good order not only as regards health, but is also free and devoid of all the cares and worries that disturb the senses from without. It could also serve to promote this end if we are thinking of things which especially arouse ideas similar to these. For example, if while conversing with any person we hear groans, it will generally happen that when we again think of that same man, the groans which we heard while speaking to him are likely to come back to mind. This dear friend, is my opinion on the question that you raise. I have been very brief, I confess, but deliberately so, in order to give you material for writing to me at the first opportunity, etc.

Voorburg, 20 July 1664.

---

90. This occasion is lost to us. Gueroult (1974) suggests (and warns) his readers that this letter was written before Spinoza's philosophy was fully matured, since no part of it as explained in this passage appears in the *Ethics*. Another reason, then, along with our note above that "On doit donc rester prudent en ce qui concerne les commentaires conjecturaux auxquels cette *Lettre* peut donner lieu" (Gueroult, 1974, 577).

LETTER 18
To the esteemed B.d.S., from William de Blyenbergh.

[Known only from the O.P. The original, which
is lost, was written in Dutch, but may be
what is in the Dutch edition of the O.P. The
Latin is a translation from the Dutch.]

Sir and unknown Friend,[91]

I have now several times had the privilege of perusing your recently published *Treatise* with its Appendix,[92] giving it close attention. It would be more seemly to tell others rather than yourself of the great solidity I found there, and the satisfaction it gave me. But I cannot refrain from saying this much, that the more frequently I peruse it with attention, the more it pleases me, and I am continually finding something that I had not noticed before. However, lest in this letter I appear a flatterer, I will not express too much admiration for the author; I know what price in toil the gods demand for all they give.

But not to keep you too long wondering who it is and how it happens that a stranger should assume the great liberty of writing to you, I will tell you that it is one who, impelled only by desire for pure truth, strives in this brief and transitory life to set his feet on the path to knowledge, so far as our human intelligence permits; one who in his search for truth has no other aim than truth itself; one who seeks to acquire for himself through science neither honours nor riches but truth alone, and the peace of mind that results from truth; one who among all truths and sciences takes pleasure in none more than metaphysical studies – if not in all of them, at least in some part of them – and finds all his pleasure in life in devoting thereto all the leisure hours that can be spared. But not everyone is as blessed as you, and not everyone applies himself as diligently as I imagine you have done, and

---

91. See section 4 of the introduction for a general overview of the correspondence on faith and theology with Blyenbergh, for which this letter itself constitutes the historical introduction.
92. This is the PPC, with the *Cogitata Metaphysica* appended. See Ep13 and our notes thereto.

therefore not everyone has attained the degree of perfection which I
see from your work you have attained. In a word, it is one whom you
would get to know more closely if you would graciously oblige him so
very much as to help open a way and pierce through the tangle of his
thoughts.

But to return to the Treatise. Just as I found therein many things
which appealed very much to my taste, so I also encountered some
things which I found difficult to digest. It would not be right for me, a
stranger to you, to raise these matters, the more so because I do not
know whether or not this would be acceptable to you. That is why I am
sending this preliminary letter, with the request that, if in these winter
evenings you have the time and the inclination to oblige me so much as
to reply to the difficulties which I still find in your book, I may be permitted to send you some of them. But I adjure you not to be hindered
thereby from any more necessary or more agreeable pursuit; for I
desire nothing more eagerly than the fulfillment of the promise made
in your book,[93] the fuller explication and publication of your views.
What I am now at last entrusting to pen and paper I would rather have
put to you in person on greeting you; but because first of all I did not
know your address, and then the epidemic and finally my own duties
prevented me, this was put off time after time.

But in order that this letter may not be entirely without content,
and in the hope that you will not find this unwelcome, I shall raise only
this one point. In several places both in the *Principia*[94] and in the *Cogitata Metaphysica*,[95] in explaining either your own opinion or Descartes',
whose philosophy you were expounding, you maintain that to create
and to preserve are one and the same thing (which is so self-evident to
those who have turned their minds to it that it is a fundamental notion)
and that God has created not only substances but the motions in substances; that is, that God not only preserves substances in their state by
a continuous creation but also their motion and their striving. For
instance, God, through his immediate will or action (whichever you like
to call it), not only brings it about that the soul continues to exist and
perseveres in its state, but is also related in the same way to the motion

---

93. The promise for a fuller development was actually made by Meyer in his preface
   to the PPC.
94. See PPC1P12.
95. See CM2, Chapters 7, 10, and 11.

of the soul. That is, just as God's continuous creation brings it about that things go on existing, so also the striving and motion of things is due to the same cause, since outside God there is no cause of motion. Therefore it follows that God is not only the cause of the substance of the mind but also of every striving or motion of the mind, which we call the will, as you everywhere maintain. From this statement it also seems to follow necessarily either that there is no evil in the motion or will of the soul or that God himself is the immediate agent of that evil. For those things that we call evil also come about through the soul, and consequently through this kind of immediate influence and concurrence of God.

For example, the soul of Adam wants to eat of the forbidden fruit. According to the above statements, it is through God's influence that no only does Adam will, but also (as will immediately be shown) that he wills thus. So either Adam's forbidden act, in so far as God not only moved his will but also in so far as he moved it in a particular way, is not evil in itself, or else God himself seems to bring about what we call evil. And it seems to me that neither you nor Monsieur Descartes solve this difficulty by saying that evil is a non-being with which God does not concur.[96] For whence, then, did the will to eat come, or the Devil's will to pride? Since the will, as you rightly observe, is not anything different from the mind, but is this or that motion or striving of the mind, it has as much need of God's concurrence for the one motion as for the other. Now God's concurrence, as I understand from your writings, is nothing but the determining of a thing by his will in this or that manner. It therefore follows that God concurs with, that is, determines, the evil will in so far as it is evil no less than the good will. For the will of God, which is the absolute cause of all things that exist both in substance and in its strivings, seems to be the prime cause of the evil will in so far as it is evil.

Again, there occurs no determination of will in us without God's having known it from eternity; otherwise, if he did not know it, we are ascribing imperfection to God. But how could God have known it except through his decrees? So his decrees are the cause of our determinations, and thus it once again seems to follow that either the evil will is not anything evil or that God is the immediate cause of that evil.

---

96. See CM2, Ch. 3; and CM3, Chs. 7, 10, and 11.

And here the Theologians' distinction regarding the difference between the act and the evil adhering to the act has no validity. For God decreed not only the act but also the manner of the act; that is, God decreed not only that Adam should eat, but also that he necessarily ate contrary to command, so that it again seems to follow that either Adam's eating the apple contrary to command is no evil, or that God himself wrought that evil.

This much in your Treatise, esteemed Sir, is for the present incomprehensible to me; for the extremes on both sides are hard to maintain. But I expect from your penetrating judgment and diligence a reply that will satisfy me, and I hope to show you in the future how much I shall be obligated to you thereby.

Be assured, esteemed Sir, that my questions are prompted only by zeal for truth, and for no other personal interest. For I am a free person, not dependent on any profession, supporting myself by honest trading and devoting my spare time to these matters. I also humbly ask that my difficulties should not be unwelcome to you; and if you are minded to reply, as is my heartfelt desire, please write to W.v.B. etc.

Meanwhile, I shall be and remain,

Your devoted servant,
W.v.B.

Dordrecht, 12 December 1664.

LETTER 19
To the learned and sagacious William de Blyenbergh, from B.d.S.

[Known only from the O.P. The original, which is lost, was
written in Dutch, but may be printed in the Dutch edition
of the O.P. The Latin is a translation from the Dutch, perhaps
by Spinoza. The last paragraph appears only in the Dutch edition.]

My unknown friend,

Your letter of the 12th December, enclosed in another letter dated the 21st of the same month, I finally received on the 26th of that month while at Schiedam. I gathered from it that you are deeply devoted to truth, which you make the sole aim of all your endeavours. Since I have exactly the same objective, this has determined me not only to grant without stint your request to answer to the best of my ability the questions which you are now sending me and will send me in the future, but also to do everything in my power conducive to further acquaintance and sincere friendship. For my part, of all things that are not under my control, what I most value is to enter into a bond of friendship with sincere lovers of truth. For I believe that such a loving relationship affords us a serenity surpassing any other boon in the whole wide world. The love that such men bear to one another, grounded as it is in the love that each has for knowledge of truth, is as unshakable as is the acceptance of truth once it has been perceived. It is, moreover, the highest source of happiness to be found in things not under our command, for truth more than anything else has the power to effect a close union between different sentiments and dispositions. I say nothing of the considerable advantages that derive therefrom, not wishing to detain you any longer on a matter on which you need no instruction. This much I have said so that you may better understand how pleased I am, and shall continue to be, to have the opportunity of serving you.

To avail myself of the present opportunity, I shall now go on to answer your question. This seems to hinge on the following point, that it seems clearly to follow, both from God's providence, which is identical with his will, and from God's concurrence and the continuous creation of things, either that there is no such thing as sin or evil, or that God brings about that sin and that evil. But you do not explain what you mean by evil, and as far as one can gather from the example of Adam's determinate will, by evil you seem to mean the will itself in so far as it is conceived as determined in a particular way, or in so far as it is in opposition to God's command. So you say it is quite absurd (and I would agree, if the case were as you say) to maintain either of the following alternatives, that God himself brings to pass what is contrary to his will, or else that what is opposed to God's will can nevertheless be good. For my own part, I cannot concede that sin and evil are anything positive, much less than anything can be or come to pass against God's will. On the contrary, I not only assert that sin is not anything positive; I maintain that it is only by speaking improperly or in merely human fashion that we say that we sin against God, as in the expression that men make God angry.[97]

For as to the first point, we know that whatever is, when considered in itself without regard to anything else, possesses a perfection coextensive in every case with the thing's essence; for its essence is not the same thing. I take as an example Adam's resolve or determinate will to eat of the forbidden fruit. This resolve or determinate will, considered solely in itself, contains in itself perfection to the degree that it expresses reality. This can be inferred from the fact that we cannot conceive imperfection in things except by having regard to other things possessing more reality.[98] For this reason, when we consider Adam's decision in itself without comparing it with other things more perfect or displaying a more perfect state, we cannot find any imperfection in it. Indeed, we may compare it with innumerable other things much more lacking in perfection in comparison with it, such as stones, logs, and so forth. In actual practise, too, this is universally conceded. For everybody beholds with admiration in animals what he dislikes and regards with aversion in men, like the warring of bees, the jealousy of doves, and so on. In men such things are detested, yet we esteem animals as more perfect because of them. This being the case, it clearly follows that sin, since it indicates only imperfection, cannot consist in anything that expresses reality, such as Adam's decision and its execution.

Furthermore, neither can we say that Adam's will was at variance with God's law, and was evil because it was displeasing to God. It would argue great imperfection in God if anything happened against

---

97. The anthropomorphism of ordinary language in dealing with God is dealt with in the Appendix to the first part of the *Ethics*, as well as in TTP2 and TTP7.
98. See the introduction to the fourth part of the *Ethics* for a more detailed exposition of the sense in which 'imperfection' is a creature of imagination.

his will, or if he wanted something he could not possess, or if his nature were determined in such a manner that, just like his creatures, he felt sympathy with some things and antipathy to others. Furthermore, this would be in complete contradiction to the nature of God's will; for since his will is identical with his intellect, it would be just as impossible for anything to take place in opposition to his will as in opposition to his intellect. That is to say, anything that would take place against his will would have to be of such a nature as likewise to be in opposition to his intellect, as, for example, a round square. Therefore since Adam's will or decision, regarded in itself, was neither evil nor yet, properly speaking, against God's will, it follows that God can be – or rather, according to the reasoning you refer to, must be – the cause of it. But not in so far as it was evil, for the evil that was in it was simply the privation of a more perfect state which Adam was bound to lose because of his action.[99]

Now it is certain that privation is not something positive, and is so termed in respect of our intellect, not God's intellect. This is due to the fact that we express by one and the same definition all the individual instances of the same genus[100] – for instance, all that have the outward appearance of men – and we therefore deem them all equally capable of the highest degree of perfection that can be inferred from that particular definition. Now when we find one thing whose actions are at variance with that perfection, we consider that it is deprived of that perfection and is astray from its own nature. This we would not do if we had not referred the individual to that particular definition and ascribed to it such a nature. Now God does not know things in abstraction, nor does he formulate general definitions of that sort, and things possess no more reality than that with which God's intellect and potency have endowed them, and which he has assigned to them in actual fact. From this it clearly follows that the privation in question is a term applicable in respect of our intellect only, and not of God's.

This, I believe, is a complete answer to the question. However, to make the path smoother and to remove every shadow of doubt, I think

99. A detailed analysis of Spinoza's use of the term *privatio* is given by Raphael Demos, "Spinoza's Doctrine of Privation," *Philosophy* 8 (1933), 155-166; reprinted in *Studies in Spinoza*, ed. Paul Kashap (Berkeley: University of California Press, 1972), 276-88.
100. Spinoza here anticipates Frege's definition of 'number', and derives from it a strongly nominalistic interpretation of general terms.

I ought still to answer the following two questions: First, why does Holy Scripture say that God requires the wicked to turn from their evil ways, and why, too, did he forbid Adam to eat of the fruit of the tree when he had ordained the contrary? Secondly, it seems to follow from what I have said that the wicked serve God by their pride, greed, and desperate deeds no less than the good by their nobleness, patience, love, etc. For they, too, carry out God's will.

In reply to the first question, I say that Scripture, being particularly adapted to the needs of the common people, continually speaks in merely human fashion, for the common people are incapable of understanding higher things. That is why I think that all that God has revealed to the Prophets as necessary for salvation is set down in the form of law, and in this way the Prophets made up a whole parable depicting God as a king and lawgiver, because he had revealed the means that lead to salvation and perdition, and was the cause thereof. These means, which are simply causes, they called laws, and wrote them down in the form of laws; salvation and perdition, which are simply effects necessarily resulting from these means, they represented as reward and punishment. All their words were adjusted to the framework of this parable rather than to truth. They constantly depicted God in human form, sometimes angry, sometimes merciful, now looking to what is to come, now jealous and suspicious, and even deceived by the Devil. So philosophers and likewise all who have risen to a level beyond law, that is, all who pursue virtue not as a law but because they love it as something very precious, should not find such words a stumbling-block.

Therefore the command given to Adam consisted solely in this, that God revealed to Adam that eating of that tree brought about death, in the same way that he also reveals to us through our natural understanding that poison is deadly. If you ask to what end he made this revelation, I answer that his purpose was to make Adam that much more perfect in knowledge. So to ask God why he did not give Adam a more perfect will is no less absurd than to ask why he has not bestowed on a circle all the properties of a sphere, as clearly follows from what I have said above, and as I have demonstrated in the Scholium to Proposition 15 of my *Principles of Cartesian Philosophy Demonstrated in Geometrical Form*, Part 1.

As to the second difficulty, it is indeed true that the wicked express God's will in their own way, but they are not for that reason at all comparable with the good; for the more perfection a thing has, the more it participates in Deity, and the more it expresses God's perfection. Since, then, the good have incomparably more perfection than the wicked, their virtue cannot be compared with the virtue of the wicked, because the wicked lack the love of God that flows from the knowledge of God, and by which alone, within the limits of our human intellect, we are said to be servants of God. Indeed, not knowing God, the wicked are but an instrument in the hands of the Maker, serving unconsciously and being used up in that service, whereas the good serve consciously, and in serving become more perfect.[101]

This, Sir, is all I can now put forward in answer to your question. I desire nothing more than that it may satisfy you. But if you still find any difficulty, I beg you to let me know, to see if I can remove it. You on your side need have no hesitation, but as long as you think you are not satisfied, I would like nothing better than to know the reasons for it, so that truth may finally come to light. I would have preferred to write in the language[102] in which I was brought up; I might perhaps express my thoughts better. But please excuse this, and correct the mistakes yourself, and consider me,

> Your devoted friend and servant,
> B. de Spinoza.

The Long Orchard, 5 January 1665.

I shall be staying at this Orchard for another three or four weeks, and then I intend to return to Voorburg. I believe I shall receive an answer from you before then, but if your affairs do not permit it, please write to Voorburg with this address – to be delivered to Church Lane at the house of Mr. Daniel Tydeman, painter.

---

101. Spinoza's account of the nature of evil is more complicated than this passage suggests, but perhaps he is attempting to adjust his expression to what he perceives as the limitations in Blyenbergh's comprehension. See William K. Frankena, "Spinoza on the Knowledge of Good and Evil," *Philosophia* 7 (1977), 15-44; and Wim Klever, "Blijenbergh's Tussing with Evil and Spinoza's Response," *Tijdschrift voor filosofie* 55 (1993), 307-329.

102. Namely, Portuguese. See W. G. van der Tak, "Spinoza's Payments to the Portuguese-Israelitic Community; and the Language in Which He Was Raised," *Studia Rosenthalia* 16 (1982), 190-195.

LETTER 20
To the esteemed B.d.S., from Willem de Blyenbergh

[This letter was written in Dutch. The original is extant.
The Latin version in the O.P. is a translation from the Dutch.]

Sir, and esteemed Friend,

When first I received your letter and read it through hastily, I intended not only to reply at once but also to make many criticisms. But the more I read it, the less matter I found to object to; and great as had been my longing to see it, so great was my pleasure in reading it.

But before I proceed to ask you to resolve certain further difficulties for me, you should first know that there are two general rules which always govern my endeavours to philosophise. One is the clear and distinct conception of my intellect, the other is the revealed Word, or will, of God. In accordance with the one, I try to be a lover of truth, while in accordance with both I try to be a Christian philosopher. And whenever it happens that after long consideration my natural knowledge seems either to be at variance with this Word or not very easily reconcilable with it, this Word has so much authority with me that I prefer to cast doubt on the conceptions I imagine to be clear rather than to set these above and in opposition to the truth which I believe I find prescribed for me in that book. And little wonder, since I wish to continue steadfast in the belief that that Word is the Word of God, that is, that it has proceeded from the highest and most perfect God who possesses far more perfection than I can conceive, and who has perhaps willed to predicate of himself and his works more perfection than I with my finite intellect can today perceive. I say 'can today perceive', because it is possible that by my own doing I have deprived myself of greater perfection, and so if perchance I were in possession of the perfection whereof I have been deprived by my own doing, I might realise that everything presented and taught to us in that Word is in agreement with the soundest conceptions of my mind. But since I now suspect myself of having by continual error deprived myself of a better state, and since you assert in *Principia*, Part 1, Proposition 15 that our knowledge, even when most clear, still contains imperfection, I prefer to turn to that Word even without reason, simply on the grounds that it has proceeded from the most perfect Being (I take this for granted at present, since its proof would here be inappropriate or would take too long) and therefore must be accepted by me.

If I were now to pass judgment on your letter solely under the guidance of my first rule, excluding the second rule as if I did not have it or as if it did not exist, I should have to agree with a great deal of it, as indeed I do, and admire your subtle conceptions; but my second rule causes me to differ more widely from you. However, within the limits of a letter, I shall examine them somewhat more extensively under the guidance of both the rules.

First of all, in accordance with the first stated rule, I asked whether, taking into account your assertions that creation and preservation are one and the same thing and that God causes not only things, but the motions and modes of things, to persist in their state (that is, concurs with them) it does not seem to follow that *there is no evil* or else that *God himself brings about that evil*. I was relying on the rule that nothing can come to pass against God's will, since otherwise it would involve an imperfection; or else the things that God brings about, among which seem to be included those we call evil, would also have to be evil. But since this too involves a contradiction, and however I turned it I could not avoid a contradiction, I therefore had recourse to you, who should be the best interpreter of your own conceptions.

In reply you say that you persist in your first presupposition, namely, that nothing happens or can happen against God's will. But when an answer was required to this problem, whether God then does not do evil, you say that sin is not anything positive, adding that only very improperly can we be said to sin against God. And in the Appendix, Part 1, Chapter 6 you say that *there is no absolute evil, as is self-evident*; for whatever exists, considered in itself without relation to anything else, possesses perfection, which in every case is co-extensive with the thing's essence. Therefore it clearly follows that sins, inasmuch as they denote nothing but imperfections, *cannot consist in anything that expresses essence*. If sin, evil, error, or whatever name one chooses to give it, is nothing else but the loss or deprivation of a more perfect state, then of course it seems to follow that to exist is indeed not an evil or imperfection, but that some evil can arise in an existing thing. For that which is perfect will not be deprived of a more perfect state through an equally perfect action, but through our inclination towards something imperfect because we misuse the powers granted us. This you seem to call not evil, but merely a lesser good, because things considered in themselves contain perfection, and secondly because, as you say, no more essence belongs to things than the divine intellect and power assigns to them and gives them in actual fact, and therefore they can display no more existence in their actions than they have received essence. For if the actions I produce can be no greater or lesser than the essence I have received, it cannot be imagined that there is a privation of a more perfect state. If nothing comes to pass contrary to God's will, and if what comes to pass is governed by the amount of essence granted, in what conceivable way can there be evil, which you call privation of a better state? How can anyone suffer the loss of a more perfect state through an act thus constituted and dependent? Thus it seems to me that you must maintain one of two alternatives: either that there is some evil, or, if not, that there can be no privation of a better state. For that there is no evil, and that there is privation of a better state, seem to be contradictory.

But you will say that, through privation of a more perfect state, we fall back into a lesser good, not into an absolute evil. But you have taught me (Appendix, Part 1, Chapter 3) that one must not quarrel over words. Therefore I am not now arguing as to whether or not it should be called an absolute evil, but whether the decline from a better to a worse state is not called by us, and ought rightly to be called, a worse state, or a state that is evil. But, you will reply, this evil state yet contains much good. Still, I ask whether that man who through his own folly has been the cause of his own deprivation of a more perfect state and is consequently now less than he was before, cannot be called evil.

To escape from the foregoing chain of reasoning since it still confronts you with some difficulties, you assert that *evil does indeed exist, and there was evil in Adam, but it is not something positive, and is called evil in relation to our intellect, not to God's intellect.* In relation to our intellect it is privation (but only in so far as we thereby deprive ourselves of the best freedom which belongs to our nature and is within our power), but in relation to God it is negation.

But let us here examine whether what you call evil, if it were evil only in relation to us, would be no evil; and next, whether evil, taken in the sense you maintain, ought to be called mere negation in relation to God.

The first question I think I have answered to some extent in what I have already said. And although I conceded that my being less perfect than another being cannot posit any evil in me because I cannot demand from my Creator a better state, and that it causes my state to differ only in degree, nevertheless I cannot on that account concede that, if I am now less perfect than I was before and have brought this imperfection on myself through my own fault, I am not to that extent the worse. If, I say, I consider myself as I was before ever I lapsed into imperfection and compare myself with others who possess a greater perfection than I, that lesser perfection is not an evil but a lower grade of good. But if, after falling from a more perfect state and being deprived thereof by my own folly, I compare myself with my original more perfect condition with which I issued from the hand of my Creator, I have to judge myself to be worse than before. For it is not my Creator, but I myself, who has brought me to this pass. I had power enough, as you yourself admit, to preserve myself from error.

To come to the second question, namely, whether the evil which you maintain consists in the privation of a better state – which not only Adam but all of us have lost through rash and ill-considered action – whether this evil, I say, is in relation to God a mere negation. Now to submit this to a thorough examination, we must see how you envisage man and his dependency on God prior to any error, and how you envisage the same man after error. Before error you depict him as possessing no more essence than the divine intellect and power has assigned to him and in actual fact bestows on him. That is, unless I mistake your meaning, man can possess no more and no less perfection than is the essence with which God has endowed him; that is to say, you make man dependent on God in the same way as elements, stones, plants, etc. But if that is your opinion, I fail to understand the meaning of *Principia*, Part 1, Proposition 15 where you say, "Since the will is free to determine itself, it follows that we have the power of restraining our faculty of assent within the limits of the intellect, and therefore of bringing it about that we do not fall into error." Does it not seem a contradiction to make the will so free that it can keep itself from error, and at the same time to make it so dependent on God that it cannot manifest either more or less perfection than God has given it essence?

As to the other question, namely, how you envisage man after error, you say that man deprives himself of a more perfect state by an over-hasty action, namely, by not restraining his will within the limits of his intellect. But it seems to me that both here and in the *Principia* you should have shown in more detail the two extremes of this privation, what he possessed before the privation and what he still retained after the loss of that perfect state, as you call it. There is indeed something said about what we have lost, but not about what we have retained, in *Principia*, Part 1, Proposition 15: *So the whole imperfection of error consists solely in the privation of the best freedom, which is called error.* Let us take a look at these two statements just as they are set out by you. You maintain not only that there are in us such very different modes of thinking, some of which we call willing and others understanding, but also that their proper ordering is such that we ought not to will things before we clearly understand them. You also assert that if we restrain our will within the limits of our intellect we shall never err, and, finally, that it is within our power to restrain the will within the limits of the intellect.

When I give earnest consideration to this, surely one of two things must be true: either all that has been asserted is mere fancy, or God has implanted in us this same order. If he has so implanted it, would it not be absurd to say that this has been done to no purpose, and that God does not require us to observe and follow this order? For that would posit a contradiction in God. And if we must observe the order implanted in us, how can we then be and remain thus dependent on God? For if no one shows either more or less perfection than he has received essence, and if this power must be known by its effects, he who lets his will extend beyond the limits of his intellect has not received sufficient power from God; otherwise he would also have put it into effect. Consequently, he who errs has not received from God the perfection of not erring; if he had, he would not have erred. For according to you there is always as much of essence given us as there is of perfection realised.

Secondly, if God has assigned us as much essence as enables us to observe that order, as you assert we are able to do, and if we always produce as much perfection as we possess essence, how comes it that we transgress that order? How comes it that we are able to transgress that order and that we do not always restrain the will within the limits of the intellect?

Thirdly, if, as I have already shown you to assert, I am so dependent on God that I cannot restrain my will either within or beyond the limits of my intellect unless God has previously given me so much essence and, by his will, has predetermined the one course or the other, how then, if the matter be deeply considered, can freedom of will be available to me? Does it not seem to argue a contradiction in God, to lay down an order for restraining our will within the limits of our intellect, and not to vouchsafe us as much essence or perfection as to enable us to observe that order? And if, in accordance with your opinion, he has granted us that much perfection, we surely could never have erred. For we must produce as much perfection as we possess essence, and always manifest in our actions the power granted us. But our errors are a proof that we do not possess a power of the kind that is thus dependent on God, as you hold. So one of these alternatives must be true: either we are not dependent on God in that way, or we do not have in ourselves the power of being able not to err. But on your view we do have the power not to err. Therefore we cannot be dependent on God in that way.

From what has been said I think it is now clear that it is impossible that evil, or being deprived of a better state, should be a negation in relation to God. For what is meant by privation, or the loss of a more perfect state? Is it not to pass from a greater to a lesser perfection, and consequently from a greater to a lesser essence, and to be placed by God in a certain degree of perfection and essence? Is that not to will that we can acquire no other state outside his perfect knowledge, unless he had decreed and willed otherwise? Is it possible that this creature, produced by that omniscient and perfect Being who willed that it should retain a certain state of essence – indeed, a creature with whom God continually concurs so as to maintain it in that state – that this creature should decline in essence, that is, should be diminished in perfection, without God's knowledge? This seems to involve an absurdity. Is it not absurd to say that Adam lost a more perfect state and was consequently incapable of practising the order which God had implanted in his soul, while God had no knowledge of that loss and of that imperfection? Is it conceivable that God should constitute a being so dependent that it would produce just such an action and then should lose a more perfect state because of that action (of which God, moreover, would be an absolute cause), and yet God would have no knowledge of it?

I grant that there is a difference between the act and the evil adhering to the act; but that 'evil in relation to God is negation' is beyond my comprehension. That God should know the act, determine it and concur with it, and yet have no knowledge of the evil that is in the act nor of its outcome – this seems to me impossible in God.

Consider with me that God concurs with my act of procreation with my wife; for that is something positive, and consequently God has clear knowledge of it. But in so far as I misuse this act with another woman contrary to my promise and vow, evil accompanies the act. What could be negative here in relation to God? Not the act of procreation; for in so far as that is positive, God concurs with it. Therefore the evil that accompanies the act must be only that, contrary to my own pledge or God's command, I do this with a woman with whom this is not permissible. Now is it conceivable that God should know our actions and concur with them, and yet not know with whom we engage in those actions – especially since God also concurs with the action of the woman with whom I transgressed? It seems hard to think this of God.

Consider the act of killing. In so far as it is a positive act, God concurs with it. But the result of that action, namely, the destruction of a being and the dissolution of God's creature – would God be unaware of this, as if his own work could be unknown to him? (I fear that here I do not properly understand your meaning, for you seem to me too subtle a thinker to perpetrate so gross an error). Perhaps you will reply that those actions, just as I present them, are all simply good, and that no evil accompanies them. But then I cannot understand what it is you call evil, which follows on the privation of a more perfect state; and furthermore the whole world would then be put in eternal and lasting confusion, and we men would become beasts. Consider, I pray, what profit this opinion would bring to the world.

You also reject the common description of man, and you attribute to each man as much perfection of action as God has in fact bestowed on him to exercise. But this way of thinking seems to me to imply that the wicked serve God by their works just as well as do the godly. Why? Because neither of them can perform actions more perfect than they have been given essence, and which they show in what they practise. Nor do I think that you give a satisfactory reply to my question in your second answer, where you say: – *The more perfection a thing has, the more it participates in Deity, and the more it expresses God's perfection. Therefore since the good have incalculably more perfection than the wicked, their virtue cannot be compared with that of the wicked. For the latter are but a tool in the hands of the master, which serves unconsciously and is consumed in serving. But the good serve consciously, and in serving become more perfect.* In both cases, however, this much is true – they can do no more; for the more perfection the one displays compared with the other, the more essence he has received compared with the other. Do not the godless with their small store of perfection serve God equally as well as the godly? For according to you God demands nothing more of the godless; otherwise he would have granted them more essence. But he has not given them more essence, as is evident from their works. Therefore he asks no more of them. And if it is the case that each of them after his kind does what God wills, neither more nor less, why should he whose achievement is slight, yet as much as God demands of him, not be equally acceptable to God as the godly?

Furthermore, as according to you we lose a more perfect state by our own folly through the evil that accompanies the act, so here too you appear to assert that by restraining the will within the limits of the intellect we not only preserve our present perfection but we even become more perfect by serving. I believe there is a contradiction here, if we are so dependent on God as to be unable to produce either more or less perfection than we have received essence – that is, than God has willed – and yet we should become worse through our folly, or better through our prudence. So if man is such as you describe him, you seem to be maintaining nothing other than this, that the ungodly serve God by their works just as much as the godly by their works, and in this way we are made as dependent on God as elements, plants, stones, etc. Then what purpose will our intellect serve? What purpose the power to restrain the will within the limits of the intellect? Why has that order been imprinted in us?

And see, on the other side, what we deprive ourselves of, namely, painstaking and earnest deliberation as to how we may render ourselves perfect in accordance with the rule of God's perfection and the order implanted in us. We deprive ourselves of the prayer and yearnings towards God wherefrom we perceive we have so often derived a wonderful strength. We deprive ourselves of all religion, and all the hope and comfort we expect from prayer and religion. For surely if God has no knowledge of evil, it is still less credible that he will punish evil. What reasons can I have, then, for not eagerly committing all sorts of villainy (provided I can escape the judge)? Why not enrich myself by abominable means? Why not indiscriminately do whatever I like, according to the promptings of the flesh? You will say, because virtue is to be loved for itself. But how can I love virtue? I have not been given that much essence and perfection. And if I can gain just as much contentment from the one course as the other, why force myself to restrain the will within the limits of the intellect? Why not do what my passions suggest? Why not secretly kill the man who gets in my way? See what an opportunity we give to all the ungodly, and to godlessness. We make ourselves just like logs, and all our actions like the movements of a clock.

From what has been said it seems to me very hard to maintain that only improperly can we be said to sin against God. For then what is the significance of the power granted to us to restrain the will within the limits of the intellect, by transgressing which we sin against that order? Perhaps you will reply, this is not a case of sinning against God, but against ourselves; for if it could properly be said that we sin against God, it must also be said that something happens against God's will, which according to you is an impossibility, and therefore so is sinning. Still, one of these alternatives must be true: either God wills it, or he does not. If God wills it, how can it be evil in respect to us? If he does not will it, on your view it would not come to pass. But although this, on your view, would involve some absurdity, nevertheless it seems to me very dangerous to admit therefore all the absurdities already stated. Who knows whether, by careful thought, a remedy may not be found to effect some measure of reconciliation?

With this I bring to an end my examination of your letter in accordance with my first general rule. But before proceeding to examine it according to the second rule, I have yet two points to make which are relevant to the line of thought of your letter, both set forth in your *Principia*, Part 1, Proposition 15. First, you affirm that 'we can keep the power of willing and judging within the limits of the intellect'. To this I cannot give unqualified agreement. For if this were true, surely out of countless numbers at least one man would be found who would show by his actions that he had this power. Now everyone can discover in his own case that, however much strength he exerts, he cannot attain this goal. And if anyone has any doubt about this, let him examine himself and see how often, in despite of his intellect, his passions master his reason even when he strives with all his might.

But you will say that the reason we do not succeed is not because it is impossible, but because we do not apply enough diligence. I reply that if it were possible, then at least there would be one instance found out of so many thousands. But from all men there has not been, nor is there, one who would venture to boast that he has never fallen into error. What surer arguments than actual examples could be adduced to prove this point? Even if there were just a few, then there would be at least one to be found; but since there is not a single one, then likewise there is no proof.

But you will persist and say: if it is possible that, by suspending judgment and restraining the will within the bounds of the intellect, I can once bring it about that I do not err, why could I not always achieve this by applying the same diligence? I reply that I cannot see that we have this day as much strength as enables us to continue so always. On one occasion, by putting all my effort into it, I can cover two leagues in one hour; but I cannot always manage that. Similarly on one occasion I can by great exertion keep myself from error, but I do not always have the strength to accomplish this. It seems clear to me that the first man, coming forth from the hand of that perfect craftsman, did have that power; but (and in this I agree with you) either by not making sufficient use of that power or by misusing it, he lost his perfect state of being able to do what had previously been within his power. This I could confirm by many arguments, were it not too lengthy a business. And in this I think lies the whole essence of Holy Scripture, which we ought therefore to hold in high esteem, since it teaches us what is so clearly confirmed by our natural understanding, that our fall from our first perfection was due to our folly. What then is more essential than to recover from that fall as far as we can? And that is also the sole aim of Holy Scripture, to bring fallen man back to God.

The second point from the *Principia*, Part 1, Proposition 15 affirms that *to understand things clearly and distinctly is contrary to the nature of man,* from which you finally conclude that *it is far better to assent to things even though they are confused, and to exercise our freedom, than to remain for ever indifferent, that is, at the lowest degree of freedom.* I do not find this clear enough to win my assent. For suspension of judgment preserves us in the state in which we were created by our Creator, whereas to assent to what is confused is to assent to what we do not understand, and thus to give equally ready assent to the false as to the true. And if (as Monsieur Descartes somewhere teaches us[103]) we do not in assenting comply with that order which God has given us in respect of our intellect and will, namely, to withhold assent from what is not clearly perceived, then even though we may chance to hit upon truth, yet we are sinning in not embracing truth according to that order which God has willed. Consequently, just as the withholding of assent preserves us in the state in which we were placed by God, so assenting to things confused puts us in a worse position. For it lays the foundations of error whereby we thereafter lose our perfect state.

But I hear you say, is it not better to render ourselves more perfect by assenting to things even though confused than, by not assenting, to remain always at the lowest degree of perfection and freedom? But apart from the fact that we have denied this and in some measure have shown that we have rendered ourselves not better but worse, it also seems to us an impossibility and practically a contradiction that God should make the knowledge of things determined by himself extend beyond the knowledge that he has given us. Indeed, God would thus contain within himself the absolute cause of our errors. And it is not inconsistent with this that we cannot complain of God that he did not bestow on us more than he has bestowed, since he was not bound so to do. It is indeed true that God was not bound to give us more than he has given us; but God's supreme perfection also implies that a creature

---

103. See Descartes' *Principles of Philosophy* I, XXXI; and also Spinoza's scholium to PPC1P15.

proceeding from him should involve no contradiction, as would then appear to follow. For nowhere in created Nature do we find knowledge other than in our own intellect. To what end could this have been granted us other than that we might contemplate and know God's works? And what seems to be a more certain conclusion than that there must be agreement between things to be known and our intellect?

But if I were to examine your letter under the guidance of my second general rule, our differences would be greater than under the first rule. For I think (correct me if I am wrong) that you do not ascribe to Holy Scripture that infallible truth and divinity which I believe lies therein. It is indeed true that you declare your belief that God has revealed the things of Holy Scripture to the prophets, but in such an imperfect manner that, if it were as you say, it would imply a contradiction in God. For if God has revealed his Word and his will to men, then he has done so for a definite purpose, and clearly. Now if the prophets have composed a parable out of the Word which they received, then God must either have willed this, or not willed it. If God willed that they should compose a parable out of his Word, that is, that they should depart from his meaning, God would be the cause of that error and would have willed something self-contradictory. If God did not will it, it would have been impossible for the prophets to compose a parable therefrom. Moreover, it seems likely, on the supposition that God gave his Word to the prophets, that he gave it in such a way that they did not err in receiving it. For God must have had a definite purpose in revealing his Word; but his purpose could not have been to lead men into error, thereby, for that would be a contradiction in God. Again, man could not have erred against God's will, for that is impossible according to you. In addition to all this, it cannot be believed of the most perfect God that he should permit his Word, given to the prophets to communicate to the people, to have a meaning given it by the prophets other than what God willed. For if we maintain that God communicated his Word to the prophets, we thereby maintain that God appeared to the prophets, or spoke with them, in a miraculous way. If now the prophets composed a parable from the communicated Word, – that is, gave it a meaning different from that which God intended them to give – God must have so instructed them. Again, it is as impossible in respect of the prophets as it is contradictory in respect of God, that the prophets could have understood a meaning different from that which God intended.

You also seem to provide scant proof that God revealed his Word in the manner you indicate, namely, that he revealed only salvation and perdition, decreeing the means that would be certain to bring this about, and that salvation and perdition are no more than the effects of the means decreed by him. For surely if the prophets had understood God's word in that sense, what reasons could they have had for giving it another meaning? But I do not see you produce a single proof to persuade us that we should prefer your view to that of the prophets. If you think your proof to consist in this, that otherwise the Word would include many imperfections and contradictions, I say that this is mere assertion, not proof. And if both meanings were squarely before us, who knows which would contain fewer imperfections? And finally, the supremely perfect Being knew full well what the people could understand, and therefore what must be the best method of instructing them.

As to the second part of your first question, you ask yourself why God forbade Adam to eat of the fruit of the tree when he had nevertheless decreed the contrary; and you answer that the prohibition to Adam consisted only in this, that God revealed to Adam that the eating of the fruit of the tree caused death just as he reveals to us through our natural intellect that poison is deadly for us. If it is established that God forbade something to Adam, what reasons are there why I should give more credence to your account of the manner of the prohibition than to that given by the prophets to whom God himself revealed the manner of the prohibition? You will say that your account of the prohibition is more natural, and therefore more in agreement with truth and more befitting God. But I deny all this. Nor can I conceive that God has revealed to us through our natural understanding that poison is deadly; and I do not see why I would ever know that something is poisonous if I had not seen and heard of the evil effects of poison in others. Daily experience teaches us how many men, not recognising poison, unwittingly eat it and die. You will say that if people knew it was poison, they would realise that it is evil. But I reply that no one knows poison, or can know it, unless he has seen or heard that someone has come to harm by using it. And if we suppose that up to this day we had never heard or seen that someone had done himself harm by using this kind of thing, not only would we be unaware of it now but we would not be afraid to use it, to our detriment. We learn truths of this kind every day.

What in this life can give greater delight to a well-formed intellect than the contemplation of that perfect Deity? For being concerned with that which is most perfect, such contemplation must also involve in itself the highest perfection that can come within the scope of our finite intellect. Indeed, there is nothing in my life for which I would exchange this pleasure. In this I can pass much time in heavenly joy, though at the same time being much distressed when I realise that my finite intellect is so wanting. Still, I soothe this sadness with the hope I have – a hope that is dearer to me than life – that I shall exist hereafter and continue to exist, and shall contemplate that Deity more perfectly than I do today. When I consider this brief and fleeting life in which I look to my death at any moment, if I had to believe that there would be an end of me and I should be cut off from that holy and glorious contemplation, then surely I would be more wretched than all creatures who have no knowledge of their end. For before my death, fear of death would make me wretched, and after my death I would be nothing, and therefore wretched in being deprived of that divine contemplation.

Now it is to this that your opinions seem to lead, that when I cease to be here, I shall for ever cease to be. Against this the Word and will of God, by their inner testimony in my soul, give me assurance that after this life I shall eventually in a more perfect state rejoice in contemplation of the most perfect Deity. Surely, even if that hope should turn out to be false, yet it makes me happy as long as I hope. This is the only thing I ask of God, and shall continue to ask, with prayers, sighs and earnest supplication (would that I could do more to this end!) that as long as there is breath in my body, it may please him of his goodness to make me so fortunate that, when this body is dissolved, I may still remain an intellectual being able to contemplate that most perfect Deity. And if only I obtain that, it matters not to me what men here believe, and what convictions they urge on one another, and whether or not there is something founded on our natural intellect and can be grasped by it. This, and this alone, is my wish, my desire, and my constant prayer, that God should establish this certainty in my soul. And if I have this (and oh! if I have it not, how wretched am I!), then let my soul cry out, "As the hart panteth after the water-brook, so longeth my soul for thee, O living God. O when will come the day when I shall be with thee and behold thee?"[104] If only I attain to that, then have I all the aspiration and desire of my soul. But in your view such hopes are

---

104. Compare Psalms 42:1-2. The quotation is not exact.

not for me, since our service is not pleasing to God. Nor can I understand why God (if I may speak of him in so human a fashion) should have brought us forth and sustained us, if he takes no pleasure in our service and our praise. But if I have misunderstood your views, I should like to have your clarification.

But I have detained myself, and perhaps you as well, far too long; and seeing that my time and paper are running out, I shall end. These are the points in your letter I would still like to have resolved. Perhaps here and there I have drawn from your letter a conclusion which may chance not to be your own view; but I should like to hear your explanation regarding this.

I have recently occupied myself in reflecting on certain attributes of God, in which your appendix has given me no little help. I have in effect merely paraphrased your views, which seem to me little short of demonstrations. I am therefore very much surprised that L. Meyer says in his Preface that this does not represent your opinions, that you were under an obligation thus to instruct your pupil in Descartes' philosophy, as you had promised, but that you held very different views both of God and the soul, and in particular the will of the soul. I also see stated in that Preface that you will shortly publish the *Cogitata Metaphysica* in an expanded form. I very much look forward to both of these, for I have great expectations of them. But it is not my custom to praise someone to his face.

This is written in sincere friendship, as requested in your letter, and to the end that truth may be discovered. Forgive me for having written at greater length than I had intended. If I should receive a reply from you, I should be much obliged to you. As to writing in the language in which you were brought up, I can have no objection, if at least it is Latin or French. But I beg you to let me have your answer in this same language, for I have understood your meaning in it quite well, and perhaps in Latin I should not understand it so clearly. By so doing you will oblige me, so that I shall be, and remain,

    Your most devoted and dutiful,
    Willem Van Blyenbergh.
    Dordrecht, 16 January 1665.

In your reply I should like to be informed more fully what you really mean by negation in God.

LETTER 21
To the learned and accomplished
Willem Van Blyenbergh, from B.d.S.

[Known only from the O.P. The original, which is lost,
was written in Dutch, and translated into Latin, perhaps
by Spinoza. The version in the Dutch edition appears
to be a re-translation from the Latin.]

Sir, and friend,

When I read your first letter, I had the impression that our views were
nearly in agreement. From your second letter, however, which I
received on the 21st of this month, I realise that this is far from being
so, and I see that we disagree not only in the conclusions to be drawn
by a chain of reasoning from first principles, but in those very same
first principles, so that I hardly believe that our correspondence can be
for our mutual instruction. For I see that no proof, however firmly
established according to the rules of logic, has any validity with you
unless it agrees with the explanation which you, or other theologians of
your acquaintance, assign to Holy Scripture. However, if it is your conviction that God speaks more clearly and effectually through Holy
Scripture than through the light of the natural understanding which he
has also granted us and maintains strong and uncorrupted through his
divine wisdom, you have good reason to adapt your understanding to
the opinions which you ascribe to Holy Scripture. Indeed, I myself
could do no other. For my part, I plainly and unambiguously avow that
I do not understand Holy Scripture, although I have devoted quite a
number of years to its study. And since I am conscious that when an
indisputable proof is presented to me, I find it impossible to entertain
thoughts that cast doubt upon it, I entirely acquiesce in what my intellect shows me without any suspicion that I am deceived therein, or that
Holy Scripture, without my even examining it, can contradict it. For
truth is not at odds with truth, as I have made clear in my Appendix (I

cannot indicate the chapter, for I do not have the book here with me in the country).[105] And even if I were once to find untrue the fruits which I have gathered from my natural understanding, they would still make me happy; for I enjoy them, and seek to pass my life not in sorrowing and sighing, but in peace, joy and cheerfulness, and so I ascend a step higher. Meanwhile I realise (and this gives me the greatest satisfaction and peace of mind) that all things come to pass as they do through the power of a most perfect Being and his immutable decree.

To return to your letter, I owe you many and sincere thanks for having confided in me in time your method of philosophising, but I do not thank you for attributing to me the sort of opinions you want to read into my letter. What grounds did my letter give you for attributing to me these opinions: that men are like beasts, that men die and perish after the manner of beasts, that our works are displeasing to God, and so forth? (It is in this last point that our disagreement is most striking, for I take your meaning to be that God is pleased with our works just like someone who has attained his end when things fall out as he wished). For my part, surely I have clearly stated that the good worship God, and by their constancy in worship they become more perfect, and that they love God. Is this to liken them to beasts, or to say that they perish in the manner of beasts, or that their works are not pleasing to God?

If you had read my letter with more care, it would have been obvious to you that our point of disagreement lies in this alone: are the perfections received by the good imparted to them by God in his capacity as God, that is, by God taken absolutely without ascribing any human attributes to him – this is the view I hold – or by God in his capacity of judge? The latter is what you maintain, and for this reason you take the line that the wicked, because they do whatever they can in accordance with God's decree, serve God no less than the good serve him. But this in no way follows from what I say. I do not bring in the notion of God as judge, and so my evaluation of works turns on the quality of the works, not on the potency of the doer, and the reward that follows from the action does so by the same necessity as it follows from the nature of a triangle that its three angles have to be equal to two right angles. This will be obvious to everyone who attends simply to the

---

105. Spinoza is probably referring to CM2, Chapter 8.

following point, that our supreme blessedness consists in love towards God, and that this love flows necessarily from the knowledge of God that is so heartily urged on us. This can be readily demonstrated in a general way if only one has regard to the nature of God's decree, as I have explained in my Appendix.[106] I admit, however, that all those who confuse God's nature with the nature of man are quite unqualified to understand this.

I had intended to end this letter here, so as not to bore you any further with matters which (as is evident from the very devout addition at the end of your letter) serve for jest and derision, and are of no value. But not to reject your request entirely, I shall proceed further to explain the terms 'negation' and 'privation', and attempt briefly to throw more light on any obscurities in my previous letter.

First, then, I say that privation is not an act of depriving; it is nothing more than simply a state of want, which in itself is nothing. It is only a construct of the mind (*ens rationis*) or a mode of thinking which we form from comparing things with one another.[107] For instance, we say that a blind man is deprived of sight because we readily imagine him as seeing. This imagining may arise from comparing him with those who can see, or from comparing his present state with a past state when he could see. When we consider the man from this perspective, comparing his nature with that of others or with his own past nature, we assert that sight pertains to his nature, and so we say that he is deprived of it. But when we consider God's decree and God's nature, we can no more assert of that man that he is deprived of sight than we can assert it of a stone. For to say that sight belongs to that man at that time is quite as illogical as to say that it belongs to a stone, since nothing more pertains to that man, and is his, than that which God's intellect and will has assigned to him. Therefore God is no more the cause of his not seeing than of a stone's not seeing, this latter being pure negation. So, too, when we consider the nature of a man who is governed by a lustful desire and we compare his present desire with the desire of a good man, or with the desire he himself once had, we assert

---

106. See CM1, Chapter 3; and CM2, Chapter 11. For the intellectual love of God, see also E5P30-P36.
107. The notion of 'evil' or 'privation' as arising from the formation of universal concepts is discussed in the Preface to E4. See also E4P64 ("Knowledge of evil is inadequate knowledge") and E4P64Cor ("Hence it follows that if the human mind had only adequate ideas, it could not form any notion of evil").

that this man is deprived of the better desire, judging that a virtuous desire belonged to him at that point of time. This we cannot do if we have regard to the nature of the decree and intellect of God. For from that perspective the better desire pertains to that man's nature at that point of time no more than to the nature of the Devil or a stone. Therefore from that perspective the better desire is not a privation but a negation. So privation is simply to deny of a thing something that we judge pertains to its nature, and negation is to deny something of a thing because it does not pertain to its nature.

From this it is clear why Adam's desire for earthly things was evil only in respect to our intellect, not God's intellect. For granted that God knew the past and present state of Adam, this does not mean that he understood Adam as deprived of a past state, that is, that the past state pertained to his nature. If that were so, God would be understanding something that was contrary to his will, that is, he would be understanding something that was contrary to his own understanding. Had you grasped this point, and also that I do not concede the sort of freedom that Descartes ascribes to the mind – as L. Meyer testified on my behalf in his Preface – you would have found no trace of contradiction in what I have said. But I see now that it would have been far better if in my first letter I had adhered to Descartes' line, that we cannot know in what way our freedom, and whatever stems from it, can be reconciled with the providence and freedom of God (see my Appendix, various passages). Consequently, we cannot find any contradiction between God's creation and our freedom because it is beyond us to understand how God created the world and – which is the same thing – how he preserves it. I thought you had read the Preface, and that I would be failing in the duty of friendship, which I sincerely offered, if I did not give you my genuine opinion. But no matter.

However, as I see that you have not yet thoroughly understood Descartes' meaning, I ask you to give careful consideration to the following two points. First, neither Descartes nor I have ever said that it pertains to our nature to restrain our will within the limits of the intellect, but only that God has given us a determinate intellect and an indeterminate will, yet in such a way that we know not to what end he has created us. Further, an indeterminate or perfect will of that kind not only renders us more perfect but is also very necessary for us, as I shall point out in due course.

Secondly, our freedom lies not in a kind of contingency nor in a kind of indifference, but in the mode of affirmation and denial, so that the less indifference there is in our affirmation or denial, the more we are free. For instance, if God's nature is known to us, the affirmation of God's existence follows from our nature with the same necessity as it results from the nature of a triangle that its three angles are equal to two right angles. Yet we are never so free as when we make an affirmation in this way. Now since this necessity is nothing other than God's decree, as I have clearly shown in my Appendix, hence we may understand after a fashion how we act freely and are the cause of our action notwithstanding that we act necessarily and from God's decree. This, I repeat, we can understand in a way when we affirm something that we clearly and distinctly perceive. But when we assert something that we do not clearly and distinctly grasp – that is, when we suffer our will to go beyond the bounds of our intellect – then we are not thus able to perceive that necessity and God's decrees; however, we do perceive the freedom of ours that is always involved in the will (in which respect alone our actions are termed good or bad). If we then attempt to reconcile our freedom with God's decree and his continuous creation, we confuse that which we clearly and distinctly understand with that which we do not comprehend, and so our effort is in vain. It is therefore sufficient to us to know that we are free, and that we can be so notwithstanding God's decree, and that we are the cause of evil; for no action can be called evil except in respect of our freedom. So much I have said concerning Descartes in order to show that in this matter his position is perfectly consistent.

Turning now to my own position,[108] I shall first briefly draw attention to an advantage that accrues from my view, an advantage that lies chiefly in this, that by this view of things our intellect places our mind and body in God's hands free from all superstition. Nor do I deny the utility for us of prayer,[109] for my intellect does not extend so far as to embrace all the means that God possesses for bringing men to the love of himself, that is, to salvation. My opinion is so far from being pernicious that, on the contrary, for those who are not hampered by prejudices and childish superstition it is the one means of obtaining the highest degree of blessedness.

---

108. In the previous two paragraphs, Spinoza has been summarising Descartes' position, in order to contrast it with his own, which follows. He provides a more detailed summary of Descartes' position on error in PPC1P15Schol.
109. Prayer for Spinoza is not a means of influencing or securing favour with God.

When you say that by making men so dependent on God I reduce them to the level of elements, plants and stones, this is enough to show that you have completely misunderstood my views and are confusing the field of intellect with that of the imagination. If you had apprehended by pure intellect the meaning of dependence on God, you would certainly not think that things, in so far as they depend on God, are dead, corporeal and imperfect. (Who has ever dared to speak so basely of the supremely perfect Being?) On the contrary, you would realise that it is for this reason, and in so far as they depend on God, that they are perfect. So this dependence on God and necessity of action through God's decree can be best understood when we have regard, not to logs and plants, but to created things of the highest degree of intelligibility and perfection. This is quite clear from my second observation on the meaning of Descartes, which you should have noted.

I am bound to express astonishment at your saying that if God does not punish wrongdoing (that is, in the way that a judge inflicts a punishment which is not entailed by the wrongdoing itself, for this alone is the point at issue), what consideration hinders me from plunging headlong into all sorts of crime? Surely, he who refrains from so doing by fear of punishment − which I do not impute to you − in no way acts from love and by no means embraces virtue. For my own part I refrain, or try to refrain, from such behaviour because it is directly opposed to my particular nature,[110] and would cause me to stray from the love and knowledge of God.

Again, if you had given a little thought to the nature of man and had understood the nature of God's decree as explained in my Appendix,[111] and had finally known how inference should be made before a conclusion is reached, you would not have so rashly asserted that my view puts us on a level with logs and the like, nor would you have saddled me with all the absurdities you imagine.

With regard to the two points which, before proceeding to your second rule, you say you fail to understand, I reply first that Descartes suffices for arriving at your conclusion, namely, that if only you pay

---

110. Spinoza again emphasizes the extent to which Blyenbergh's concept of evil and privation rests on inadequate universal concepts, rather than an adequate knowledge of particular things.
111. See CM2, Chapters 7-9.

attention to your nature, you experience the ability to suspend judgment. But if you are saying that you do not find in your own experience that our power over reason today is great enough to enable us always to do the same in the future, to Descartes this would be the same as to say that we cannot see today that as long as we exist we shall always be thinking things, or retain the nature of a thinking thing – which surely involves a contradiction.

To your second point I say, with Descartes, that if we could not extend our will beyond the bounds of our very limited intellect, we should be in a most wretched plight. It would not be in our power even to eat a piece of bread, or to move a step, or to halt.[112] For all things are uncertain, and fraught with peril.

I pass on now to your second rule, and I assert that for my part, while I do not ascribe to Scripture the sort of truth that you believe to be contained in it, yet I think that I ascribe to it as much authority, if not more, and that I am far more cautious than others in not assigning to it certain childish and absurd doctrines, for which one must needs be supported either by a thorough knowledge of philosophy or by divine revelation. So I am quite unmoved by the explanations of Scripture advanced by the common run of theologians, especially if they are of the kind that always take Scripture literally by its outward meaning. Apart from the Socinians,[113] I have never found any theologian so stupid as not to see that Holy Scripture very often speaks of God in merely human style and expresses its meaning in parables.

As for the contradiction which you vainly, in my opinion, try to show, I think that by parable you understand something quite different from what is generally accepted. Who has ever heard that a man who expresses his concepts in parables goes astray from his intended meaning? When Micaiah told King Ahab that he had seen God sitting on his throne and the celestial hosts standing on his right hand and on his left, and that God asked them who would deceive Ahab,[114] that was surely a parable wherein the Prophet on that occasion (which was not one for teaching the high doctrines of theology) sufficiently expressed the main

---

112. It is in this sense, and this sense only, that Spinoza can agree with Descartes that will extends beyond intellect. He amplifies this point in his discussion of various objections to his own position on the identity of will and intellect in E2P49Schol, where he criticizes Descartes.
113. See section 8 of our introduction.
114. See I Kings 22:19 and II Chronicles 18:18.

purport of the message he was charged to deliver in God's name. So in no way did he stray from his intended meaning. Likewise the other prophets by God's command made manifest to the people the Word of God in this way, as being the best means – though not means enjoined by God – of leading people to the primary objective of Scripture, which according to Christ himself[115] consists of loving God above all things, and your neighbour as yourself. High speculative thought, in my view, has nothing to do with Scripture. For my part I have never learned, nor could I have learned, any of God's eternal attributes from Holy Scripture.

As to your fifth argument (namely, that the prophets made manifest the Word of God in that way), since truth is not contrary to truth it only remains for me to prove (as anyone will agree who understands the methodology of proof) that Scripture, as it stands, is the true revealed Word of God. A mathematically exact proof of this proposition can be attained only by divine revelation. I therefore said, 'I believe, but do not know in a mathematical way, that all things revealed by God to the prophets. . .' etc. For I firmly believe, but do not know in a mathematical way, that the prophets were the trusted counsellors and faithful messengers of God. So there is no contradiction whatsoever in what I have affirmed, whereas many contradictions can be found on the other side.

The rest of your letter, namely, where you say, 'Finally, the supremely perfect being knew. . . ' etc., and thereafter what you adduce against the example of poison, and lastly, what concerns the Appendix, and what follows on that, – none of this, I say, is relevant to the question at issue. With regard to Meyer's Preface, it is certainly also shown therein what Descartes had yet to prove in order to construct a solid demonstration concerning free-will, and it adds that I favour a contrary opinion, and how so. This I shall perhaps explain in due course, but at present this is not my intention.

I have not thought about the work on Descartes[116] nor have I given it any further consideration since it was published in Dutch. I have good reason for this, which it would take too long to discuss here. So there remains nothing more to say than that I am, etc.

[Schiedam, 28 January 1665].

---

115. See Matthew 22:37.
116. The reference is to the Dutch translation by P. Balling (1664) of the PPC.

LETTER 22
To the highly esteemed B.d.S.,
from Willem Van Blyenbergh

[The original, which is extant, was written in Dutch
and was printed in the Dutch edition of the O.P.
The Latin version is a translation from the Dutch.[117]]

Sir, and worthy friend,

I received your letter of 28 January in good time, but affairs other
than my studies have prevented me from replying sooner. And since
your letter was liberally besprinkled with sharp reproofs, I scarce knew
what to make of it. For in your first letter of 5 January you very generously offered me your sincere friendship, assuring me that not only
was my letter of that time very welcome, but also any subsequent
letters. Indeed, I was urged in a friendly way to put before you freely
any further difficulties I might wish to raise. This I did at some greater
length in my letter of 16 January. To this I expected a friendly and
instructive reply, in accordance with your own request and promise.
But on the contrary I received one that does not savour overmuch of
friendship, stating that no demonstrations, however clear, avail with
me, that I do not understand Descartes' meaning, that I am too much
inclined to confuse corporeal with spiritual things, etc., so that our
correspondence can no longer serve for our mutual instruction.

To this I reply in a friendly way that I certainly believe that you
understand the above-mentioned things better than I, and that you are
more accustomed to distinguish corporeal from spiritual things. For in
metaphysics, where I am a beginner, you have already ascended to a
high level, and that is why I sought the favour of your instruction. But
never did I imagine that I would give offence by my frank objections. I
heartily thank you for the trouble you have taken with both your letters,

---

117. The Dutch original was in the possession of the United Baptists of Amsterdam.
A number of letters from or to Spinoza were discovered at a Collegiant
Orphanage (*De Oranjeappel*) in Amsterdam, which was built in 1675. Jarig Jelles
is known to have contributed to its maintenance. It is also possible that he,
Schuller, and Meyer worked there when they prepared the *Opera Posthuma*.

especially the second, from which I grasped your meaning more clearly than from the first.[118] Nevertheless, I still cannot assent to it unless the difficulties I yet find in it are removed. This neither should nor can give you cause for offence, for it is a grave fault in our intellect to assent to a truth without having the necessary grounds for such assent. Although your conceptions may be true, I ought not to give assent to them as long as there remain with me reasons for obscurity or doubt, even if those doubts arise not from the matter as presented, but from the imperfection of my understanding. And since you are very well aware of this, you should not take it amiss if I again raise some objections, as I am bound to do as long as I cannot clearly grasp the matter. For this I do to no other end than to discover truth, and not to distort your meaning contrary to your intention. I therefore ask for a friendly reply to these few observations.

You say that no more pertains to the essence of a thing than that which the divine will and power allows it and in actual fact gives to it, and when we consider the nature of a man who is governed by desire for sensual pleasure, comparing his present desires with those of the pious or with those which he himself had at another time, we then assert that that man is deprived of a better desire, because we judge that at that time the virtuous desire pertains to him. This we cannot do if we have regard to the nature of the divine decree and intellect. For in this respect the better desire no more pertains to that man at that time than to the nature of the Devil, or a stone, etc. For although God knew the past and present state of Adam, he did not on that account understand Adam as deprived of a past state, that is, that the past state pertained to his present nature, etc. From these words it seems to me clearly to follow, subject to correction, that nothing else pertains to an essence than that which it possesses at the moment it is perceived. That is, if I have a desire for pleasure, that desire pertains to my essence at that time, and if I do not have that desire, that non-desiring pertains to my essence at the time when I do not desire. Consequently, it must also infallibly follow that in relation to God I include as much perfection

---

118. In the preceding letter Spinoza had taken more care to distinguish his position carefully from that of Descartes on the nature of will. Even with that qualification, however, some of the difficulties which Blyenbergh has are due to Spinoza's truncated statements in the second letter. Part of this is no doubt due to Spinoza's desire to terminate the correspondence.

(differing only in degree) in my actions when I have a desire for pleasure as when I have no such desire, when I engage in all kinds of villainy as when I practise virtue and justice. For at that time there pertains to my essence only as much as is expressed in action, for, on your view, I can do neither more nor less than what results from the degree of essence I have in actual fact received. For since the desire for pleasure and villainy pertains to my essence at the time of my action, and at that time I receive that essence, and no more, from the divine power, it is only those actions that the divine power demands of me. Thus it seems to follow clearly from your position that God desires villainy in exactly the same way as he desires those actions you term virtuous.

Let us now take for granted that God, as God and not as judge, bestows on the godly and the ungodly such and so much essence as he wills that they should exercise. What reasons can there be why God does not desire the actions of the one in the same way as the actions of the other? For since God gives to each one the quality for his action, it surely follows that from those to whom he has given less he desires only proportionately the same as from those to whom he has given more. Consequently God, regarded only in himself, wills the greater and the lesser perfection in our actions, wills the desires for pleasure and the virtuous desires, all alike. So those who engage in villainy must of necessity engage in villainy because nothing else pertains to their essence at that time, just as he who practises virtue does so because the divine power has willed that this should pertain to his essence at that time. So again I cannot but think that God wills equally and in the same way both villainy and virtue, and in so far as he wills both, he is the cause of both, and to that extent they must both be pleasing to him. It is too hard for me to conceive this of God.

I see indeed that you say that the pious serve God. But from your writings I can only understand that serving God is merely to carry out such actions as God has willed us to do, and this is what you also ascribe to the impious and the licentious. So what difference is there in relation to God between the service of the pious and the impious? You say too that the pious serve God, and by their service continually become more perfect. But I cannot see what you understand by 'becoming more perfect', nor what is meant by 'continually becoming more perfect'. For the impious and the pious both receive their essence, and likewise their preservation or continual creation of their essence, from God as God, not as judge, and both fulfill God's will in the same way, that is, in accordance with God's decree. So what difference can there be between the two in relation to God? For the 'continually becoming more perfect' derives not from their actions but from the will of God. So if the impious through their actions become more imperfect, this derives not from their actions but only from the will of God; and both only carry out God's will. So there can be no difference between the two in relation to God. What reasons are there, then, why these should become continually more perfect through their actions, and the others be consumed in serving?

But you seem to locate the difference between the actions of the one and the other in this point, that the one includes more perfection than the other. I am quite sure that herein lies my error, or yours, for I cannot find in your writings any rule whereby a thing is called more or less perfect except as it has more or less essence. Now if this is the standard of perfection, then surely in relation to God's will villainy is equally as acceptable to him as the actions of the pious. For God as God, that is, in regard only to himself, wills them in the same way, since in both cases they derive from his decree. If this is the only standard of perfection, errors can only improperly be so called. In reality there are no errors, in reality there are no crimes; everything contains only that essence, and that kind of essence, which God has given it; and this essence, be it as it may, always involves perfection. I confess I cannot clearly comprehend this. You must forgive me if I ask whether murder is equally as pleasing to God as almsgiving, and whether, in relation to God, stealing is as good as righteousness. If not, what are the reasons? If you say yes, what reasons can I have which should induce me to perform one action which you call virtuous rather than another? What law or rule forbids me the one more than the other? If you say it is the law of virtue itself, I must certainly confess that by your account I can find no law whereby virtue is to be delineated or recognised. For everything depends inseparably on God's will, and consequently the one action is equally as virtuous as the other. Therefore I do not understand your saying that one must act from love of virtue, for I cannot comprehend what, according to you, is virtue, or the law of virtue. You do indeed say that you shun vice or villainy because they are opposed to your own particular nature and would lead you astray from the knowledge and love of God.[119] But in all your writings I find

---

119. As the following lines make clear, Blyenbergh is still having difficulty understanding the full extent of Spinoza's nominalism, though this is partly due to Spinoza's failure to make his own position clear to his correspondent. Blyenbergh wants to approach virtue and vice through the concept of a generic 'human nature' common to all humans, and interprets Spinoza as holding that there may be some human beings with whose nature vicious action may accord; whereas

no rule or proof for this. Indeed, forgive me for having to say that the contrary seems to follow from your writings. You shun the things I call wicked because they are opposed to your particular nature, not because they contain vice in themselves. You avoid them just as we avoid food that we find disgusting. Surely he who avoids evil things just because they are repugnant to his nature can take little pride in his virtue.

Here again a question can be raised; if there were a mind to whose particular nature the pursuit of pleasure or villainy was not repugnant but agreeable, could he have any virtuous motive that must move him to do good and avoid evil? But how is it possible that one should be able to relinquish the desire for pleasure when this desire at that time pertains to his essence, and he has in actual fact received it from God and cannot free himself from it?

Again, I cannot see in your writings that it follows that the actions which I call wicked should lead you astray from the knowledge and love of God. For you have only done what God willed, and could not have done more, because at that time no more was assigned to your essence by the divine power and will. How can an action so determined and dependent make you stray from the love of God? To go astray is to be confused, to be non-dependent, and this according to you is impossible. For whether we do this or that, manifest more or less perfection, that is what we receive for our essence at that point of time immediately from God. How, then, can we go astray? Or else I do not understand what is meant by going astray. However, it is here, and here alone, that must lurk the cause of either my or your misapprehension.

At this point there are still many other things I should like to say and ask.

1. Do intelligent substances depend on God in a way different from lifeless substances? For although intelligent beings contain more essence than the lifeless, do they not both stand in need of God and God's decrees for their motion in general and for their particular motions? Consequently, in so far as they are dependent, are they not dependent in one and the same way?

Spinoza insists on looking at each nature as distinctive and operating from the rules of its own essence. See Steven Barbone, "Virtue and Sociality in Spinoza," *Iyyun* 42 (1993), 383-395; and Lee Rice, "Le nominalisme de Spinoza," *Canadian Journal of Philosophy* 24 (1994), 19-32. Spinoza's position for affective responses on the part of individual natures is most clearly stated in E3P57.

2. Since you do not allow to the soul the freedom that Descartes ascribed to it, what difference is there between the dependence of intelligent substances and that of soulless substances? And if they have no freedom of will, in what way do you conceive dependence on God, and in what way is the soul dependent on God?

3. If our soul does not have that freedom, is not our action properly God's action, and our will God's will?

There are many other questions I should like to raise, but I dare not ask so much of you. I simply look forward to receiving first of all your answer to the foregoing pages. Perhaps thereby I shall better be able to understand your views, and then we could discuss these matters rather more fully in person. For when I have received your answer, I shall have to go to Leiden in a few weeks, and shall give myself the honour of greeting you in passing, if that is acceptable to you. Relying on this, with warm salutations I say that I remain,

> Your devoted servant,
> W.v. Blyenbergh.
> Dordrecht, 19 February 1665.

If you do not write to me under cover, please write to Willem Van Blyenbergh, Grainbroker, near the great Church.

P.S. In my great haste I have forgotten to include this question, whether we cannot by our prudence prevent what would otherwise happen to us.

LETTER 23
To the learned and accomplished
Willem Van Blyenbergh, from B.d.S.

[Reply to the preceding.[120]]

Sir and Friend,

This week I have received two letters from you; one of 9 March, which served only to inform me of the other of 19 February, sent to me from Schiedam. In the latter I see that you complain of my having said that 'no demonstration can avail with you', etc., as if I had said that with regard to my reasoning because it did not immediately satisfy you. That is far from my meaning. What I had in mind were your own words, 'And if ever after long consideration it should come about that my natural knowledge should appear to be either at variance with that Word or not easily. . . etc., that Word has so much authority with me that I prefer to cast doubt on the conceptions I imagine to be clear rather than. . . etc.' So I only repeated briefly your own words. Therefore I do not believe that I have given the slightest reason for offence, the more so because I adduced these words as an indication of the great difference between us.

Moreover, since you said at the end of your second letter that your only wish is to persevere in your belief and hope, and that other matters which we discuss with one another concerning our natural understanding are indifferent to you, I thought, as I still think, that no advantage could come of my writings, and it would therefore be more sensible for me not to neglect my studies (which I must otherwise relinquish for so long) for things which cannot yield any profit. And this does not contradict my first letter, for then I regarded you as a pure philosopher who (as is granted by many who consider themselves Christians) has no other touchstone for truth than our natural understanding, not theology. But you have taught me otherwise, showing me that the foundation on which I intended to build our friendship was not

---

120. The original letter is in the State Library in Berlin. Spinoza appears to have translated it into Latin himself.

laid as I thought. Lastly, with regard to the other remarks, this happens quite commonly in the course of disputation without on that account exceeding the bounds of courtesy, and I have therefore ignored such things in your second letter and shall also do likewise with this one. So much regarding your displeasure, so as to show that I have given no reason for it, and far less for thinking that I cannot brook any contradiction. Now I shall turn again to answering your objections.

First, then, I assert that God is absolutely and effectively the cause of everything that has essence, be it what it may. If now you can demonstrate that evil, error, villainy and so on are something that expresses essence, I will entirely agree with you that God is the cause of villainy, evil, error, etc. I think I have sufficiently shown that that which constitutes the specific reality of evil, error and villainy does not consist in anything that expresses essence, and therefore it cannot be said that God is its cause. For example, Nero's matricide, in so far as it contained something positive, was not a crime; for Orestes too performed the same outward act and had the same intention of killing his mother, and yet he is not blamed, or at least not as Nero. What then was Nero's crime? Nothing else than that by that deed he showed that he was ungrateful, devoid of compassion and obedience. Now it is certain that none of these things express any essence. Therefore neither was God the cause of any of them, but only of Nero's action and intention.[121]

Furthermore, I should like it here to be noted that while we are speaking philosophically, we ought not to use the language of theology. For since theology has usually, and with good reason, represented God as a perfect man, it is therefore natural for theology to say that God desires something, that God is displeased with the deeds of the impious and pleased with those of the pious. But in philosophy, where we clearly understand that to ascribe to God those attributes which make a man perfect would be as wrong as to ascribe to a man the attributes that make perfect an elephant or an ass, these and similar words have no place, and we cannot use them without utterly confusing our concepts. So, speaking philosophically, we cannot say that God wants something from somebody, or that something is displeasing or pleasing to him. For these are all human attributes, which have no place in God.

---

121. Again Spinoza simplifies his own position. See William Frankena, "Spinoza on the Knowledge of Good and Evil," *Philosophia* 7 (1977), 15-44.

Finally, I should like it to be noted that although the actions of the pious (that is, those who have a clear idea of God in accordance with which all their actions and thoughts are determined) and of the impious (that is, those who have no idea of God but only confused ideas of earthly things, in accordance with which all their actions and thoughts are determined), and, in short, the actions of everything that exists, follow necessarily from God's eternal laws and decrees and constantly depend on God, they nevertheless differ from one another not only in degree but in essence. For although a mouse is as dependent on God as an angel, and sorrow as much as joy, yet a mouse cannot on that account be a kind of angel, nor sorrow a kind of joy.

Herewith I think I have answered your objections (if I have rightly understood them, for I am sometimes in some doubt as to whether the conclusion you reach does not differ from the proposition you seek to prove). But that will be more clearly evident if, from this basis, I reply to the questions you propose:

1. Is murder as pleasing to God as almsgiving?
2. Is stealing, in relation to God, as good as righteousness?
3. If there were a mind to whose particular nature the pursuit of pleasure and villainy was not repugnant, but agreeable, could it have any virtuous motive that must move it to do good and avoid evil?

To the first I reply that (speaking philosophically) I do not know what you mean by 'pleasing to God'. If the question is whether God does not hate the one and love the other, or whether the one has not done God an injury and the other a favour, then I answer No. If the question is whether men who murder and men who give alms are equally good and perfect, again I answer No.

As to the second question, I say that if 'good in relation to God' means that the righteous man does God some good and the thief some evil, I reply that neither the righteous man nor the thief can cause God pleasure or displeasure. But if the question is whether both actions, in so far as they are something real and caused by God, are not equally perfect, then I say that if we attend only to the actions and the way they are done, it may well be that they are both equally perfect. If you then ask whether the thief and the righteous man are not equally perfect and blessed, I answer No. For by a righteous man I understand one who has a steadfast desire that each should possess his own, which desire I show in my *Ethics*[122] (which I have not yet published) arises necessarily in the pious from the clear knowledge they have of themselves and of God. And since the thief has no such desire, he necessarily lacks the knowledge of God and of himself; that is, he lacks the principal thing that makes us men.

If, however, you still ask what can move you to perform the action which I call virtuous rather than the other, I reply that I cannot know which way, out of the infinite ways there are, God uses to determine you to such actions. It may be that God has clearly imprinted in you the clear idea of himself, and through love of himself makes you forget the world and love the rest of mankind as yourself; and it is clear that such a constitution of mind is opposed to all else that men call evil, and so they cannot subsist in the same subject.

But this is not the place to explain the fundamentals of Ethics, or to prove everything I say; for I am concerned simply to answer your objections and defend my position.

Finally, as to your third question, it presupposes a contradiction. It is just as if someone were to ask me whether, if it accorded better with a man's nature that he should hang himself, there would be any reason why he should not hang himself. However, suppose it possible that there could be such a nature. Then I say (whether I grant free will or not) that if anyone sees that he can live better on the gallows than at his own table, he would be very foolish not to go and hang himself. And he who saw clearly that he would in fact enjoy a more perfect and better life or essence by engaging in villainy than by pursuing virtue would also be a fool if he did not do just that. For in relation to such a perverted human nature, villainy would be virtue.

As to your other question which you added at the end of your letter, since one could ask a hundred such questions an hour without arriving at the conclusion of any one of them, and since you yourself do not press for an answer, I shall leave it unanswered.

---

122. The version of the *Ethics* which we possess has nothing which states this in the manner Spinoza does here. But see E4P37Schol2 and E4P72.

For the present I shall only say that I shall expect you at about the time as arranged, and that you will be very welcome. But I should like it to be soon, for I am already planning to go to Amsterdam for a week or two. Meanwhile I remain, with cordial greetings,

Your friend and servant,
B. de Spinoza.
Voorburg, 13 March 1665.

LETTER 24
To the esteemed B.d.S., from Willem Van Blyenbergh

[The original, which was written in Dutch, is extant,
and is printed in the Dutch edition of the O.P.
The Latin is a translation.]

Sir and Friend,

When I had the honour of visiting you, time did not allow me to stay
longer with you. And far less did my memory permit me to retain all
that we discussed, even though on parting from you I immediately
gathered all my thoughts so as to be able to remember what I had
heard. So on reaching the next stopping-place I attempted on my own
to commit your views to paper, but I found that in fact I had not
retained even a quarter of what was discussed. So please forgive me if
once again I trouble you by raising questions regarding matters where I
did not clearly understand your views, or did not well remember them.
(I wish I could do you some service in return for your trouble.) These
questions are:

First, when I read your *Principia* and *Cogitata Metaphysica*, how can
I distinguish between what is stated as Descartes' opinions and what is
stated as your own?

Second, is there in reality such a thing as error, and wherein does it
consist?

Third, in what way do you maintain that the will is not free?

Fourth, what do you mean by having Meyer say in the Preface[123]
"that you do indeed agree that there is a thinking substance in Nature,
but you nevertheless deny that this constitutes the essence of the
human mind. You hold that just as Extension is infinite, so Thought is
not limited, and therefore just as the human body is not Extension
absolutely but only Extension determined in a definite way according
to the laws of extended Nature through motion and rest, so too the
human mind is not Thought absolutely but only Thought determined in

---

123. The quotation following is from Balling's Dutch translation of the PPC and CM.
    In his previous letters, Blyenbergh has quoted the original Latin edition.

a definite way according to the laws of thinking Nature through ideas; and this mind is necessarily inferred to exist when the human body comes into being"?

From this I think it seems to follow that just as the human body is composed of thousands of small bodies, so too the human mind is composed of thousands of thoughts; and just as the human body on its disintegration is resolved into the thousands of bodies of which it was composed, so too our mind, when it leaves the body, is resolved again into the multitude of thoughts of which it was composed. And just as the separated bodies of our human body no longer remain united with one another and other bodies come between them, so it also seems to follow that when our mind is disintegrated, the innumerable thoughts of which it was composed are no longer united, but separated. And just as our bodies, on disintegrating, do indeed remain bodies but not human bodies, so too after death our thinking substance is dissolved in such a way that our thoughts or thinking substances remain, but their essence is not what it was when it was called a human mind. So it still appears to me as if you maintained that man's thinking substance is changed and dissolved like corporeal substances, and indeed in some cases, as you (if my memory serves me) maintained of the wicked, they are even entirely annihilated and retain no thought whatever. And just as Descartes, according to Meyer, merely assumes that the mind is an absolutely thinking substance, so it seems to me that both you and Meyer in these statements are also for the most part merely making assumptions. Therefore I do not here clearly understand your meaning.

Fifth, you maintained both in our conversation and in your last letter of 13 March that from the clear knowledge that we have of God and of ourselves there arises our steadfast desire that each should possess his own. But here you have still to explain how the knowledge of God and of ourselves produces in us the steadfast desire that each should possess his own; that is, in what way it proceeds from the knowledge of God, or lays us under the obligation, that we should love virtue and abstain from those actions we call wicked. How does it come about (since in your view killing and stealing, no less than almsgiving, contain within them something positive) that killing does not involve as much perfection, blessedness, and contentment as does almsgiving?

Perhaps you will say, as you do in your last letter of 13 March, that this question belongs to Ethics, and is there discussed by you. But since without an explanation of this question and the preceding questions I am unable to grasp your meaning so clearly that there still do not remain absurdities which I cannot reconcile, I would ask you kindly to give me a fuller answer, and particularly to set out some of your principal definitions, postulates and axioms on which your *Ethics*, and this question in particular, is based. Perhaps you will be deterred by the amount of trouble and will excuse yourself, but I beseech you to grant my request just this once, because without the solution of this last question I shall never be able to understand what you really mean. I wish I could offer you some recompense in exchange. I do not venture to limit you to one or two weeks, I only beg you to let me have your answer here before your departure to Amsterdam. By so doing you will lay me under the greatest obligation, and I shall show you that I am, and remain, Sir,

Your most devoted servant,
Willem Van Blyenbergh.
Dordrecht, 27 March.

To Mr. Benedictus de Spinoza, staying at Voorburg. Per couverto.

LETTER 25
To the esteemed B.d.S., from Henry Oldenburg.

[Known only from the O.P. The original is lost.]

Esteemed Sir, and very dear Friend,

It gave me great pleasure to learn from a recent letter from Mr. Serrarius[124] that you are alive and well and remember your Oldenburg.
But at the same time I bitterly blamed my fortune (if it is right to use
such a word) for my having been deprived over so many months of that
most welcome correspondence which I previously enjoyed with you.
The fault is to be assigned partly to the accumulation of business, partly
to some dreadful domestic misfortunes,[125] for my abundant devotion to
you and my faithful friendship will always stand on a firm footing and
continue unshaken. Mr. Boyle and I often talk about you, your learning and your profound reflections. We should like to see the offspring
of your talent brought to birth and entrusted to the warm embrace of
the learned, and we are confident that you will not disappoint us in this.

There is no reason why Mr. Boyle's essay on Nitre, on Solidity and
Fluidity should be printed in Holland, for it has already been published
here in Latin, and there only lacks opportunity for sending you copies. I
therefore ask you not to let any of your printers attempt such a thing.
Boyle has also published a notable Treatise on Colours,[126] both in
English and Latin, and at the same time Experimental Observations on
Cold, Thermometers, etc.,[127] which contains many excellent things, and
much that is new. Nothing but this unfortunate war[128] prevents my
sending you these books. There has also appeared a notable treatise on
sixty Microscopic observations,[129] where there are many bold but

---

124. See the notes to Ep14.
125. Oldenburg had serious difficulties in earning a living, but the specific misfortune
    to which he here refers is not known.
126. The exact title was *Experiments and Considerations touching Colours* (1664).
127. *New Experiments and Observations upon Cold* (1665).
128. England declared war against the Netherlands in January of 1665.
129. Robert Hooke's *Micrographia* (1665). Hooke (1635-1703) was a collaborator
    with Boyle in the construction of the air-pump, and when Oldenburg died in 1677,
    Hooke succeeded him as Secretary of the Royal Society.

philosophical assertions, that is, in accordance with mechanical principles. I hope that our booksellers will find a way of sending copies of all
these to your country.

I long to receive from you yourself what you have been doing or
have in hand. I am,

Your devoted and affectionate,
Henry Oldenburg.
London, 28 April 1665.

LETTER 26
To the noble and learned Henry Oldenburg, from B.d.S.

[Known only from the O.P. The original is lost.
The letter is undated, but the opening sentence
indicates that it must be May 1665.]

Most honourable friend,

A few days ago a friend of mine said he had been given your letter of 28 April by an Amsterdam bookseller, who had doubtless received it from Mr. Serrarius.[130] I was very glad to be able to hear at last from you yourself that you are well, and that you are as kindly disposed to me as ever. For my part, whenever opportunity arose, I never failed to ask after you and your health from Mr. Serrarius and Christiaan Huygens, Z.D.,[131] who had also told me that he knows you. From the same Mr. Huygens I also gathered that the learned Mr. Boyle is alive and has published in English that notable Treatise on Colours, which he would lend me if I understood English. So I am pleased to know from you that this Treatise, together with the other on Cold and Thermometers (of which I had not yet heard) have been granted Latin citizenship and common rights. The book on microscopic observations is also in Mr. Huygens' possession, but, unless I am mistaken, it is in English.

He has told me some wonderful things about these microscopes, and also about certain telescopes made in Italy,[132] with which they have been able to observe eclipses of Jupiter caused by the interposition of satellites,[133] and also a kind of shadow on Saturn as if made by a ring.[134] These events cause me to wonder not a little at the rashness of

---

130. For Serrarius see the notes to Ep14.
131. 'Z.D.' stands for *Zeelhemi Dominum* (Squire of Züylichem), where Huygens' father had an estate.
132. These were constructed by Giuseppe Compani in Rome. Huygens tried and failed to learn how they were made. Huygens was himself quite secretive about his own work on lenses, and warned his brother not to impart any information about them to either John Hudde (see section 7 of our introduction) or Spinoza.
133. Jupiter's satellites were first discovered by Galileo, who observed only four of them. The shadow cast on Jupiter by its satellites, which were also called the Medicean stars, was first announced by Dominico Cassini in Rome (1665).
134. Galileo had mistaken Saturn's rings for projections or satellites. They were first clearly observed by Huygens in 1656.

Descartes,[135] who says that the reason why the planets next to Saturn (for he thought that its projections were planets, perhaps because he never saw them touch Saturn) do not move may be because Saturn does not rotate on its own axis. For this is not in agreement with his own principles, and he could very easily have explained the cause of the projections from his own principles had he not been labouring under a false preconception, etc.

(Voorburg, May 1665).

---

135. See Descartes' *Principles of Philosophy*, III, 154.

LETTER 27
To the courteous and accomplished
Willem Van Blyenbergh, from B.d.S.

[The original, written in Dutch, is extant. The
Latin translation in the O.P. was perhaps made
by Spinoza. The text of the Dutch edition appears
to be a retranslation from the Latin.]

Sir and Friend,

When I received your letter of 27 March, I was about to leave for
Amsterdam, and so I left it at home only half-read, intending to answer
it on my return and thinking that it contained only matters relating to
the first question. But later on reading it through, I found that its contents were quite different. Not only did it ask for proof of those things I
had caused to be included in the Preface – intending only to indicate
to everyone my thoughts and opinions, but not to prove or explain them
– but also proof of a large part of the *Ethics*, which as everyone knows
must be based on metaphysics and physics. I therefore could not make
up my mind to satisfy you on this matter, but looked for an opportunity
of asking you in person in a friendly way to desist from your request,
while at the same time giving you reason for my refusal and finally
pointing out that these matters do not contribute to the solution of
your first question, but on the contrary for the most part depend on
that question. So it is by no means the case that my opinion regarding
the necessity of things cannot be understood without the solution to
these new questions; for the solution of the latter and of what pertains
to them cannot be grasped without first understanding the necessity of
things. For, as you know, the necessity of things touches metaphysics,
and knowledge of this must always come first.

However, before I could obtain the desired opportunity, I received
another letter this week under cover from my landlord. This seems to
indicate some displeasure at the delay, and has therefore compelled me
to write these few lines informing you briefly of my decision and intention. This I have now done. I hope that when you have thought the
matter over you will willingly desist from your request, while nevertheless retaining your good will towards me. For my part, I shall show in
every way I can or may, that I am,

Your well disposed friend and servant,
B. de Spinoza.

To Mr. Willem Van Blyenbergh, Grainbroker, at Dordrecht, near the great church.
Voorburg, 3 June 1665.

LETTER 28
To the learned and experienced Johan Bouwmeester, from B.d.S.

[This letter is extant, but does not appear in the O.P. It was first published by Van Vloten in 1860. On the back of the letter is a note, presumably by one of the editors of the O.P., to the effect that the letter was 'of no value'. Hence its omission. It is undated, but can be assigned to June 1665.]

My very special friend,

I don't know whether you have completely forgotten me, but there are many circumstances which make me think so. First, when I was about to set out on my journey and wanted to bid you good-bye, and felt sure, being invited by you yourself, that I would find you at home, I was told that you had gone to the Hague. I returned to Voorburg, confident that you would at least call on me in passing; but you, if it pleases the gods, have returned home without greeting your friend. Finally, I have waited three weeks, and in all that time I have seen no letter from you. So if you want to banish this opinion of mine, you will easily do so by a letter, in which you can also indicate some way of arranging our correspondence, of which we once talked in your house.

Meanwhile I should like to ask you in all earnestness, indeed, to beseech and urge you by our friendship, to apply yourself with real energy to serious work, and to prevail on yourself to devote the better part of your life to the cultivation of your intellect and your soul. Now, I say, while there is yet time, and before you complain that time, and indeed you yourself, have slipped by.

Next, to say something about our proposed correspondence so as to encourage you to write more freely, you should know that I have previously suspected and am practically certain that you have rather less confidence in your abilities than is right, and that you are afraid that you may ask or propose something unbefitting a man of learning. But is it not seemly for me to praise you to your face and recount your gifts. Still, if you fear that I may communicate your letters to others to whom you would then become a laughing-stock, on this matter I give you my word that I shall henceforth regard them as sacred and shall not communicate them to any mortal without your leave. On these terms you can begin our correspondence, unless perchance you doubt my good faith, which I don't believe. However, I look to hear your views on this from your first letter.

At the same time I also expect some of the conserve of red roses[136] which you promised, although I have now for a long time felt better. On leaving there, I opened a vein once, but the fever did not abate (although I was somewhat more active even before the bloodletting because of the change of air, I think). But I have suffered two or three times with tertian fever, though by good diet I have at last rid myself of it and sent it packing. Where it went I know not, but I don't want it back.

With regard to the third part of my Philosophy, I shall soon be sending some of it to you, if you wish to be its translator, or to our friend de Vries.[137] Although I had decided to send none of it until I had finished it, yet since it is turning out to be longer than expected, I don't want to keep you waiting too long. I shall send it up to about the eightieth proposition.[138]

I hear much about English affairs,[139] but nothing certain. The people do not stop suspecting all kinds of evil, and no one can find any reason why the fleet does not set sail. And indeed the situation does not yet seem secure. I fear that our side want to be too wise and far-sighted. Still, the event will show in due course what they have in mind and what they are after – may the gods prosper it.[140] I should like to know what our people there are thinking, and what they know for

---

136. Bouwmeester was a physician (see our introduction, section 3), and, as it was held that a conserve of red roses is remedial for diseases of the lungs, he probably prescribed this remedy to Spinoza. Note that this letter is the earliest indication we have of the tuberculosis which eventually killed Spinoza.

137. Concerning de Vries, see our introduction, section 3.

138. The third part of the *Ethics* has only 59 propositions, not 80. We believe that Spinoza had originally thought that this work would include only three parts and that he decided to divide it into five parts.

139. At the time, the Dutch were at war with the English, and the Dutch navy remained in the harbours instead of engaging the English. Spinoza's worries turned out to be reasonable since when the Dutch did finally attack on June 13, 1665, it was a disastrous defeat for them.

140. There is more than one passage in which Spinoza refers to the gods (*dei*). Rather than reflecting any type of polytheism on Spinoza's part, it was probably just an idiomatic expression. Certainly Spinoza could not say 'God willing' and remain consistent with his own teaching. 'May the gods prosper it' is just a way of expressing a certain hope for the future.

certain, but more than that, and above all else, that you consider me. . .
etc.

(Voorburg, June 1665).

LETTER 29
To the esteemed B.d.S., from Henry Oldenburg.

[Not in the O.P. First published in 1860 by Van Vloten.]

Excellent Sir, and honoured friend,

From your last letter, written to me on 4 September,[141] it is clear that your devotion to our affairs goes very deep indeed. You have laid under an obligation not only me but the most noble Boyle, who joins me in sending you the warmest thanks on this account, and will repay your courtesy and kindness with whatever service he can render when opportunity arises. You can rest assured that this applies to me as well. As regards that over-officious man who, in spite of the translation of the *Treatise on Colours*[142] which has already been prepared here, has nevertheless determined to provide another, he will perhaps realise that he has done himself no good by his absurd over-eagerness. For what will happen to his translation if our Author enlarges the Latin version, prepared here in England, with a considerable number of experiments that are not to be found in the English version? It is inevitable that our version, soon to be distributed, will then have complete preference over his, and be held in much higher esteem by all men of good sense. But let him please himself, if he so wishes; we shall look to our own affairs in the way we think best.

Kircher's *Subterranean World*[143] has not yet appeared in our English world because of the plague, which hinders almost all communication. Then there is also this terrible war, which brings with it a veritable *Iliad* of woes, and very nearly eliminates all culture from the world.

---

141. We do not possess this letter by Spinoza, but it is clear from Oldenburg's remarks that it dealt in part with Spinoza's intentions for the TTP.
142. See notes to Ep25.
143. Athanasius Kircher (1601-1680) was born in Germany and educated by the Jesuits at Fulda, joined the Jesuit Order in Mainz, and later became Professor of Philosophy, Mathematics, and Oriental Languages at Würzburg. Because of the Thirty Years' War, he fled to Avignon in 1631 and settled in Rome four years later. This work, published in 1665, deals with forces and processes inside the earth.

Meanwhile, however, although our Philosophical Society holds no public meetings in these dangerous times, yet there are some of its Fellows who do not forget that they are such. So some are privately engaged in experiments on Hydrostatics, some on Anatomy, some on Mechanics, some in other experiments. Mr. Boyle has conducted an investigation into the origin of Forms and Qualities as it has hitherto been treated in the Schools and by teachers, and he has composed a treatise on this subject,[144] no doubt a notable one, which will shortly go to press.

I see that you are not so much philosophising as theologising, if one may use that term, for you are recording your thoughts about angels, prophecy and miracles. But perhaps you are doing this in a philosophic way. Of whatever kind it be, I am sure that the work is worthy of you and will fulfil my most eager expectations. Since these difficult times are a bar to freedom of intercourse, I do at least ask you please to indicate in your next letter your plan and object in this writing of yours.

Here we are daily expecting news of a second naval battle,[145] unless perchance your fleet has again retired into harbour. The courage which you hint is the subject of debate among you is of a bestial kind, not human. For if men acted under the guidance of reason, they would not so tear one another to pieces, as anyone can see. But why do I complain? There will be wickedness as long as there are men: but even so, wickedness is not without pause, and is occasionally counterbalanced by better things.

While I was writing this, a letter was delivered to me from that distinguished astronomer of Danzig, Mr. John Hevel.[146] In this he tells me among other things that his *Cometography*, consisting of twelve books, has already been in the press for a whole year, and that four hundred pages, or the first nine books, are completed. He also tells me that he has sent me some copies of his *Prodromus Cometicus*, in which he gives

---

144. Published in 1666. See notes to Ep3.
145. The Dutch fleet set out on 14 August 1665 to engage the English fleet, but due to poor weather no battle occurred.
146. Johann Hevelius (or Hevel, or Höwelcke), 1661-1687. He studied jurisprudence at Leiden, and lived in Danzig. In 1641 he built a private observatory, equipped with a large telescope, and published many observations. He discovered four comets and suggested that they had a parabolic orbit. His *Prodromus Cometicus* (1668) dealt with a comet observed in 1664. In 1668 he published *Cometographia*, which dealt with comets generally.

a full description of the first of the two recent comets; but these have not yet come to hand. He has decided, moreover, to publish another book concerning the second comet also, and to submit it to the judgment of the learned.

What, I pray you, do your people think of the pendulums of Huygens,[147] and particularly of those that are said to show the measure of time so exactly that they can serve to find the longitude at sea?[148] And also what is happening about his *Dioptrics* and his *Treatise on Motion*, both of which we have been long awaiting? I am sure he is not idle; I would only like to know what he is about.

Keep well, and continue to love,

> Your most devoted,
> H.O.

To Mr. Benedictus Spinosa,
In the Baggyne Street,
At the house of Mr. Daniel, painter, in Adam and Eve.

---

147. Huygens' *Horologium* (1658) described the pendulum clock which he invented in 1656. The *Dioptrics* was begun in 1654, the *De Motu Corporum* in 1663, and both were published posthumously in 1700.
148. The method which Huygens proposed for measuring longitudes at sea by means of pendulum clocks was described in detail in his *Brevis Institutio de usu Horologiorum ad Inveniendas Longitudines*, which is summarised in the *Philosophical Transactions of the Royal Society* #47, 10 May 1669.

LETTER 30
To the noble and learned Henry Oldenburg, from B.d.S.

[Not in the O.P. This is part of a letter which survives in
a letter from Oldenburg to Boyle (published in *The Works
of Robert Boyle*, 1772). In his letter Oldenburg quotes from
a letter he had written to Sir Robert Moray, wherein is quoted
a long extract from a letter which Spinoza had written to
Oldenburg (in Latin). Spinoza's letter is clearly a reply to
Letter 29. A conjectural date is autumn, 1665.]

... I rejoice that your philosophers are alive, and are mindful of themselves and their republic. I shall expect news of what they have recently
done, when the warriors are sated with blood and are resting so as to
renew their strength somewhat. If that famous scoffer[149] were alive
today, he would surely be dying of laughter. For my part, these troubles
move me neither to laughter nor again to tears, but rather to philosophising, and to a closer observation of human nature. For I do not
think it right to laugh at nature, and far less to grieve over it, reflecting
that men, like all else, are only a part of nature, and that I do not know
how each part of nature harmonises with the whole, and how it coheres
with other parts. And I realise that it is merely through such lack of
understanding that certain features of nature – which I thus perceived
only partly and in a fragmentary way, and which are not in keeping with
out philosophical attitude of mind – once seemed to me vain, disordered and absurd. But now I let everyone go his own way. Those who
wish can by all means die for their own good, as long as I am allowed
to live for truth.

I am now writing a treatise on my views regarding Scripture.[150] The
reasons that move me to do so are these:

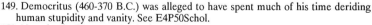

1. The prejudices of theologians. For I know that these are the
   main obstacles which prevent men from giving their minds to

---

149. Democritus (460-370 B.C.) was alleged to have spent much of his time deriding
   human stupidity and vanity. See E4P50Schol.
150. Namely, the *Tractatus theologico-politicus*.

philosophy. So I apply myself to exposing such prejudices and removing them from the minds of sensible people.

2. The opinion of me held by the common people, who constantly accuse me of atheism. I am driven to avert this accusation, too, as far as I can.

3. The freedom to philosophise and to say what we think. This I want to vindicate completely, for here it is in every way suppressed by the excessive authority and egotism of preachers.[151]

I have not yet heard that any Cartesian explains the phenomena of the recent comets on Descartes' hypothesis,[152] and I doubt whether they can thus be properly explained . . . .

---

151. The clergy of the Calvinist Church exploited the war between Holland and England in order to overthrow the De Witts and their party, which defended religious liberty.

152. The reference is to Descartes' account of vortices, by which he tried to account for planetary revolution and also the motion of comets. Spinoza's inability to see how the account could explain planetary motion probably explains why the PPC remained unfinished (the third part, of which only several pages were written, was to deal with vortices). Newton spends time in the General Appendix to the *Principia* deriding the inadequacies of the 'hypothesis of vortices'.

LETTER 30A
To Henry Oldenburg, from B.d.S.

[Not in the O.P. nor in Gebhardt. The letter from Oldenburg
to Sir Robert Moray mentioned in the preamble to Letter 30
has been recovered, and was printed by Wolf in 1935. In this
letter, dated 7 October 1665, another extract from Spinoza's
letter is quoted. This does not appear in Gebhardt.]

... I have seen Kircher's *Subterranean World*[153] with Mr. Huygens,
who has a higher regard for his piety than for his abilities. This may be
because Kircher discusses pendulums and concludes that they can be of
no use to determine longitude, an opinion quite opposed to that of
Huygens. You want to know what our people here think of Huygens'
pendulums. As yet I cannot give you any definite information on this
subject, but this much I know, that the craftsman who has the sole right
to manufacture them has stopped work altogether because he cannot
sell them. I don't know whether this is due to the interruption of com-
merce or to the excessively high price he is demanding, for he values
them at three hundred Caroline florins each. When I asked Huygens
about his *Dioptrics* and about another treatise dealing with Parhelia, he
replied that he was still seeking the answer to a problem in *Dioptrics*,
and that as soon as he found the solution he would set that book in
print together with his treatise on Parhelia. However, for my part I
believe he is more concerned with his journey to France (he is getting
ready to go to live in France as soon as his father has returned) than
with anything else. The problem which he says he is trying to solve in
Dioptrics is as follows: Is it possible to arrange the lenses in telescopes
in such a way that the deficiency in the one will correct the deficiency
in the other, and thus bring it about that all parallel rays passing
through the objective lens will reach the eye as if they converged on a
mathematical point? As yet this seems to me impossible. Further,
throughout his *Dioptrics*, as I have both seen and gathered from him
(unless I am mistaken), he treats only of spherical figures. As for the
Treatise on Motion about which you also ask, I think you may look for it

___
153. See notes to Ep29.

in vain. It is quite a long time since he began to boast that his calculations had shown that the rules of motion and the laws of nature are
very different from those given by Descartes, and that those of Descartes are almost all wrong. Yet up to now he has produced no evidence on this subject. I know that about a year ago he told me that all
his discoveries made by calculation regarding motion he had since
found verified by experiment in England. This I can hardly believe, and
I think that regarding the sixth rule of Motion in Descartes,[154] both he
and Descartes are quite in error. . . .

---

154. See *Principia* II, 50.

LETTER 31
To the esteemed B.d.S., from Henry Oldenburg.

[Known only from the O.P. The original is lost.]

Most excellent Sir, and valued friend,

In loving good men you are doing what beseems a wise man and a philosopher, and you have no reason to doubt that they love you in return
and value your merits as they should. Mr. Boyle joins with me in sending cordial greetings, and urges you to pursue your philosophising with
energy and rigour. Above all, if you have any light to cast on the
difficult question as to how each part of Nature accords with its whole,
and the manner of its coherence with other parts, please do us the
favour of letting us know your views.

The reasons which you mention as having induced you to compose
a treatise on Scripture have my entire approval, and I am desperately
eager to see with my own eyes your thoughts on that subject. Mr. Serrarius[155] will perhaps soon be sending me a little parcel. If you think it
proper, you may safely entrust to him what you have already written on
this matter, and you can be assured of our readiness to render services
in return.

I have read some of Kircher's *Subterranean World*,[156] and although
his arguments and theories do not indicate great talent, the observations and experiments we find therein are a credit to the author's diligence and his will to deserve well of the republic of philosophers. So
you see that I attribute to him something more than piety, and you can
easily discern the intention of those who besprinkle him with this Holy
Water.

When you speak of Huygens' *Treatise on Motion*,[157] you imply that
Descartes' Rules of motion are nearly all wrong. I do not have to hand
the little book which you published some time ago on 'Descartes' *Principia* demonstrated in geometric fashion'. I cannot remember whether

---

155. See notes to Ep14.
156. See notes to Ep29.
157. See notes to Ep29.

you there point out that error, or whether you followed Descartes closely so as to gratify others. Would that you may at last bring to birth the offspring of your own mind and entrust it to the world of philosophers to cherish and foster! I recall that you somewhere indicated that many of those matters of which Descartes himself affirmed that they surpass human comprehension – indeed, even other matters more sublime and subtle – can be plainly understood by men and clearly explained.[158] Why do you hesitate, my friend, what do you fear? Make the attempt, go to it, bring to completion a task of such high importance, and you will see the entire company of genuine philosophers supporting you. I venture to pledge my word, which I would not do if I doubted my ability to redeem it. In no way could I believe that you have in mind to contrive something against the existence and providence of God, and with these crucial supports intact religion stands on a firm footing, and any reflections of a philosophical nature can either be readily defended or excused. So away with delays, and suffer nothing to divert you.

I think it likely you will soon hear what is to be said about the new comets. Hevel of Danzig and the Frenchman Auzout,[159] both learned men and mathematicians, are at odds regarding the observations that were made. At present the controversy is under examination, and when the dispute is decided the entire affair, I imagine, will be communicated to me, and by me to you. This much I can already assert, that all astronomers – or at any rate those known to me – are of the opinion that there were not one but two comets, and I have not yet met anyone who has tried to explain their phenomena according to the Cartesian hypothesis.[160]

If you receive any more news regarding the studies and work of Mr. Huygens and of the success of his pendulums in the matter of ascertaining longitude, and of his removing to France,[161] I beg you please to

---

158. Spinoza states this in the Preface to PPC1.
159. Adrien Auzout (d. 1691) was a member of the Paris Academy. Hevelius (see notes to Ep29) claimed that the comet observed in 1664 had appeared near the first star of the constellation Aries, and Auzout argued that it appeared near the bright star in the left horn of that constellation. The Royal Academy took up the matter in *Philosophical Transactions of the Royal Society*, IX, 12 February 1666, and decided in favour of Auzout.
160. See notes to Ep30.
161. When Jean Baptiste Colbert became Controller-General of France in 1665, he made an effort to bring to Paris many foreign scholars and scientists. Huygens was invited there in 1665, and moved to Paris in 1666.

let me know as soon as possible. To this add also, I pray you, what is perhaps being said in your country about a peace treaty, about the intentions of the Swedish army[162] which has been sent to Germany, and about the progress of the Bishop of Munster.[163] I believe that the whole of Europe will be involved in war next summer, and everything seems to be tending towards a strange transformation. As for us, let us serve the supreme Deity with a pure mind, and cultivate a philosophy that is true, sound, and profitable. Some of our philosophers who followed the King to Oxford hold frequent meetings there, and are concerned to promote the study of physics. Among other things, they have recently begun to investigate the nature of sounds. They will be making experiments, I believe, to find out in what proportion weights must be increased, without any other force, to stretch a string so that its tension may produce a higher note of a kind that has a set consonance with the previous sound. More about this another time. Farewell, and remember your most devoted

Henry Oldenburg.
London, 12 October 1665.

---

162. During the war with Holland, the British attempted to persuade the Swedish government to send an army to attack the Dutch, but no army was ever sent.
163. Christoph Bernhard von Galen (1606-1678), the Bishop of Munster, invaded Holland in 1665 at the encouragement of his British allies.

LETTER 32
To the most noble and learned Henry Oldenburg, from B.d.S.

[The original of this letter is extant, and held by the
Royal Society, London. Spinoza retained a slightly
different version of it, and it is from this that the text
of the O.P. is printed. The differences are unimportant.]

Most noble Sir,

Please accept my most grateful thanks for the kind encouragement
which you and the most noble Mr. Boyle have given me in the pursuit
of philosophy. As far as my poor abilities will allow, I shall continue in
this way, with the assurance meanwhile of your assistance and good
will.

When you ask for my views on 'how we know the way in which each
part of Nature accords with the whole, and the manner of its coherence
with other parts', I presume that you are asking for the grounds of our
belief that each part of Nature accords with the whole and coheres with
other parts. As to knowing the actual manner of this coherence and the
agreement of each part with the whole, I made it clear in my previous
letter that this is beyond my knowledge. To know this it would be
necessary to know the whole of Nature and all its parts. So I shall
attempt to give the reasoning that compels me to this belief. But I
would first ask you to note that I do not attribute to Nature beauty,
ugliness, order or confusion. It is only with respect to our imagination
that things can be said to be beautiful, ugly, well-ordered or confused.[164]

By coherence of parts I mean simply this, that the laws or nature of
one part adapts itself to the laws or nature of another part in such wise
that there is the least possible opposition between them. On the question of whole and parts, I consider things as parts of a whole to the
extent that their natures adapt themselves to one another so that they

---

164. See E4Pref for a more expanded statement of the themes contained in this paragraph. Oldenburg refers to this letter as being 'on the unity of nature' in a letter
to Boyle dated 21 November 1665.

are in the closest possible agreement. In so far as they are different from one another, to that extent each one forms in our mind a separate idea and is therefore considered as a whole, not a part. For example, when the motions of particles of lymph, chyle, etc. adapt themselves to one another in accordance with size and shape so as to be fully in agreement with one another and to form all together one single fluid, to that extent only are the chyle, lymph, etc. regarded as parts of the blood. But in so far as we conceive the particles of lymph as different from the particles of chyle in respect of shape and motion, to that extent we regard them each as a whole, not a part.

Now let us imagine, if you please, a tiny worm living in the blood,[165] capable of distinguishing by sight the particles of the blood – lymph, etc. – and of intelligently observing how each particle, on colliding with another, either rebounds or communicates some degree of its motion, and so forth. That worm would be living in the blood as we are living in our part of the universe, and it would regard each individual particle of the blood as a whole, not a part, and it could have no idea as to how all the parts are controlled by the overall nature of the blood and compelled to mutual adaptation as the overall nature of the blood requires, so as to agree with one another in a definite way. For if we imagine that there are no causes external to the blood which would communicate new motions to the blood, nor any space external to the blood, nor any other bodies to which the parts of the blood could transfer their motions, it is beyond doubt that the blood would remain indefinitely in its present state and that its particles would undergo no changes other than those which can be conceived as resulting from the existing relation between the motion of the blood and of the lymph, chyle, etc. Thus the blood would always have to be regarded as a whole, not a part. But since there are many other causes which do in a definite way modify the laws of the nature of the blood and are reciprocally

---

165. For an analysis of the analogy of the worm (we would say 'micro-organism' today) in the bloodstream, see Lee C. Rice, "Spinoza on Individuation," in *Spinoza: Essays in Interpretation*, ed. M. Mandelbaum and E. Freeman (LaSalle: Open Court, 1975), 195-214; William Sacksteder, "Spinoza on Part and Whole: The Worm's Eye View," in *Spinoza: New Perspectives*, ed. R. Shahan and J. Biro (Norman: University of Oklahoma Press, 1978), 139-160; and Charles Ramond, *Qualité et quantité dans la philosophie de Spinoza* (Paris: Presses Universitaires de France, 1995), 203-230. The basic physical model for his theory of individuation is provided by Spinoza in the scholia and lemmata following E2P13.

modified by the blood, it follows that there occur in the blood other motions and other changes, resulting not solely from the reciprocal relation of its particles but from the relation between the motion of the blood on the one hand and external causes on the other. From this perspective the blood is accounted as a part, not as a whole. So much, then, for the question of whole and part.

Now all the bodies in Nature can and should be conceived in the same way as we have here conceived the blood; for all bodies are surrounded by others and are reciprocally determined to exist and to act in a fixed and determinate way, the same ratio of motion to rest being preserved in them taken all together, that is, in the universe as a whole.[166] Hence it follows that every body, in so far as it exists as modified in a definite way, must be considered as a part of the whole universe, and as agreeing with the whole and cohering with the other parts. Now since the nature of the universe, unlike the nature of the blood, is not limited, but is absolutely infinite, its parts are controlled by the nature of this infinite potency in infinite ways, and are compelled to undergo infinite variations. However, I conceive that in respect to substance each individual part has a more intimate union with its whole. For, as I endeavoured to show in my first letter written some time ago when I was living at Rijnsburg, since it is of the nature of substance to be infinite, it follows that each part pertains to the nature of corporeal substance,[167] and can neither be nor be conceived without it.

So you see in what way and why I hold that the human body is a part of Nature. As regards the human mind, I maintain that it, too, is a part of Nature; for I hold that in Nature there also exists an infinite power[168] of thinking which, in so far as it is infinite, contains within itself the whole of Nature ideally, and whose thoughts proceed in the

---

166. See E2p13Schol for the axioms and definitions upon which this paragraph is based.

167. By 'corporeal substance' Spinoza means the attribute of extension.

168. The notion of 'power' (*potentia*) here is not a mathematical notion of 'potency' or 'possibility', but rather a physical notion of force. It is further developed along two distinct lines by Spinoza: beginning at E3P6 as the account of *conatus* or psychological drive, and beginning at E4Def8 as the basis of his theory of virtue. For the former development, see Lee C. Rice, "Emotion, Appetition, and Conatus in Spinoza," *Revue Internationale de Philosophie* 31 (1977), 101-116. For the latter development, see Steven Barbone, "Virtue and Sociality in Spinoza," *Iyyun* 42 (1993), 383-395.

same manner as does Nature, which is in fact the object of its thought.[169]

Further, I maintain that the human mind is that same power of thinking, not in so far as that power is infinite and apprehends the whole of Nature, but in so far as it is finite, apprehending the human body only. The human mind, I maintain, is in this way part of an infinite intellect.[170]

However, to provide here an explanation and rigorous proof of all these things and of other things closely connected with this subject would take far too long, and I do not imagine that you expect this of me at this moment. Indeed, I am not sure that I have rightly understood your meaning, and my reply may not be an answer to your question. This I should like you to let me know.

As to what you say about my hinting that the Cartesian Rules of motion are nearly all wrong, if I remember correctly I said that Mr. Huygens thinks so, and I did not assert that any of the Rules were wrong except for the sixth,[171] regarding which I said I thought that Mr. Huygens too was in error. At that point I asked you to tell me about the experiment which you have conducted in your Royal Society according to this hypothesis. But I gather that you are not permitted to do so, since you have made no reply on this matter.[172]

The said Huygens has been, and still is, fully occupied in polishing dioptrical glasses. For this purpose he has devised a machine in which he can turn plates, and a very neat affair it is. I don't yet know what success he has had with it, and, to tell the truth, I don't particularly want to know. For experience has taught me that in polishing spherical

---

169. The application of the physical model to cognition is given in E2P14-E2P22.
170. The infinite intellect is introduced in E2P4-E2P6.
171. The sixth law states: "If a body C was at rest and exactly equal in size to a body B which moves towards it, then it must in part be pushed by B and in part cause B to rebound; so that if B approaches C with four degrees of velocity, it must transfer one degree to it and return in the direction from which it had come through the other three degrees" (*Principia* II, 50).
172. For Huygens' experiments at the Royal Society, see the notes to Ep33. Huygens mentioned Spinoza at several points in his letters to his brother Constantyn, asking that he secure as much information from Spinoza while giving Spinoza as little information as possible. The letters of Huygens in which Spinoza is mentioned are those dated 9 September 1667, 14 October 1667, 4 November 1667, 2 December 1667, 6 April 1668, and 11 May 1668; all printed in Huygens' *Oeuvres Complètes*, Vol. 6 (The Hague: Nijhoff, 1895).

plates a free hand yields safer and better results than any machine. Of the success of his pendulums and the time of his moving to France I have no definite news as yet.

The Bishop of Munster, having made an ill-advised incursion into Frisia like Aesop's goat into the well, has met with no success.[173] Indeed, unless winter begins very early, he will not leave Frisia without great loss. There is no doubt that he embarked on this audacious venture through the persuasion of some traitor or other. But all this is too stale to be written as news, and for the last week or two there has been no new development worth mentioning. There appears to be no hope of peace with the English. But a rumour has recently been spread because of conjectures concerning the sending of a Dutch ambassador to France,[174] and also because the people of Overijsel, who are making every effort to bring in the Prince of Orange – in order, as many think, to annoy the Dutch rather than to benefit themselves – have thought up a certain scheme, namely, to send the said Prince to England as mediator. But the facts are quite otherwise. The Dutch at present have no thoughts of peace, unless matters should reach such a point that they would buy peace. There is as yet some doubt as to the plans of the Swede.[175] Many think that he is making for Metz, others for Holland. But these are simply guesses.

I wrote this letter last week, but I could not send it because the wind prevented my going to the Hague. This is the disadvantage of living in the country. Rarely do I receive a letter at the proper time, for unless an opportunity should chance to arise for sending it in good time, one or two weeks go by before I receive it. Then there is frequently a difficulty preventing me from sending a reply at the proper time. So when you see that I do not reply to you as promptly as I should, you must not think that this is because I forget you. Meanwhile, time presses me to close this letter; of the rest on another occasion. Now I can say no more than to ask you to give my warm greetings to the most noble Mr. Boyle, and to keep me in mind, who am,

---

173. See our notes to Ep31. The unsuccessful invasion of Holland took place on 23 September 1665. After several failed efforts, the Bishop made peace with the Dutch on 18 April 1666.
174. See Wolf (1928) 426.
175. See our notes to Ep31.

In all affection yours,
B. de Spinoza.
Voorburg, 20 November 1665.

I should like to know whether the belief that there were two comets is held by all astronomers as a result of their motion, or in order to preserve Kepler's hypothesis.[176]

To Mr. Henry Oldenburg,
Secretary of the Royal Society,
In the Pall Mall,
in St. James' Fields,
London.

---

176. Despite his revolutionary three laws of motion, Kepler (1571-1630) remained something of a 'closet Aristotelian' in holding that the fixed stars were parts of a solid sphere with the sun as its centre. The interior of this sphere was filled with the ether. He attempted to account for the origin of comets as the condensates of the ether at random points, which were eventually destroyed by the light of the sun.

LETTER 33
To the highly esteemed B.d.S., from Henry Oldenburg

[Known only from the O.P. The original is lost.]

Excellent Sir, much cherished friend,

Your philosophical thoughts on the agreement of the parts of Nature with the whole and on their interconnection are much to my liking, although I do not quite follow how we can banish order and symmetry from Nature, as you seem to do, especially since you yourself admit that all its bodies are surrounded by others and are reciprocally determined both to exist and to act in a definite and regular manner, while at the same time the same proportion of motion to rest is preserved in them all. This itself seems to me good grounds for true order. But perhaps I do not here understand you sufficiently, any more than in your previous writing regarding Descartes' laws. I wish you would undertake the task of making clear to me wherein you consider that both Descartes and Huygens went wrong in regard to the laws of motion. By rendering this service you would do me a great favour, which I would strive with all my might to deserve.

I was not present when Mr. Huygens here in London carried out the experiments confirming his hypothesis.[177] I have since learned that, among other experiments, someone suspended a ball of one pound weight in the manner of a pendulum, and, on being released, it struck another ball similarly suspended but weighing only half a pound, at an angle of forty degrees, and that Huygens, making a brief algebraic calculation, had predicted the result, which answered exactly to his prediction. A certain distinguished person, who had proposed many such experiments which Huygens is said to have solved, is away.[178] As soon as I can meet this absent person, I shall perhaps give you a fuller and clearer account of this affair. Meanwhile I do most earnestly beseech you not to refuse the above-mentioned request of mine, and also to be

---

177. These experiments are summarised in the *Philosophical Transactions*, 46 (12 April 1669), p. 100.
178. The reference may be to Lord Brouncker (1620-1684).

kind enough to let me know whatever else you have discovered about Huygens' success in polishing telescopic glasses. Now that by the grace of God the plague is markedly less violent, I hope that our Royal Society will soon return to London and resume its weekly meetings. You can rest assured that I shall communicate to you whatever of its proceedings is worth knowing.

I have previously made mention of anatomical observations. No so long ago Mr. Boyle (who sends you his very kind greetings) wrote to me that some distinguished anatomists of Oxford had informed him that they had found the windpipe of certain sheep and also oxen crammed with grass,[179] and that a few weeks ago the said anatomists[180] were invited to view an ox which for almost two or three days on end had held its neck rigid and upright, and had died of a disease quite unknown to its owners. When the parts relating to the neck and throat were dissected, they were surprised to find that the windpipe deep inside the very trunk was stuffed with grass, as if someone had forcibly rammed it in. This provided just cause for an enquiry as to how such a great quantity of grass could have got there, and also, when it had got there, how such an animal could have survived so long.

Moreover, the same friend told me that a certain doctor of an enquiring nature, likewise of Oxford, has found milk in human blood. He relates how a girl, having eaten an ample breakfast at seven in the morning, was bled in the foot at eleven on the same day. The first blood was collected in a dish, and after a short space of time assumed a white colour; some later blood was gathered in a smaller vessel which, unless I am mistaken, they call an 'acetabulum' (in English, saucer), and immediately assumed the form of a milky cake. Five or six hours later the doctor returned and examined both lots of blood. That which was in the dish was half blood and half chyliform, and this chyle floated in the blood like whey in milk, whereas that which was in the 'saucer' was entirely chyle, without any appearance of blood. When he heated each of the two separately over a fire, both liquids solidified. The girl was quite well, and was bled only because she had never menstruated, although she had a good colour.

But I turn to politics. Here there is a wide-spread rumour that the Israelites, who have been dispersed for more than two thousand years,

---

179. Reported in the *Philosophical Transactions*, 6 (6 November 1665).
180. These were Josiah Clark (1639-1714) and Richard Lower (1631-1691).

are to return to their homeland.[181] Few hereabouts believe it, but many wish it. Do let your friend know what you hear about this matter, and what you think. For my part, I cannot put any faith in this news as long as it is not reported by trustworthy men from the city of Constantinople, which is most of all concerned in this matter. I am anxious to know what the Jews of Amsterdam have heard about it, and how they are affected by so momentous an announcement, which, if true, is likely to bring about a world crisis.

There seems as yet no hope of peace between England and the Netherlands.

Tell me, if you can, what the Swede and the Brandenburger are about,[182] and believe me to be

Your most devoted,
Henry Oldenburg.
London, 8 December 1665.[183]

P.S. I shall shortly let you have news, God willing, as to what our philosophers think about the recent comets.

---

181. The reference is to a movement led by Sabbatai Zevi (1626-1676), who was a false messiah rather than a proto-Zionist. Spinoza's reply to this letter, unfortunately, is lost; but we know (see the TTP, Chapter 3) that he had no sympathy for proto-Zionism. For a summary of the Marrano origins of many of the Zionist movements in the seventeenth century, see Gabriel Albiac, *La synagogue vide: Les sources marranes du spinozisme*, trs. M.-L. Copete and J.-F. Schaub (Paris: Presses Universitaires de France, 1994). On Zevi see Gershom Scholem, *Sabbatai Sevi: The Mystical Messiah* (Princeton: Princeton University Press, 1973 [note spelling as 'Sevi']. Contemporary sources of Zevi's works include *The Restauration of the Jewes* (London: R.R., 1665); *Several New Letters Concerning the Jevves* (London: Printed by A. Maxwel, 1666); and *God's Love of His People Israel* (London: Printed by A. Maxwell, 1666) [note different spellings of 'Maxwel(l)']. Peter Serrarius was no doubt Oldenburg's main source of information regarding Zevi. He was known to have been in contact with Oldenburg.
182. The reference is to strained relations between Sweden and Brandenburg concerning the possession of Hither Pomerania.
183. Following this letter there is a gap of approximately ten years in the correspondence between Spinoza and Oldenburg. This gap is partly explained by the war between England and Holland (1665-1667), the Great Fire (1666), and the imprisonment of Oldenburg in the Tower of London (30 June until 26 August 1667).

LETTER 34
To the highly esteemed and sagacious John Hudde,
from B.d.S.

[The original of this letter is extant, and held by the
Royal Society, London. Spinoza retained a slightly different
version of it, and it is from this that the text of the O.P.
is printed. The differences are unimportant.]

Most esteemed Sir,

The proof of the unity of God on the ground that his nature involves
necessary existence, which you asked for and I undertook to provide, I
have hitherto been unable to send you because of other demands on
my time. To engage upon it now, I shall make the following assumptions:[184]

1. The true definition of each single thing includes nothing other
than the simple nature of the thing defined. Hence it follows that:

2. No definition involves or expresses a plurality, or a fixed number
of individuals, since it involves and expresses only the nature of the
thing as it is in itself. For example, the definition of a triangle includes
nothing but the simple nature of a triangle, and not a fixed number of
triangles, just as the definition of mind as a thinking thing or the
definition of God as a perfect Being includes nothing other than the
nature of mind and of God, and not a fixed number of minds or Gods.

3. There must necessarily be a positive cause of each thing, through
which it exists.

4. This cause must either be placed in the nature and definition of
the thing itself (because in effect existence belongs to its nature or is
necessarily included in it) or outside the thing.

From these assumptions it follows that if in Nature there exists a
fixed number of individuals, there must be one or more causes which
could have produced exactly that number of individuals, no more and
no less. For example, if there should exist in Nature twenty men

---

184. The numbered assumptions and immediate consequences which Spinoza draws
from them are further expanded in E1P8Schol2.

(whom, to avoid confusion, I shall suppose to exist all at the same time and to be the first men in Nature), to account for the existence of these twenty it would not be enough to conduct an investigation into the cause of human nature in general. A reason must also be sought as to why twenty men, not more and not less, exist; for (in accordance with the third hypothesis) a reason and cause must be assigned for the existence of every man. But this cause (in accordance with the second and third hypothesis) cannot be contained in the nature of man himself, for the true definition of man does not involve the number of twenty men. So (in accordance with the fourth hypothesis) the cause of the existence of these twenty men, and consequently of each single man individually, must lie outside them. Therefore we must conclude absolutely that all things which are conceived to exist as a plurality are necessarily produced by external causes, and not by virtue of their own nature. Now since (according to our hypothesis) necessary existence pertains to God's nature, it must be that his true definition should also include necessary existence, and therefore his necessary existence must be concluded from his true definition. But from his true definition (as I have already proved from the second and third hypothesis) the necessary existence of many Gods cannot be concluded. Therefore there follows the existence of one God only. Q.E.D.

This, esteemed Sir, seems to me at present the best way of proving the proposition. On a previous occasion[185] I have proved this same proposition in a different way, making use of the distinction between essence and existence; but having regard to the consideration which you pointed out to me, I have preferred to send you this proof. I hope it will satisfy you, and, awaiting your judgment on it, I remain meanwhile, etc.

Voorburg, 7 January 1666.

---

185. The proof to which Spinoza alludes is probably like that given as E1P7Dem.

LETTER 35
To the highly esteemed and sagacious John Hudde, from B.d.S.

[The original, written in Dutch, is lost. The Latin
version in the O.P. was probably made by Spinoza.
The Dutch edition of the O.P. prints a text that
appears to be a re-translation from the Latin.]

Most esteemed Sir,

In your last letter dated 30 March[186] you have made perfectly clear
what I found rather obscure in the letter you wrote me on 10 February.
So since I now know what is your real line of thought, I shall frame the
question in the form in which it presents itself to you, namely, whether
there is only one Being which subsists through its own sufficiency or
force. This I not only affirm, but undertake to prove from this basis,
that its nature involves necessary existence. This may be most easily
proved from God's understanding (as I did in Proposition 11 of my
Geometrical Proofs of Descartes' *Principia*), or from others of God's
attributes.[187] To embark upon this task, I shall first of all briefly show
what properties must be possessed by a Being that includes necessary
existence. These are:

1. It is eternal. For if a determinate duration were ascribed to it,
beyond the bounds of its determinate duration this Being would be
conceived as not existing, or as not involving necessary existence, and
this would be in contradiction with its definition.[188]

2. It is simple, and not composed of parts. For in respect of their
nature and our knowledge of them component parts would have to be
prior to that which they compose. In the case of that which is eternal by
its own nature, this cannot be so.[189]

---

186. No such letter from Hudde to Spinoza is extant. It was probably destroyed by
the editors of the O.P.
187. Spinoza has "ex aliis Dei attributis," clearly indicating that the proof would go
through with any of the others (plural), though he claims that only one other
(extension) is known to the human mind.
188. See E1P19.
189. See E1P15.

3. It cannot be conceived as determinate, but only as infinite. For if the nature of that Being were determinate, and were also conceived as determinate, that nature would be conceived as not existing beyond those limits. This again is in contradiction with its definition.[190]

4. It is indivisible.[191] For if it were divisible, it would be divided into parts either of the same or of a different nature. In the latter case it could be destroyed, and thus not exist, which is contrary to the definition. In the former case, every part would include necessary existence through itself, and in this way one could exist, and consequently be conceived, without another. Therefore that nature could be understood as finite, which, by the foregoing, is contrary to the definition. Hence it can be seen that if we were to ascribe any imperfection to such a Being, we would at once fall into a contradiction. For whether the imperfection we would ascribe to such a nature lay in some defect, or in some limitations which such a nature would possess, or in some change which it might undergo from external causes through its lack of force, we are always reduced to saying that this nature which involves necessary existence does not exist, or does not exist necessarily.[192] Therefore I conclude that –

5. Everything that includes necessary existence can have in itself no imperfection, but must express pure perfection.[193]

6. Again, since it can only be the result of its perfection that a Being should exist by its own sufficiency and force, it follows that if we suppose that a Being which does not express all the perfections exists by its own nature, we must also suppose that a Being which comprehends in itself all the perfections exists as well. For if that which is endowed with less power exists by its own sufficiency, how much more does that exist which is endowed with greater power.[194]

To come now to the point at issue, I assert that there can only be one Being whose existence pertains to its own nature, namely, that

---

190. See E1P20-P21.
191. See E1P15.
192. The account of the indivisibility of substance (and of *res extensa*) is further amplified in E1P15Schol. The existence proof is given in E1P7. The fact that Spinoza has here reversed the order indicates that he did not regard the order or status (as axioms or theorems) of the propositions in the *Ethics* to be invariant.
193. This claim is expanded in E1P17Schol.
194. See E1P17Schol, and also the third of the three versions of the ontological proof which Spinoza gives in E1P11.

Being which possesses in itself all perfections, and which I shall call God. For if there be posited a Being to whose nature existence pertains, that Being must contain in itself no imperfection, but must express every perfection (Note 5). And therefore the nature of that Being must pertain to God (whom, by Note 6, we must also claim to exist), since he possesses in himself all perfections and no imperfections. Nor can it exist outside God; for if it were to exist outside God, one and the same nature involving necessary existence would exist in double form, and this, according to our previous demonstration, is absurd. Therefore nothing outside God, but only God alone, involves necessary existence.[195] This is what was to be proved.

These, esteemed Sir, are at present the points I can put before you to prove what I have undertaken. I should like occasion to prove to you that I am, etc.

Voorburg, 10 April 1666.

---

195. The contrary of 'necessary existence' here is not contingency (whose existence Spinoza denies: see E1P29), but perhaps 'consequential existence'. The line of development is given in E1P21-E1P24.

LETTER 36
To the highly esteemed and sagacious John Hudde,
from B.d.S.

[The original, written in Dutch, is lost. The Latin
version in the O.P. was perhaps made by Spinoza.
The text of the Dutch edition of the O.P. appears
to be a re-translation from the Latin.]

Most esteemed Sir,

Something has prevented me from replying any sooner to your letter
dated 19 May. As I understand that for the most part you suspend
judgment about the proof which I sent you (because of the obscurity, I
imagine, which you find in it), I shall here endeavour to explain its
meaning more clearly.

First, then, I enumerated four properties which must be possessed
by a Being existing through its own sufficiency or force. These four
properties and the other properties similar to them I reduced to one in
the fifth note. Then, in order to deduce from a single assumption
everything necessary for the proof, in the sixth note I endeavoured to
prove the existence of God from the given hypothesis; and then, taking
nothing more as known except the bare meaning of words, I reached
the conclusion which was sought.

This in short was my intention, this my aim. I shall now clarify the
meaning of each link individually, and first I shall begin with the
assumed properties.

In the first you find no difficulty; it is nothing but an axiom, as is
the second. For by simple I mean only that which is not composite or
composed of parts that are different in nature, or of other parts that
agree in nature. The proof is certainly of universal application.[196]

---

196. Individuation on the basis of parts of *different* natures is the basis of the physical
account of material bodies following E2P13Schol. The social account of the origin of the civil community given beginning at E4P37Schol2 is based on parts (i.e.,
citizens) of *similar* natures. There is an ambiguity here in Spinoza's treatment
which leads to two rather different accounts of the nature of civil society. The
communitarian account is developed and defended by Alexandre Matheron, *Individu et communauté chez Spinoza* (Paris: Editions de Minuit, 1969), esp. pp. 241-
284. A more individualistic account is given by Lee C. Rice in "Individual and
Community in Spinoza's Social Psychology," in *Spinoza: Issues and Directions*, ed.

The meaning of the third note you have understood very well, in so far as it makes the point that, if the Being is Thought, it cannot be conceived as determined in Thought, but only as undetermined, and if the Being is Extension it cannot be conceived as determined in Extension, but only as undetermined. And yet you deny that you understand the conclusion, which is simply based on this, that it is a contradiction to conceive under the negation of existence something whose definition includes existence, or (which is the same thing) affirms existence. And since 'determinate' denotes nothing positive, but only the privation of existence of that same nature which is conceived as determinate, it follows that that whose definition affirms existence cannot be conceived as determinate. For example, if the term 'extension' includes necessary existence, it is just as impossible to conceive extension without existence as extension without extension. If this is granted, it will also be impossible to conceive determinate extension. For if it were conceived as determinate, it would have to be determined by its own nature, that is, by extension, and this extension by which it would be determined would have to be conceived under the negation of existence. This, according to the hypothesis, is a manifest contradiction.

In the fourth note I intended only to show that such a Being cannot be divided into parts of the same nature or into parts of a different nature, whether or not those parts of a different nature involve necessary existence. For in the latter case, I said, it could be destroyed, since to destroy a thing is to resolve it into such parts that none of them express the nature of the whole, while the former case would be inconsistent with the three properties already established.

In the fifth note I have only assumed that perfection consists in being, and imperfection in the privation of being. I say 'privation'; for although Extension, for instance, denies of itself Thought, this is not an imperfection in it. But if it were deprived of extension, this would indeed argue imperfection in it, as would be the case if it were determinate. And the same would apply if it were to lack duration, position, etc.

E. Curley and P.-F. Moreau (Leiden: E. J. Brill, 1990), 271-285. A summary of the divergences between the two interpretations, with extensive bibliography, is given by Steven Barbone and Lee Rice, "La naissance d'une nouvelle politique," in a forthcoming volume devoted to Matheron and edited by P.-F. Moreau (Paris: Presses Universitaires de France, 1995).

You grant the sixth note absolutely, and yet you say that your difficulty remains quite unresolved, namely, as to why there could not be several beings existing through themselves but of different natures, just as Thought and Extension are different and perhaps can subsist through their own sufficiency. From this I cannot but believe that you understand this in a sense far different from mine. I think I can see in what sense you understand it; but in order not to waste time, I shall only make clear my own meaning. I say, then, with regard to the sixth note, that if we suppose that something which is indeterminate and perfect only in its own kind exists by its own sufficiency, then we must also grant the existence of a being which is absolutely indeterminate and perfect.[197] This Being I shall call God. For example, if we are willing to maintain that Extension or Thought (which can each be perfect in its own kind, that is, in a definite kind of being) exist by their own sufficiency, we shall also have to admit the existence of God who is absolutely perfect, that is, the existence of a being who is absolutely indeterminate.

At this point I would have you note what I recently said regarding the word 'imperfection'; namely, that it signifies that a thing lacks something which nevertheless pertains to its nature. For example, extension can be said to be imperfect only in respect of duration, position, or magnitude; that is to say, because it does not last longer, because it does not retain its position, or because it is not greater. But it will never be said to be imperfect because it does not think, for nothing like this is demanded of its nature which consists solely in extension, that is, in a definite kind of being, in which respect alone it can be said to be determinate or indeterminate, imperfect or perfect. And since God's nature does not consist in one definite kind of being, but in being which is absolutely indeterminate, his nature also demands all that which perfectly expresses being; otherwise his nature would be determinate and deficient. This being so, it follows that there can be only one Being, God, which exists by its own force. For if, let us say, we suppose that Extension involves existence, it must needs be eternal and indeterminate, and express absolutely no imperfection, but only perfection. And so Extension will pertain to God, or will be something that expresses God's nature in some way; for God is a Being which is

---

197. This claim is the converse of E1P9.

indeterminate in essence and omnipotent absolutely, and not merely in a particular respect. And thus what is said of Extension (arbitrarily chosen) must also be affirmed of everything which we shall take to be of a similar kind. I therefore conclude, as in my former letter, that nothing outside God, but God alone, subsists by its own sufficiency. I trust that this is enough to clarify the meaning of my former letter; but you will be the better judge of that.

I might have ended here, but since I am minded to get new plates made for me for polishing glasses, I should very much like to have your advice in this matter. I cannot see what we gain by polishing convex-concave glasses. On the contrary, if I have done my calculations correctly, convex-plane glasses are bound to be more useful. For if, for convenience, we take the ratio of refraction[198] as 3 to 2, and in the accompanying diagram we insert letters according to your arrangement in your little *Dioptrics*, it will be found on setting out the equation that NI or, as it is called $z = \sqrt{[(9/4)zz - xx]} - \sqrt{[1 - xx]}$.[199] Hence it follows that if $x = 0$, $z = 2$, which then is also the longest. And if $x = {}^3/_5$, z will be ${}^{43}/_{25}$, or a little more; that is, if we suppose that the ray BI does not undergo a second refraction when it is directed from the glass towards I. But let us now suppose that this ray issuing from the glass is refracted at the plane surface BF, and is directed not towards I but towards R. If therefore the lines BI and BR are in the same ratio as is the refraction – that is, as is here supposed, a ratio of 3 to 2 – and if we then follow out the working of the equation, we get $NR = \sqrt{(zz - xx)} - \sqrt{(1 - xx)}$. And if again, as before, we take $x = 0$, then $NR = 1$, that is, equal to half the diameter.

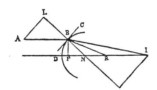

198. This ratio has the sine of the angle of incidence as numerator, and the sine of the angle of refraction as denominator.
199. Spinoza uses 'xx' where we would use an exponential for squaring. The exponential notation had been introduced by Descartes, but was not widely adopted until after the seventeenth century.

But if x = $3/5$, NR will be $20/25$ + $1/50$, which shows that this focal length is less than the other, although the optic tube is less by a whole semi-diameter. So if we were to make a telescope as long as DI by making the semi-diameter = $1^1/2$ while the aperture BF remained the same, the focal length would be much less. A further reason why convex-concave glasses are less satisfactory, apart from the fact that they require twice the labour and expense, is that the rays, being not all directed to one and the same point, never fall perpendicularly on the concave surface. However, as I have no doubt that you have long since considered these points and have made more rigorous calculations about them, and have reached a decision on this question, I seek your opinion and advice regarding it, etc.

[Date probably June 1666].

LETTER 37
To the learned and experienced
Johan Bouwmeester, from B.d.S.

[The original is lost, but an old copy is extant,
differing in a few details from the O.P. text.
The last sentence appears only in the old copy.]

Most learned Sir, and very special friend,[200]

I have been unable to reply any sooner to your last letter which reached
me quite some time ago. Various concerns and troubles have kept me
so occupied that it is only with difficulty that I have at last managed to
extricate myself. However, since I have now obtained some degree of
respite, I will not fail in my duty, but I want first of all to express my
very warm thanks for your love and devotion towards me which you
have abundantly shown so often by deeds, and now by letter, etc.

I pass on to your question, which is as follows: whether there is or
can be a method such that thereby we can make sure and unwearied
progress in the study of things of the highest importance; or whether
our minds, like our bodies, are at the mercy of chance, and our
thoughts are governed more by fortune than by skill. I think I shall give
a satisfactory answer if I show that there must necessarily be a method
whereby we can direct and interconnect our clear and distinct perceptions, and that the intellect is not, like the body, at the mercy of chance.
This is established simply from the following consideration, that one
clear and distinct perception, or several taken together, can be absolutely the cause of another clear and distinct perception. Indeed, all
the clear and distinct perceptions that we form can arise only from
other clear and distinct perceptions which are in us, and they acknowledge no other cause outside us. Hence it follows that the clear and distinct perceptions that we form depend only on our nature and its
definite and fixed laws, that is, on our power itself alone, and not on
chance, that is, on causes which, although acting likewise by definite
and fixed laws, are yet unknown to us and foreign to our nature and

---

200. See our introduction, section 3, for information on Bouwmeester.

power. As for the other perceptions, I do admit that they depend in the highest degree on chance. From this it is quite clear what a true method must be and in which it should especially consist, namely, solely in the knowledge of pure intellect and its nature and laws.[201] To acquire this, we must first of all distinguish between intellect and imagination,[202] that is, between true ideas and the others – fictitious, false, doubtful, and, in sum, all ideas which depend only on memory. To understand these things, at least as far as the method requires, there is no need to get to know the nature of mind through its first cause; it is enough to formulate a brief account of the mind or its perceptions in the manner expounded by Verulam.[203]

I think that in these few words I have explained and demonstrated the true method, and at the same time shown the way to attain it. It remains, however, for me to advise you that for all this there is needed constant meditation and a most steadfast mind and purpose, to acquire which it is most important to establish a fixed way and manner of life, and to have a definite aim in view. But enough of this for the present.

Farewell, and love him who has for you a sincere affection.

Bened. de Spinoza.
Voorburg, 10 June 1666.

---

201. The brief summary of his method given here is further developed in the unfinished *Tractatus de intellectus emendatione* (DIE). Three important commentaries on this method are given in B. Spinoza, *Traité de la réforme de l'entendement*, texte, traduction, introduction, et commentaires par Bernard Rousset (Paris: Vrin, 1992); Pierre-François Moreau, *Spinoza: L'expérience et l'éternité* (Paris: Presses Universitaires de France, 1994), pp. 1-225; and Theo Zweerman, *L'Introduction à la philosophie selon Spinoza: Analyse structurelle de l'introduction de la Réforme de l'entendement suivie d'un commentaire de ce texte* (Louvain: Presses Universitaires de Louvain, 1993). See also Anthony Beavers and Lee Rice, "Doubt and Belief in the *Tractatus de intellectus emendatione*," *Studia Spinozana* 4 (1988), 93-120.
202. See E2P40Schol, where Spinoza develops the distinction among three kinds of knowledge (imagination, reason, intuition). The term *imaginatio* in Spinoza refers most generally to sensory perception. See Michèle Bertrand, *Spinoza et l'imaginaire* (Paris: Presses Universitaires de France, 1983), for a detailed analysis of the complexities of the distinction which Spinoza is drawing in this brief passage.
203. I.e., Francis Bacon, in the *Organon*.

LETTER 38
To the accomplished John Van der Meer, from B.d.S.

[The original, written in Dutch, is lost.
The Latin is a translation.]

Sir,[204]

While living in solitude here in the country, I reflected on the problem you once put to me, and found that it was very simple. The proof, universally stated, is based on this, that the fair gambler[205] is one who makes his chance of winning or losing equal to that of his opponent. This equality is to be measured by the chances of winning and the money which the opponents stake and risk; that is, if the chances are the same for both sides, each should stake and risk the same sum of money, but if the chances are unequal, one must stake and lay down as much more money as his chances are greater. Thus the prospects on both sides are equal, and consequently the game will be fair. If, for example, A playing against B has two chances of winning and only one of losing, and B on the other hand has only one chance of winning and two of losing, it seems clear that A should risk as much for each chance of winning as B for his; that is, A must wager twice as much as B.

In order to show this more clearly, let us suppose that three persons, A, B and C, are playing together with equal chances and each lays down an equal sum of money. It is clear that, since each lays an equal stake, each also risks only one third in order to gain two thirds, and that, since each is playing against two, each has only one chance of winning against two or losing. If we suppose that one of the three, say C, withdraws before the beginning of play, it is clear that he should take

---

204. Nothing whatever is known about John Van der Meer, to whom this letter is addressed.

205. The history of the calculus of probability began with reflections on betting odds of the sort which Spinoza here offers. Huygens and many others of Spinoza's contemporaries dealt with the subject. A tract on the calculation of chances (*Reeckening van Kanssen*) was published in 1687 and attributed to Spinoza together with a short treatise on the rainbow (*Stelkonstige Reeckening can den Reegenbog*). Neither work had appeared in the O.P. The treatise on the rainbow has gained general acceptance as being Spinoza's, whereas the authorship of the tract on chance has been more widely disputed.

back only what he has staked, that is, a third part, and that B, if he wants to buy C's chance and take his place, must put down as much as C withdraws. To this A cannot object, for it makes no difference to him whether he must play with his one chance against the two chances of two different men or against two chances of one man alone. If this is the case, it follows that if one person holds out his hand for another to guess one out of two numbers, winning a certain sum of money if he guesses right or losing a like sum if he is wrong, the chances on both sides are equal, as well for him who invites the guess as for him who is to make the guess. Again, if he holds out his hand for the other to guess at the first attempt one out of three numbers and to win a certain sum of money if he guesses right or to lose half that sum if he guesses wrong, the chances will be equal on both sides, just as both sides have an equal chance if he who holds out his hand allows the other two guesses on condition that, if he guesses right, he wins a certain sum of money, or if he is wrong, he loses twice that amount.

The chances are also equal if he allows him three guesses at one of four numbers so as to win a certain sum of money if he is right or to lose three times as much if he is wrong; or to have four guesses at one of five numbers so as to win one amount if he is right or lose four times that amount if he is wrong, and so on. From all this is follows that for him who holds out his hand it is all the same if the other has as many guesses as he likes at one out of many numbers provided that, in return for the number of times he proposes to guess, he also stakes and risks an amount which is equivalent to the number of tries divided by the sum of the numbers. If, for instance there are five numbers and the guesser is allowed only one guess, he must stake $1/5$ against the other's $4/5$; if he is to make two guesses, he must stake $2/5$ against the other's $3/5$; if three guesses, then $3/5$ against $2/5$, and, by continuation, $4/5$ against $1/5$ and $5/5$ against 0.[206] Consequently, for him who invites the guess, if, for example, he risks only $1/6$ of the stake to win $5/6$, it will be just the same whether one man guesses five times or five men each guess once, which is the point at issue in your problem.

1 October 1666.

---

206. Within the context of the Bayesian calculus of probability, the property to which Spinoza is appealing is the 'value of a wager', defined as the product of the probability of winning and the payoff.

LETTER 39
To the worthy and sagacious Jarig Jelles, from B.d.S.

[The original, written in Dutch, is lost. It may
be the text reproduced in the Dutch edition
of the O.P. The Latin is a translation.]

Worthy Sir,[207]

Various obstacles have hindered me from replying any sooner to your
letter. I have checked the points you made regarding Descartes' *Dioptrics*. On the question as to why the images at the back of the eye
become larger or smaller, he takes account of no other cause than the
crossing of the rays proceeding from the different points of the object,
according as they begin to cross one another nearer to or further from
the eye, and so he does not consider the size of the angle which the
rays make when they cross one another at the surface of the eye. And
although this last cause is the most important to be considered in the
case of telescopes, yet he seems deliberately to have passed it over in
silence because, I imagine, he knew of no means of gathering rays
proceeding in parallel from different points onto as many other points,
and therefore he could not determine this angle mathematically.

Perhaps he was silent so as not to give any preference to the circle
above other figures which he introduced; for there is no doubt that in
this matter the circle surpasses all other figures that can be discovered.
For the circle, being everywhere the same, has everywhere the same
properties. For example, the circle ABCD has the property that all the
rays coming from the direction A and parallel to the axis AB are
refracted at its surface in such a manner that they all thereafter come
together at point B. Likewise, all rays coming from the direction C and
parallel to the axis CD are refracted at the surface in such a way that
they all come together at point D.

---

207. See our introduction, section 3, for information on Jarig Jelles, who was one of
the editors of the O.P.

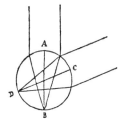

This can be said of no other figure, although hyperbolae and ellipses have infinite diameters. So the case is as you describe; that is, if no account is taken of anything except the length of the eye or of the telescope, we should be obliged to manufacture very long telescopes before we could see objects on the moon as distinctly as those on earth. But, as I have said, the chief consideration is the size of the angle made by the rays issuing from different points when they cross one another at the surface of the eye. And this angle also becomes greater or less as the foci of the glasses fitted in the telescope differ to a greater or lesser degree. If you desire to see the proof of this I am ready to send it to you whenever you wish.

Voorburg, 3 March 1667.

LETTER 40
To the worthy and sagacious Jarig Jelles, from B.d.S.

[The original, written in Dutch, is lost. It may
be the text reproduced in the Dutch edition
of the O.P. The Latin is a translation.]

Worthy friend,

I have duly received your last letter dated the 14th of this month, but
various obstacles have prevented me from replying sooner.

With regard to the Helvetius affair,[208] I have spoken about it with
Mr. Vossius,[209] who (not to recount in a letter all that passed between
us) laughed heartily at it, and even expressed surprise that I should
question him about such a silly thing. However, disregarding this, I
went to the silversmith named Brechtelt, who had tested the gold. Taking quite a different view from Vossius, he said that between the melting and the separation the gold had increased in weight, and had
become that much heavier as was the weight of the silver he had introduced into the crucible to effect the separation. So he firmly believed
that the gold which had transmuted his silver into gold contained something singular. He was not the only one of this opinion; various other
persons present at the time also found that this was so. Thereupon I
went to Helvetius himself, who showed me the gold and the crucible
with its interior still covered with a film of gold, and told me that he
had introduced into the molten lead scarcely more than a quarter of a
grain of barley or of mustard-seed. He added that he would shortly
publish an account of the whole affair, and went on to say that in

---

208. Johannes Fridericus Helvetius was physician to the Prince of Orange. Huygens
knew him and had no faith in him. In 1680, Helvetius published a book (*Philosophia theologica*) attacking the philosophies of both Descartes and Spinoza. The
details of the experiment to which Spinoza is here referring are not known,
though alchemical experiments designed to convert baser metals into gold were
common at the time.
209. Isaac Vossius (1618-1689). He wrote on the Septuagint and on poetry, and was
made Canon of Windsor in 1673.

Amsterdam a certain man (he thought it was the same man who had visited him) had performed the same operation, of which you have no doubt heard. This is all I have been able to learn about this matter.

The writer of the book you mention (in which he presumes to show that Descartes' arguments in the Third and Fifth Meditation proving the existence of God are false) is assuredly fighting his own shadow, and will do more harm to himself than to others. Descartes' axiom is, I admit somewhat obscure and confused as you have also remarked, and he might have expressed it more clearly and truthfully thus: 'The power of thought to think or to comprehend things is no greater than the power of Nature to be and to act'.[210] This is a clear and true axiom, whence the existence of God follows most clearly and forcefully from the idea of him. The argument of the said author as related by you shows quite clearly that he does not yet understand the matter. It is indeed true that we could go on to infinity if the question could thus be resolved in all its parts, but otherwise it is sheer folly. For example, if someone were to ask through what cause a certain determinate body is set in motion, we could answer that it is determined to such motion by another body, and this again by another, and so on to infinity. We could reply in this way, I say, because the question is only about motion, and by continuing to posit another body we assign a sufficient and eternal cause of this motion. But if I see a book containing excellent thoughts and beautifully written in the hands of a common man and I ask him whence he has such a book, and he replies that he has copied it from another book belonging to another common man who could also write beautifully, and so on to infinity, he does not satisfy me.[211] For I am asking him not only about the form and arrangement of the letters,

---

210. What is at issue here is Descartes' use of the notion of 'difficulty' in describing acts of comprehension (as well as divine conservation). Spinoza criticizes the anthropomorphism implicit in the notion in PPC1P7Schol, but goes on to suggest there, as here, that the underlying point is valid despite the misleading metaphor.

211. The argument refers to the explanation of the representational content of a cognition or idea, which Spinoza – following Descartes – calls its 'objective reality'. The objective reality of a representation cannot be explained by an infinite series of causes, although just such a series does explain its formal reality. In PPC1 Spinoza uses the example of an ordered series of books, each a copy of its predecessor. The $n-1$ predecessors in the series causally explain the n-th member's existence or formal reality, but not its contents or objective reality. The argument is *not* against the possibility of the series being infinite, since in fact for Spinoza *every* such causal series is infinite. See E1P28.

with which alone his answer is concerned, but also about the thoughts and meaning expressed in their arrangement, and this he does not answer by his progression to infinity. How this can be applied to ideas can easily be understood from what I have made clear in the ninth axiom of my Geometrical Proofs of Descartes' *Principles of Philosophy.*

I now proceed to answer your other letter, dated 9 March, in which you ask for a further explanation of what I wrote in my previous letter concerning the figure of a circle. This you will easily be able to understand if you will please note that all the rays that are supposed to fall in parallel on the anterior glass of the telescope are not really parallel because they all come from one and the same point. But they are considered to be so because the object is so far from us that the aperture of the telescope, in comparison with its distance, can be considered as no more than a point. Moreover, it is certain that, in order to see an entire object, we need not only rays coming from a single point but also all the other cones of rays that come from all the other points. And therefore it is also necessary that, on passing through the glass, they should come together in as many other foci. And although the eye is not so exactly constructed that all the rays coming from different points of an object come together in just so many foci at the back of the eye, yet it is certain that the figures that can bring this about are to be preferred above all others. Now since a definite segment of a circle can bring it about that all the rays coming from one point are (using the language of Mechanics) brought together at another point on its diameter, it will also bring together all the other rays which come from other points of the object, at so many other points. For from any point on an object a line can be drawn passing through the centre of the circle, although for that purpose the aperture of the telescope must be made much smaller than it would otherwise be made if there were no need of more than one focus, as you may easily see.

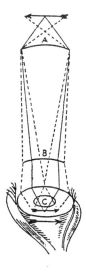

What I here say of the circle cannot be said of the ellipse or the hyperbola, and far less of other more complex figures, since from one single point of the object only one line can be drawn passing through both the foci. This is what I intended to say in my first letter regarding this matter.

From the attached diagram you will be able to see the proof that the angle formed at the surface of the eye by rays coming from different points becomes greater or less according as the difference of the foci is greater or less. So, after sending you my cordial greetings, it remains only for me to say that I am etc.

Voorburg, 25 March 1667.

LETTER 41
To the worthy and sagacious Jarig Jelles, from B.d.S.

[The original, written in Dutch, is lost. The Dutch
edition of the O.P. probably reproduces the original
text, and the Latin version is a translation from this.]

Most worthy Sir,

I shall here relate in brief what I have discovered by experiment
regarding the question which you first put to me in person, and later in
writing; and to this I shall add my present opinion on this subject.[212]

I had a wooden tube made for me, 10 feet long with a bore of $1\frac{2}{3}$
inches, to which I affixed three perpendicular tubes, as in the accompanying figure.

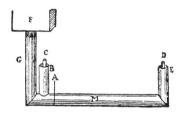

---

212. This is the sole letter surviving from the period 1668-1670. Simon de Vries died
in 1667, Balling died in 1669, and Oldenburg was imprisoned in 1667. Adriaan
Koerbagh, a friend of Spinoza, was imprisoned in Amsterdam in 1668, and died
there under extreme conditions in 1669. It was one of the several periods of religious repression in Holland, and people were cautious of corresponding with one
another on any subject which might draw the attention of the religious authorities. Spinoza was also busy with the writing of the *Tractatus theologico-politicus*,
which was to reflect much of the religious dissension of the period. See Gerrit H.
Jongeneelen, "An Unknown Pamphlet of Adriann Koerbagh," *Studia Spinozana*
3 (1987), 405-414, for a summary of the available historical data on both Koerbaghs.

In order first to find out whether the pressure of the water in the tube B was as great as in E, I closed the tube at A with a piece of wood made for the purpose. Then I made the mouth of B so narrow that it could hold a small glass tube, like C. Then, having filled the tube with water by means of the vessel F, I noted the height to which the water rose through the narrow tube C. Then I closed the tube B, and, removing the stopper at A, I allowed the water to flow into the tube E which I had fitted up in the same way as B, and when I refilled the whole tube with water, I found that it rose to the same height in D as it had done in C. This led me to believe that the length of the tube was no hindrance, or very little.

But to make a more rigorous investigation, I also sought to find out whether the tube E could fill a vessel of a cubic foot, which I had made for the purpose, in as short a time as tube B. In order to measure the time, not having a pendulum clock to hand, I made do with a bent glass tube, like H, whose shorter part was immersed in water while the longer was suspended in open air. When I had made these preparations, I first let the water flow through the tube B in a stream equal to the bore of the tube until the vessel of a cubic foot was full. Then with accurate scales I weighed the amount of water that had meanwhile flowed into the bowl L, and found that it weighed about four ounces.

Then I closed the tube B, and let the water flow through the tube E, in an equally dense stream, into the cubic foot vessel. When this was full, I weighed again, as before, the water which had meanwhile flowed into the small basin, and I found that it did not weigh even half an ounce more. But since the steams from both B and E had not constantly flowed with the same force, I repeated the operation, and first brought as much water as we had found from our first experiment we needed to have at hand. There were three of us as busy as could be, performing the aforementioned experiment more accurately than before, but not as accurately as I could wish. Still, I obtained sufficient information to reach a fairly sure conclusion, for I found practically the same difference on the second occasion as on the first.

On consideration of this matter and these experiments, I find myself forced to the conclusion that the difference that can be produced by the length of the tube has an effect only at the beginning, that is, when the water begins its flow; but when it has been flowing for a short while, it will flow with as much force through a very long tube as through a short tube. The reason for this is that the pressure of the higher water always retains the same force, and that all the motion which it communicates it continually regains through the action of gravity; and so it will also continually communicate this motion to the water in the tube until the latter, being forced forward, has gained as much speed as is equivalent to the force of gravity which the higher water can impart to it. For it is certain that, if the water in the tube G in the first moment imparts to the water in the long tube M one degree of speed, then in the second moment, if it retains its original force as it is presumed to do, it will communicate four degrees of speed to the same water, and so on until the water in the longer tube M has acquired exactly the degree of speed that the gravitational force of the higher water in tube G can give it.

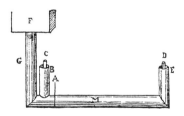

Therefore the water flowing through a tube forty thousand feet long, after a short space of time and solely through the pressure of the higher water, would acquire as much speed as if the tube M were only one foot long. If I had been able to get more exact instruments, I could have determined the time needed for the water in the longer tube to acquire so much speed. However, I do not think this is necessary, since the main point is adequately determined, etc.

Voorburg, 5 September 1669.

LETTER 42
To the learned and accomplished Jacob Ostens,
from Lambert de Velthuysen, M. Dr.

[Known only from the O.P. The original is lost.]

Most learned Sir,

Having at last obtained some free time, I at once turned my attention to satisfying your wishes and requests.[213] You ask me to let you know my opinion and the verdict I pronounce on the book entitled *Discursus Theologico-Politicus*[214] and this I am now resolved to do as far as my time and my ability permit. I shall not go into every detail, but I shall give a summarised account of the author's thinking and his attitude to religion.

I do not know of what nationality he is or what manner of life he pursues, and this is not of any importance. The methodical reasoning of the book itself is evidence enough that he is not unintelligent, and that his discussion and close examination of the controversies among Christians in Europe is not careless and superficial. The writer of this book is convinced that, in making assessment of the opinions which cause men to break forth into factions and divide into parties, he will achieve greater success if he puts aside and renounces prejudice. Therefore he has energetically striven to rid his mind of all superstition. But in seeking to show himself free from superstition, he has gone too far in the opposite direction, and, to avoid the accusation of superstition, I think he has renounced all religion. At any rate, he does not rise above the religion of the Deists, of whom there are considerable numbers everywhere (so deplorable is the morality of our age), and especially in France. Mersenne[215] has published a treatise against them, which I

---

213. Lambert Van Velthuysen (1622-1685) studied philosophy, theology, and medicine at the University of Utrecht. While his liberal views brought him into conflict with the Calvinists, he regarded the TTP as both atheistic and fatalistic. After Spinoza's death, Velthuysen wrote a treatise which attacked the *Ethics*. See Wim Klever, *Verba et sententiae Spinozae or Lambert van Velthuysen (1662-1685) on Benedictus de Spinoza* (Amsterdam: APA – North Holland, 1991).

214. *Discursus* should of course be *Tractatus*.

215. Marin Mersenne (1588-1648) was educated at a Jesuit college and wrote various theological treatises. He was a friend of Descartes, and defended him against charges of unorthodoxy. In 1624 Mersenne published an attack on freethinkers,

remember once reading. But I think that scarcely anyone of the Deists has written on behalf of that evil cause so maliciously, so cleverly and cunningly as the author of this dissertation. Furthermore, unless I am mistaken, this man does not rank himself among the Deists, and does not suffer men to retain the slightest portions of religious worship.

He acknowledges God and declares him to be the maker and founder of the universe. But he asserts that the form, appearance and order of the world are wholly necessary, equally with God's nature and the eternal truths, which he holds to be established independently of God's control. And so he also explicitly declares that all things come to pass by an invincible necessity and ineluctable fate. And he asserts that for those who think aright no room is left for precepts and command-ments, but men's want of understanding has brought such expressions into use, just as the ignorance of the multitude has given rise to modes of speech whereby emotions are ascribed to God. And so God likewise adapts himself to men's understanding when he exhibits to men in the form of command those eternal truths and the other things that must necessarily come to pass. He tells us that the necessity of the occurrence of those things that are governed by laws and are thought to be not amenable to the will of men is the same as the necessity of the nature of a triangle. And so what is embodied in the precepts does not depend on man's will, nor will any good or evil befall men as they neglect or heed them, any more than God's will can be influenced by prayer or his eternal and absolute decrees be mutable. So precepts are in like case with decrees and have this in common, that men's ignorance and lack of understanding has moved God to allow them to be of some use to those who cannot form more perfect thoughts about God and need wretched aids of this kind to excite in them a love of vir-tue and a hatred of vice. And so we can see that the author makes no mention in his writing of the use of prayer, just as he makes no mention of life or death or of any reward or punishment which must be allotted to men by the judge of the universe.

And this he does in accordance with his principles. For what place can there be for the last judgment? Or what expectation of reward or punishment, when all is attributed to fate, and when it is asserted that

---

L'Impiété des déistes, athées et libertins combattue et renversée. See Meinsma, 47-53, for more information on the work and its supposed targets (of which Spinoza was only one).

all things emanate from God by an ineluctable necessity, or rather, when he asserts that this universe in its entirety is God? For I fear that our author is not very far removed from that opinion; at any rate there is not much difference between asserting that all things necessarily emanate from God's nature and that the universe itself is God.

However, he locates man's highest pleasure in the cultivation of virtue, which he says is its own reward and the stage for the display of all that is finest. And so he holds that the man who understands things aright ought to devote himself to virtue not because of God's precepts and law, nor through hope of reward or fear of punishment, but because he is enticed by the beauty of virtue and the joy which a man feels in the practise of virtue.

He therefore asserts that it is only to outward appearance that God, through the prophets and through revelation, exhorts men to virtue by the hope of reward and the fear of punishment, two things that are always conjoined in law. For in the case of men of the common sort their minds are so constituted and so ill-trained that they can be urged to the practise of virtue only by arguments deriving from the nature of law, and from fear of punishment and hope of reward. But men of true judgment understand that there is no truth or force underlying such arguments.

Nor does he think it of any importance even if it correctly follows from this axiom of his that the prophets and the holy teachers – and so God himself, who spoke to men through their mouths – employed arguments which, if their nature be considered, are in themselves false. For quite openly and in many places, when occasion offers, he proclaims and emphasizes that Holy Scripture is not intended to teach truth and the natures of things which are mentioned therein, and which it uses for its own purpose to train men to virtue. And he denies that the prophets were so learned as to be quite free from the errors of the common people when they constructed arguments and devised reasons whereby they exhorted men to virtue, although the nature of moral virtues and vices was clearly discerned by them.

So the author furthermore tells us that even when the prophets were admonishing of their duty those to whom they were sent, they were not free from mistakes of judgment. Yet this did not detract from their holiness and credibility, although they employed speech and arguments that were not true, but were adapted to the preconceived beliefs of those whom they were addressing, thereby urging men to those virtues which no one ever doubts and are not the subject of any controversy among mankind. For the purpose of the prophet's mission was to promote the cultivation of virtue among men, and not to teach any truth. So he considers that such error and ignorance on the part of the prophet was not injurious to his hearers whom he was inspiring to virtue, for he thinks it matters little what arguments incite us to virtue provided that they are not subversive of moral virtue, for the encouragement of which they were devised and promulgated by the prophet. For he thinks that the grasping of truth in regard to other matters makes no contribution to piety, since moral holiness is not in fact to be found in such truth, and he holds that knowledge of truth, and also of mysteries, is necessary only to the extent that it promotes piety.

I think the author has in mind the axiom of those theologians who make a distinction between the words of the prophet when he is proclaiming doctrine and his words when he is merely narrating something. This distinction, if I am not mistaken, is accepted by all theologians, and he quite wrongly believes that his own doctrine is in agreement with this.

He therefore considers that all those who deny that reason and philosophy are the interpreters of Scripture will be on his side. For it is generally agreed that in Scripture there are predicated of God a great many things which are not applicable to God, but are adapted to human understanding in such a way that men may be moved by them and be awakened to the love of virtue. This being so, he thinks it must be accepted that the holy teacher intended by these untrue arguments to educate men to virtue, or else anyone who reads Holy Scripture is entitled to judge the intended meaning of the holy teacher according to the principles of his own reason. This latter view the author utterly condemns and rejects, and along with it the view of those who agree with the paradoxical theologian[216] that reason is the interpreter of Scripture. For he considers that Scripture must be understood literally, and that men must not be granted freedom to interpret as they please in a rationalistic way what is to be understood by the words of the prophet,

---

216. The 'paradoxical theologian' is Lodewijk Meyer (see section 3 of our introduction), whose *Philosophia Sanctae Scripturae Interpres* appeared in 1666. The author of this letter, however, simply misunderstands the position defended by Spinoza in the TTP, which is in direct contrast to the position taken by Meyer in his work. A translation with notes of Meyer's work is available: Louis Meyer, *La philosophie interprète de l'Ecriture Sainte*, traduction, notes et présentation par Jacqueline Lagrée et Pierre-François Moreau (Paris: Intertextes Editeur, 1988).

so as to decide in the light of their own reasoning and acquired knowledge when it is that the prophets spoke literally and when figuratively. But there will be opportunity to discuss this later.

To return to the theme from which I have digressed somewhat, the author, adhering to his principles of the fatalistic necessity of all things, denies that any miracles occur contrary to the laws of Nature.[217] For, as I have already remarked above, he asserts that the natures of things and their order are something no less necessary than the nature of God and the eternal truths. So he teaches that for something to depart from the laws of Nature is just as impossible as that the three angles of a triangle should not be equal to two right angles, that God cannot bring it about that a lighter weight should raise a heavier weight, or that a body moving with two degrees of motion can overtake a body moving with four degrees of motion. Therefore he asserts that miracles are subject to the universal laws of Nature, which he says are just as immutable as the very natures of things, these natures being contained within the laws of Nature. He does not admit any other power of God than the regular one which is displayed in accordance with Nature's laws, and he thinks that no other can be imagined, because it would destroy the natures of things and would be self-contradictory.

In the author's view, then, 'a miracle is an unexpected occurrence whose cause is unknown to the common people'.[218] Thus, when it appears that after prayers have been offered in due form an imminent disaster has been averted or a much desired good has been obtained, this same common people attributes it to the power of prayer and God's special dispensation, whereas, according to the author, God has already decreed absolutely from eternity that those things should come to pass which the common people attribute to his special intervention and display of power. For the prayers are not the cause of the decree: the decree is the cause of the prayers.

All this doctrine of fate and the invincible necessity of things, both in respect to the natures of things and also their occurrence in our daily lives, he bases on the nature of God, or to speak more clearly, on the

---

217. Spinoza's note at this point: "He is unjust in so saying, for I have expressly proved that miracles afford no knowledge of God. God is far better comprehended from the constant order of Nature."

218. The references in this and the discussion following are to TTP6, which is devoted to miracles. The author misinterprets Spinoza at many points, but Spinoza himself (see Ep43) corrects the majority of these misunderstandings.

nature of God's will and intellect which, while nominally different, are in reality identical in God. So he asserts that God has willed this universe and all that successively happens in it with the same necessity as that by which he knows this same universe. Now if God necessarily knows this universe and its laws, as also the eternal truths contained in those laws, he concludes that God could no more have created a different universe than he could overturn the natures of things and make twice three equal to seven. And therefore, just as we could not conceive anything different from this universe and the laws that govern the coming into being and the perishing of things, and anything of this kind imaginable by us would be self-defeating, so he tells us that the nature of the divine intellect, of the entire universe, and of those laws which Nature obeys is so constituted that God could no more have understood by his intellect any things different from those that now exist than it is possible for things now to be different from themselves. He therefore concludes that, just as God cannot now bring about things that are self-destructive, so God can neither invent nor know natures different from those that now exist. For the comprehension and understanding of such natures is just as impossible (since in the author's view it posits a contradiction) as the production of things different from those which now exist is impossible now. For all such natures, if conceived as different from those which now exist, would necessarily be opposed to those which now exist, because the natures of things contained in this universe being in the author's view necessary, they cannot possess that necessity from themselves but only from God's nature, from which they necessarily emanate. For he does not follow the line of Descartes – whose doctrine he nevertheless wants to appear to have accepted – that just as the natures of all things are different from the nature and essence of God, so their ideas are freely in the divine mind.

By these arguments, which I have now recounted, the author has paved the way to what he has to tell us in the final section of the book, towards which all the teachings of the preceding chapters are directed. There it is his aim to convince the magistrate and all mankind of this axiom, that to the magistrate belongs the right of establishing the divine worship which must be publicly observed in the state. Further, it is right for the magistrate to permit citizens to think and to speak of religion as their mind and feelings bid them, and this freedom should also be granted to subjects in the matter of external acts of worship, to the extent that this does not detract from their devotion to moral virtue or piety. For since there can be no controversy about these virtues, and the knowledge and practise of other things do not hold any moral virtue, he concludes that God cannot be displeased at whatever religious rites men additionally adopt. Here the author is speaking of those religious rites that do not constitute moral virtue and are not relevant to it, and which are not opposed to virtue or alien to it, but which men adopt and profess as aids to true virtue so that they may thus become acceptable and pleasing to God through their devotion to these virtues. For God is not offended by devotion to and practise of rites which, while they are indifferent and have no bearing on virtue or vice, men nevertheless associate with the practise of piety, and employ as a help towards the cultivation of virtue.

To prepare men's minds for the acceptance of these paradoxical views, the author first asserts that the entire form of worship established by God and delivered to the Jews – that is, to the citizens of the Israelite commonwealth – was designed only that they might live happily in their commonwealth, but that for the rest the Jews were not dear and pleasing to God above other nations. God, he says, has frequently made this known to the Jews through the prophets, rebuking them for their ignorance and error in identifying holiness and piety with the form of worship established and prescribed for them by God, whereas the former should have been located only in devotion to the moral virtues, that is, in the love of God and regard for one's neighbour.

And since God has instilled into the minds of all nations the principles and, as it were, the seeds of virtue so that, of their own accord and almost without any instruction, they may judge of the difference between good and evil, from this he concludes that God has not left other nations destitute of the means of gaining true blessedness, but has shown himself equally beneficent to all men.

Indeed, to affirm the equality of Gentiles with Jews in all matters which can in any way be of assistance and use in the pursuit of true happiness, he declares that the Gentiles have not been without prophets, and this he proceeds to prove by examples. He goes so far as to intimate that God exercised his sovereignty over other nations through the medium of good angels whom, following the usage of the Old Testament, he calls Gods. So the religious rites of other nations, he says, were not displeasing to God as long as they were not so corrupted by human superstition as to estrange men from true holiness, and did not incite men to engage in such acts in their worship as were inconsistent with virtue. But for special reasons peculiar to that people, God forbade the Jews to worship the Gods of the Gentiles who, under God's ordinance and superintendence, were worshipped by the Gentiles with the same right as those angels, appointed as guardians of the Jewish commonwealth, were accounted as Gods by the Jews in their own way, and were afforded divine honours.

And since the author thinks it commonly accepted that external forms of worship are not in themselves pleasing to God, he dismisses as unimportant what rites are involved in this external form of worship, provided that it is of a kind so conformable with God as to arouse reverence for God in men's minds and to incite them to the love of virtue.

Again, since he thinks that the whole substance of religion is contained in the cultivation of virtue, and regards as pointless all knowledge of mysteries that is not inherently adapted to promote virtue, and holds as more important and essential the sort of knowledge that is more effective in teaching men virtue and inspiring them thereto, he concludes that we should approve, or at least not reject, all those opinions touching God, his worship, and all matters concerning religion which are held to be true by those who cherish them, and whose purpose is that uprightness may thrive and flourish. In support of this doctrine he cites the prophets themselves as authors and supporters of his view. Being instructed that God does not regard as important what kind of thoughts men entertain about religion, but that he finds acceptable that form of worship and all these opinions which proceed from love of virtue and reverence for the divine, the prophets have even gone so far as to advance arguments for promoting virtue which are not in themselves true, but were considered to be so by those they were addressing, and which were intrinsically of a kind to spur men on to a more eager devotion to virtue. He therefore assumes that God left the choice of arguments to the prophets, who would employ those suited to the times and to the modes of thought of their particular audiences who, in accordance with their understanding, would regard such arguments as good and effective.

This he thinks to be the reason why different divine teachers employed different and often mutually conflicting arguments, why Paul taught that man was not justified by works whereas James urged the opposite. For James, so the author thinks, saw that Christians were distorting the doctrine of justification by faith, and he therefore insisted that man is justified by faith and by works. For he realised that it was not in the interests of Christians of his time to stress and to expound, as Paul had done, the doctrine of faith whereby men calmly rested on God's mercy and paid little attention to good works. Paul had to deal with the Jews, who erroneously placed their justification in the works of the Law especially delivered to them by Moses. Thinking that they

were thus raised above the Gentiles and that they had a way of blessedness prepared for them alone, they rejected the method of salvation by
faith whereby they were put on a level with the Gentiles and stripped
bare of all special status. Since therefore, taking into account the
difference of the times and audiences and other factors, both these
teachings, that of Paul and James, met with great success in turning
men to piety, the author thinks that it was part of apostolic wisdom to
employ now the one, now the other.

And this is one of the reasons why the author thinks it quite inconsistent with truth to try to explain the sacred text by means of reason
and to make reason the interpreter of Scripture, or to interpret one
holy teacher with the aid of another; for they are of equal authority,
and the words they employed are to be explained by the mode of
speech and peculiarity of expression which came naturally to those
teachers. In investigating the true meaning of Scripture we must pay
heed not to the nature of the case, but only to the literal meaning.

Therefore, since Christ himself and the other divinely sent teachers[219] instructed us and showed by their own example and way of life
that only by love of virtue do men attain happiness, and that other
things should be regarded as of little account, the author proposes that
the sole concern of the magistrate should be that justice and uprightness should flourish in the commonwealth. The magistrate should not
regard it as any part of his duty to deliberate as to what form of worship and what doctrines are most in accord with truth, but should
ensure that such are not adopted as place an obstacle in the way of virtue, even though they are favoured by those who profess them. Thus,
without any offence to the Deity, the magistrate has no difficulty in
allowing different religious rites in his commonwealth. In order to
make his point, the author takes the following line. He holds that the

---

219. The suggestion here that Christ's role for Spinoza is little more than that of
teacher is also not a correct reading of Spinoza, for whom Christ occupies a
unique position not equivalent to that of prophet or apostle. See TTP4, and also
Alexandre Matheron, *Le Christ et le salut des ignorants* (Paris: Aubier, 1971), esp.
85-141. This is not to suggest, however, that Spinoza countenances the inconsistent notion of a 'god-man': see Ep73 to Oldenburg. Deciphering Spinoza's pre-
cise position on Christ's nature is problematic partly due to the absence of a pro-
longed discussion on his part. For further details, and an enumeration of the
problematic texts, see Sylvain Zac, *Spinoza et l'interprétation de l'Ecriture* (Paris:
Presses Universitaires de France, 1965), esp. 190-199.

character of those moral virtues whose practise has social implications and which are concerned with external actions is such that their exercise should not fall within the scope of anyone's private judgment and decision; the cultivation, exercise and practical application of these virtues should depend on the sovereign power of the magistrate. For this there are two reasons: externally directed acts of virtue derive their nature from the circumstances of their performance, and secondly, a man's duty to perform such external actions is measured by the good or harm arising therefrom, with the result that those externally directed actions, if not performed at the appropriate time, lose the character of virtuous action and their opposites must be reckoned as virtues. The author thinks that there are other kinds of virtue whose existence is confined to the mind; these always preserve their character, and do not depend on the changing state of external circumstance.

A disposition to cruelty and harshness, a failure in love of one's neighbour and of truth, is never to be countenanced. But occasions may arise when it is permissible, not indeed to abandon this attitude of mind and love of the said virtues, but either to restrict their application in regard to external actions or even to engage in actions which, to outward appearance, are thought to be inconsistent with these virtues. And so it may come about that it is not then the duty of an upright man to set truth in the public domain, and in speech or writing to let citizens share in that truth and to communicate it to them, if we think that more harm than good will ensue for the citizens from that promulgation. And although individuals have the duty to embrace all men in love and never to be divorced from that sentiment, it frequently happens that we may be justified in dealing severely with some men when it is established that we would suffer great harm from a display of clemency. In the same way it is universally agreed that it is not at all times opportune to proclaim all truths, whether they pertain to religion or to civil life. And he who teaches that roses should not be cast before swine if there is any danger that the swine will savage those offering the roses, likewise considers that it is not the duty of a good man to instruct the common people on certain religious questions which, published and spread abroad among the populace, could well cause such disturbance in the commonwealth or Church as to bring more injury than benefit on the citizens and the godly.

Now civil societies, from whom sovereign power and authority to pass laws cannot be disjoined, among other things have established that it must not be left to individuals to decide what is for the good of men who are united in a civic body, but that this must be entrusted to the rulers. The author therefore argues that it is the right of the magistrate to decide which and what kind of doctrines should be publicly taught in the commonwealth, and that it is the duty of subjects, so far as concerns public pronouncement, to refrain from teaching and professing doctrines which the magistrate has by law forbidden to be publicly professed. For God has no more entrusted this to the judgment of private individuals than he has allowed them, contrary to the views and decrees of the magistrate or the opinion of judges, to engage in actions which render ineffective the force of law, and frustrate the intention of magistrates. For the author considers that, in such matters as concern external forms of worship and public pronouncements thereon, there can be general agreement, and that the question of external forms of divine worship is entrusted to the magistrate's judgment with as much confidence as there is granted him the right and power to evaluate injury done to the state and to punish it by force. For just as a person of private station is not bound to adjust to the magistrate's judgment his own judgment as to injury done to the state, but can entertain his own opinion, while yet being bound in some circumstances to lend assistance in carrying out the magistrate's sentence, in the same way, so the author thinks, it is the prerogative of those of private station in the commonwealth to judge as to the truth and falsity, as also of the necessity, of any doctrine. And a private person cannot be bound by the laws of the state to hold the same views on religion, although the magistrate must judge what doctrines are to be publicly proclaimed, and it is the duty of private persons not to voice their own views on religion when these differ from those of the magistrate, and to do nothing whereby the laws concerning worship enacted by the magistrate may lose their effectiveness.

But since it may happen that the magistrate, differing from many of the populace on points of religion, decides that certain doctrines should be publicly taught which are not favoured by the populace, and the magistrate nevertheless believes that respect for the Deity demands the public profession of those doctrines in his commonwealth, the author has seen that there remains the problem that citizens may suffer considerable harm because of the differing judgments of magistrate and populace. Therefore to the preceding proposals the author adds another which may satisfy magistrate and subjects and also preserve religious freedom intact, namely, that the magistrate need not fear God's wrath even if he allows in his commonwealth the practise of sacred rites which in his judgment are wrong – provided that they are not opposed to the moral virtues and do not subvert them. The grounds for this view cannot escape you, since I have already recounted them at some length. For the author asserts that God is indifferent and unconcerned as to what religious beliefs men cherish, favour and defend, or what religious rites they publicly practise. All such things are to be accounted as having no affinity with virtue and vice, although it is everyone's duty to make his own dispositions with view to choosing those doctrines and that form of worship which will enable him to make the greatest progress in the love of virtue.

Here, most accomplished Sir, you have in brief space a summary of the doctrine of the political-theologian, which in my judgment banishes and thoroughly subverts all worship and religion, prompts atheism by stealth, or envisages such a God as can not move men to reverence for his divinity, since he himself is subject to fate; no room is left for divine governance and providence, and the assignment of punishment and reward is entirely abolished. This, at the very least, is evident from the author's writing, that by his reasoning and arguments the authority of all Holy Scripture is impaired, and is mentioned by the author only for form's sake; and it similarly follows from the position he adopts that the Koran, too, is to be put on a level with the Word of God. And the author has not left himself a single argument to prove that Mahomet was not a true prophet. For the Turks, too, in obedience to the command of their prophet, cultivate those moral virtues about which there is no disagreement among nations, and, according to the author's teaching, it is not uncommon for God, in the case of other nations to whom he has not imparted the oracles given to the Jews and Christians, to lead them by other revelations to the path of reason and obedience.

So I think I have not strayed far from the truth, nor am I unfair to the author, if I denounce him as teaching sheer atheism with furtive and disguised arguments.

L. v. V.
Utrecht, 24 January 1671 (Old style).

LETTER 43
To the learned and accomplished Jacob Ostens, from B.d.S.

[The original is extant, and differs in unimportant
details from the Latin text of the O.P. The date is
uncertain, but is probably 1671.[220]]

Most learned Sir,

You are doubtless surprised that I have kept you waiting so long, but I
can hardly bring myself to answer that man's letter, which you kindly
sent me. Nor do I do so now for any other reason than to keep my
promise. But to satisfy myself, too, as far as that can be, I shall
discharge my debt in as few words as possible, and briefly show how
perversely he has misinterpreted my meaning – whether from malice
or ignorance, I cannot say. But to the matter in hand.

First, he says 'it is of no importance to know of what nationality I
am, or what manner of life I pursue'. But surely if he had known this,
he would not have been so readily convinced that I teach atheism. For
atheists are usually inordinately fond of honours and riches,[221] which I
have always despised, as is known to all who are acquainted with me.
Then, to pave the way to the end he has in view, he says that I am not
unintelligent, doubtless so that he may more easily establish that I have
argued cleverly, cunningly, and with evil intent on behalf of the evil
cause of the Deists. This is a clear indication that he has not understood my line of reasoning. For who can be so clever and so astute as to
pretend to present so many powerful arguments in support of something he deems false? Whom, I say, will he hereafter believe to have
written in all sincerity, if he thinks that the fictitious can be proved as

---

220. The original draft of the letter is in the Orphanage of the Baptist Collegiants in
Amsterdam. A facsimile was printed in W. Meyer's edition of 1903, and also in
Van Vloten's *Ad Benedicti de Spinoza Opera Supplementum* (1860).
221. On the seventeenth century use of the term 'atheist', see Meinsma, 21-46; and
Gabriel Albiac, *La synagogue vide*, tr. M.-L. Copete and J.-F. Schaub (Paris:
Presses Universitaires de France, 1994), 327-347.

soundly as the true? But this does not now surprise me, for thus was Descartes once maligned by Voetius,[222] and this is what often happens to all good men.

He then continues, 'to avoid the accusation of superstition, I think he has renounced all religion'. What he understands by religion and what by superstition, I do not know. Does that man, pray, renounce all religion, who declares that God must be acknowledged as the highest good, and that he must be loved as such in a free spirit? And that in this alone does our supreme happiness and our highest freedom consist? And further, that the reward of virtue is virtue itself,[223] while the punishment of folly and weakness is folly itself? And lastly, that everyone is in duty bound to love his neighbour and obey the commands of the sovereign power? I not only said this explicitly, but also proved it with the strongest arguments. But I think I see in what mire this man is stuck. He finds nothing to please him in virtue itself and in intellect, and would choose to live under the impulsion of his passions but for one obstacle, his fear of punishment. So he abstains from evil deeds and obeys the divine commandments like a slave, reluctantly and waveringly, and in return for this servitude he expects to reap rewards from God far sweeter to him than the divine love itself, and the more so as he dislikes the good that he does, and does it unwillingly.[224] Consequently, he believes that all who are not restrained by this fear lead unbridled lives and renounce all religion. But I let this pass, and turn to his conclusion, where he seeks to prove that I teach atheism by clandestine and disguised arguments.

---

222. Gysbertus Voetius (1588-1676), a Dutch theologian who studied in Leiden. He became Pastor of Blynen in 1611 and played a role in the Synod of Dort. In 1634 he became Professor of Theology and Oriental Studies at the University of Utrecht and three years later became Vicar of Utrecht. An extreme Calvinist, he succeeded in persuading the University of Utrecht to condemn the philosophy of Descartes in 1642. The following year there appeared a pamphlet, of his authorship or inspiration, attacking the Cartesian philosophy as the root of atheism. Descartes replied to the pamphlet in his *Epistola ad celeberrimum virum D. Gisbertim Voetium*. His work, *Selectarum disputationum theologicarum de Atheismo*, published in 1648, continued the assault on Descartes' philosophy. For further details, see Meinsma, 43-46.

223. See E5P41-P42.

224. This theme, the attitude of the *vulgus* to the practise of religion based on fear and expectancy of reward, is developed in E5P41Schol.

The basis of his reasoning is this, that he thinks that I do away with God's freedom and subject him to fate. This is completely false. For I have asserted that everything follows by an inevitable necessity from God's nature in just the same way that all assert that it follows from God's nature that he understands himself. Surely no one denies that this necessarily follows from the divine nature, and yet no one conceives that God, in understanding himself, is under the compulsion of some fate; it is conceived that he does so altogether freely, although necessarily. Here I find nothing that is beyond anyone's perception. And if he still believes that these assertions are made with evil intent, what does he think of his own Descartes,[225] who declared that nothing is done by us that is not pre-ordained by God; nay, that we are at every single moment created by God anew, as it were, and that nevertheless we act from freedom of our own will.[226] This is surely something, as Descartes himself admits, that no one can understand.

Furthermore, this inevitable necessity of things does not do away with either divine or human laws. For moral precepts, whether or not they receive the form of law from God himself, are still divine and salutary. And whether the good that follows from virtue and love of God is bestowed on us by God as judge, or whether it emanates from the necessity of the divine nature, it will not on that account be more or less desirable, just as on the other hand the evils that follow from evil deeds are not less to be feared because they necessarily follow from them. And finally, whether we do what we do necessarily or freely, we are still led by hope or by fear. Therefore he is wrong in saying that 'I assert that no room is left for precepts and commandments', or, as he goes on to say, 'there is no expectation of reward or punishment when all is attributed to fate, or when it is asserted that all things emanate from God by an inevitable necessity'.

I do not here inquire why it is the same, or not very different, to assert that all things emanate necessarily from God's nature and that the universe is God, but I should like you to note that which he adds in no less malignant vein, 'that I hold that a man ought to devote himself to virtue not because of God's commandment and law, nor through hope of reward or fear of punishment, but ... etc.' This you will

---

225. See Descartes' *Principia* I, 39.
226. Divine conservation in Descartes is further discussed by Spinoza in PPC1P12, and preordination in PPC1P19.

certainly find nowhere in my Treatise; on the contrary, in chapter 4 I expressly said that the substance of the divine law (which is divinely inscribed in our minds, as I said in chapter 12) and its supreme commandment is to love God as the highest good; that is, not from fear of some punishment (for love cannot spring from fear) nor from love of something else from which we hope to derive pleasure – for then we should be loving the object of our desire rather than God himself. And in the same chapter I showed that God has revealed this very law to his prophets, and whether I maintain that this law of God received its authoritative form from God himself or whether I conceive it to be like the rest of God's decrees which involve eternal necessity and truth, it will nevertheless remain God's decree and a teaching for salvation. And whether I love God freely or through the necessity of God's decree, I shall still love God, and I shall be saved. Therefore I can now say that this man is to be classed with those of whom I said at the end of my Preface[227] that I would prefer them to leave my book entirely alone rather than make themselves a nuisance by misinterpreting it, as is their wont in all cases, and hinder others without any benefit to themselves.

Although I think that this suffices to show what I intended, I consider it worthwhile to add some brief observations. He is wrong in thinking that I am referring to that axiom of the theologians who make a distinction between the words of a prophet when he is proclaiming dogma and his words when he is merely narrating something. If by this axiom he means the one which I attributed in chapter 15 to a certain Rabbi Judah Alpakhar,[228] how could I have thought that my view agrees with this when in the same chapter[229] I rejected it as false? But

---

227. In the penultimate paragraph of the Preface to the TTP, Spinoza admonishes the reader that the work is not intended for the common public or for the superstitious.

228. Alpakhar (sometimes also found in its Arabic form, 'Alfakhar') was a distinguished rabbi of Toledo, and physician to King Ferdinand III. An opponent of Maimonides' Aristotelianism, he died in 1235. The opening pages of TTP15 offer a summary of his position as Spinoza understood it. His own views are expressed in his correspondence with David Kimhi, contained in *Kovets Teshuvot ha-Rambam ve-Igrotav* ("Collection of Responsa and Letters of Maimonides"), 3 vols. in 1 (Leipzig, 1859), 3:1a-4b.

229. Maimonides is also criticized in TTP15. The general claim that philosophy is the proper interpreter of Scripture was defended by Lodewijk Meyer in his *Philosophia Sanctae Scripturae Interpres* (Amsterdam, 1666). See section 3 of our Introduction. The French edition of Meyer's treatise (by Jacqueline Lagrée and Pierre-François Moreau; Paris: Intertextes Editeur, 1988) contains a discussion of the relationship between it and the TTP.

if he is thinking of some other axiom, I confess that I still do not know of it, and so I could hardly have been referring to it.

Furthermore, I do not see why he says that I think that all those will agree with me who deny that reason and philosophy are the interpreters of Scripture. For I have refuted the views both of these and of Maimonides.[230]

It would take too long to review all his remarks which indicate that it is in no equable spirit that he has passed judgment on me. So I move on to his conclusion where he says that 'I have left myself with no argument to prove that Mahomet was not a true prophet', which he tries to prove from the views I have expressed. Yet from these it clearly follows that Mahomet was an impostor, since he completely abolishes the freedom which is granted by that universal religion revealed by the natural and prophetic light, and which I have shown ought to be fully granted. And even if this were not so, am I bound, pray, to show that some prophet is false? On the contrary, the prophets were bound to show that they were true prophets. And if he replies that Mahomet, too, taught the divine law and gave sure signs of his mission as did the other prophets, there is certainly no reason for him to deny that Mahomet was a true prophet.

As for the Turks and the other Gentiles, if they worship God by the exercise of justice and by love of their neighbour, I believe that they possess the spirit of Christ and are saved, whatever convictions they may hold in their ignorance regarding Mahomet and the oracles.

So you see, my friend, that this man has strayed far from the truth. Yet I grant that he does me no injury, but much to himself, when he is not ashamed to proclaim that I teach atheism with clandestine and disguised arguments.

---

230. For Spinoza's understanding of and relation to Maimonides, see Jacob Dienstag, "The Relations of Spinoza to the Philosophy of Maimonides: An Annotated Bibliography," *Studia Spinozana* 2 (1986), 375-418; Jean Robelin, *Maimonide et le langage religieux* (Paris: Presses Universitaires de France, 1991); and Leon Roth, *Spinoza, Descartes, and Maimonides* (Oxford: Clarendon Press, 1924). Some commentators suggest that Spinoza's position is closer to that of Maimonides than his critique in TTP16 would suggest. See Sylvain Zac, "Maimon, Spinoza et Kant," in *Spinoza entre Lumières et Romantisme*, ed. J. Bonnamour (Fontenay-aux-Roses: Ecole Normale Supérieure, 1985), 65-76; O. Hamelin, "Sur une des origines du spinozisme," *L'Année Philosophique* 11 (1901), 15-28; and Warren Z. Harvey, "A Portrait of Spinoza as a Maimonidean," *Journal of the History of Philosophy* 19 (1981), 151-172.

In general, I do not think that you will here find any expression which you might consider over-harsh against this man. However, if you come across anything of that sort, please either delete it or amend it as you think fit. It is not my intention to provoke him, whoever he may be, and to get for myself enemies of my own making. It is because this is often the result of disputes of this kind that I could scarcely prevail on myself to reply, and I would not have done so had I not promised.

Farewell. To your prudence I entrust this letter, and myself, who am. . . etc.

LETTER 44
To the most worthy and judicious Jarig Jelles, from B.d.S.

[The original, written in Dutch, is lost. The Dutch
edition of the O.P. probably reproduces the original
text, and the Latin version is a translation from this.]

Worthy Friend,

When Professor N.N.[231] recently paid me a visit, he told me, among
other things, that he had heard that my *Tractatus Theologico-Politicus*
had been translated into Dutch, and that somebody, he did not know
who, proposed to get it printed. I therefore beg you most earnestly
please to look into this, and, if possible, to stop the printing. This is not
only my request but that of many of my good friends who would not
wish to see the book banned, as will undoubtedly happen if it is published in Dutch. I have every confidence that you will do me and our
cause this service.[232]

Some time ago one of my friends sent me a little book entitled
Homo Politicus, or *Political Man*,[233] of which I had already heard a
great deal. I have read it through, and found it the most pernicious
book that can be devised by man. The highest good of the man who
wrote it is wealth and honours. To this he shapes his doctrine, and
shows the way to attain them, and that is, by inwardly rejecting all religion and outwardly assuming such as will best serve his advancement,
and furthermore by keeping faith with no one except in so far as it con-
duces to his advantage. For the rest, his highest praise is reserved for
dissembling, breaking promises he has made, lying, perjuring, and
many other such things. When I read this, I had some thought of writing a short book indirectly criticising it, in which I would treat of the

---

231. Wolf (1928, 438-439) conjectures that this may have been Professor Theodorus
  Kraanen (also spelled 'Craanen'), a Cartesian at the University of Leiden.
232. For the subsequent fate of this Dutch translation (which did finally appear in
  1693), see section 6 of our Introduction.
233. Believed to have been written by Christophorus Rapp, this book appeared in
  1644 and was published anonymously. For further information, see our introduction, section 3, and also Wolf (1928), 439.

highest good, and then indicate the restless and pitiable condition of those who are greedy for money and covet honours, and finally, prove by clear reasoning and abundant examples that through insatiable desire for honours and greed for riches commonwealths must necessarily perish, and have perished.

How far superior, indeed, and excellent were the reflections of Thales of Miletus[234] compared with this writer is shown by the following account. All things, he said, are in common among friends. The wise are the friends of the Gods, and all things belong to the Gods; therefore all things belong to the wise. In this way this wise man makes himself the richest, by nobly despising riches instead of greedily pursuing them. But on another occasion he proved that it is not out of necessity but by choice that the wise possess no riches. When his friends reproached him for his poverty, he answered them, "Do you want me to show you that I can acquire that which I consider unworthy of my effort, and which you so eagerly seek?" And when they assented to this, he hired all the presses throughout Greece; for being well versed in the courses of the stars, he had seen that in the current year there would be a great abundance of olives, which had been very scarce in the preceding years. Then he let out at a high price the presses which he had hired cheaply, for people needed them to press the oil out of the olives. In this way in one year he acquired great wealth, which he then distributed with a liberality equal to the shrewdness by which he had acquired it.

I conclude by assuring you that I am, etc.

The Hague.
17 February 1671.

---

234. Thales of Miletus, (circa 600 B.C.) was as much an astronomer as he was a philosopher, and he is given credit for writing an almanac and for introducing the Phoenician practise of navigation using the Little Dipper. The story repeated here by Spinoza is found in Diogenes Laertes' *Lives of the Philosophers*, I, 26.

LETTER 45
To the illustrious and esteemed B.d.S.,
from Gottfried Leibniz

[The original is extant. The Latin text of
the O.P. differs from it only slightly,
omitting Hudde's name and the postscript.]

Illustrious and most honoured Sir,

Among your other achievements which fame has spread abroad I
understand is your remarkable skill in optics. For this reason I venture
to send this essay, such as it is, to you, than whom I am not likely to
find a better critic in this field of study. This paper which I send you,
and which I have entitled *A Note on Advanced Optics*,[235] I have published in order to communicate more conveniently with friends or
interested parties. I hear that the highly accomplished Hudde,[236] too,
is eminent in this field, and he is doubtless well known to you. So if you
can also obtain for me his judgment and approval, you will add
immensely to your kindness.

The paper itself explains very well what it is about, ...

I believe you have received the *Prodromus* of Francis Lana, S.J.,[237]
written in Italian, which also contains some notable suggestions on
Dioptrics. But John Oltius,[238] too, a young Swiss, who is very learned
in these matters, has published his *Physical-Mechanical Reflections on
Vision*, in which he promises a certain machine for polishing all kinds
of glasses, which is very simple and of general application. He also says
that he has discovered a method for gathering *all* the rays coming from
all the points of an object into as many other corresponding points. But
this applies only to an object at a certain distance and of a certain
shape.

---

235. Leibniz' *Notitia opticae promotae* was published in 1671.
236. See section 7 of our Introduction.
237. Franciscus Lana (1631-1687) was Professor of Philosophy and of Mathematics in
   Rome. The *Prodromo, overo Saggio di alcune inventioni nuove premesse all'Arte
   maestra* was published in Brescia in 1677.
238. This person is unknown.

However, the point of my proposal is this, not that all the rays from *all* the points should be gathered again – for this is impossible, as far as our present knowledge goes, in the case of objects at every distance and of every shape – but that the rays should be gathered equally from points outside the optic axis as from on the optic axis, and therefore the apertures of the glasses can be of any size without impairing distinctness of vision. But this will await your expert judgment.

Farewell, honoured Sir, and favour

> Your faithful admirer,
> Gottfried William Leibniz,
> Doctor of Laws and Councillor of Mainz.
> Frankfurt, 5 October 1671 (New Style).

P.S. If you will favour me with an answer, the most noble Diemerbroek,[239] Lawyer, will, I hope, be willing to take charge of it. I think you have seen my new *Physical Hypothesis*; if not, I will send it.

To Mr. Spinosa, celebrated doctor and profound philosopher.
At Amsterdam.
Per couverto.

---

239. J. de Diemerbroek was a lawyer in Utrecht.

To the most learned and noble Gottfried Leibniz, Doctor of Laws and Councillor of Mainz, from B.d.S.

[The original is extant. The O.P. Latin text seems
to have been composed from Spinoza's own copy.
There are some slight differences.]

Most learned and noble Sir,

I have read the paper which you kindly sent me, and I am very grateful
to you for letting me have it. I regret that I have not been able fully to
grasp your meaning, though I believe you have explained it clearly
enough. I therefore beg you to answer these few queries. Do you
believe that there is a reason for restricting the size of the aperture of
the glasses other than that the rays coming from a single point are not
collected precisely at another point but over a small space (which we
usually call a mechanical point), whose size varies with that of the
aperture? Secondly, do those lenses which you call 'pandochal'[240]
correct this fault? That is, does the mechanical point, or the small
space at which the rays coming from the same point are gathered after
refraction, remain the same size whether the aperture is great or
small? For if the lenses achieve this, one may enlarge their aperture as
much as one likes, and they will therefore be far superior to lenses of
any other shape known to me; otherwise I do not know why you so
warmly commend them above ordinary lenses. For circular lenses have
everywhere the same axis, and so when we employ them, all the points
of an object must be considered as if placed in the optic axis. And
although all the points of an object are not equidistant, the resulting
difference cannot be perceptible in the case of far distant objects,
because then the rays coming from a single point would be regarded as
entering the glass in parallel. However, in cases where we wish to
apprehend several objects at one glance (as happens when we employ
very large circular convex lenses), I believe your lenses can be effective
in representing the entire field more distinctly. But I shall suspend

---

240. The term 'pandochal' means 'all-receptive' (for rays of light).

judgment on all these points until you explain your meaning more clearly, as I earnestly beg you to do.

I sent the other copy to Mr. Hudde, as you requested. He has replied that he does not have time at present to examine it, but hopes to be free to do so in a week or two.

The *Prodromus* of Francis Lana has not yet come into my hands, nor the *Physico-Mechanical Reflections* of John Oltius; and, which is more to be regretted, neither have I been able to see your *Physical Hypothesis*. At any rate, it is not on sale here at the Hague. I shall be most grateful if you send it to me, and if I can be of service to you in any other way, you will always find that I am,

> Most honourable Sir,
> Yours entirely,
> B. De Spinoza.
> The Hague, 9 November 1671.

Mr. Dimerbruck[241] does not live here, so I am forced to give this to the ordinary letter-carrier. I have no doubt that you know somebody here at the Hague who would be willing to take charge of our correspondence. I should like to know who it is, so that our letters can be dispatched more conveniently and safely. If the *Tractatus Theologico-Politicus* has not yet reached you, I shall send you a copy if you care to have it. Farewell.

To the most noble and eminent Mr. Gottfried William Leibniz, Doctor of Laws and Councillor of Mainz.

Dispatched on 8 December 1671.

---

241. This is the same 'Dimerbroek' of the previous letter, but Spinoza has altered the spelling.

LETTER 47
To the acute and renowned philosopher, B.d.S.
from J. Louis Fabritius

[Known only from the O.P. The original is lost.[242]]

Renowned Sir,

His Serene Highness the Elector Palatine,[243] my most gracious lord, has commanded me to write to you who, while as yet unknown to me, are strongly recommended to his Serene Highness, and to ask you whether you would be willing to accept a regular Professorship of Philosophy in his illustrious University. The annual salary will be that currently paid to regular Professors. You will not find elsewhere a Prince more favourably disposed to men of exceptional genius, among whom he ranks you. You will have the most extensive freedom in philosophising, which he believes you will not misuse to disturb the publicly established religion. I have pleasure in complying with the request of the most wise Prince. Therefore I do most earnestly beg you to let me have your answer as soon as possible, and to entrust your answer to the care of Mr. Grotius, His Serene Highness the Elector's resident at the Hague, or to Mr. Gilles Van der Mek, to be forwarded to me in the packet of letters regularly sent to the Court, or else to avail yourself of any other convenient means you deem most suitable. I will add only this, that if you come here, you will have the pleasure of living a life worthy of a philosopher, unless everything turns out contrary to our hope and expectation.

And so farewell, with my greetings, most honoured Sir,

From your most devoted,

J. Louis Fabritius.

Professor at the University of Heidelberg

and Councillor to the Elector Palatine.

Heidelberg, 16 February 1673.

---

242. See section 7 of our Introduction for information on Fabritius.

243. This was Karl Ludwig, the brother of Queen Christina of Sweden, who was Descartes' patroness. For information on the source and political inspiration of the invitation (which was probably inspired by the appearance of Spinoza's TTP), see Meinsma, 406-409.

LETTER 48
To the most honourable and noble Mr. J. Louis Fabritius, Professor in the University of Heidelberg and Councillor to the Elector Palatine, from B.d.S.

[Known only from the O.P. The original is lost.]

Most honourable Sir,

If I had ever had any desire to undertake a professorship in any faculty, I could have wished for none other than that which is offered me through you by His Serene Highness the Elector Palatine, especially on account of the freedom to philosophise which this most gracious Prince is pleased to grant, not to mention my long-felt wish to live under the rule of a Prince whose wisdom is universally admired. But since I have never intended to engage in public teaching, I cannot induce myself to embrace this excellent opportunity, although I have given long consideration to the matter.[244] For, first, I reflect that if I am to find time to instruct young students, I must give up my further progress in phiphy. Secondly, I do not know within what limits the freedom to philosophise must be confined if I am to avoid appearing to disturb the publicly established religion. For divisions arise not so much from an ardent devotion to religion as from the different dispositions of men, or through their love of contradiction which leads them to distort or to condemn all things, even those that are stated aright. Now since I have already experienced this while leading a private and solitary life, it would be much more to be feared after I have risen to this position of eminence. So you see, most Honourable Sir, that my reluctance is not due to the hope of some better fortune, but to my love of peace, which I believe I can enjoy in some measure if I refrain from lecturing in public. Therefore I most earnestly beg you to pray His Serene Highness the Elector to grant me more time to deliberate on this matter. And

---

244. Spinoza's caution was in fact validated by subsequent events. The year after this letter was written the French seized Heidelberg and closed the university there.

please continue to commend to the favour of the most gracious Prince his most devoted admirer, whereby you will oblige even more,

Most honourable and noble Sir,

Yours entirely,
B.d.S.
The Hague, 30 March 1673.

LETTER 48A
Confession of the Universal and Christian Faith, contained in a letter to N.N. from Jarig Jelles.

[Not in the O.P. Published by Jan Rieuwertsz.[245]]

Worthy Friend,

(1) I have complied with your earnest request desiring me to let you know by letter[246] my sentiments regarding my faith or religion, and all the more readily since you declare that your motive for so asking is that some persons are trying to persuade you that the Cartesian philosophers (among whom you are pleased to number me) entertain a strange opinion, lapsing into the ancient heathendom, and that their propositions and basic principles are opposed to the basic principles of the Christian Religion and of Piety, etc. In my own defence, then, I shall first of all say that the Cartesian philosophy touches religion so little that Descartes' propositions find followers not only among various religious persuasions but also among Roman Catholics, so that what I

---

245. Ep48a and the first fragment of Ep48b were published by Rieuwertsz, a significant fact inasmuch as he had physical possession of the Spinoza correspondence. The reliability of these passages is thus as high as those published in the O.P. Things stand differently with respect to the second fragment of Ep48b, since our text is based on Hallmann's notes and partial transcription. The two fragments of Ep48b differ so remarkably in content that we suspect that they may actually be drawn from two different letters, one referring to an early version of Jelles' *Confession*, and the other to a later and revised text.

246. The letter is mentioned in Bayle's Dictionary (see Wolf 1928, 442-443), from which Wolf drew a summary of it. An edition of the letter was published by F. Akkerman, H. G. Hubbeling, and A. G. Westerbrink in 1977 (Spinoza, *Briefwisseling*. Amsterdam: Wereldbibliotheek, pp. 303-309). The text of the letter was first published in Jarig Jelles' *Belydenisse des Algemeenen en Christelyken Geloofs, Vervattet in een Brief aan N.N.* (Amsterdam: by Jan Rieuwertsz, 1684), a copy of which can be found in the Leiden University Library. Except for minor differences of punctuation and a typographical error in Rieuwertsz's version, this version is identical to that published by Akkerman, Hubbeling, and Westerbrink. The first paragraph (up to "... in this letter") is found in the unpaginated front matter of the book, the remainder on pp. 159-161. Our thanks to Francis Pastijn (Marquette University) for his comparative work on the two versions and for assistance in the translation.

shall say about religion should be taken as my own particular view, not that of the Cartesians. And although I do not seek to engage in controversy with others and to stop the mouths of calumniators, I shall however be pleased to satisfy you and others like you. And while it is not my intention to prescribe a universal creed, or again to determine the essential, fundamental and necessary doctrinal tenets, but only to acquaint you with my views, I shall still endeavour, as well as I can, to comply with the terms which, according to Jacobus Acontius, are required for a universal Confession acceptable to all Christians, namely, that it should contain only that which must necessarily be known, that which is quite true and certain, that which is attested and confirmed by testimonies, and, finally, that which is expressed as far as possible in the same words and phrases as were used by the Holy Spirit. Here, then, is a Confession which I think to be of this kind. Read it attentively, judge it not lightly, and be assured that, just as I have taken my stand on truth, so shall I seek to impart it to you in this letter.

[The body of the *Confession* follows here, concluding with these words:]

(2) I trust that herewith I shall have accomplished even more than you yourself had expected, and that you will therefore deem that I have fulfilled that which you asked of me.

(3) In return I ask of you only that you will please consider carefully and prudently what I have said, and then judge of the reports you have received concerning my religious opinion.

(4) If you find anything here that may seem to you false or in opposition to Holy Scripture, I beg you to let me know this, and also the reason why it seems so to you, so that I can look into it. Those who hold as opposed to Holy Scripture and false whatever does not accord with their Formulations[247] or Confessions of faith will doubtless judge that much contained in my letter is of this kind. But I am confident that those who test it against truth (which I have shown above to be the only unerring measure and touchstone for truth and falsity, for honesty and dishonesty, etc.) will judge differently, which I also expect of you.

(5) Here you have my view as far as concerns the Christian religion, and also the proofs and reasoning on which it rests. It is now for you to judge whether those who build on such a groundwork and try to live in

---

247. The *Formulieren* was often a formal summary of beliefs published as a pamphlet [note supplied by Francis Pastijn].

accordance with such understanding are Christians or not, and whether there is any truth in the reports which some people have made to you regarding my opinions.

(6) Finally, for my part I ask you to examine all this carefully and dispassionately. I wish you enlightenment of understanding, and conclude by testifying that I am, etc.,

Your devoted friend,
Jarig Jelles.
[Amsterdam 1673].

LETTER 48B
To the most courteous and learned Jarig Jelles, from B.d.S.

[Not in the O.P. These are fragments of a letter
written in Dutch by Spinoza to Jarig Jelles, in
response to Jelles' request for his opinion of
Jelles' book *Confession of Faith*.[248]]

(1) Sir and most illustrious friend,

It is with pleasure that I have read through the writings that you sent
me, and found them such that I can suggest no alterations in them.[249]

(2) The date of the letter was 19 April 1673, dispatched from the
Hague and addressed to Jarig Jelles, who had sent him his *Confession
of the Universal Christian Faith*, and had asked him his opinion. In this
reply Spinoza gave him no praise nor many indications of approval, but
merely stated that "it is open to some criticism. On page 5 of the
manuscript you assert that man is inclined by nature to evil, but
through the Grace of God and the Spirit of Christ he becomes
indifferent to good and evil. This, however, is contradictory, because he
who has the Spirit of Christ is necessarily impelled only to good." In
this letter Spinoza also makes reference to Mr. Kerckring,[250] a doctor,

---

248. The fragments here translated were reported by (1) Bayle, in his *Historical and
Critical Dictionary*, 1702, and by (2) Dr. Hallmann, who found the letter in the
possession of Rieuwertsz junior in 1703. The first fragment, minus the salutation,
appears in Dutch in the editor's afterword (*Na-Reden*) to Jelles' *Belydenisse*, p.
164 (see our note to Ep48A). It is very likely that this was Bayle's source. The text
is: "Ik heb met vermaak UE. Schriften overgelezen, en zodanig bevonden, dat ik
'er niets in kan veranderen."
249. The first fragment of this letter leaves it rather ambiguous whether Spinoza
actually agrees with Jelles' *Confession* or whether he merely suggests no changes.
Rieuwertsz's postscript includes a short statement which appears to support the
first interpretation, and which is followed by the first of the two fragments of this
letter.
250. Dirck Kerckring (1639-1693) was a physician who had studied Latin at Van den
Enden's school at about the same time Spinoza was there. His first name is also
given as Theodoor or Theodorus (of which 'Dirck' was a common Dutch
equivalent). Several of his treatises were found in Spinoza's library, so it is
presumed that the two friends maintained contact throughout the years. As a
note of interest, Kerckring married Van den Enden's daughter, Clara Maria, in
1671.

whom he had consulted on some anatomical questions. Near the end of the letter to Jelles he wrote, "I will send you the *Known Truth*[251] as soon as Mr. Vallon[252] returns my copy. But if he takes too long over it, I will make arrangements through Mr. Bronckhorst[253] for you to get it." The ending was, "I remain, with cordial greetings,

> Your devoted servant,
> B. Spinoza."

---

251. There are no extant copies of this book or manuscript.
252. We are not sure who this man was. Conjectures are that he may have been a professor friend of Spinoza's at the University of Leiden or that 'Vallon' is a corruption of 'De Vallan' who was a professor at the University of Ultrecht, or of 'De Volder' who taught at the University of Leiden. Other possibilities have also been suggested, but who exactly this man was remains still a mystery.
253. Probably this was Hendrick Van Bronckhurst. He wrote the poem which introduced the Dutch translation of the PPC.

LETTER 49
To the esteemed John George Graevius, from B.d.S.

[Not in the O.P. The original is extant.]

Most esteemed Sir,

Please send me as soon as you can the letter concerning the death of Descartes, of which I think you have long ago made a copy; for Mr. de V. has several times asked me to return it. If it were my own, I should not be in any hurry. Farewell, honoured Sir, and remember me, your friend, who am,

       Yours in all love and devotion,
       Benedictus De Spinoza.
       The Hague, 14 December 1673.

Mr. John George Graevius,[254]
Regular Professor of Rhetoric, at Utrecht.

---

254. For John Graevius, see Meinsma, 390-392, and section 7 of our Introduction.

LETTER 50
To the most worthy and judicious Jarig Jelles, from B.d.S.

[The original, written in Dutch, is lost. The O.P. gives
a Latin translation. The text of the Dutch edition of
the O.P. appears to be a re-translation from the Latin.]

Most worthy Sir,

With regard to political theory, the difference between Hobbes[255] and
myself, which is the subject of your inquiry, consists in this, that I
always preserve the natural right in its entirety, and I hold that the
sovereign power in a State has right over a subject only in proportion to
the excess of its power over that of a subject. This is always the case in
a state of nature.[256]

---

255. Thomas Hobbes (1588-1679) was a celebrated political philosopher whose works
include *Leviathan, Behemoth, De corpore, De homine* and *De cive* (Spinoza had a
copy of the last-mentioned book in his library). His philosophy was empirical,
nominalistic, and materialistic; his objections to Descartes' philosophy are
included along with Descartes' replies in the *Meditations*. Hobbes' famous statement, "that life of man [is] solitary, poor, nasty, brutish, and short" (*Leviathan* I,
13) is meant to show that people in the state of nature, that is, as individuals
before the creation of society or the political state, live in a constant war-like state
in which the most powerful are free to do as they please. People form political
states and societies as a means to ensure relatively peaceful lives by surrendering
all their rights (except for the right not to do impossible things, e.g., perform
patricide upon request) to the sovereign who/which (since the sovereign need not
necessarily be a person) then exercises total control and power over the ruled.
While there are many similarities between Spinoza and Hobbes, the two are very
different. Spinoza holds that a person *never* loses his or her rights, whether in the
state of nature (Hobbes' war-like state) or in community. Further differences and
similarities between the philosophers are noted in Alexandre Matheron *Individu
et communauté chez Spinoza* (Paris: Editions de Minuit, 1969), 151-179; and S.
Barbone and L. Rice, "La naissance d'une nouvelle politique" (forthcoming,
1995). See also Gilbert Boss, "Les fondements de la politique selon Hobbes et
selon Spinoza," *Les Etudes Philosophiques* 1994, 171-190.
256. The psychological concept of the state of nature is introduced in E4P37Schol,
and further developed in TTP16, but is notably absent in the unfinished TP. Alexandre Matheron (*Individu et communauté chez Spinoza*, 287-354) argues that
there is no change of position between the two works, but rather a difference of
emphasis. The relation between Hobbes' and Spinoza's political philosophy is
more difficult than Spinoza's brief remark here suggests. See E. Giancotti Bos-
cherini, "La naissance du matérialisme moderne chez Hobbes et Spinoza," *Revue
Philosophique* 1985/2, 136-148; Gilbert Boss, "Les principes de la philosophie
chez Hobbes et chez Spinoza," *Studia Spinozana* 3 (1987), 87-124; M. de Souza

Further, with regard to the demonstration that I establish in the Appendix to my Geometrical Proof of Descartes' Principles, namely, that God can only improperly be called one or single,[257] I reply that a thing can be called one or single only in respect of its existence, not of its essence. For we do not conceive things under the category of numbers unless they are included in a common class.[258] For example, he who holds in his hand a penny and a dollar will not think of the number two unless he can apply a common name to this penny and dollar, that is, pieces of money or coins. For then he can say that he has two pieces of money or two coins, because he calls both the penny and the dollar a piece of money or a coin. Hence it is clear that a thing cannot be called one or single unless another thing has been conceived which, as I have said, agrees with it. Now since the existence of God is

---

Chaui, "Direito natural e direito civil en Hobbes e Espinoza," *Revista latino-americana de filosofía* 6 (1980), 57-71; Douglas Den Uyl and Stuart D. Warner, "Liberalism and Hobbes and Spinoza," *Studia Spinozana* 3 (1987), 261-318; B. H. Kazemier, *De Staat bij Spinoza en Hobbes* (Leiden: Brill, 1952); and F. Tinland, "Hobbes, Spinoza, Rousseau, et la formation de l'idée de démocratie comme mesure de la légitimité du pouvoir politique," *Revue Philosophique* 1985/2, 195-222. Volume 3 (1987) of *Studia Spinozana* is devoted entirely to Hobbes and Spinoza.

257. Some commentators see in this letter evidence that Spinoza is not a monist, that is, that he holds that there is more than one substance. While Spinoza does write, "[A] thing can be called one or single only in respect of its existence, not of its essence," we take him to mean that substance is one in respect to its existence (since there is only one), but that there is nothing in the essence of substance which requires that it alone exist. Whether or not substance may essentially exist singularly or not does not alter the fact that Spinoza does hold that substance is singular (see Ep12, E1P14), and so in one sense he is certainly a monist. We remind the reader, nevertheless, that a monist need not necessarily believe that any substance exists, but only that there cannot be two or more of them. For an alternate reading which does argue that Spinoza is not a monist, see Pierre Macherey, "Spinoza est-il moniste?" in *Spinoza: puissance et ontologie*, ed. Myriam Revault D'Allonnes (Paris: Editions Kimé, 1993), 39-53.

258. As the example following makes clear, Spinoza is here anticipating the Fregean or Russellian definition of number in terms of a property (or better, class) of classes. So the number one is the set of all singletons, two the set of all pairs, etc. So God cannot be properly called 'one' insofar as he is not the member of any class of beings. Implicit in Spinoza's analysis is his rejection of the modern notion of a unit set (used to define individuals in some axiomatisations of set theory). Spinoza also rejects the claim that an infinite set can properly be *numbered* (or counted), hence his conclusion that 'infinite number' is a contradictory concept.

his very essence, and since we can form no universal idea of his essence, it is certain that he who calls God one or single has no true idea of God, or is speaking of him very improperly.

With regard to the statement that figure is a negation and not anything positive, it is obvious that matter in its totality, considered without limitation, can have no figure,[259] and that figure applies only to finite and determinate bodies. For he who says that he apprehends a figure, thereby means to indicate simply this, that he apprehends a determinate thing and the manner of its determination. This determination therefore does not pertain to the thing in regard to its being; on the contrary, it is its non-being. So since figure is nothing but determination, and determination is negation, figure can be nothing other than negation, as has been said.

The book which the Utrecht Professor[260] wrote against mine and has been published after his death, I have seen in a bookseller's window. From the little that I then read of it, I judged it not worth reading through, and far less answering. So I left the book lying there, and its author to remain such as he was. I smiled as I reflected that the ignorant are usually the most venturesome and most ready to write. It seemed to me that the .... set out their wares for sale in the same way as do shopkeepers, who always display the worse first. They say the devil is a crafty fellow, but in my opinion these people's resourcefulness far surpasses him in cunning.

Farewell.
The Hague, 2 June 1674.

---

259. The failure to distinguish the infinite from the unbounded was common to seventeenth-century physics, and displayed by Newton also. It is in part due to the implicit euclideanism assumed for space. On the question of Spinoza's euclideanism, Bennett is probably correct in claiming that Spinoza's system is at least open to non-euclidean geometry, unlike Kant's, although Spinoza never in fact raised the issue of the epistemological status of geometry. See Jonathan Bennett, *A Study of Spinoza's Ethics* (Indianapolis: Hackett, 1984), 85-92.

260. This was Regner Van Mansvelt, who published *Adversus Anonymum Theologico-Politicum, Liber Singularis* (One Book against the anonymous *Theological-political* [*Tractate*]) in 1674. Is it coincidental that Spinoza would use the image of a shopkeeper to his friend Jelles who had been a spice merchant before taking up philosophy?

LETTER 51
To the most acute philosopher B.d.S., from Hugo Boxel

[The original, written in Dutch, is lost. The O.P. gives
a Latin translation. The text of the Dutch edition of
the O.P. appears to be a re-translation from the Latin.]

Most esteemed Sir,

My reason for writing to you is that I should like to know your opinion
of apparitions and spectres,[261] or ghosts; and if they exist, what you
think regarding them, and how long they live; for some think that they
are immortal, while others think they are mortal. In view of my doubt
as to whether you admit their existence, I shall proceed no further.
However, it is certain that the ancients believed in their existence.
Theologians and philosophers of our times still believe in the existence
of creatures of this kind, although they do not agree as to the nature of
their essence. Some assert that they are composed of very delicate and
fine matter, while others think that they are spiritual beings. But, as I
began by saying, we are much at variance on this subject, for I am
doubtful as to whether you grant their existence; yet it cannot escape
you that there are to be found throughout antiquity so many instances
and stories of them that it would indeed be difficult either to deny
them or to call them into doubt. This much is certain, that if you admit
their existence, you still do not believe that some of them are the souls
of the dead, as the upholders of the Roman faith will have it.

Here I will end, and await your reply. I will say nothing about the
war,[262] nothing about rumours, for it is our lot to live in such times. . .
etc.

Farewell.
14 September 1674.

---

261. For Boxel see section 7 of our Introduction. The correspondence between Spinoza and Boxel on the question of the supernatural has been studied in detail by
Alain Billecoq, *Spinoza et les spectres* (Paris: Presses Universitaires de France,
1987). As Billecoq notes, Spinoza's careful discussion with Boxel provides many
insights into Spinoza's view of the nature of philosophical method in general.
262. This is the continuing war between Holland and France.

LETTER 52
To the highly esteemed and judicious Hugo Boxel, from B.d.S.

[The original, written in Dutch, is lost, but is
probably reproduced in the Dutch edition of the O.P.
The Latin is a translation.]

My dear Sir,

Your letter, which I received yesterday, was most welcome, both because I wanted to have news of you and because it assures me that you have not entirely forgotten me. And although some might think it a bad omen that ghosts or spectres should have been the occasion of your writing to me, I, on the contrary, discern in this something of greater significance; for I reflect that not only real things but trifles and fancies can turn to my advantage.

But let us set aside the question as to whether ghosts are delusions and fancies, since it seems to you strange not only to deny such things but even to cast doubt on them, being convinced as you are by the numerous stories related by ancients and moderns. The great respect in which I have always held you, and still hold you, does not permit me to contradict you, still less to humour you. The middle course which I shall take between the two is to ask you please to select, from the numerous ghost stories you have read, one or two that are least open to doubt and which prove most clearly the existence of ghosts. For, to tell the truth, I have never read a trustworthy author who showed clearly that they exist. I still do not know what they are, and no one has ever been able to inform me. Yet it is certain that in the case of a thing so clearly demonstrated by experience we ought to know what it is; otherwise we can hardly conclude from a story that ghosts exist, but only that there is something, but no one knows what it is. If philosophers want to call these things we do not know 'ghosts'. I shall not be able to refute them, for there are an infinite number of things of which I have no knowledge.

Finally, my dear Sir, before I go further into this matter, I beg you to tell me what kind of things are these ghosts or spirits. Are they children, fools, or madmen? For what I have heard of them seems to suggest silly people rather than intelligent beings, or, at best childish games or the pastime of fools. Before concluding, I shall put before you one further consideration, namely, that the desire men commonly have to narrate things not as they are but as they would like them to be can nowhere be better exemplified than in stories about spirits and ghosts. The main reason for this is, I believe, that since stories of this kind have no other witnesses than the narrators, the author of such stories can add or suppress circumstantial details as he pleases without having to fear that anyone will contradict him. In particular, he makes things up to justify the fear that has seized him regarding his dreams and fancied apparitions, or also to confirm his courage, his credibility and his esteem. Besides this I have found other reasons that move me to doubt, if not the stories themselves, at least the details included therein, which serve most of all to support the conclusion meant to be drawn from these stories. Here I shall stop, until I hear from you what are the stories which have so convinced you that you think it absurd even to doubt them.

[The Hague, September 1674].

LETTER 53
To the very sagacious philosopher B.d.S., from Hugo Boxel

[The original, written in Dutch, is extant. The Latin
version in the O.P. may have been made by Spinoza.]

Most sagacious Sir,

The reply you have sent me is just what I expected from a friend, and
one who holds an opinion at variance with mine. This latter point is of
no importance, for friends may well disagree on indifferent matters
without ever impairing their friendship.

Before you give your own opinion, you ask me to say what sort of
things ghosts are, whether they are children, fools or madmen, and so
forth, and you add that all that you have heard of them seems to
proceed from lunatics rather than from intelligent beings. The old
proverb is true, that a preconceived opinion hinders the search for
truth.

I say that I believe that there are ghosts. My reasons are, first, that
it contributes to the beauty and perfection of the universe that they
should exist. Second, it is probable that the Creator has created them
because they resemble him more closely than do corporeal creatures.
Third, just as there is a body without soul, so there is a soul without
body. Fourth and last, I believe that there is no dark body in the upper
air, region or space that is without its inhabitants, and therefore the
immeasurable space extending between us and the stars is not empty
but filled with inhabitants that are spirits. The highest and uppermost
are true spirits, while the lowest in the nethermost region of air are
possibly creatures of very delicate and fine substance, and also invisible. So I think that there are spirits of all kinds, except perhaps of the
female sex.

This reasoning will not convince those who perversely believe that
the world was made by chance. Besides these arguments, our daily
experience shows that there are ghosts, of whom there are many
stories, old and modern, and even present-day. They are related in
Plutarch's treatise *On Famous Men* and in other of his works, by

Suetonius in his *Lives of the Caesars*, by Wierus in his books on ghosts[263] and also by Lavater,[264] who deal with this subject at length, drawing on other writers. Cardanus, too,[265] celebrated for his learning, speaks of them in his books *De Subtilitate* and *De Varietate* and in his autobiography, where he recounts the appearances of ghosts in his own case and in that of his relations and friends. Melanthon,[266] a lover of truth and a man of understanding, and many others bear witness as to their own experiences. A certain burgomaster of Sc., a learned and wise man who is still alive, once told me that work was heard going on at night in his mother's brewery in the same way as it was heard by day when brewing was taking place, and swore to me that this occurred on several occasions. The same sort of thing has happened to me more than once, which I shall never forget. These experiences and the aforementioned reasons have convinced me that there are ghosts.

As regards devils who torment poor people in this life and the next, that is another question, as also is the practise of magic. I consider that stories told on these matters are fables. Sir, in treatises concerning ghosts you will find an abundance of details. Besides those I have mentioned, you can look up, if you please, the younger Pliny, Book 7, his letter to Sura, Suetonius' *Life of Caesar*, chapter 32, Valerius Maximus, Book 1, chapter 8, sections 7 and 8, and also the *Dies Geniales* of Alexander ab Alexandro.[267] No doubt you have access to these books. I make no mention of monks and clerics, who report so many apparitions and sightings of spirits, ghosts and devils, and so many stories, or rather, fables of spectres that people are bored by them and sick of reading them. These things are also dealt with by the Jesuit Thyraeus

---

263. Johannes Wierus (b. 1515 or 1516) was a physician in Düsseldorf. He published *De praestigiis Daemonum* in 1563 as a protest against the prosecution of witches. The book was followed on *De lamiis* (*On Ghosts*) and *Pseudomonarchia daemonum* (*On the Hierarchy of Hell*). The original text of this letter has 'Wierius', which is corrected to 'Wierus' in the O.P.

264. Ludwig Lavater (1527-1586), a Protestant Minister in Zurich, wrote a treatise on ghosts, *Tractatus de Spectris, Lemuribus, Fragoribus, Variisque Praesagiis* (Geneva, 1580).

265. Girolamo Cardanus (1501-1576) became Professor of Medicine in Pavia in 1547. His *De Subtilitate Rerum* appeared in 1551, and *De Rerum Varietate* in 1557. Although he insisted on the inviolability of laws of nature, he claimed that he had the assistance of a guardian daemon.

266. This is probably the German Reformer Philipp Melanchton (1497-1560).

267. Alexander ab Alexandro (1461-1523) was an Italian lawyer. His *Genialium Dierum, Libri Sex*, dealing mostly with antiquities, was published in 1522.

in his book which he entitles *Apparitiones Spirituum*.[268] But these people expound such subjects merely for their own gain, and to prove that there is a purgatory, which is for them a mine from which they extract so much silver and gold. This, however, is not true of the above-mentioned writers and other writers of our times, who deserve more credibility for being without any such motivation.

You say at the end of your letter that to commend me to God is something you cannot do without smiling.[269] But if you are still mindful of the conversation we had some time ago, you will realise that there is no need for alarm over the conclusion I reached at the time in my letter, etc.

In answer to the passage in your letter where you speak of fools and lunatics, I will state the conclusion of the learned Lavater with which he ends his first book on *Night Ghosts*. It goes as follows. "He who ventures to repudiate so many unanimous witnesses, both ancient and modern, seems to me undeserving of belief in anything he asserts. For just as it is a mark of rashness to give unquestioning belief to all those who assert that they have seen ghosts, so on the other hand it would be sheer effrontery to contradict, rashly and shamelessly, so many historians, Fathers, and others of great authority."

21 September 1674.

---

268. Petrus Thyraeus (1546-1601), professor at Würzburg, published the *De Apparitionibus Spirituum* in 1600 at Cologne.

269. The last two paragraphs of this letter are in the original but not in the O.P. The reference to Spinoza's letter is obscure.

LETTER 54
To the highly esteemed and judicious Hugo Boxel, from B.d.S.

[The original, written in Dutch, is lost. The O.P.
gives a Latin version, perhaps by Spinoza, and this
has been re-translated into Dutch in the Dutch edition.
Conjectural date, September 1674.]

Most esteemed Sir,

Relying on what you say in your letter of the 21st of last month, that friends may disagree on an indifferent matter without impairing their friendship, I will clearly state what I think of the arguments and stories from which you conclude that 'there are ghosts of all kinds, but perhaps not of the female sex'. The reason for my not having replied sooner is that the books you quoted are not to hand, and I have found none but Pliny[270] and Suetonius. But these two will save me the trouble of consulting the others, for I am sure that they all talk the same sort of nonsense, and love tales of extraordinary events which astonish men and compel their wonder. I confess that I was not a little amazed, not at the stories that are narrated, but at those who write them. I am surprised that men of ability and judgment should squander their gift of eloquence and misuse it to persuade us of such rubbish.

Still, let us dismiss the authors and turn to the issue itself, and I shall first devote a little time to a discussion of your conclusion. Let us see whether I, who deny that there are ghosts or spirits, am thereby failing to understand those writers who have written on this subject, or whether you, who hold that such things exist, are not giving the writers more credibility than they deserve. On the one hand you do not doubt the existence of spirits of the male sex, while on the other hand you doubt the existence of any of the female sex. This seems to me more like caprice than genuine doubt, for if this were really your opinion, it would be more in keeping with the popular imagination which makes God masculine rather than feminine. I am surprised that those who

---

270. A copy of Pliny's *Letters* is listed in the inventory of Spinoza's library compiled after his death.

have seen naked spirits have not cast their eyes on the genital parts; perhaps they were too afraid, or ignorant of the difference.

You will retort that this is to resort to ridicule, not to argue the case; and so I see that your reasons appear to you so strong and so well-founded that no one, at least in your judgment, can contradict them unless there is someone who perversely thinks that the world was made by chance. This impels me, before I deal with your preceding arguments, to give a brief account of my view on the question as to whether the world was made by chance. My answer is that, as it is certain that chance and necessity are two contrary terms, so it is also clear that he who affirms that the world is the necessary effect of the divine nature is also denying absolutely that the world was made by chance, whereas he who affirms that God could have refrained from creating the world is declaring in an indirect way that it was made by chance, since it proceeded from an act of will which might not have been.[271] Since this belief and this view is quite absurd, it is commonly and unanimously admitted that God's will is eternal and has never been indifferent, and therefore they must also necessarily grant (note this well) that the world is the necessary effect of the divine nature. Let them call it will, intellect, or any name they please, they will still in the end come to realise that they are expressing one and the same thing by different names. For if you ask them whether the divine will does not differ from the human will, they will reply that the former has nothing in common with the latter but the name; and furthermore they will mostly admit that God's will, intellect, and essence or nature are one and the same thing.[272] And I, too, to avoid confusing the divine nature with human nature, do not ascribe to God human attributes – will, intellect, attention, hearing, etc. I therefore say, as I have already said, that the world is the necessary effect of the divine nature, and was not made by chance.

This, I think, is enough to convince you that the opinion of those (if indeed such there be) who say that the world was made by chance is

---

271. The position described and criticized here is in fact the one espoused by Leibniz in the *Theodicy*. It is criticized further in E1P33Schol2.
272. That intellect and will are predicated equivocally of God and of finite things is argued in E1P17Schol, where Spinoza makes the claim that, "They could be no more alike than the celestial constellation of the Dog and the dog that barks." See Alexandre Koyré, "Le chien, constellation céleste, et le chien, animal aboyant," *Revue de Métaphysique et de Morale* 55 (195), 50-59.

entirely opposed to my opinion, and on this basis I proceed to examine the arguments from which you infer that there exist ghosts of all kinds. As a general remark, I would say of them that they seem to be conjectures rather than reasons, and I find it very difficult to believe that you take them to be conclusive arguments. However, whether they be conjectures or reasons, let us see whether they can be accepted as well-founded.

Your first reason is that it pertains to the beauty and perfection of the universe that ghosts should exist. Beauty, most esteemed Sir, is not so much a quality in the perceived object as an effect in him who perceives.[273] If we were more long-sighted or more short-sighted, or if we were differently constituted, the things which we now think beautiful would appear ugly, and the ugly, beautiful. The most beautiful hand, seen through a microscope, would appear repulsive. Some things seen at a distance are beautiful, but when viewed at close range, ugly. So things regarded in themselves, or as related to God, are neither beautiful nor ugly. Therefore he who says that God has created the world so as to be beautiful must necessarily affirm one of two alternatives: either that God made the world so as to suit the desire and the eyes of men, or the desire and the eyes of men to suit the world. Now whichever of these alternative views we adopt, I do not see why God had to create ghosts and spirits in either case. Perfection and imperfection are designations not much different from beauty and ugliness. Therefore, not to be tedious, I merely ask which would contribute more to the adornment and perfection of the world – that there should be ghosts, or that there should be a multiplicity of monsters, such as Centaurs, Hydras, Harpies, Griffins, Arguses, and other such absurdities?

---

273. The claim that 'beauty is in the eye of the beholder' is also made in the Appendix to E1. Some commentators argue that it does not imply, as it is commonly assumed, that aesthetic properties are wholly subjective. See Alain Billecoq, "L'idée de beauté chez Spinoza," *l'Art*, ed. C. G. Gaultier (Paris: Breal, 1984), 33-35; Laurent Bove, ed., *Théâtre et justice* (Paris: Quintette, 1991); and Filippo Mignini, "Le problème de l'esthétique spinoziste à la lumière de quelques interprétations, de Leibniz à Hegel," in *Spinoza entre Lumières et Romantisme*, ed. J. Bonnamour (Fontenay-aux-Roses: École Normale Supérieure, 1985), 123-42. The subjectivist interpretation of Spinoza is argued by J. C. Morrison, "Why Spinoza Had No Aesthetics," *Journal of Aesthetics and Art Criticism* 47 (1989), 359-365.

Truly, the world would have been handsomely embellished if God, to suit our fancy, had adorned and furnished it with things which anyone can easily imagine and dream of, but no one can ever understand!

Your second reason is that, since spirits express God's image more than do other corporeal creatures, it is also likely that God has created them. I frankly confess that I still do not understand in what respect spirits express God more than do other creatures. This I do know, that between the finite and the infinite there is no relation, so that the difference between God and the greatest and most excellent created thing is no other than that between God and the least created thing. This argument, therefore, is wide of the mark. If I had as clear an idea of ghosts as of a triangle or a circle, I should not hesitate to affirm that they have been created by God. However, since the idea I have of them is just like the ideas of Harpies, Griffins, Hydras, etc. which I form in my imagination, I cannot consider them as anything other than dreams, which are as different from God as being from non-being.

Your third reason (that just as a body can exist without soul, so a soul must exist without body) seems to me equally absurd. Tell me, pray, whether it is not also probable that memory, hearing, sight, etc. can exist without bodies, since some bodies are found to be without memory, hearing, sight, etc.? Or a sphere exist without a circle, because a circle exists without a sphere?

Your fourth and last reason is the same as the first, and I refer you to my answer. Here I shall merely observe that I do not know which are those highest and lowest regions which you conceive in infinite matter, unless you take the Earth to be the centre of the universe. For if the Sun or Saturn is the centre of the universe, then the Sun or Saturn, not the Earth, will be the lowest. Therefore, leaving aside this and any remaining consideration, I conclude that these and similar arguments will not convince anyone that ghosts and spectres of all kinds exist, except those who, shutting their ears to the voice of reason, suffer themselves to be led astray by superstition, which is so hostile to right reason that, so as to lower the prestige of philosophers, it prefers to believe old wives' tales.

As regards the stories, I have already said in my first letter that I do not altogether deny them, but only the conclusion drawn from them. I may add that I do not consider them so trustworthy as not to doubt many of the circumstantial details, which are often added for adornment rather than to render more plausible the truth of the story or the inference to be drawn therefrom. I had hoped that from so many stories you would have produced one or two which are least open to doubt, and which would have clearly proved the existence of ghosts or spectres. The case of the burgomaster, who was ready to conclude that they exist because he heard them working by night in his mother's brewery just as he was wont to hear work going on by day, seems to me ridiculous. Similarly, it would also be too tedious to examine here all the stories that have been written about these silly incidents. So, to be brief, I refer to Julius Caesar who, as Suetonius tells us, laughed at such things, and yet was favoured by fortune, according to what Suetonius relates of that Prince in his biography, chapter 59. In the same way, all who reflect on the effects of mortal imaginings and emotions must laugh at such things, whatever may be adduced to the contrary by Lavater and others who share his delusions on this subject.

To the most sagacious philosopher, B.d.S., from Hugo Boxel

[The original, written in Dutch, is lost. The O.P. gives
a Latin version, perhaps by Spinoza, and this has been
re-translated into Dutch in the Dutch edition.
Conjectural date, September 1674.]

Most sagacious Sir,

I am later than expected in replying to your letter because a slight illness has deprived me of the pleasure of study and meditation, and has
prevented me from writing to you. Now, thanks be to God, I have
recovered my health. In this reply I shall follow your letter step by
step, passing over your outcry against those who have written about
ghosts.

I say, then, that I think there are no ghosts of the female sex
because I deny that they give birth. As to their shape and constitution I
say nothing, because this does not concern me. A thing is said to happen fortuitously when it comes about regardless of the doer's intention.
When we dig the ground to plant a vine or to make a pit or a grave, and
find a treasure of which we have never had a thought, this is said to
happen by chance. He who acts of his own free will in such a way that
he can either act or not act can never be said to act by chance if he
chooses to act; for in that case all human actions would be by chance,
which would be absurd. 'Necessary' and 'free', not 'necessary' and 'for-
tuitous', are contrary terms. Granted that God's will is eternal, it still
does not follow that the world is eternal, for God could have determined from eternity to create the world at a set time.

You go on to deny that God's will has ever been indifferent, which I
dispute; nor is it as necessary as you think to pay such strict attention to
this point. Neither does everyone agree that God's will is necessary, for
this involves the concept of necessity. Now he who attributes will to
someone means thereby that he can either act or not, according to his
will; but if we ascribe necessity to him, he must act of necessity.

Finally, you say that you avoid granting any human attributes in
God lest you should confuse the divine nature with human nature. Thus
far I agree, for we do not apprehend in what way God acts, or in what
way he wills, understands, thinks, sees, hears, etc. However, if you completely deny of God these activities and our most sublime conceptions

of him, and you assert that these are not in God eminently and in a metaphysical sense, then I do not understand your God, or what you mean by the word 'God'. What we fail to apprehend ought not to be denied. Mind, which is spirit and incorporeal, can act only along with the most subtle bodies, namely, the humours. And what is the relation between body and mind? In what way does mind act along with bodies? For without these the mind is at rest, and when these are in a disordered state the mind does what it should not have done. Show me how this comes about. You cannot, and neither can I. Yet we see and sense that the mind does act, and this remains true in spite of our failure to perceive how this acting comes about. In the same way, although we do not understand how God acts and we refrain from ascribing to him human activities, yet we ought not to deny of him that, in an eminent way and beyond our comprehension, these activities are in accord with our own, such as willing, understanding, seeing and hearing with the intellect, though not with eyes or ears. Similarly, wind and air can destroy, and even overthrow, lands and mountains without the use of hands or other tools; yet this is impossible for men without the use of hands and machines. If you attribute necessity to God and deprive him of will and free choice, this raises some doubt as to whether you are not depicting and representing as a monster him who is an infinitely perfect being. To attain your purpose you will need other arguments to form a basis, for in my opinion those you have advanced have no solidity. And even if you can prove them, there are perhaps other arguments to counterbalance yours. But setting this aside, let us proceed.

To establish the existence of spirits in the world, you demand conclusive proofs. There are few of these in the world, and, apart from mathematics, none of these are as certain as we would wish. Indeed, we are satisfied with probable conjectures which are likely to be true. If the arguments by which things were proved were quite conclusive, only the foolish and the obstinate would be found to contradict them. But, my dear friend, we are not as fortunate as that. In this world we are less demanding; to some extent we rely on conjecture, and in our reasoning we accept the probable in default of demonstrative proof. This is evident from all the sciences, both human and divine, which abound in controversies and disputes whose prevalence is the reason why so many different opinions are everywhere to be found. That is why, as you know, there were once philosophers called Sceptics who doubted everything. They used to debate the case for and against so as to arrive at the merely probable in default of true reasons, and each of them believed what he thought more probable. The moon is situated directly below the sun, and therefore the sun will be obscured in some region of the earth, and if the sun is not obscured in daytime, then the moon is not situated directly below it. This is conclusive proof, reasoning from cause to effect and from effect to cause. There are some proofs of this sort, but very few, which cannot be contradicted by anyone if only he grasps them.

With regard to beauty, there are some things whose parts are in proportion with one another, and are better composed than others. God has bestowed on man's understanding and judgment a sense of agreeableness and harmony with that which is well-proportioned, and not with that which lacks proportion. This is the case with harmonious and discordant sounds, where our hearing can well distinguish between harmony and discord because the former brings pleasure and the latter annoyance. A thing's perfection is also beautiful, in so far as it lacks nothing. Of this there are many examples, which I omit to avoid prolixity. Let us only consider the world, to which we apply the term Whole or Universe. If this is true, as indeed is the case, the existence of incorporeal things does not spoil it or degrade it. Your remarks as to Centaurs, Hydras, Harpies, etc. are quite misplaced, for we are speaking of the most universal genera, of the prime grades of things, which comprehend under them various and innumerable species: we are speaking of the eternal and the temporal, cause and effect, finite and infinite, animate and inanimate, substance and accident[274] or mode, the corporeal and the spiritual, and so on.

I say that spirits are like God because he also is spirit. You demand as clear an idea of spirits as of a triangle, which is impossible. Tell me, I beg you, what idea you have of God, and whether it is as clear to your intellect as is the idea of a triangle. I know that you have none such, and I have said that we are not so fortunate as to be able to apprehend things by means of conclusive proofs, and that, for the most part, the probable holds sway in this world. Nevertheless, I affirm that just as body can exist without memory, etc., so can memory, etc. exist without body, and that just as a circle can exist without a sphere, so too can a sphere exist without a circle. But this is to descend from the most universal genera to particular species, which are not the object of this discussion.

---

274. The terminology is mediaeval. See our notes to Ep4.

I say that the Sun is the centre of the world, that the fixed stars are more distant from the earth than is Saturn, and Saturn than Jupiter, and Jupiter than Mars. So in the limitless air some bodies are more distant from us and some nearer to us, and these we term higher and lower.

It is not the upholders of the existence of spirits who discredit philosophers, but those who deny it; for all philosophers, both of ancient and modern times, think themselves convinced of the existence of spirits. Plutarch bears witness to this in his treatises on the opinions of philosophers and on the daemon of Socrates, and so do all the Stoics, Pythagoreans, Platonists, Peripatetics, Empedocles, Maximus Tyrius, Apuleius and others. Of modern philosophers not one denies spectres. Reject, then, the testimony of so many wise men who had eyes and ears, reject the narratives of so many philosophers, so many historians. Assert that they are all foolish and crazy like the common herd – and yet your answers are unconvincing, even absurd, and generally irrelevant to the main point at issue, and you fail to produce any proof to confirm your view. Caesar, along with Cicero and Cato, does not laugh at spectres, but at omens and presentiments. And yet, if he had not mocked at Spurina[275] on the day he was to die, he would not have suffered all those stab-wounds from his enemies. But let this suffice for the time, etc.

---

275. The story is related in Suetonius' *Caesar*, chapter 81.

LETTER 56
To the highly esteemed and judicious Hugo Boxel, from B.d.S.

[The original, written in Dutch, is lost. The O.P. gives
a Latin version, perhaps by Spinoza, and this has been
re-translated into Dutch in the Dutch edition.
Conjectural date, September 1674.]

Most esteemed Sir,

I hasten to reply to your letter received yesterday, for if I delay any
further I shall have to postpone my reply longer than I could wish. I
should have been anxious about your health, had I not learned that you
are better. I hope that you are by now completely recovered.

When two people follow different first principles, the difficulty they
experience in coming together and reaching agreement in a matter
involving many other questions might be shown simply from this discussion of ours, even if it were not confirmed by rational considerations. Tell me, pray, whether you have seen or read any philosophers
who have maintained that the world was made by chance, taking
chance in the sense you give it, that God had a set aim in creating the
world and yet departed from his resolve. I am unaware that any such
idea has ever entered the thoughts of any man. I am similarly at a loss
to understand the reasoning whereby you try to convince me that
chance and necessity are not contraries. As soon as I perceive that the
three angles of a triangle are necessarily equal to two right angles, I
also deny that this comes about by chance; likewise, as soon as I perceive that heat is the necessary effect of fire, I also deny that this happens by chance. That 'necessary' and 'free' are contraries seems no less
absurd and opposed to reason. Nobody can deny that God freely knows
himself and all other things, and yet all are unanimous in granting that
God knows himself necessarily. Thus you fail, I think, to make any distinction between constraint (*coactio*) or force, and necessity.[276] That a

---

276. Spinoza constantly inveighs against the confusion between external coercion and
internal necessity. The libertarian notion of a freedom of indifference makes freedom into random activity or caprice. Spinoza's efforts to reorient the concept of
liberty toward self-determination are studied by Jean Préposiet, *Spinoza et la
liberté des hommes* (Paris: Gallimard, 1967).

man wills to live, to love, etc., does not proceed from constraint, but is nevertheless necessary, and far more so is God's will to be, to know and to act. If, in addition to these points, you reflect that a state of indifference is nothing but ignorance or a condition of doubt, and that a will that is always constant and determined in all things is a virtue and a necessary property of the intellect, you will see that my view is in complete accord with the truth. If we maintain that God was able not to will what he willed, but that he was not able not to understand what he willed, we are attributing to God two different kinds of freedom, the freedom of necessity, and the freedom of indifference. Consequently, we shall conceive God's will as different from his essence and his intellect, and in this way we shall fall into one absurdity after another.

The attention which I requested in my former letter you have not deemed necessary, and it is for this reason that you have failed to direct your thoughts to the main point at issue, and have disregarded what was most relevant.

Further, when you say that you do not see what sort of God I have if I deny in him the actions of seeing, hearing, attending, willing, etc. and that he possesses those faculties in an eminent degree, I suspect that you believe there is no greater perfection than can be explicated by the aforementioned attributes. I am not surprised, for I believe that a triangle, if it could speak, would likewise say that God is eminently triangular, and a circle that God's nature is eminently circular. In this way each would ascribe to God its own attributes, assuming itself to be like God and regarding all else as ill-formed.

The briefness of a letter and the pressure of time do not permit me to deal with my view of the divine nature and with the questions you have propounded; anyway, to bring up difficulties is not to advance rational arguments. It is true that in this world we often act from conjecture, but it is not true that philosophical thinking proceeds from conjecture. In the common round of life we have to follow what is probable, but in speculative thought we have to follow what is true. A man would perish of hunger and thirst if he refused to eat and drink until he had obtained perfect proof that food and drink would be good for him, but this does not hold in the field of contemplation. On the contrary, we should take care not to admit as true anything that is merely probable. When one false proposition is allowed entry, innumerable others follow.

Again, because the sciences of things divine and human abound with quarrels and controversies, it cannot be concluded therefrom that the whole of the subject-matter with which they deal is uncertain.

There have been many whose zeal for controversy was such that they even scoffed at geometrical proof. Sextus Empiricus and other Sceptics whom you quote say that it is false that the whole is greater than its part, and they pass similar judgment on other axioms.

However, leaving aside and granting the fact that in default of proof we must be content with the probable, I say that a probable proof must be such that, although open to doubt, it cannot be contradicted; for that which can be contradicted is akin, not to truth, but to falsehood. If, for example, I say that Peter is alive because I saw him yesterday in good health, this is indeed probable in so far as nobody is able to contradict me. But if somebody else says that yesterday he saw Peter unconscious, and that he believes that since then Peter has died, he makes my statement seem false. That your conjecture regarding spectres and ghosts seems false and has not even a show of truth, I have demonstrated so clearly that I find nothing in your reply worthy of consideration.

To your question as to whether I have as clear an idea of God as of a triangle, I reply in the affirmative. But if you ask me whether I have as clear a mental image of God as of a triangle, I reply in the negative.[277] We cannot imagine God, but we can apprehend him by the intellect. Here it should also be observed that I do not claim to have complete knowledge of God, but that I do understand some of his attributes – not indeed all of them, or the greater part – and it is certain that my ignorance of very many attributes does not prevent me from having knowledge of some of them. When I was studying Euclid's *Elements*, I understood early on that the three angles of a triangle are equal to two right angles, and I clearly perceived this property of a triangle although I was ignorant of many others.

As regards spectres or ghosts, I have not as yet heard of any intelligible property of theirs; I have heard only of fantasies beyond anyone's understanding. In saying that spectres or ghosts here below (I follow your usage of words, though I do not know why matter here below should be inferior to matter above) are made of very tenuous, rarefied and subtle substance, you seem to be speaking of spiders' webs, air, or mist. To say that they are invisible is, in my view, tantamount to saying not what they are, but what they are not. But perhaps you wish to

---

277. See E2P47: "The human mind has an adequate knowledge of the eternal and infinite essence of God."

indicate that they render themselves visible or invisible as and when they please, and that our imagination will find no more difficulty in this than in other impossibilities.

The authority of Plato, Aristotle and Socrates[278] carries little weight with me. I should have been surprised if you had produced Epicurus, Democritus, Lucretius or one of the Atomists or defenders of the atoms.[279] It is not surprising that those who have thought up occult qualities, intentional species, substantial forms and a thousand more bits of nonsense[280] should have devised spectres and ghosts, and given credence to old wives' tales with view to disparaging the authority of Democritus, whose high reputation they so envied that they burned all the books which he had published amidst so much acclaim.[281] If you are minded to put your trust in such people, what reason have you to deny the miracles of the Holy Virgin and all the saints? These have been reported by so many renowned philosophers, theologians and historians that I could produce a hundred of these latter to scarcely one of the former.

In conclusions, most esteemed Sir, I find that I have gone further than I intended, and I will trouble you no longer with matters which I know you will not concede, your first principles being far different from my own, etc.

---

278. The inventory of Spinoza's library contains a Latin translation of the complete works of Aristotle, but nothing whatever by Plato.
279. Epicurus (341-271 B.C.), Democritus (460-370 B.C.), and Lucretius (99-55 B.C.) all supported the atomic theory, and were accordingly held in favour by seventeenth-century scientists.
280. The terms 'intentional species' and 'substantial forms' are mediaeval. They were widely criticized in the seventeenth century as involving an appeal to unknown and unknowable ("occult") qualities of things which explain nothing. This is the same accusation which the Cartesians (and Leibniz) were to make against Newton's theory of gravitation as a *vis insita*.
281. The story comes from Diogenes Laertes, *Lives of the Philosophers*.

LETTER 57
To the most distinguished and acute philosopher, B.d.S., from Ehrenfried Walther von Tschirnhaus

[Known only from the O.P. The original is lost. The
letter was addressed to Schuller, who transmitted
to Spinoza the part that concerned him.[282]]

Distinguished Sir,

It surprises me, to say the least, that when philosophers demonstrate
that something is false, at the same time they are showing its truth.
For Descartes, at the beginning of his Method,[283] thinks that the certainty of the intellect is equal for all, and in the *Meditations* he proves
it. The same line is taken by those who think that they can prove something to be certain on the grounds that it is accepted by separate individuals as being beyond doubt.

But setting this aside, I appeal to experience, and I humbly request
you to give careful consideration to the following. For thus it will be
found that if of two men one affirms something and the other denies it,
and they are fully conscious of what it is they are saying, although they
appear verbally to contradict each other, yet when we consider what is
in their minds they are both speaking the truth, each according to his
own thinking.[284] I bring up this point because it is of immeasurable
value in our common dealings, and if this single fact were taken into
account, innumerable controversies and the ensuing disputes would be
averted, even though this truth in conception is not always true in an
absolute sense, but is taken as true only on the basis of what is assumed
to be in a man's understanding. This rule is of such general application

---

282. As reported in our introduction, section 4, much of the Spinoza/Tschirnhaus
correspondence was conducted through Schuller as an intermediary.
283. The Dutch version has 'in the same paragraph' instead of 'at the beginning of his
Method'. The opening paragraphs of this letter have been obviously omitted, and
probably referred to specific passages in Descartes. The Dutch editors probably
made the change in the light of the omission.
284. This passage is treated by some commentators as obscure, but Tschirnhaus
seems to be making roughly the same point as Spinoza does in E2P47Schol:
"Dum sibi maxime contradicunt, vel eadem, vel diversa cogitant."

that it holds good in the case of all men, even those who are mad or are asleep. For whatever they say they see (although it may not appear so to us) or have seen, it is quite certain that this is really so.

This is also seen very clearly in the case under consideration, that of Free Will. For both he who argues for and he who argues against seem to me to speak the truth, according to how one conceives freedom. Descartes says that that is free which is not compelled by any cause, whereas you say that it is that which is not determined to something by any cause. I agree with you that in all things we are determined to something by a definite cause, and that thus we have no free will. But on the other hand I also agree with Descartes that in certain matters (as I shall soon make clear) we are not in any way compelled, and so have free will. The present question will furnish me with an example.

The problem is of a threefold nature.[285] First, do we have in an absolute sense a power over things which are external to us? This is denied. For example, that I am at this moment writing a letter is not something that is absolutely within my power, since I would certainly have written sooner had I not been prevented either by my being away or by the company of friends. Secondly, do we have in an absolute sense power over the movements of our bodies which follow when the will determines them thereto? I reply affirmatively with this reservation – if we are in good health; for if I am well, I can always set myself to write, or not. Thirdly, when I am in a position to exercise my reason, can I do so quite freely, that is, absolutely? I reply in the affirmative. For who would tell me, without gainsaying his own consciousness, that I can not in my thoughts think that I want to write or not to write? And

---

285. Here Tschirnhaus betrays his own Cartesianism. According to Descartes, the universe is divided into three types of substances: extension (matter), thought (mind), and that special union of the two, human beings. Thus Tschirnhaus uses three examples to illustrate the possible cases of freedom. First, there is physical causality in which all physical effects have physical causes; inasmuch as we are bodies, we are subject to external physical forces which limit our putative freedom to act as bodies. The second case he examines is the relation between pure mind and body; here he states that there is only partial freedom since the effects of the body do affect the ability of the mind to act freely with regard to the body. Finally, he examines whether the mind itself is free, and here he claims is where freedom lies since he believes that the mind is unconstrained by any forces external to it. For Spinoza, however, there is only one unique substance, not a multiplicity of three kinds, and the causal order in the physical universe is the same as that in the mental universe.

with regard to the act of writing, too, since external causes permit (and this concerns the second question) that I should possess the capacity both to write and not to write, I agree with you that there are causes which determine me to write just now – that you wrote to me in the first place and in that letter requested me to reply as soon as I could, and, with the present opportunity arising, I would not willingly let it pass. I also agree with Descartes, on the testimony of my conscious-ness, that things of that kind do not on that account constrain me, and that I can still (as seems impossible to deny) really refrain from writing, in spite of those considerations. And, again, if we were under the com-pulsion of external circumstances, who could possibly acquire the habit of virtue? Indeed, if this point were granted, all wickedness would be excusable. But does it not frequently come about that, being deter-mined to something by external things, we still resist this with a firm and steady mind?

To give a clearer explanation of the above rule, you are both telling the truth according to your own conception, but if we look to absolute truth, this belongs only to Descartes' view. For in your mind you are assuming as certain that the essence of freedom consists in our not being determined by any thing. On this assumption both sides are in the right. However, the essence of any thing consists in that without which it cannot even be conceived, and freedom can surely be clearly conceived, even though in our actions we are determined to something by external causes, or even though there are always causes which incite us to act in a certain way, but without being completely dominant. But freedom cannot be conceived at all on the assumption that we are under compulsion. See, in addition, Descartes, Volume 1, letters 8 and 9, and also Volume 2, page 4. But let this suffice. I beg you to reply to the difficulties here raised, and you will find me not only grateful, but also, health permitting,[286]

Your most devoted,
N.N.
8 October 1674.

---

286. The last phrase, beginning 'and you will find me . . . ', is found only in the Dutch edition.

LETTER 58
To the most learned and wise G. H. Schuller, from B.d.S.

[Known only from the O.P. The original is lost.]

Most wise Sir,

Our friend J.R.[287] has sent me the letter which you were kind enough to write to me, together with your friend's judgment of the views expressed by Descartes and myself on the question of free will, for which I am most grateful. Although I am at present fully occupied with other matters and my health is also causing me some concern, I feel impelled both by your exceptional courtesy and by your devotion to truth, which I particularly value, to satisfy your wish as far as my slender abilities allow. Indeed, I do not know what your friend means in the section preceding his appeal to experience and his request for careful attention. As to what he goes on to say, 'if one of two men affirms something of a thing and the other denies it' etc., this is true if he means that the two men, while using the same words, nevertheless have different things in mind. I once sent some examples of this to our friend J. R., and I am now writing to him to let you have them.

So I now pass on to that definition of freedom which he ascribes to me, but I do not know whence he has taken it, I say that that thing is free which exists and acts solely from the necessity of its own nature,[288] and I say that that thing is constrained (*coactus*) which is determined by something else to exist and to act in a fixed and determinate way.

---

287. Most likely this is Jan Rieuwertsz of Amsterdam, who was a bookseller and a publisher. His bookstore was a centre for liberal thinkers, and he published all Spinoza's works (though in secret except for the PPC). On Schuller see part 5 of our Introduction. For a detailed historical summary of the problems relating to understanding Schuller's relationship to Spinoza and to the publication of the O.P., see Piet Steenbakkers, *Spinoza's Ethica from manuscript to print* (Assen: Van Gorcum, 1994), 50-63.
288. The definition of 'freedom' is given in E1Def7, and E1P17 states that "God acts solely from the laws of his own nature, constrained by none." For more information on God's free but necessary nature, see Gary Finn, "The Order of Nature and the Nature of Order in the Philosophy of Spinoza," and Steven Barbone, "Putting Order in Order," in *North American Spinoza Society Monographs* 2 (1994); pp. 3-16 and 17-22 respectively.

For example, although God exists necessarily, he nevertheless exists freely because he exists solely from the necessity of his own nature. Similarly, too, God freely understands himself and all things absolutely, because it follows solely from the necessity of his own nature that he should understand all things. So you see that I place freedom, not in free decision, but in free necessity.

However, let us move down to created things, which are all determined by external causes to exist and to act in a fixed and determinate way. To understand this clearly, let us take a very simple example. A stone receives from the impulsion of an external cause a fixed quantity of motion whereby it will necessarily continue to move when the impulsion of the external cause has ceased. The stone's continuance in motion is constrained, not because it is necessary, but because it must be defined by the impulsion received from the external cause. What here applies to the stone must be understood of every individual thing, however complex its structure and various its functions. For every single thing is necessarily determined by an external cause to exist and to act in a fixed and determinate way.[289]

Furthermore, conceive, if you please, that while continuing in motion the stone thinks, and knows that it is endeavouring, as far as in it lies, to continue in motion. Now this stone, since it is conscious only of its endeavour[290] and is not at all indifferent, will surely think it is completely free, and that it continues in motion for no other reason than that it so wishes. This, then, is that human freedom which all men boast of possessing, and which consists solely in this, that men are conscious of their desire and unaware of the causes by which they are determined. In the same way a baby thinks that it freely desires milk, an angry child revenge, and a coward flight. Again, a drunken man believes that it is from his free decision that he says what he later, when sober, would wish to be left unsaid. So, too, the delirious, the loquacious, and many others of this kind believe that they act from

---

289. See E1P28, which asserts that the chain of causes is infinite.
290. Here 'endeavour' is *conatus*, which is introduced beginning at E3P6 and plays a major role not just in Spinoza's psychology but also in the account of virtue central to his moral philosophy. See Lee Rice, "Emotion, Appetition, and Conatus in Spinoza," *Revue Internationale de Philosophie* 31 (1977), 101-116. In E3P9Schol Spinoza defines desire as conscious appetite. Some commentators see the doctrine as anticipatory of Freud's theory of innate drives. See Stuart Hampshire, *Spinoza* (Baltimore: Penguin Books, 951), esp. 141-144.

their free decision, and not that they are carried away by impulse. Since this preconception is innate in all men, they cannot so easily be rid of it. For although experience teaches us again and again that nothing is less within men's power than to control their appetites, and that frequently, when subject to conflicting emotions, they see the better course and pursue the worse,[291] they nevertheless believe themselves to be free, a belief that stems from the fact that in some cases our desire has no great force and can easily be checked by the recurrence to mind of some other thing which is frequently in our thoughts.

I have now, if I am not mistaken, sufficiently set forth my views on free and constrained necessity and on imaginary human freedom, and with this your friend's objections are readily answered. For when he says, along with Descartes,[292] that the free man is he who is not constrained by any external cause, if by constrained he means acting against one's will, I agree that in some cases we are in no way constrained and that in this sense we have free will. But if by constrained he means acting necessarily, though not against one's will, I deny that in any instance we are free, as I have explained above.

But your friend, on the contrary asserts that 'we can employ our rational faculty in complete freedom, that is, absolutely', in which assertion he is somewhat overconfident. 'For who', he says, 'would deny, without gainsaying his own consciousness, that with my thoughts I can think that I want to write, or do not want to write?' I should very much like to know what consciousness he is talking about, apart from that which I illustrated above with the example of the stone. For my part, not to gainsay my own consciousness – that is, reason and experience – and not to cherish prejudice and ignorance, I deny that, by any absolute power of thought, I can think that I want, or do not want, to write. But I appeal to the consciousness of the man himself, who has doubtless experienced in dreams that he has not the power to think that he wants, or does not want, to write, and that, when he dreams that he wants to write, he does not have the power not to dream that

---

291. Viz., "meliora videant et deteriora sequantur." Spinoza uses this expression elsewhere; see E3P2schol. It is original to Spinoza in this form, but is found in Ovid, (*Metamorphoses*, VII, 20) in another form: "*Video meliora proboque, deteriora sequor*" (I see and approve the better, but I follow the worse). Cf. Paul's Epistle to the Romans, 7:15-19.
292. A more extended critique of Descartes' account of freedom is given in E1P33Schol2.

he wants to write. I think that he must likewise have experienced that the mind is not at all times equally fitted to thinking of the same object, but that just as the body is more fitted to have the image of this or that object aroused in it, so the mind is more apt to regard this or that object.

When he further adds that the causes of his resolving to write have indeed urged him to write, but have not constrained him, if you will weigh the matter impartially he means no more than this, that his mind was at the time in such a state that causes which might not have swayed him at other times – as when he is assailed by some strong emotion – were at this time easily able to sway him. That is, causes which might not have constrained him at other times did in fact constrain him then, not to write against his will, but necessarily to want to write.

When he goes on to say that 'if we were constrained by external causes, nobody could acquire the habit of virtue', I do not know who has told him that we cannot be of strong and constant mind from the necessity of fate, but only from free will.

As to his final remark, that 'on this basis all wickedness would be excusable', what of it? Wicked men are no less to be feared and no less dangerous when they are necessarily wicked. But on this point please see my Appendix to Books 1 and 2 of *Principia Cartesiana* demonstrated in geometric form, Part II, Chapter 8.[293]

Lastly, I should like your friend who raises these objections to tell me how he reconciles the human virtue that springs from free decision with God's pre-ordainment. If he admits with Descartes that he does not know how to effect this reconciliation, then he is trying to hurl against me the weapon by which he himself is already transfixed. But to no purpose. If you will examine my view attentively, you will see that it is quite consistent.

The Hague.
[October 1674].

---

293. The appendix to the PPC is entitled *Cogitata Metaphysica* (CM). CM2.8 is entitled, "Of the Will of God."

LETTER 59
To the most distinguished and acute philosopher, B.d.S., from Ehrenfried Walther von Tschirnhaus

[Known only from the O.P. The original is lost.]

Most distinguished Sir,

When shall we have your Method of rightly directing the reason in acquiring knowledge of unknown truths, and also your General Treatise on Physics? I know that you have but recently made great advances in these subjects. I have already been made aware of the former, and the latter is known to me from the lemmata attached to the second part of your *Ethics*,[294] which provide a ready solution to many problems in physics. If time and opportunity permit, I humbly beg you to let me have the true definition of motion, together with its explanation. And since extension when conceived through itself is indivisible, immutable, etc., how can we deduce a priori the many and various forms that it can assume, and consequently the existence of figure in the particles of a body, which yet are various in any body and are different from the figures of the parts which constitute the form of another body?

In our conversation you pointed out to me the method you adopt in seeking out truths as yet unknown. I find this method to be of surpassing excellence, and yet quite simple, as far as I understand it; and I can say that by following this single procedure I have made considerable advances in mathematics. I would therefore like to have from you the true definition of an adequate, a true, a false, a fictitious and a doubtful idea. I have sought the difference between a true and an adequate idea, but as yet I have not been able to discover anything but this: on investigating a thing and a definite concept or idea, then (in order further to discover whether this true idea was also the adequate idea of some

---

294. These are the axioms, lemmata, and definitions following E2P13, which deal with the principle of individuation as Spinoza conceives it and also offer a basic outline of Spinoza's physics. See Lee Rice, "Spinoza on Individuation," in *Spinoza: Essays in Interpretation*, ed. M. Mandelbaum and E. Freeman (La Salle: Open Court, 1975), 195-214; and André Lécrivain, "Spinoza et la physique cartésienne," *Cahiers Spinoza* 1 (1977), 235-266, and 2 (1978), 93-206.

thing) I asked myself what was the cause of this idea or concept. On discovering this, I again asked what was the cause of this further concept, and thus I continued enquiring into the causes of the causes of ideas until I could come upon a cause for which I could not again see any other cause than this, that out of all possible ideas which I had at my command, this one alone also positively existed. If, for example, we ask wherein consists the true source of our errors, Descartes will reply that it consists in our giving assent to things not yet clearly perceived. But although this be a true idea of the matter in question, I shall still be unable to determine all that it is necessary to know on this subject unless I also possess an adequate idea of this matter. To acquire this I again ask what is the cause of this concept – that is, why we give assent to things not clearly understood, and I reply that this comes about through our lack of knowledge. But at this point we cannot raise the further question as to what is the cause of our not knowing some things, and therefore I realise that I have discovered the adequate idea of our errors.

Here, incidentally, let me put this question to you. Since it is established that many things expressed in an infinite number of ways have an adequate idea of themselves, and that from any adequate idea all that can possibly be known of the thing can be inferred, though they can be more easily elicited from one idea than from another, is there any means of knowing which idea should be utilised in preference to another? For example, an adequate idea of a circle consists in the quality of its radii, but it also consists in the equality with one another of an infinite number of rectangles constructed from the segments of intersecting chords. One could go on and say that the adequate idea of a circle can be expressed in an infinite number of ways, each of which explicates the adequate nature of a circle. And although from each of these everything else knowable about a circle can be deduced, this comes about more easily from one idea than from another. So, too, one who considers the applicates of curves[295] will make many inferences

---

295. The method of exhaustion was the oldest method for measuring the area under a curve by evaluating the perimeter of polygons tangential to the curve as their sides increased until a limit was reached. The method of applicates (or ordinates) involved drawing lines at right angles across the curves so as to be bisected by their diameters. The method of exhaustion led to the integral calculus (developed by Leibniz and Newton), whereas that of applicates developed into co-ordinate geometry.

concerning the measurements of curves, but this will be done more effectively if we consider tangents, etc.

In this way I have tried to give some indication of the progress I have made in this study. I await its completion, or if I am anywhere in error, its correction, and also the definition I have asked for. Farewell.

5 January 1675.

LETTER 60
To the noble and learned Ehrenfried Walther von Tschirnhaus, from B.d.S.

[Known only from the O.P. The original is lost.]

Most noble Sir,

Between a true and an adequate idea I recognise no difference but this, that the word 'true' has regard only to the agreement of the idea with its object (*ideatum*), whereas the word 'adequate' has regard to the nature of the idea in itself.[296] Thus there is no real difference between a true and an adequate idea except for this extrinsic relation.

Next, in order that I may know which out of many ideas of a thing will enable all the properties of the object to be deduced, I follow this one rule, that the idea or definition of the thing should express its efficient cause.[297] For example, in order to investigate the properties of a circle, I ask whether from the following idea of a circle, namely, that it consists in an infinite number of rectangles, I can deduce all its properties; that is to say, I ask whether this idea involves the efficient cause of a circle. Since this is not so, I look for another cause, namely, that a circle is the space described by a line of which one point is fixed and the other moveable. Since this definition now expresses the efficient cause, I know that I can deduce from it all the properties of a circle, etc. So, too, when I define God as a supremely perfect Being,[298] since this definition does not express the efficient cause (for I take it that an efficient cause can be internal as well as external), I shall not be able to extract therefrom all the properties of God, as I can do when I define God as a Being, etc. (see *Ethics*, Part 1, Definition 6).[299]

---

296. See E2Def4.
297. From an axiomatic perspective, this claim amounts to the requirement that all definitions be constructive. Spinoza's understanding of geometrical construction follows closely that of Thomas Hobbes. See Martial Gueroult, *Spinoza: Dieu* (*Ethique, 1*) (Paris: Aubier-Montaigne, 1968), esp. 19-48.
298. Spinoza here gives his own reasons for rejecting this definition, used by Descartes (see the third Meditation). For Spinoza, the definition of a thing is that from which all the properties of that thing can be deduced. Cf. E1P8Schol2.
299. E1Def6: "By God I mean an absolutely infinite being; that is, substance consisting of infinite attributes, each of which expresses eternal and infinite essence." See Martial Gueroult, *Spinoza: Dieu* (*Ethique, 1*), 67-75.

As for your other questions, namely, concerning motion, and those which concern method, since my views on these are not yet written out in due order, I reserve them for another occasion.

As to your remarks that he who considers the applicates of curves[300] will make many deductions regarding the measurement of curves, but will find this easier by considering tangents, etc., I think, on the contrary, that the consideration of tangents will make it more difficult to deduce the many other properties than the consideration of a succession of applicates; and I assert absolutely that from certain properties of a thing (whatever be the given idea) some things can be discovered more easily and others with greater difficulty – though they all concern the nature of that thing. But this one point I consider should be kept in mind, that one must seek such an idea that everything can be elicited therefrom, as I have said above. For if one is to deduce from some thing all that is possible, it necessarily follows that the last will prove more difficult than the earlier, etc.

The Hague.
[January 1675].

---

300. See note 295 to Ep59 on the method of applicates.

LETTER 61
To the esteemed B.d.S., from Henry Oldenburg

[Known only from the O.P. The original is
lost. The date, wrongly given in the Latin,
is correctly given in the Dutch edition.]

With hearty greetings.

As the learned Mr. Bourgeois, Doctor of Medicine of Caen and an
adherent of the reformed religion, is about to leave for Holland, I cannot let pass this convenient opportunity of letting you know that some
weeks ago I expressed my gratitude to you for the Treatise you sent me
(though it was never delivered), but that I have some doubt as to
whether my letter duly reached you.[301] In that letter I indicated my
opinion of the Treatise. This opinion, anyway, now that I have given
more proper attention and thought to the matter, I have come to consider far too premature. At the time some things seemed to me to
tend to the endangerment of religion, when I was assessing it by the
standard set by the common run of theologians and the accepted for-
mulae of the Creeds (which seem to me far too influenced by partisan
bias). But on reconsidering the whole matter more closely, I find much
that convinces me that, so far from intending any harm to true religion
and sound philosophy, on the contrary you are endeavouring to commend and establish the true purpose of the Christian religion, together
with the divine sublimity and excellence of a fruitful philosophy. So
since I now believe this to be your set intention, I most earnestly beg
you to be good enough to explain what you are now preparing and have
in mind to this end, writing regularly to your old and sincere friend who
wholeheartedly longs for a most successful outcome for such a divine
undertaking. I promise on my sacred oath that I will divulge nothing of
this to any mortal, if you enjoin silence on me, and that I will strive only
for this, gradually to prepare the minds of good and wise men to
embrace those truths which you will one day bring forth into the

---

301. There is no trace of this letter, presumably written in 1670 following the publication of the TTP.

broader light of day, and to dispel the prejudices which have been conceived against your thoughts.

If I am not mistaken, I think you have a very profound insight into
the nature and powers of the human mind, and its union with the body.
I earnestly beg you to let me have your thoughts on this subject.
Farewell, distinguished Sir, and continue to think well of the most
devoted admirer of your teaching and your virtue, Henry Oldenburg.

London, 8 June 1675.

LETTER 62
To the esteemed B.d.S., from Henry Oldenburg

[Known only from the O.P. The original is lost.]

Now that our epistolary intercourse has been so happily resumed, most esteemed Sir, I would not want to fail in the duty of a friend by any interruption in our correspondence. Since I understand from your reply dated 5 July[302] that it is your intention to publish the five-part Treatise of yours,[303] please allow me, out of your genuine affection for me, to advise you not to include in it anything that may seem in any way to undermine the practise of religious virtue. This I strongly urge because there is nothing our degenerate and wicked age looks for more eagerly than the kind of doctrines whose conclusions may appear to give encouragement to prevalent vices.[304]

For the rest, I shall not decline to receive some copies of the said Treatise. I would only ask this of you, that in due course they should be addressed to a certain Dutch merchant staying in London, who will then have them sent to me. There would be no need to mention the fact that the particular books have been forwarded to me; for, provided that they reach me safely, I have no doubt that I shall easily arrange to distribute them among my various friends, and to obtain a fair price for them. Farewell, and when you have time, write back to,

Your most devoted,
Henry Oldenburg.

London, 22 July 1675.

---

302. This letter is unknown.
303. In Ep28 (1665, to Bouwmeester), Spinoza's plans appear to have been to divide the *Ethics* into three parts. By 1675 its division was the fivefold one in which it was finally published after his death.
304. For the historical reasons for Oldenburg's adopting of a more cautious and perhaps even fearful attitude than that expressed in his earlier letters, see our Introduction, section 2.

LETTER 63
To the distinguished and acute philosopher
B.d.S., from G.H. Schuller

[The original is extant. The O.P. text is somewhat
abridged. The translation is taken from the original.]

Most noble and distinguished Sir,

I should blush for my long spell of silence which has exposed me to the
charge of ingratitude for the favour which, of your kindness, you have
extended to my undeserving self, if I did not reflect that your generous
courtesy inclines to excuse rather than accuse, and if I did not know
that, for the common good of your friends, you are engaged in important studies such that it would be culpable and wrong to disturb without
good cause. For this reason I have kept silent, being content meanwhile
to learn from friends of your good health. But the purpose of this letter
is to inform you that our noble friend Mr. von Tschirnhausen,[305] who is
in England and still, like us, enjoying good health, has three times in his
letters to me bidden me to convey to you, Sir, his dutiful regards and
respectful greetings. He repeatedly asks me to put before you the following difficulties, and at the same time to ask for the reply he seeks
from you.

Would you, Sir, please convince him by a positive proof,[306] and not
by *reductio ad absurdum*, that we cannot know any more attributes of
God than thought and extension? Further, does it follow from this that
creatures constituted by other attributes cannot on their side have any
idea of extension? If so, it would seem that there must be constituted
as many worlds as there are attributes of God.[307] For example, our

---

305. For information concerning Tschirnhaus, see our Introduction, section 5.
306. Note printed in the O.P.: "I earnestly beg you please to solve the problems here
    raised, and to send me your reply."
307. A common misinterpretation of Spinoza is to see each attribute as constituting a
    distinct world or substance, and this view has its historic roots in these remarks by
    Tschirnhaus. Part of the difficulty, however, lies in the incompleteness of
    Spinoza's own explanation of the nature of the attributes, and perhaps more has
    been written on this aspect of his metaphysics than on any other. It is common to
    distinguish a 'subjective' from an 'objective' interpretation of the attributes. For
    more details see Jacob Adler, "Divine Attributes in Spinoza: Intrinsic and Rela-
    tional," *Philosophy & Theology* 4 (1989), 33-52; Virgil Aldrich, "Categories and
    Spinoza's Attributes," *Pacific Philosophical Quarterly* 61 (1980), 156-166;

world of extension, to call it so, is of a certain size; there would exist worlds of that same size constituted by different attributes. And just as we perceive, apart from thought, only extension, so the creatures of those worlds must perceive nothing but their own world's attribute, and thought.

Secondly, since God's intellect differs from our intellect both in essence and existence, it will therefore have nothing in common with our intellect, and therefore (Book 1, Proposition 3)[308] God's intellect cannot be the cause of our intellect.

Thirdly, in the Scholium to Proposition 10[309] you say that nothing in Nature is clearer than that each entity must be conceived under some attribute (which I understand very well), and that the more reality or being it has, the more attributes appertain to it. It would seem to follow from this that there are entities which have three, four, or more attributes, whereas from what has been demonstrated it could be inferred that each entity consists of only two attributes, namely, a certain attribute of God and the idea of that attribute.

Fourthly, I should like to have examples of those things immediately produced by God, and of those things produced by the mediation

---

Jonathan Bennett, "Spinoza's Mind-Body Identity Thesis," *Journal of Philosophy* 78 (1981), 573-584; Carroll R. Bowman, "Spinoza's Doctrine of Attributes," *Southern Journal of Philosophy* 5 (1967), 59-71; Victor Delbos, "La doctrine spinoziste des attributs de Dieu," *L'Année Philosophique* 23 (1913), 1-17; Alan Donagan, "Essence and the Distinction of Attributes in Spinoza's Metaphysics," in *Spinoza*, ed. Marjorie Grene (Garden City: Doubleday, 1973), 164-181; Paul Eisenberg, "On the Attributes and Their Alleged Independence of One Another," in *Spinoza: Issues and Directions*, ed. Edwin Curley and Pierre-François Moreau (Leiden: E. J. Brill, 1990), 1-15; Charles E. Jarrett, "Some Remarks on the 'Objective' and 'Subjective' Interpretation of the Attributes," *Inquiry* 20 (1977), 447-456; Thomas C. Mark, "The Spinozistic Attributes," *Philosophia* 7 (1977), 55-82; Stanley A. Martens, "Spinoza on Attributes," *Synthese* 37 (1978), 107-111; Timothy L. Sprigge, "Spinoza's Identity Theory," *Inquiry* 20 (1977), 419-445; and A. Wolf, "Spinoza's Conception of the Attributes of Substance," in *Studies in Spinoza*, ed. Paul Kashap (Berkeley: University of California Press, 1972), 16-27.

308. In its final form E1P3 says only that two substances having different attributes have nothing in common. E1P17Schol deals with the predication of 'intellect' to both finite modes and to God.

309. E1P10schol. The proposition asserts that each attribute must be conceived through itself.

of some infinite modification. It seems to me that thought and extension are of the first kind, and of the latter kind, intellect in thought and motion in extension, etc.[310]

These are the questions, distinguished Sir, which our aforementioned Tschirnhausen joins with me in asking you to elucidate, if it should be that you have time to spare. He further relates that Mr. Boyle[311] and Oldenburg[312] had formed a very strange idea[313] of your character. He has not only dispelled this, but has furthermore given them reasons that have induced them to return to a most worthy and favourable opinion of you, and also to hold in high esteem the *Tractatus Theologico-Politicus*. In view of your directions,[314] I did not venture to inform you of this.

Be assured that I am in all things at your service, and that I am, most noble Sir,

       Your most devoted servant,
       G.H. Schuller.

Amsterdam, 25 July 1675.

Mr. A. Gent[315] and J. Rieuw.[316] send their dutiful greetings.

---

310. Note printed in the O.P.: "The face of the whole of Nature, which, although varying in infinite ways, always remains the same. See Part 2, Proposition 13, Scholium."
311. Consult the notes to Ep5 and Ep6 for information about Boyle.
312. Concerning Oldenburg, see our Introduction, section 2.
313. Given the conservative religious nature of these two men, it is hardly surprising that they should form some unflattering ideas about the author of the TTP. More surprising is that Tschirnhaus was able to dissuade them of it. We conjecture that it was through Tschirnhaus' intervention at this point that the Oldenburg-Spinoza correspondence was renewed.
314. Had Spinoza requested that Schuller and Tschirnhaus not speak about him or his works? This is also suggested in Ep70 and Ep72.
315. We are unable to identify this man.
316. Jan Rieuwertsz. See our note above to Ep58 for more information.

LETTER 64
To the learned and experienced G.H. Schuller, from B.d.S.

[Known only from the O.P. The original is lost.]

Most experienced Sir,

I am glad that you have at last found opportunity to favour me with one of your letters, always most welcome to me. I earnestly beg you to do so regularly. . . , etc.

And now to the questions you raise. To the first I say that the human mind can acquire knowledge only of those things which the idea of an actually existing body involves, or what can be inferred from this idea. For the power of any thing is defined solely by its essence (Prop. 7, Part III, *Ethics*),[317] and the essence of mind consists (Prop. 13, II)[318] solely in its being the idea of an actually existing body. Therefore the mind's power of understanding extends only as far as that which this idea of the body contains within itself, or which follows therefrom. Now this idea of the body involves and expresses no other attributes of God than extension and thought. For its ideate (*ideatum*), to wit, the body (Prop. 6, II) has God for its cause in so far as he is considered under the attribute of extension, and not under any other attribute. So (Ax. 6, I)[319] this idea of the body involves knowledge of God only in so far as he is considered under the attribute of extension. Again, this idea, in so far as it is a mode of thinking, also has God for its cause (same Prop.) in so far as he is a thinking thing, and not in so far as he is considered under any other attribute. Therefore (same Axiom) the idea of this idea involves knowledge of God in so far as he is considered under the attribute of thought, and not under any other attribute. It is thus clear that the human mind – i.e., the idea of the human body – involves and expresses no other attributes of God except these two. Now (by Prop. 10, II),[320] no other attribute[321] of God can be inferred or conceived

---

317. E3P7: "The conatus with which each thing endeavours to persist in its own being is nothing but the actual essence of the thing itself."
318. E2P13: "The object of the idea constituting the human mind is the body – i.e., a definite mode of extension actually existing, and nothing else."
319. E1Ax6: "A true idea must agree with its ideate."
320. E2P10: "The being of substance does not pertain to the essence of man; i.e., substance does not constitute the form of man."
321. Spinoza speaks in the opening definitions and propositions of E1 of an "infinity

from these two attributes, or from their affections. So I conclude that the human mind can attain knowledge of no other attribute of God than these two, which was the point at issue. With regard to your further question as to whether there must therefore be constituted as many worlds as there are attributes, I refer you to the Scholium on Prop. 7, II of the *Ethics*.[322]

Moreover, this proposition could be more easily demonstrated by *reductio ad absurdum*, a style of proof I usually prefer to the other in the case of a negative proposition, as being more appropriate to the character of such propositions. But you ask for a positive proof only, and so I pass on to the second question, which asks whether, when both their essence and existence are different, one thing can be produced from another, seeing that things that differ thus from one another appear to have nothing in common. I reply that since all particular things, except those that are produced by like things, differ from their causes both in essence and existence, I see no difficulty here. As to the sense in which I understand God to be the efficient cause of both the essence and existence of things, I think I have made this quite clear in the Scholium and Corollary to Prop. 25, I of the *Ethics*.[323]

The axiom in the Scholium to Prop. 10, I, as I have indicated towards the end of the said Scholium, derives from the idea we have of an absolutely infinite Entity, and not from the fact that there are, or may be, entities having three, four, or more attributes.[324]

Lastly, the examples you ask for of the first kind are: in the case of thought, absolutely infinite intellect; in the case of extension, motion and rest. An example of the second kind is the face of the whole universe, which, although varying in infinite ways, yet remains always the same. See Scholium to Lemma 7 preceding Prop. 14, II.[325]

---

of infinite attributes." Though he cannot speak of the *number* of attributes as infinite, this is because his concept of number is finitary. E1P9 clearly requires that the attributes be infinite in number in the modern (transfinite) sense of this term.

322. E2P7 is the famous proposition expressing the parallelism: "The order and connection of ideas is the same as the order and connection of things."

323. E1P25 states that God is efficient cause both of the existence and the essence of things.

324. E1P10Schol in fact denies Tschirnhaus' interpretation of an infinity of attributes as constitutive of an infinity of entities.

325. In E2P13Schol, Spinoza does not use the expression, 'face of the entire universe', but speaks of conceiving the whole of nature as one infinite individual whose parts vary in infinite ways without any change in nature itself. Motion-and-rest and infinite intellect are called immediate infinite modes (of extension and thought respectively), but it is curious that Spinoza gives an example only for

Thus, most excellent Sir, I think I have answered your objections and those of our friend. If you think there still remains any difficulty, I hope you will not hesitate to tell me, so that I may remove it if I can. Farewell, etc.

The Hague, 29 July, 1675.

---

extension of an infinite mediate mode. Jean-Marie Beyssade, commenting on this letter, conjectures that the infinite mediate mode of thought is in fact the infinite love of God given in E5P36. See his "Sur le mode infini médiat dans l'attribut de la pensée," *Revue Philosophique de la France et de l'Etranger* 1994#1, 23-26.

LETTER 65
To the acute and learned philosopher B.d.S., from Ehrenfried Walther von Tschirnhaus

[Known only from the O.P. The original is lost.]

Most esteemed Sir,

Will you please let me have a proof of your assertion that the soul cannot perceive any more attributes of God than extension and thought. Although I can understand this quite clearly, yet I think that the contrary can be deduced from the Scholium to Prop. 7, Part II of the *Ethics*, perhaps only because I do not sufficiently perceive the correct meaning of this Scholium. I have therefore resolved to explain how I come to this conclusion, earnestly begging you, esteemed Sir, to come to my aid with your customary courtesy wherever I do not rightly follow your meaning.

My position is as follows. Although I do indeed gather from your text that the world is one, it is also no less clear therefrom that the world is expressed in infinite modes, and that therefore each single thing is expressed in infinite modes. Hence it seems to follow that, although the particular modification which constitutes my mind and the particular modification which expresses my body are one and the same modification, this is expressed in infinite modes – in one mode through thought, in another through extension, in a third through some attribute of God unknown to me, and so on to infinity. For there are infinite attributes of God, and the order and connection of their modifications seems to be the same in all cases. Hence there now arises the question as to why the mind, which represents a particular modification – which same modification is expressed not only by extension but by infinite other modes – why, I ask, does the mind perceive only the particular modification expressed through extension, that is, the human body, and not any other expression through other attributes?

But time does not permit me to pursue this subject any further. Perhaps these difficulties will all be removed by continued reflection.

London, 12 August 1675.

LETTER 66
To the noble and learned Ehrenfried Walther von Tschirnhaus, from B.d.S.

[Known only from the O.P. The original is lost.]

Most noble Sir,

. . . However, in reply to your objection, I say that although each thing is expressed in infinite modes in the infinite intellect of God, the infinite ideas in which it is expressed cannot constitute one and the same mind of a particular thing, but an infinity of minds. For each of these infinite ideas has no connection with the others, as I have explained in that same Scholium to Proposition 7, Part II of the *Ethics*,[326] and as is evident from Prop. 10, Part I.[327] If you will give a little attention to these, you will see that no difficulty remains, etc.

The Hague, 18 August 1675.

---

326. The brevity of Spinoza's answer to Tschirnhaus ignores the fact that Spinoza himself writes, at the end of E2P7Schol, "For the present, I cannot give a clearer explanation." Errol Harris [*Salvation from Despair* (The Hague: Nijhoff, 1973), pp. 70-71] uses this brief letter as a central support for his idealistic reading of Spinoza. Harris' reading is criticized by James Thomas, "Spinoza's Letter 66 and Its Idealistic Reading," *Idealistic Studies* 24 (1994), 191-196. The proposition cited by Spinoza in reference to Tschirnhaus' question (E2P7) makes no mention of the *ideae idearum* or 'infinity of minds', so the sense of Spinoza's reply is somewhat baffling. For more details, see also Errol Harris, "Infinity of Attributes and *Idea Ideae*," *Neue Hefte für Philosophie* 12 (1977), 9-20; and Lee C. Rice, "Reflexive Ideas in Spinoza," *Journal of the History of Philosophy* 28 (1990), 201-211. Rice supports a non-idealistic reading.
327. E1P10: "Each attribute of substance must be conceived through itself."

LETTER 67
To the learned and acute B.d.S., from Alfred Burgh

[Known only from the O.P. The original is lost.]

Many greetings.

On leaving my country[328] I promised to write to you, should anything worthy of note occur during my journey. Since such an occasion has now arisen, and one of the greatest importance, I am discharging my debt. I have to tell you that, through God's infinite mercy, I have been brought back to the Catholic Church and have been made a member thereof. As to how this came about, you will be able to learn in more detail from the letter I have sent to the illustrious and wise Mr. Craenen, Professor at Leiden. I will here add these few remarks which have regard to your own good.

The more I have admired you in the past for the penetration and acuity of your mind, the more do I now moan and lament for you. For although you are a man of outstanding talent, with a mind on which God has bestowed splendid gifts, a lover of truth and indeed a most eager one, yet you allow yourself to be entrapped and deceived by that most wretched and arrogant Prince of evil spirits. For what does all your philosophy amount to, except sheer illusion and chimera? Yet you entrust to it not only your peace of mind in this life, but the eternal salvation of your soul. See on what a poor foundation is grounded all that is yours. You claim to have finally discovered the true philosophy. How do you know that your philosophy is the best out of all those that have ever been taught in this world, are at present being taught, or will ever be taught in the future? To say nothing of possible future philosophies, have you examined all those philosophies, throughout the entire world? And even if you have examined them properly, how do you know that you have chosen the best? You will say, my philosophy is in agreement with right reason, while the rest are opposed to it. But all other philosophers except for your followers disagree with you, and with the same right they claim for themselves and their philosophy exactly what you

---

328. On Burgh see section 7 of our Introduction, and Meinsma, 451-458 and 475-478.

claim for yours, and accuse you of falsity and error just as you do them. It is therefore clear that, to make manifest the truth of your philosophy, you have to propound arguments which are not shared by other philosophies but are peculiar to your own; otherwise it must be admitted that your philosophy is as unsure and as futile as all the others.

However, I shall now confine myself to your book, to which you have given that impious title, and in this I shall make no distinction between your philosophy and your theology since you yourself do in fact confuse one with the other, though with diabolical cunning you pretend to claim that they are distinct from one another and that they have different principles. I proceed as follows.

Perhaps you will say, others have not read Holy Scripture as many times as I, and it is from Holy Scripture itself, the recognition of whose authority constitutes the difference between Christians and other peoples of the whole world, that I prove my case. But how? I explain Holy Scripture, you say, by placing the clear passages side by side with the more obscure, and by this method of interpretation I reach my conclusions, or confirm those that are already formed in my brain. I beseech you to think carefully what you are saying. For how do you know that you are making correct use of that comparison, and again, that the comparison even when properly made suffices to interpret Holy Scripture and thus allows you to make a correct interpretation of Holy Scripture? Especially since Catholics say – and this is very true – that the entire Word of God was not committed to writing, and thus Holy Scripture cannot be explained through Holy Scripture alone, I will not say by one man, but even by the Church itself, which is the sole interpreter of Holy Scripture. For the Apostolic traditions, too, must be taken into account, as is proved from Holy Scripture itself and the testimony of the Holy Fathers, and as is also in accord both with right reason and with experience. Now since the principle you adopt is utterly false, leading to perdition, where stands all your teaching, based and built as it is on this false foundation?

So then, if you believe in Christ crucified, acknowledge your most evil heresy, regain your senses after this distortion of your true nature, and be reconciled with the Church.

In what way does the method you use to prove your teachings differ from that which all heretics who have ever left the Church of God, are now leaving it, or will ever leave it, have used, are using, or will use? For, like you, they all adopt the same principle, that is, they rely on Holy Scripture alone to form and lend weight to their doctrines.

Do not be beguiled because maybe the Calvinists or so-called Reformers, or the Lutherans or the Mennonites or the Socinians, etc., cannot refute your doctrine. For these, as I have said, are in the same hapless plight as you, and sit under the shadow of death.

But if you do not believe in Christ, you are more wretched than I can say. Yet there is an easy remedy; turn away from your sins, try to realise the deadly arrogance of your wretched, insane way of reasoning. You do not believe in Christ; why is this? You will say, because the teaching and life of Christ does not agree with my principles, and the teaching of Christians about Christ does not agree with my teaching. But again I say, do you then dare to think yourself greater than all those who have ever arisen in the State or the Church of God, the patriarchs, prophets, apostles, martyrs, doctors, confessors and virgins, the countless saints, and even, blasphemously, our Lord Jesus Christ himself? Do you alone surpass them in doctrine, in manner of life, and in all else? Will you, a sorry little creature, a vile little worm of the earth, nay, mere ashes and food for worms, in your unspeakable blasphemy claim pre-eminence over the Incarnate Infinite Wisdom of the Eternal Father? Will you alone think yourself wiser and greater than all who have ever been in the Church of God from the beginning of the world, and have believed, or even now believe, in the Christ to come, or in the Christ who has already come? On what foundation rests this arrogance of yours, so rash, so mad, to be deplored and execrated?

You deny that Christ is the son of the living God, the Word of the Father's eternal wisdom, made manifest in the flesh, and that he suffered and was crucified for mankind. Why? Because all this is not in harmony with your principles. But apart from the fact that it is now proved that your principles are not true, but false, rash, and absurd, I now say further that even if you relied on true principles and built all your philosophy on them, you could not any the more explain through them all those things that are in the world, have happened or are happening, nor could you brazenly assert, when something appears to be in contradiction with those principles, that this is therefore impossible in actuality, or false. For there are very many things, innumerable things, which, even if there is some degree of certainty in our knowledge of natural things, you will never be able to explain, nor even to remove the obvious contradiction there is between such phenomena and your explanations of the rest, explanations which you regard as most certain. From your principles you will never give a satisfactory explanation of the things done in witchcraft, and in spells simply by the utterance of certain words, or by merely carrying on one's person those words or inscriptions marked out on some material, or of the amazing behaviours shown by those possessed by demons. Of all these I have seen various examples, and I am well acquainted with the indubitable testimony of many trustworthy persons in countless such cases, who speak with one voice.

How can you reach conclusions regarding the essences of all things, granted that some ideas in your mind do adequately agree with the essences of those things of which they are the ideas? For you can never be sure whether ideas of all created things are there in the human mind naturally, or whether many of them, if not all, can be produced in the mind, and are in fact produced, by external objects, and even through the agency of good or evil spirits, and through clear divine revelation. How, then, while disregarding the testimony and experience of other men, to say nothing about submitting your judgment to the divine omnipotence – can you from your principles define precisely and establish with certainty the actual existence or non-existence, the possibility or impossibility of existence, of the following things (that is, that they actually exist or not, or that they may exist or not, in Nature) – a divining rod for detecting metals and underground waters, the stone sought by the alchemists, the power of words and inscriptions, apparitions of various spirits, both good and evil, and their power, skill, and ability to possess people, the restoration of plants and flowers in a glass jar after they have been burned, sirens, the frequent appearance of little men in mines, as is reported, the antipathies and sympathies of so many things, the impenetrability of a human body, and so on? No, my philosopher, even if you were gifted above others with a mind a thousand times more subtle and acute than that which you possess, you would not be able to account for any of these things. And if in passing judgment on these and like matters you are relying solely on your intellect, then assuredly you are now adopting the same attitude to those matters which are beyond your knowledge and understanding, and which you therefore regard as impossible, and which in truth you ought to regard as unsubstantiated only until you are convinced by the testimony of numerous trustworthy witnesses. Yours is the way, I imagine, that Julius Caesar would have thought if someone had told him that a powder can be manufactured, and would become common in future ages, whose power could be so effective that it would blow up castles, entire cities, even the very mountains, and which, being confined in any place, when ignited would expand in an extraordinary way, shattering everything that might impede its action. Julius Caesar would never have believed this; he would have laughed this man to scorn, as one seeking to convince him of something contrary to his own judgment, his experience, and his supreme military knowledge.

But let us return to our theme. If you have no understanding of the things aforementioned and cannot judge of them, why will you, wretched man swollen with diabolical pride, rashly judge of the awesome mysteries of the life and passion of Christ, which Catholic teachers themselves declare to be beyond our understanding? Why will you keep on raving, with your idle and futile chatter on the subject of the countless miracles and signs which, after Christ, his apostles and disciples and thereafter many thousands of saints have performed through the omnipotent power of God in witness to and confirmation of the truth of the Catholic Faith, and which, through that same omnipotent mercy and goodness of God, occur even in our day in countless numbers throughout the whole world? And if you cannot contradict these, as you certainly cannot, why do you keep on with your clamour? Surrender, turn away from your errors and sins; put on humility, and be born again.

But furthermore, let us come down to the question of factual truth, which is the real foundation of the Christian religion. How will you dare deny, if you give it proper attention, the import of the consensus of so many myriads of men, some thousands of whom have vastly surpassed you, and do now surpass you, in doctrine, in learning, in solidity that is truly subtle, and in the perfection of their lives? Unanimously, with a single voice, they all affirm that Christ, the incarnate Son of the living God, suffered, was crucified, and died for the sins of mankind, rose again, was transfigured, and reigns in heaven as God along with the eternal Father in unison with the Holy Spirit. And other things relating to this they also affirm, that by the same Lord Jesus, and later in his name by the Apostles and the rest of the saints, through the omnipotent power of God countless miracles have been wrought in the Church of God, and are still being wrought, which not only exceed human understanding but are opposed to ordinary sense. (Even to this day there remain innumerable material indications of them and visible signs scattered far and wide throughout the world.) Taking your line, might I not deny that there ever were ancient Romans in the world, and that the Emperor Julius Caesar suppressed their free republic and changed their government to monarchy? Of course, I would be taking no account of the many monuments that meet our eyes, which time has bequeathed us in witness of Roman power, or again of the testimony of all those weighty authors who have written histories of the Roman republic and monarchy, and in particular those that relate the many deeds of Julius Caesar. I would be taking no account of the judgment of so many thousands of men who have either seen for themselves the said monuments, or have believed, and still believe, in their existence (this being vouched for by countless witnesses) just as much as in the said histories. And on what grounds? That last night I had dreamed that the monuments surviving from the time of the Romans are not real things but mere illusions, and likewise that the stories told of the Romans are just like those childish stories told in books called romances about Amadis de Galliis and heroes of that sort; and also that Julius Caesar either never existed in the world or, if he existed, was a man of melancholic temperament who did not really crush the freedom of the Romans and raise himself to the throne of imperial majesty, but was led to believe that he had accomplished these mighty deeds by his own foolish imagination or by the persuasion of flattering friends. Again, might I not in like manner deny that the kingdom of China was occupied by the Tartars, that Constantinople is the seat of the Turkish Empire, and any number of such things? If I were to deny these things, would anyone think me in control of my senses, or regard me as other than a pitiable case of madness? For all these matters are based on the consensus of belief of several thousands of men, and therefore their certainty is indubitable, since it is impossible that all who make these assertions, and indeed many more assertions, have deceived themselves, or have deliberately deceived others for so many centuries in succession – indeed, for the many centuries that stretch from the world's earliest years right up to the present day.

Consider, secondly, that the Church of God, continuing an uninterrupted existence from the beginning of the world right up to this day, persists unmoved and stable, whereas all other religions, pagan or heretical, have had at least a later beginning, if not already an end, and the same must be said of royal dynasties and the opinions of all philosophers whatever.

Consider, thirdly, that through the advent of Christ in the flesh the Church of God was advanced from the religion of the Old Testament to that of the New Testament, and was founded by Christ himself, Son of the living God, and thereafter was continued by the apostles and their disciples and successors. These were men regarded by the world as untaught, who yet confounded all philosophers, although they taught a Christian doctrine opposed to ordinary sense, exceeding and transcending all human reasoning. They were regarded by the world as abject, lowly, of humble birth, unassisted by the power of early kings or

princes; on the contrary, they endured from them every form of persecution, and suffered all other worldly adversities. The more the most
powerful Roman Emperors exerted themselves to hinder and indeed to
suppress their work, putting to death with every form of martyrdom as
many Christians as they could, the more that work flourished. Thus in
a short space of time the Church of Christ spread throughout the
world, and finally, with the conversion to the Christian faith of the
Roman Emperor himself and the Kings and Princes of Europe, the
Ecclesiastical Hierarchy attained to that vastness of power such as we
may admire today. All this was done through charity, gentleness, patience, trust in God, and the other Christian virtues (and not by the
clash of arms, the violence of mighty armies, and the devastation of ter-
ritories, which is the way that worldly Princes extend their boundaries),
and, according to Christ's promise, the gates of Hell did not prevail
against the Church. Here, too, ponder over the frightful and unspeak-
ably stern punishment which has reduced the Jews to the ultimate
degree of wretchedness and disaster because they were responsible for
the crucifixion of Christ. Read through, consider again and again the
histories of all the ages, and you will not find there the faintest suggestion of anything like this occurring in the case of any other association.

Observe, in the fourth place, that there are included in the nature
of the Catholic church, and in fact inseparable from that church, the
following characteristics; its antiquity, whereby, succeeding to the Jewish religion, which was at that time the true religion, it reckons its
beginning from Christ sixteen and a half centuries ago, throughout
which time it traces an uninterrupted line of succession of Pastors, so
that as a result this Church alone possesses sacred and divine books,
pure and uncorrupted, along with the equally sure and immaculate
tradition of the unwritten Word of God. Next, its immutability,
whereby its teaching, and the ministering of the Sacraments just as was
ordained by Christ himself and the Apostles, is preserved inviolate and,
as is agreed, in full vigour. Next, its infallibility, whereby it determines
and decides all things pertaining to the Faith with supreme authority,
sureness and truth, in accordance with the power bestowed on it to this
end by Christ himself, and the guidance of the Holy Spirit, whose bride
the Church is. Next, its status as above reform, for since it cannot be
corrupted or be deceived or deceive others, it obviously can never stand
in need of reform. Next, its unity, whereby all its members hold the
same beliefs, teach the same faith, have one and the same altar and all
the Sacraments in common, and finally, are united by mutual obedience to pursue one and the same end. Next, the inseparability of any

soul from the Church, on any pretext whatsoever, without its immediately incurring eternal damnation, unless it be re-united to the Church before death by repentance. This makes it clear that all heresies are a deviation from the Church, whereas the Church remains ever consistent with itself and firmly based, in as much as it is built on a Rock. Next, its vast extension, whereby it is spread throughout the world, and visibly so. This cannot be affirmed of any other association, schismatic, heretical or pagan, or of any political government or philosophical doctrine, just as neither is it true that any of the said characteristics of the Catholic Church belong to, or can belong to, any other association. And finally, its continued duration to the end of the world, which was assured for it by the Way, the Truth and the Life,[329] and which is also clearly demonstrated by recognition of all the said characteristics, likewise promised to it and granted by the same Christ through the Holy Spirit.

In the fifth place, reflect that the admirable order by which the Church, a body of such immensity, is guided and governed, clearly shows that it has a very special dependence on God's Providence, and that its administration is wonderfully arranged, protected and guided by the Holy Spirit, in the same way that the harmony discerned in all the arrangements of this universe points to the Omnipotence, Wisdom and Infinite Providence which created all things, and still preserves them. In the case of no other association is there preserved such an order, so beautiful, so close-knit and uninterrupted.

In the sixth place, consider that apart from the fact that innumerable Catholics of both sexes (of whom there are still many about today, some of whom I myself have seen and know) have lived admirable and holy lives, and through the omnipotent power of God have wrought many miracles in the worshipful name of Jesus Christ, and also that every day there still take place instantaneous conversions of very many people from a wicked life to a better, truly Christian and holy life – consider, I say, that Catholics as a class are the more humble as they are more holy and perfect, and think themselves less worthy, and assign to others the praise for a more holy life. Even the greatest sinners still constantly retain a proper respect for sacred things, confess their own wickedness, rebuke their own vices and imperfections, and desire to be

---

329. See John 14:6.

freed from these and to correct themselves. So it can be said that the most perfect heretic or philosopher that ever was can scarcely deserve to rank with the least perfect Catholics. Hence it is also clear, and most evidently follows, that the Catholic teaching is the wisest, and admirable in its profundity – in a word, it is superior to all the other teachings of this world, in that it makes men to be better than all others belonging to any association whatsoever, and teaches and communicates to them the sure way to peace of mind in this life, and to the attainment of eternal salvation of the soul thereafter.

In the seventh place, give earnest heed to the public confessions of the many heretics hardened by their obstinacy, and of philosophers of the greatest weight. These, on receiving the Catholic faith, have at last seen and realised that beforehand they were wretched, blind and ignorant – nay, foolish and mad – when, swollen with pride and inflated with their windy arrogance, they wrongly convinced themselves that they far surpassed others in the perfection of their doctrine, their learning, and their lives. Of these some thereafter lived most holy lives and left behind them the record of countless miracles, while others went to their martyrdom eagerly and with the utmost joy. Some, among whom was the Divine Augustine, even became the most discerning, profound, wise, and therefore most valuable teachers of the Church – indeed, its very pillars.

And finally, in the seventh place, reflect on the wretched and uneasy lives of atheists, though they may sometimes put on a very cheerful appearance and try to present themselves as living a joyful life, completely at peace in their hearts. Have regard especially to their most unhappy and horrifying death, of which I myself have seen many instances and am equally certain of many others – innumerable others – from other men's accounts and from history. Learn from their example to be wise in time.

Thus you see, or at least I hope you see, how rash you are to put your trust in the opinions formed by your brain. (For if Christ is the true God and at the same time man, as is most certain, see to what you are reduced. By persisting in your abominable errors and in your grievous sins, what else do you expect but eternal damnation? Reflect for yourself how horrifying this is.) Think how little reason you have to scoff at the whole world except your wretched adorers, how foolishly proud and puffed up you have become by the thought of the superiority of your talent and by men's admiration of your vain – indeed, utterly false and impious – doctrine, how basely you make yourself more wretched than the very beasts by doing away with your own freedom of will. And even if you really did not experience and acknowledge your freedom of will, yet how could you have deluded yourself into thinking that your opinions deserve the highest praise, and even rigorous imitation?

If you do not wish (banish the thought) that God or your neighbour should have pity on you, do you yourself at least have pity on your own plight, whereby you are endeavouring to make yourself more wretched than you now are, or even more wretched in the future if you continue in this way.

Come to your senses, philosopher, acknowledge the folly of your wisdom, and that your wisdom is madness. Practise humility instead of pride, and you will be healed. Pray to Christ in the Most Holy Trinity, that he may see fit to take pity on your plight and receive you. Read the Holy Fathers and the Doctors of the Church, and they will instruct you as to what to do so as not to perish, but to have eternal life. Consult Catholics who are deeply learned in their faith and of good life, and they will tell you many things that you have never known, and that will amaze you.

I have written you this letter with a truly Christian purpose, firstly, that you may know the love I bear you, Gentile though you be; and secondly, to ask you not to persist in ruining others as well as yourself.

I will therefore conclude thus: God wishes to snatch your soul from eternal damnation, if only you wish it. Do not hesitate to obey the Lord who, having called you so many times through others, is now calling you perhaps for the last time through me, one who, having achieved this grace from the ineffable mercy of God himself, whole-heartedly prays for the same for you. Do not refuse it; for if you will not hearken now to God when he calls you, the wrath of our Lord will be kindled against you, and you risk being abandoned by his Infinite Mercy to become the hapless victim of the Divine Justice that is all-consuming in its wrath. May Almighty God avert this to the greater glory of his Name and the salvation of your soul, and also as a salutary example to be imitated by your many most unhappy followers, through our Lord and Saviour Jesus Christ, who with the Eternal Father lives and reigns in unison with the Holy Spirit, God for ages without end. Amen.

Florence, 3 September 1675.

LETTER 67A
A letter from Nicholas Steno to the Reformer of the
New Philosophy, concerning the true philosophy.

[This letter was printed in Florence in 1675. The
original is not extant. There is no doubt that it was
intended for Spinoza, referred to as the 'Reformer of
the New Philosophy'. The book referred to is clearly the
Tractatus Theologico-Politicus.]

I observe that in your book[330] (of which others have told me you are
the author, and this I also suspect for various reasons) your overriding
concern is with public security, or rather, with your own security, which
according to you is the aim of public security; and yet you have advo-
cated measures that are opposed to this desired security, while altogether neglecting that part of yourself whose security should have been
your prime objective. That you have chosen measures opposed to the
security you seek is apparent from this, that while public peace is what
you seek, you are creating complete confusion, and while aiming to
free yourself from all danger, you are exposing yourself quite unneces-
sarily to the gravest danger. That you have entirely disregarded that
part of yourself which should have been your chief concern is clear
from this, that you concede to all men the right to think and say about
God whatever they please, provided it is not such as to destroy the
obedience due, according to you, not so much to God as to man. This is
the same as to confine the entire good of man within the bounds of the
goods of civil government, that is, the goods of the body. And to say
that you reserve the care of the soul for philosophy does nothing to
advance your case, for two reasons; your philosophy treats of the soul
through a system framed from suppositions, and furthermore you
abandon those unfit for your philosophy to a way of life just like that of
automata destitute of soul, born with a body only.

---

330. Clearly the TTP is intended. Wolf (465-466) conjectures that, since Steno's letter
was written at approximately the same time as Burgh's and also from Florence,
the writing of both may have been at the instigation of some Roman Catholic
authority. The first edition of this letter was edited and reproduced in facsimile by
W. Meyer in *Chronicon Spinozanum* 1 (1921). See also section 7 of our Introduction.

Since I see shrouded in such darkness a man who was once my good friend, and even now, I hope, not unfriendly to me (for I am persuaded that the memory of our former close relationship still preserves a mutual love) and since I remember how I too was once entangled, if not in exactly the same errors, yet errors of a most serious kind, the more the gravity of the dangers from which I escaped makes evident God's mercy towards me, the more I am moved by compassion for you to pray for the same heavenly grace for you which was vouchsafed me, not through my own deserts but solely through Christ's goodness. And, to add deeds to prayers, I offer myself as most ready to examine along with you all those arguments which you may be pleased to examine as to how one may discover and hold fast the true way to true security. And although your writings show you to be far removed from the truth, yet the love of peace and truth which I once perceived in you and is not yet extinguished in your darkness affords me some hope that you will give a ready hearing to our Church, provided that you are given a sufficient explanation as to what she promises to all, and what she provides for those who are willing to come to her.

As to the first, the Church promises to all a true security, an eternal security, or the abiding peace which is the accompaniment of infallible truth, and at the same time offers the means necessary for the attainment of so great a good – first, sure forgiveness for ill deeds; second, a most perfect standard for right action; third, a true practical perfection of all occupations in accordance with this standard. And this it offers not only to the learned or those endowed with subtle intellect and who are free from the distractions of business, but to all without distinction, of every age, sex and condition. Lest this should move you to wonder, know that while there is indeed required of the convert active co-operation as well as non-resistance, yet these things come to pass through the inward working of him who pronounces the outward word through visible members of the Church. And although he tells the convert that he must grieve for his sins in the eyes of God and must display before the eyes of men works that sufficiently mark this repentance, and that he must believe certain things about God, body and soul, etc., his intended meaning is not that the penitent has only his own strength in essaying these tasks. For nothing else is required of the penitent but that he should not refuse his assent and co-operation in doing and believing these things, which alone is within his power, since to will these things, and having willed them to do them, depends on the Spirit of Christ which anticipates, accompanies and perfects your co-operation. If you have not yet understood this, I am not surprised, and it is not my present objective – indeed, it is not within my capacity – to get you to understand these things. However, lest these things should appear to you entirely divorced from reason, I shall give you a brief outline of the form of Christian government, as far as this can be done by a new dweller in that state, or rather by a stranger who still tarries on the lowest benches.

The aim of this government is that man should direct not only his outward actions but also his most secret thoughts according to the order established by the author of our universe; or, what amounts to the same thing, that the soul in its every action should look to God as its author and judge. In this regard the life of every man who is tainted by sin can be divided into four stages. The first stage is one in which a man performs all his actions as if his thoughts were not subject to any judge, and this is the condition of men who are either not yet cleansed by baptism or are hardened in sin after baptism. This stage is sometimes called blindness, because the soul takes no account of God who beholds it, as when it is said in Wisdom 2, "Their wickedness blinded them";[331] sometimes it is called death, because the soul lies hidden as if buried within the pleasures that pass away, and it is in this sense that Christ said, "Let the dead bury their dead,"[332] and many other things of that sort. Nor is it inconsistent with this condition to discourse at length, and often truly, of God and the soul; but since he treats of these subjects as of things remote or external to him, this results in perpetual doubts concerning them, many contradictory ideas, and frequently occurring lapses if not in external works, at any rate in thought; and this because his soul, deprived of the spirit that lends life to action, is moved like a dead thing by every breeze of desire. The second stage is when a man, ceasing to resist the word of God, either external or internal, begins to heed his call. Recognising by the beam of this supernatural light that in his opinions there is much that is false, in his actions much that is wrong, he gives himself wholly to God who, administering to him his Sacraments through his servants, bestows on him under visible signs an invisible grace. This stage of those who are born again is called infancy and childhood, and the word of God preached to them is compared with milk. The third grade is when, through the continual exercise of virtue by mastering its desires, the mind is made ready for a

---

331. See Wisdom 2:21.
332. See Matthew 8:22; cf. also Luke 9:60.

proper understanding of the mysteries concealed in the sacred letters. These are not grasped by the soul until with a heart now clean it reaches the fourth stage, when it begins to see God and attains the wisdom of the perfect. And here there is the perpetual uniting of the will, sometimes of a mystical kind, of which there exist many examples among us even today.

So the entire established order of Christianity is directed to this end, that the soul may be taken from a state of death to a state of life, that is, that the soul which beforehand had its mind's eyes turned away from God and fixed on error should now turn its eyes away from all error and fix them steadfastly on God in all its actions of body and mind, willing and not willing whatever its author, the author of the entire order, wills and does not will. So if you will make a thorough investigation of all the facts, you will find in Christianity alone a true philosophy, teaching of God what is worthy of God, and of man what is proper to man, and guiding its adherents to true perfection in all their actions.

As for the second point, only the Catholic Church fulfils all its promises to whose who do not fight against it, for only the Catholic Church has produced perfect examples of virtue in every age, and still today, in persons of every age, sex, and condition, it is preparing what posterity must venerate. And one may not doubt its good faith in promising eternal security, seeing that it is furnishing means ancillary to this end in a miraculous way, all with the utmost fidelity. I have not yet completed my fourth year in the Church, and yet I have already seen such examples of sanctity that I must truly exclaim with David, "Thy testimonies are very sure."[333] I say nothing of bishops, I say nothing of priests, whose words heard by me in friendly intercourse, as I would testify with my own blood, were human symbols of the divine spirit, such a blameless life do they evince, such forceful eloquence. Nor shall I name the many who have embraced a way of life under the strictest rules, of whom the same could be said. I shall merely adduce examples of two kinds, one of persons converted from a most evil to a most holy way of life, the other of simple folk, as you would call them, who nevertheless without any studying have acquired the highest conceptions of God at the feet of the crucified one. Of this kind I am

---

333. See Psalms 93:5.

acquainted with some whose occupation is with the mechanical arts, bound to servile tasks, both men and women, who through the practise of the godly virtues have been raised to an understanding of the wondrous nature of God and the soul, whose life is holy, their words divine, and their deeds not infrequently miraculous, such as foretelling the future and other things which I omit for brevity's sake.

I know what objections you can raise to miracles, nor do we put our trust solely in miracles; but when we see the result of a miracle to be the perfect conversion of a soul from vice to virtue, we rightly ascribe this to the author of all virtues. For I regard as the greatest of all miracles that those who have spent thirty, forty years or more in the full gratification of their desires should in a moment of time turn away from all wickedness and become the most holy examples of virtue, such as I have seen with my own eyes and embraced with my own hands as they often moved me and others to tears of joy. There is no God like our God. Surely, if you study past history, if you study the present state of the Church, not in the books of our adversaries nor from those who are either dead among us or at any rate have not yet matured beyond childhood, but, as you would do in studying any other doctrine, from those whom your own people avow to be true Catholics, you will see that the Church has always stood by its promises and continues to do so to this day, and you will find there such proof of credibility as will satisfy you, especially since your sentiments concerning the Pope of Rome are much milder than those of our other adversaries, and you admit the necessity of good works. But do please examine our case from our own writings, as your own teachings regarding the strength of prejudice will readily persuade you to do.

I would gladly have instanced the passages of Scripture which assign authority to the Pope, which you deny for no other reason than that you do not find it so stated in the Scriptures, nor do you grant that the Christian commonwealth is like that of the Jews. But because your view on the interpretation of Scripture differs from our teaching which assigns this solely to the Church, I pass over this argument on this occasion, and I say, in the second place, that Christian government, whose one aim is the unity of the Faith, the Sacraments and Charity, admits only of one head, whose authority consist not in making arbitrary innovations – which our adversaries falsely allege – but in ensuring that matters belonging to the divine right, or necessary matters, remain always unchanged, while matters belonging to human right, or indifferent matters, may be changed as the Church shall judge with good cause to be expedient – for example, if it should see that the wicked are misusing different things for the subversion of the necessary. Hence, in interpreting Holy Scripture and in determining the dogmas of the Faith, its object is the preservation of the dogmas and interpretations handed down by God through the Apostles, and the proscription of innovative and merely human dogmas. I shall not speak of other matters subject to its authority, since the uniformity of belief and action so often taught by Christ is enough to show you the point of monarchic rule.

So if you are guided by true love of virtue, if you delight in the perfection of actions, make a thorough search of all the societies there are in the world, and nowhere else will you find that the pursuit of perfection is undertaken with such zeal, crowned with such success, as with us; and this argument by itself can serve you as a demonstration that truly "this is the finger of God."[334]

But to recognise this more readily, probe into your own self and scrutinise your soul; for a thorough investigation will show you that it is dead. You concern yourself with matter in motion as if the moving cause were absent or non-existent. For it is a religion of bodies, not of souls, that you are advocating, and in the love of one's neighbour you discern actions necessary for the preservation of the individual and the propagation of the species, whereas you pay very little or no regard to those actions whereby we acquire knowledge and love of our author. You believe that all others, too, are dead like you, you who deny to all the light of grace because you have not experienced it yourself, and you think there is no certainty except of a demonstrative kind, unaware as you are of the certainty of faith which surpasses all demonstrations. As for that demonstrative certainty of yours, within what narrow bounds is it enclosed! Scrutinise, I pray, all those demonstrations of yours and bring me just one which shows how the thinking thing and the extended thing are united, how the moving principle is united with the body that is moved. But why do I ask for demonstrations of these matters from you who cannot even give me a likely explanation of their modes, so that without the help of suppositions you cannot explain the sensation of pleasure or pain, nor the emotion of love and hatred. So the entire philosophy of Descartes, however diligently examined and reformed by you, cannot explain to me in demonstrative form even this single

---

334. See Exodus 8:19.

phenomenon, how the impact of matter on matter is perceived by a soul united to matter. But with regard to matter itself, I ask, what knowledge do you give us except for a mathematical assessment of quantity in respect of figures which are not yet proved to consist of any kind of particles, except hypothetically? What is more divorced from reason than to deny the divine words of one whose divine works are obvious to the senses, on the grounds that they are inconsistent with merely human proofs based on hypotheses? And again, though you do not even understand the physical structure of the body which enables the mind to perceive corporeal objects, yet to pronounce an opinion on this physical structure which, when glorified by change from corruptible to incorruptible, is once more to be united with the soul?

I am indeed fully convinced that to invent new principles explaining the nature of God, the soul, and the body, is just the same as to invent fictitious principles. Even reason tells us that it is inconsistent with divine providence that, while the holiest of men have failed to discover the true principles of these things for so many thousands of years, in our age they are to be disclosed for the first time by men who have not even attained to the perfection of moral virtues. Indeed, I am inclined to believe as true only those principles concerning God, the soul and the body which have been preserved from the beginning of created things until this day constantly in one and the same society, the City of God. Among the first teachers of these principles, that old man[335] who was responsible for St. Justin's move from a worldly philosophy to a Christian philosophy said, 'There have been philosophers in the ancient times, blessed, just, dear to God, who spoke with the inspiration of the Holy Spirit, and prophesied that these things would be which are now coming to pass'. It is principles propounded by such philosophers and transmitted to us through successors like them in an uninterrupted chain, and through philosophers of the same kind made available even today to him who seeks them in the spirit of right reason – it is such principles alone I would believe to be true, when sanctity of life proves the truth of doctrine. Examine thoroughly both the principles and the doctrines of this philosophy, not in the writings of its enemies nor in

---

335. The quotation following is a loose version of a passage in Justin, *Dialogue with Trypho*, VIII, 1. Justin had two teachers, the first having introduced him to Stoic, Peripatetic, and Pythagorean philosophy, and another who taught him Platonism. The reference to the 'old man', otherwise unidentified, is probably to the second.

those of its parasites, who for their wickedness are rated with the dead, or for their ignorance with children, but in the writings of its masters, perfected in all wisdom, dear to God and probably even now sharing in life eternal, and you will acknowledge that the perfect Christian is the perfect philosopher, even if it were merely an old woman, or a maid-servant busied with menial tasks, or one seeking a living by washing rags, in the world's judgment an ignorant person. And then you will cry out with St. Justin, "I find this to be the one philosophy, safe and good."[336]

If you should wish, I will gladly take upon myself the task of show-ing you how your doctrine is inferior to ours, sometimes through its contradiction, sometimes through its uncertainty. Yet I would prefer that, recognising in your doctrine a few errors as compared with the assured credibility that is a feature of ours, you would become a disci-ple of the said teachers and, as first-fruits of your repentance, offer to God a refutation of your errors which you yourself recognise through the illumination of the divine light, so that if your first writings have turned aside a thousand minds from the true knowledge of God, their recantation, corroborated by your own example, may bring back to him, accompanied by you like a second Augustine, a thousand thousand. This grace I pray for you with all my heart. Farewell.

[September 1675].

---

336. See Justin, *Dialogue with Trypho*, VIII.

LETTER 68
To the most noble and learned Henry Oldenburg, from B.d.S.

[Reply to Letter 62. Known only from
the O.P. The original is lost.]

Most noble and esteemed Sir,

At the time when I received your letter of 22 July, I was setting out for Amsterdam, intending to put into print the book of which I had written to you.[337] While I was engaged in this business, a rumour became wide-spread that a certain book of mine about God was in the press, and in it I endeavour to show that there is no God. This rumour found credence with many. So certain theologians, who may have started this rumour, seized the opportunity to complain of me before the Prince[338] and the Magistrates. Moreover, the stupid Cartesians, in order to remove this suspicion from themselves because they are thought to be on my side, ceased not to denounce everywhere my opinions and my writings, and still continue to do so.[339] Having gathered this from certain trustworthy men who also declared that the theologians were everywhere plotting against me, I decided to postpone the publication I had in hand until I should see how matters would turn out, intending to let you know what course I would then pursue. But the situation seems to worsen day by day, and I am not sure what to do about it.

Meanwhile I do not want to delay any longer my reply to your letter. First, I thank you most warmly for your friendly warning, of which, however, I should like a fuller explanation so that I may know what you believed to be the doctrines which seemed to undermine the

---

337. This was the *Ethics*. See notes to Ep62.
338. The Prince of Orange owed a considerable debt to the Calvinist clergy who helped bring about the downfall of democracy in Holland.
339. By attacking Spinoza politically the Cartesians sought to reinforce their own orthodoxy in the public eye. For further details on this aspect of the politics of Cartesianism, see Gabriel Albiac, *La synagogue vide*, tr. M.-L. Copete and J.-F. Schaub (Paris: Presses Universitaires de France, 1994), 205-222. Albiac argues that Spinoza continued to remain, even after his death, "*l'obsession refoulée du cartésianisme*" (218).

practise of religious virtue. For the things that seem to me to be in accord with reason I believe to be most beneficial to virtue. Secondly, if it is not burdensome to you, I should like you to point out to me the passages in the *Tractatus Theologico-Politicus* which have proved a stumbling-block to learned men. For I want to clarify this Treatise with some additional notes,[340] and, if possible, remove prejudices which have been conceived against it. Farewell.

[September 1675].

---

340. Notes to the TTP were inserted by Spinoza by his own hand in some versions of this letter. These notes were published in a French translation of the TTP (1678), and the original Latin notes were published in 1802 by C. T. de Murr (*Benedict de Spinoza Adnotationes ad Tractatum Theologico-Politicum*). This 1802 edition contained a facsimile of the notes in Spinoza's own writing.

LETTER 69
To the most learned Lambert Van Velthuysen, from B.d.S.

[Not in the O.P. The original came into the
possession of a Professor Tydeman of Leiden,
who published it in 1824. It is now lost.]

Most distinguished and esteemed Sir,

I am surprised that our friend Nieuwstad[341] has said that I am considering a refutation of those writings which for some time have been published against my treatise, and that among them I propose to refute your manuscript.[342] For I know that I have never had in mind to rebut any of my adversaries, so undeserving of reply did they all seem to me. Nor do I remember having said to Mr. Nieuwstad anything other than that I proposed to clarify some more obscure passages of the said treatise with some notes,[343] and to add to them your manuscript together with my reply, if you would kindly grant permission. This I asked him to seek from you, adding that if perhaps you are reluctant to grant this permission on the grounds that my reply contains some rather harsh observations, you would have complete authority to correct or delete them. But meanwhile I am not at all annoyed with Mr. Nieuwstad: I merely want to let you know how the matter stands so that, if I cannot obtain the permission I seek, I may at least make it clear that I never had any intention of publishing your manuscript against your will. And although I believe that this can be done without in any way endangering your reputation provided that your name does not appear in it, I shall do nothing unless you grant me permission to publish it. However, to confess the truth, I would be much more obliged to you if you would put in writing the arguments which you believe you can bring against my treatise and append them to your manuscript. This I most earnestly beg you to do, for there is no one

---

341. Joachim Nieuwstad was Secretary of the city of Utrecht from 1662 until 1674. Meinsma (478) suggests that Spinoza visited him during his stay in the French camp at Utrecht in 1673.
342. The manuscript to which Spinoza refers is Velthuysen's letter to Ostens, Ep42.
343. See notes to the preceding letter.

whose arguments I would more gladly consider. I know that you are devoted solely to the pursuit of truth, and that you are a man of exceptional sincerity of mind.[344] For this reason I urgently beg you not to be unwilling to undertake this labour, and believe me to be,

       With great respect,
       B. de Spinoza.

Mr. Lambert Velthuysen, Doctor of Medicine,
De Nieuwe Gracht, Utrecht.
The Hague.
[Autumn 1675].

---

344. Spinoza's attitude toward Velthuysen is far more positive than that which he displayed in Ep43. In the Preface to his own works, published in 1680, Velthuysen notes that he had many conversations with Spinoza during their joint stay in Utrecht (1673). It is not known whether Velthuysen gave to Spinoza the requested permission; but, in any case, Spinoza never had the opportunity to prepare an enlarged edition of the TTP.

LETTER 70

To the most illustrious and acute philosopher, B.d.S., from G.H. Schuller, Doctor of Medicine

[Not in the O.P. The original is extant, and was first published by Van Vloten in 1860.]

Most learned and illustrious Sir, my most venerable patron,

I hope that you have duly received my last letter, together with the *Processus* of an anonymous writer,[345] and that you still enjoy good health, as I do.

I had had no letter for three months from our friend Tschirnhaus,[346] whence I had entertained the gloomy conjecture that he had met with misfortune in journeying from England to France. But now, having received a letter, I am overjoyed and, in obedience to his request, it is my duty to convey its contents to you, and to let you know, with his most dutiful greetings, that he has arrived safely in Paris, that he has there met Mr. Huygens[347] as we had advised him to do, and has therefore made every effort to win his favour, so that he is highly regarded by him. He mentioned that you, Sir, had recommended him to seek an introduction to Huygens, for whom you have the highest regard. This pleased him very much, so that he replied that he likewise had a high regard for you, and had lately received from you the *Tractatus Theologico-Politicus*, which is esteemed by many there, and there are eager inquiries as where any more writings of the same author are published. To this Mr. Tschirnhaus has replied that he knows of none except for the 'Proofs of the First and Second Parts of Descartes' Principia'. Otherwise he said nothing about you except for the above, and hopes that this will not displease you.

---

345. This was the *Processus anonymi*, which judging from Spinoza's response in Ep72, was not written so anonymously, but by a relative of Schuller. Also judging from Spinoza's remarks, it seems that it was a book on alchemy, a discipline for which Spinoza had little interest. See our note for Ep40, the Helvetius affair.
346. Concerning Tschirnhaus, refer to our Introduction, section 5.
347. See our notes to Ep32 and Ep33.

Huygens has recently sent for our Tschirnhaus and informed him that Mr. Colbert[348] is looking for someone to instruct his son in mathematics, and if a situation of this kind was acceptable to him, he would arrange it. To this our friend replied by asking for some time to think it over, and eventually declared himself willing to accept. So Huygens came back with the answer that Mr. Colbert was very happy with this proposal, especially as his ignorance of the French language would compel him to speak to his son in Latin.

As to the objection he recently advanced, he replies that the few words I wrote at your instruction have given him a deeper understanding of your meaning, and that he has already entertained the same thoughts (since they particularly admit of explanation in these two ways), but that he had taken the line set out in his objection for the following two reasons. First, because otherwise Propositions 5 and 7 of Book II would seem to be in contradiction.[349] 'In the first of these it is maintained that *ideata* are the efficient cause of ideas, whereas in the proof of the latter this seems to be refuted by reason of the citing of Axiom 4, Part I.[350] Or else, as I am inclined to think, I am not correctly applying the axiom in accordance with the author's intention, and this I would very much like to learn from him, if his leisure permits. The second cause which has prevented me from following his explanation as set out is this, that in this way the attribute of Thought is given a much wider scope than the other attributes.[351] Now since each of the

---

348. Jean Baptiste Colbert (1619-1683) was the Chancellor of the Exchequer under the reign of Louis XIV. He attempted to draw several of the day's leading scientists and scholars to Paris.

349. As Spinoza notes in his reply (Ep72), Tschirnhaus is apparently confused. E2P5 states: "The formal being of ideas recognises God as its cause only in so far as he is considered as a thinking thing, and not in so far as he is explicated by any other attribute; that is, the ideas both of God's attributes and of individual things recognise as their efficient cause not the things of which they are ideas, – that is, the things perceived, – but God himself in so far as he is a thinking thing." E2P7 is the celebrated statement of parallelism: "The order and connection of ideas is the same as the order and connection of things."

350. E1Ax4: "The knowledge of the effect depends on, and involves, the knowledge of the cause."

351. Tschirnhaus' claim that, in allowing both ideas of things (bodies) and ideas of ideas, Spinoza had violated the parallelism by making thought more extensive than extension, has been echoed by many commentators to the present day. Seen in the light of modern set theory, the postulated violation does not exist. Two infinite sets may have the same cardinality (which is what E2P7 asserts for thought and extension) while one of them has also a one-one mapping between two of its proper subsets. But the notion of infinity had not been developed logically in the seventeenth century to a state where this claim could be demon-

attributes constitutes the essence of God, I fail to see how the one thing does not contradict the other. I will add only this, that if I may judge other minds by my own, there will be considerable difficulty in understanding Propositions 7 and 8 of Book II,[352] and this simply because the author has been pleased (doubtless because they seemed so plain to him) to explain the demonstrations attached to them so briefly and sparingly.

He further relates that in Paris he has met a man named Leibniz[353] of remarkable learning, most skilled in the various sciences and free from the common theological prejudices. He has established a close friendship with him, based on the fact that like him he is working at the problem of the perfecting of the intellect, and indeed he considers there is nothing better or more important than this. In Ethics, he says, Leibniz is most practised, and speaks solely from the dictates of reason uninfluenced by emotion. He adds that in physics and especially in metaphysical studies of God and the Soul he is most skilled, and he finally concludes that he is a person most worthy of having your writings communicated to him, if consent is first given; for he thinks that the Author will derive considerable advantage therefrom, as he undertakes to show at some length, if this should please you. But if not, have no doubt that he will honourably keep them secret in accordance with his promise, just as in fact he has made not the slightest mention of them. This same Leibniz thinks highly of the *Tractatus Theologico-*

---

strated. That the attribute of thought is 'special' is in some sense true, but as Matheron notes each of the infinite attributes is 'special' in some specific sense. See Alexandre Matheron, *Individu et communauté chez Spinoza* (Paris: Editions de Minuit, 1969), 31-35. A useful summary of the literature dealing with the problem of interpreting the parallelism is given by H. F. Hallett, *Benedict de Spinoza: The Elements of His Philosophy* (London: Athlone Press, 1957).

352. For E2P7 see above. E2P8: "The ideas of non-existing individual things must be comprehended in the infinite idea of God in the same way as the formal essences of individual things or modes are contained in the attributes of God." In his reply (Ep72), Spinoza ignores this question; but, in the scholium to E2P8, he notes, "Should anyone want an example for a clearer understanding of this matter, I can think of none at all that would adequately explicate the point with which I am here dealing." Perhaps this scholium resulted from Tschirnhaus' puzzlement.

353. Leibniz stayed in Paris from 1672 until 1676 trying to persuade Louis XIV to direct his attentions to Egypt and to leave Europe in peace. For information concerning Leibniz, refer to our introduction, section 7. The various contacts which Leibniz had with Spinoza and his friends are studied in detail by George Friedmann, *Leibniz et Spinoza*, 2nd edition (Paris: Gallimard, 1962).

Politicus,[354] on which subject he once wrote you a letter, if you remember. I would therefore ask you out of your gracious kindliness, unless there is strong reason against it, not to refuse your permission, but if you can, to let me know your decision as soon as possible. For when I have received your reply, I can send our Tschirnhaus an answer, which I am anxious to do Tuesday evening, unless you are delayed by more important business.

Mr. Bresser[355] has returned from Cleves, and has sent here a considerable quantity of the native beer. I have asked him to send you half a tun, which he has promised to do with his most friendly greetings.

Finally, I beg you to excuse the clumsiness of my style and the haste of my pen, and to command me in any service, so that I may have a real occasion of proving that I am,

> Most illustrious Sir,
> Your most ready servant,
> G.H. Schuller.

---

354. Wolf notes (469) that this was in fact not true. As a diplomat, Leibniz acquired the habit of professing whatever views were most likely to please his audience. In his own writings he described the TTP as "intolerably impudent" and "monstrous." We agree with Wolf that the caution which Spinoza displayed in dealing with him arose from sound judgment.

355. Possibly Jan Bresser who is incorrectly believed by some to have written the poem which precedes the PPC. Whether he is originally from the Cleves district or was simply visiting there is also not known, but it is coincidental that Schuller is from that area while Tschirnhaus served time in the army there.

LETTER 71
To the esteemed B.d.S., from Henry Oldenburg,
with many greetings

[Known only from the O.P. The original is lost.]

As far as I can gather from your last letter, the issuing of the book intended by you for the general public is in danger.[356] I cannot but approve your purpose in signifying your willingness to elucidate and moderate those passages in the *Tractatus Theologico-Politicus* which have proved a stumbling-block to readers. I refer in particular to those which appear to treat in an ambiguous way of God and Nature, which many people consider you have confused with each other. In addition, many are of the opinion that you take away the authority and validity of miracles, which almost all Christians are convinced form the sole basis on which the certainty of Divine Revelation can rest. Furthermore, they say that you are concealing your opinion with regard to Jesus Christ, Redeemer of the World, sole Mediator for mankind, and of his Incarnation and Atonement, and they request you to disclose your attitude clearly on these three heads. If you do so, and in this matter satisfy reasonable and intelligent Christians, I think your position will be secure. This is what I, who am devoted to you, wish you to know in brief. Farewell.

15 November 1675.

P.S. Please let me know soon that these few lines have duly reached you.

---

356. Oldenburg's naïveté is apparent here, since Spinoza never intended any of his writings after the PPC for the general public, one reason why he was opposed to the effort to publish the Dutch translation of the TTP.

LETTER 72
To the most learned and experienced
G.H. Schuller, from B.d.S.

[Not in the O.P. The original, in private hands,
was first published in 1860 by Van Vloten.]

Most experienced Sir, and honoured Friend,

I am very pleased to learn from your letter, received today, that you are well and that our friend Tschirnhaus[357] has happily accomplished his journey to France. In his conversations with Mr. Huygens he has, in my opinion, conducted himself with discretion, and furthermore I am very glad that he found so convenient an opportunity for that which he had intended.

I do not see what he finds in Axiom 4, Part I to contradict Proposition 5, Part 2. For in this proposition it is asserted that the essence of any idea has God for its cause in so far as he is considered as a thinking thing, while that axiom says that the knowledge or idea of an effect depends on the knowledge or idea of the cause. But to tell the truth, I do not quite follow the meaning of your letter in this matter, and I believe that either in your letter or in his copy there is a slip of the pen. For you write that in Proposition 5 it is asserted that *ideata* are the efficient cause of ideas, whereas this very point is expressly denied in that same proposition. I now think that the whole confusion arises from this, and so at present it would be pointless for me to try to write at greater length on this matter. I must wait until you explain his meaning to me more clearly, and until I know whether he has a sufficiently correct copy.[358]

I believe I know Leibniz, of whom he writes, through correspondence, but I do not understand why he, a councillor of Frankfurt, has gone to France.[359] As far as I can judge from his letter, he seemed to

---

357. About Tschirnhaus, see our introduction, section 5.
358. These propositions are printed as notes to Ep70. Spinoza's assumption that Tschirnhaus may have received a corrupted text of them is plausible in the light of Tschirnhaus' strange reading in Ep70.
359. See Ep70 and our notes to it for some justification for Spinoza's wariness.

me a person of liberal mind and well versed in every science. Still, I think it imprudent to entrust my writings to him so hastily. I should first like to know what he is doing in France, and to hear our friend Tschirnhaus' opinion of him after a longer acquaintance and a closer knowledge of his character. However, greet that friend of ours in my name with all my duty, and if I can serve him in any way, let him command what he will, and he will find me most ready to comply in all things.

I congratulate our most worthy friend Mr. Bresser[360] on his arrival or his return. I thank him very much for the beer that is promised, and shall repay him in whatever way I can.

Finally, I have not yet made trial of the *Process* of your kinsman,[361] nor do I think that I can turn my mind to essay it. For the more I think about it, the more I am convinced that you have not made gold, but have insufficiently separated out what was hidden in the antimony. But more of this on another occasion; at the moment I am pressed for time. Meanwhile, if I can be of service to you in any matter, here I am, whom you will always find,

    Most distinguished Sir,
    Your very good friend and ready servant,
    B. de Spinoza.

The Hague, 18 November 1675.
Mr. G. H. Schuller, Doctor of Medicine,
de Kortsteegh in de gestofeerde hoet, Amsterdam.

---

360. See our note 355 to Ep70 for information on Bresser.
361. See our note 345 to Ep70 for information on this work.

LETTER 73
To the most noble and learned Henry Oldenburg, from B.d.S.

[Printed in the O.P. The original is lost,
but a copy made by Leibniz is extant.]

Most noble Sir,

I received your very short letter, dated 15 November, last Saturday. In it you merely indicate those passages of the *Tractatus Theologico-Politicus* which have proved a stumbling-block to readers, whereas I had also hoped to learn from it what were those passages which appeared to undermine the practise of religious virtue, of which you had previously made mention.[362] However, in order to disclose to you my attitude concerning the three heads which you single out, I say in the first place that I entertain an opinion on God and Nature far different from that which modern Christians are wont to uphold. For I maintain that God is the immanent cause, as the phrase is, of all things, and not the transitive cause. All things, I say, are in God and move in God, and this I affirm together with Paul and perhaps together with all ancient philosophers, though expressed in a different way, and I would even venture to say, together with all the ancient Hebrews, as far as may be conjectured from certain traditions, though these have suffered much corruption. However, as to the view of certain people that the *Tractatus Theologico-Politicus* rests on the identification of God with Nature (by the latter of which they understand a kind of mass or corporeal matter) they are quite mistaken.

Next, as to miracles, I am on the contrary convinced that the certainty of divine revelation can be based solely on the wisdom of

---

362. Spinoza is being a consistent Spinozist here, without realising that neither Oldenburg nor the many critics of the TTP accept the divorce between obedience (which is the goal of faith) and truth (which is the goal of philosophy) whose demonstration is one of the central theses of the TTP. Oldenburg has in fact given Spinoza a list of objectionable philosophical claims, whereas what Spinoza had sought was an indication of how, in the eyes of his critics, the TTP undermined the *practise* of obedience and virtue.

doctrine, and not on miracles, that is, on ignorance, as I have shown at some length in Chapter 6, 'On Miracles'. Here I will add only this, that the chief distinction I make between religion and superstition is that the latter is founded on ignorance, the former on wisdom. And this I believe is the reason why Christians are distinguished from other people not by faith, nor charity, nor the other fruits of the Holy Spirit, but solely by an opinion they hold, namely, because, as they all do, they rest their case simply on miracles, that is, on ignorance, which is the source of all wickedness, and thus they turn their faith, true as it may be, into superstition. But I doubt very much whether rulers will ever allow the application of a remedy for this evil.[363]

Finally, to disclose my meaning more clearly on the third head, I say that for salvation it is not altogether necessary to know Christ according to the flesh; but with regard to the eternal son of God, that is, God's eternal wisdom, which has manifested itself in all things and chiefly in the human mind, and most of all in Christ Jesus, a very different view must be taken. For without this no one can attain to a state of blessedness, since this alone teaches what is true and false, good and evil. And since, as I have said, this wisdom has been manifested most of all through Jesus Christ, his disciples have preached it as far as he revealed it to them, and have shown themselves able to glory above all others in that spirit of Christ. As to the additional teaching of certain Churches, that God took upon himself human nature, I have expressly indicated that I do not understand what they say. Indeed, to tell the truth, they seem to me to speak no less absurdly than one who might tell me that a circle has taken on the nature of a square.[364]

---

363. As a good republican, Spinoza is here claiming that it is only in a democracy that government can afford to permit free access to information and universal education. His experience with the Calvinist clergy's effort to restore the monarchy certainly provided ample support for this claim in his own time.

364. While Spinoza's denial of the godhood of Christ is quite unambiguous in the TTP, Oldenburg was probably correct in claiming that the account of Christ given in the TTP is, if not ambiguous, at least not clear. See Alexandre Matheron, *Le Christ et le salut des ignorants chez Spinoza* (Paris: Aubier, 1971). The term *'salus'*, as used in the TTP, also appears to conflict with its use in the fifth part of the *Ethics*. Sylvain Zac argues that for Spinoza Christ, unlike the prophets (who had no true knowledge of God), incarnates the divine wisdom, and that such a wisdom exceeds both human wisdom and prophetic imagination. See his *Spinoza et l'interprétation de l'Ecriture* (Paris: Presses Universitaires de France, 1965), 190-199.

This, I think, suffices to explain what is my opinion on those three heads. As to whether it is likely to please the Christians of your acquaintance, you will know better than I. Farewell.

[Conjectural date, November or December 1675]

LETTER 74
To the most esteemed and learned B.d.S.,
from Henry Oldenburg

[Known only from the O.P. The original is lost.]

Many greetings.

As you seem to accuse me of excessive brevity, I shall clear myself of that charge on this occasion by excessive prolixity. You expected, I see, an account of those opinions in your writings which seem to your readers to do away with the practise of religious virtue. I will tell you what it is that particularly pains them. You appear to postulate a fatalistic necessity in all things and actions. If this is conceded and affirmed, they say, the sinews of all law, all virtue and religion are severed, and all rewards and punishments are pointless. They consider that whatever compels or brings necessity to bear, excuses; and they hold that no one will thus be without excuse in the sight of God. If we are driven by fate,[365] and if all things, unrolled by its unrelenting hand, follow a fixed and inevitable course, they do not see what place there is for blame and punishment. What wedge can be applied to this knot, it is very difficult to say. I would be glad to know and to learn from you what help you can give in this matter.

As to your views on the three heads I mentioned, which you were kind enough to disclose to me, the following questions arise. First, in what sense do you take miracles and ignorance to be synonymous and equivalent terms, as you appear to do in your last letter? For the raising of Lazarus from the dead and the resurrection of Jesus Christ from death seem to surpass all the force of created Nature and to belong only to the divine power; nor does it argue a culpable ignorance that this must necessarily exceed the bounds of an intelligence that is finite and confined within definite limits. Or do you not deem it proper for the created mind and science to acknowledge in the uncreated mind and supreme Deity such science and power that it can see deeply into

---

365. Oldenburg is interpreting Spinoza as a fatalist rather than as a determinist. See our notes to Ep56.

and bring to pass things, the reason and manner of which are beyond understanding and explanation by us petty men? We are men; we should regard as foreign to us nothing that is human.

Again, since you admit that you cannot grasp the idea that God did indeed assume human nature, may one ask in what way you understand those texts of our Gospel and the passages in the Epistle to the Hebrews, of which the former declares 'the Word was made flesh',[366] and the latter 'the Son of God took not on him the nature of angels, but he took on him the seed of Abraham'.[367] And the whole trend of the Gospel, I should think, implies that the only-begotten Son of God, the Word (who was both God and with God), manifested himself in human nature, and by his passion and death paid the ransom on behalf of us sinners, the price of redemption.[368] I would much like to learn what you have to say regarding these and similar matters that would be consistent with the truth of the Gospel and the Christian religion, to which I believe you are well disposed.

I had intended to write more fully, but I am interrupted by the visit of friends, to whom I think it wrong to refuse the duties of courtesy. But what I have already committed to paper will suffice, and will perhaps prove irksome to you as a philosopher. So farewell, and believe me to be ever an admirer of your learning and knowledge.

London, 16 December 1675.

---

366. See John 1:14.
367. See Hebrews 2:16.
368. See I Timothy 2:5-6 and Matthew 20:27.

LETTER 75
To the most noble and learned Henry Oldenburg, from B.d.S.

[Printed in the O.P. The original is lost,
but a copy made by Leibniz is extant.]

Most noble Sir,

I see at last what it was that you urged me not to publish. However, since this is the principal basis of all the contents of the treatise which I had intended to issue, I should here like to explain briefly in what way I maintain the fatalistic necessity of all things and actions.

In no way do I subject God to fate, but I conceive that all things follow with inevitable necessity from God's nature in the same way that everyone conceives that it follows from God's nature that God understands himself. Surely no one denies that this follows necessarily from God's nature, and yet no one conceives that God is forced by some fate to understand himself; it is conceived that God understands himself altogether freely, though necessarily.

Next, this inevitable necessity of things does not do away with either divine or human laws. For moral precepts, whether or not they receive from God himself the form of command or law, are none the less divine and salutary, and whether the good that follows from virtue and the divine love is bestowed on us by God as judge, or whether it emanates from the necessity of the divine nature, it will not on that account be more or less desirable, just as on the other hand the evils that follow from wicked deeds and passions are not less to be feared because they necessarily follow from them. And finally, whether we do what we do necessarily or contingently, we are still led by hope and fear.

Furthermore, men are without excuse before God for no other reason than that they are in God's hands as clay in the hands of the potter,[369] who from the same lump makes vessels, some to honour and some to dishonour. If you would give just a little attention to these few

---

369. See Romans 9:20-21.

points, I doubt not that you will find it easy to reply to all objections that are usually raised against this view, as many have already discovered along with me.

I have taken miracles and ignorance as equivalents because those who endeavour to establish the existence of God and religion from miracles are seeking to prove the obscure through the more obscure, of which they are quite ignorant; and in this way they are introducing a new style of argumentation, reduction not to the impossible, as the phrase is, but to ignorance.[370] However, I have sufficiently expressed my view on miracles, if I am not mistaken, in the *Tractatus Theologico-Politicus*. Here I will add only this, that if you will consider the following points, that Christ did not appear to the Senate, nor to Pilate, nor to any of the unbelievers, but only to the Saints, that God has neither right nor left and is not in any one place but is everywhere in accordance with his essence, that matter is everywhere the same, that God does not manifest himself in some imaginary space beyond the world, and that the frame of the human body is restrained within its proper limits only by the weight of the air, you will easily see that this appearance of Christ is not unlike that whereby God appeared to Abraham when he saw the three men whom he invited to eat with him.[371] But, you will say, all the Apostles were fully convinced that Christ rose again after death and that he really did ascend to heaven; and this I do not deny. For Abraham, too, believed that God partook of a meal with him, and all the Israelites believed that God descended from heaven to Mount Sinai in the midst of fire, and spoke to them directly. Yet these and many other events of this kind were appearances or revelations adapted to the understanding and beliefs of those men to whom God wished to reveal his mind by these means. I therefore conclude that Christ's resurrection from the dead was in fact of a spiritual kind and was revealed only to the faithful according to their understanding, indicating that Christ was endowed with eternity and rose from the dead (I here understand 'the dead' in the sense in which Christ said 'Let the dead bury their dead'),[372] and also by his life and death he provided an

---

370. The thrust of Spinoza's argument in the TTP is that belief in miracles in fact inevitably leads to disbelief in the existence of God. See Sylvain Zac, *Spinoza et l'interprétation de l'Ecriture* (Paris: Presses Universitaires de France, 1965), 199-208.

371. See Genesis 18:1-2.

372. See Matthew 8:22 and Luke 9:60.

example of surpassing holiness, and that he raises his disciples from the dead in so far as they follow the example of his own life and death.

It would not be difficult to explain the entire teaching of the Gospel in accordance with this hypothesis. Indeed, it is only on this hypothesis that Chapter 15 of the First Epistle to the Corinthians can be explained and Paul's arguments understood, which otherwise, according to the usually accepted hypothesis, appear weak and easily to be refuted, to say nothing of the fact that Christians have interpreted in a spiritual way all that the Jews have interpreted according to the flesh.

I agree with you as to human weakness. But permit me to ask you in turn, do we petty men have such an understanding of Nature that we can determine how far its force and power extend, and what is beyond its power? Since nobody can make such a claim without arrogance, one may therefore without presumption explain miracles through natural causes as far as possible; and as to those which because of their absurdity we can neither explain nor prove, it will be better to suspend judgment, and to base religion, as I have said, solely on the wisdom of doctrine.

Finally, the reason why you believe that the passages in the Gospel of John and in the Epistle to the Hebrews are opposed to the views I have expressed in this, that you interpret the phraseology of Oriental languages according to the norm of European speech; and although John wrote his Gospel in Greek, his idiom was Hebraic.[373]

Be that as it may, do you believe that when Scripture says that God manifested himself in a cloud, or that he dwelt in a tabernacle and a temple, that God assumed the nature of a cloud, a tabernacle and a temple? But the most that Christ said about himself was this, that he was the temple of God, because undoubtedly, as I have said in my previous letter, God manifested himself most of all in Christ; and John, to express this more effectually, said that the Word was made flesh. But enough for now.

[December 1675].

---

373. This theme is echoed also in the TTP, since Spinoza there claims that understanding the text of Scripture requires a knowledge of the linguistic and cultural connotations which underlie it. This is one reason why he avoids a detailed interpretation of the New Testament, for want of a knowledge of Greek.

LETTER 76
Greetings to the noble young man, Alfred Burgh, from B.d.S.

[Reply to Letter 67]
[Printed in the O.P. The original is lost,
but a copy made by Leibniz is extant.]

What I could scarcely believe when it was told me by others, I now at last learn from your letter; not only have you become a member of the Roman Church, as you say,[374] but you are also its very keen champion, and have already learned to curse and rage without restraint against your opponents. I had intended to make no reply to your letter, being convinced that time rather than argument was what you needed so as to be restored to yourself and your family, not to mention other reasons to which you once gave your approval when we were discussing the case of Steno[375] (in whose footsteps you now follow). But some of my friends, who with me had formed great hopes for you from your excellent natural abilities, have strenuously urged me not to fail in the duties of a friend, and to reflect on what you lately were rather than what you now are, and so on. These representations have at last induced me to write you these few words, which I earnestly beg you please to read with patience.

I shall not here recount the vices of priests and popes, as opponents of the Roman Church are wont to do, so as to discredit them with you. Such accusations are often advanced from unworthy motives, and are intended to annoy rather than to instruct. Indeed, I will concede that in the Roman Church there are to be found more instances of men of great learning and upright life than in any other Christian Church; for since this Church has more members, there will also be found in it more men of every character. Still, unless perchance you have lost your memory together with your reason, you will not be able to deny that in every Church there are very many honourable men who worship God with justice and charity. For we have known many such among the Lutherans, the Reformed Church, the Mennonites and the Enthusiasts,

---

374. For information on Burgh and details of his conversion, see our Introduction, section 7.
375. See Ep67A and our Introduction, section 7.

and, to say nothing of others, you know of your own relations who, in the time of the Duke of Alva, suffered every kind of torture steadfastly and freely for the sake of their religion. You must therefore grant that holiness of life is not peculiar to the Roman Church, but is common to all.

Since we know by this (to quote from the Apostle John, First Epistle, Chapter 4 verse 13) that we dwell in God and God dwells in us,[376] it follows that whatever distinguishes the Roman Church from others is of no real significance, and consequently is constructed merely from superstition. For, as I have said with John,[377] justice and charity are the one sure sign of the true catholic faith, the true fruits of the Holy Spirit, and wherever these are found, there Christ really is, and where they are not, Christ is not. For only by the Spirit of Christ can we be led to the love of justice and charity. Had you been willing to meditate aright on these things, you would not have ruined yourself nor would you have brought bitter grief on your kinsfolk who now sorrowfully bewail your plight.

But I return to your letter, in which first of all you lament that I allow myself to be ensnared by the prince of evil spirits. But please be of good cheer and come to yourself again. When you were in your senses, if I am not mistaken, you used to worship an infinite God by whose efficacy all things absolutely come into being and are preserved; but now you dream of a Prince, God's enemy, who against God's will ensnares most men (for the good are few) and deceives them, whom God therefore delivers over to this master of wickedness for everlasting torture. So divine justice permits the Devil to deceive men with impunity, but does not permit men, haplessly deceived and ensnared by the Devil, to go unpunished.

Now these absurdities might so far be tolerated if you worshipped a God infinite and eternal, not one whom Chastillon, in a town which the Dutch call Tienen, gave to horses to eat, and was not punished.[378] And do you bewail me, wretched man? And do you call my philosophy, which you have never beheld, a chimera? O youth deprived of

---

376. Spinoza inserted this verse from I John on the title-page of the TTP.
377. See TTP, Chapter XIV. The reference is to I John 4:7-8.
378. This probably refers to an incident in May of 1635 when a Franco-Dutch army attacked the Spanish army in Belgium. The French general Gaspard de Coligny was a Huguenot, and after sacking the town he ordered the eucharistic hosts to be thrown to the horses as an expression of his disgust with Catholic idolatry.

understanding, who has bewitched you into believing that you eat, and hold in your intestines, that which is supreme and eternal?

Still, you appear to be willing to resort to reason, and you ask me 'how I know that my philosophy is the best of all those that have ever been taught in this world, are now being taught, or will ever be taught in the future'. But surely I have far better right to put that question to you. For I do not presume that I have found the best philosophy, but I know that what I understand is the true one.[379] If you ask me how I know this, I reply that I know it in the same way that you know that the three angles of a triangle are equal to two right angles. That this suffices no one will deny who has a sound brain and does not dream of unclean spirits who inspire us with false ideas as if they were true. For truth reveals both itself and the false.[380]

But you, who presume that you have at last found the best religion, or rather, the best men to whom you have pledged your credulity, how do you know that they are the best out of all those who have taught other religions, are teaching them now, or will teach them in the future? Have you examined all those religions, both ancient and modern, which are taught here and in India and throughout the whole world? And even if you have duly examined them, how do you know that you have chosen the best? For you can give no grounds for your faith. You will say that you give acceptance to the inward testimony of the Spirit of God, whereas others are ensnared and deceived by the Prince of wicked spirits. But all who are outside the Roman Church claim with the same right for their church what you claim for yours.

As to what you add about the common consent of myriads of men and the uninterrupted ecclesiastical succession and so on, this is the same old song of the Pharisees.[381] Just as confidently as the adherents

---

379. Spinoza is using 'best' here in the sense of 'complete'. In fact, no philosophy (his or any other) can claim completeness on Spinoza's own count; since philosophy by its very nature is a finitary activity and deals at most with a finite number of the divine attributes. No matter how adequate or true a philosophy should be, infinite orders of nature will lie beyond its range of understanding.

380. This is a major theme of the unfinished *Tractatus de intellectus emendatione*. An idea is said to be false only in relation to a given true idea which lies at the base of human understanding. See Pierre-François Moreau, *Spinoza: L'expérience et l'éternité* (Paris: Presses Universitaires de France, 1994), 65-103.

381. Spinoza uses the term 'Pharisee' to refer to and condemn the adherents of rabbinic Judaism, which is based on the Talmud and the belief in the so-called Oral Torah (or "Law"). Central to the belief is the claim (made also by Roman Catholicism) of an unbroken chain of succession. The term is also used in this sense in the work of Gabriel da Costa (known more commonly as Uriel d'Acosta) (1585-1640), who certainly did not originate the sense. Wolf conjectures that in

of the Roman Church, they produce their myriads of witnesses who, with just as much pertinacity as the Roman witnesses, recount what they have merely heard just as if they had experienced it themselves. Again, they trace their lineage as far back as Adam. With like arrogance they boast that their Church, continuing to this day, endures unmoved and unshaken in spite of the bitter hatred of heathens and Christians. More than any other people they rely on their antiquity. With one voice they cry that their traditions were given them by God himself, that they alone preserve the Word of God, written and unwritten. No one can deny that all other sects have issued from them, while they have remained steadfast over some thousands of years with no government to constrain them, solely through the efficacy of superstition. The miracles they tell of are enough to weary a thousand tongues. But their chief source of pride is that they count far more martyrs than any other nation, a number that is daily increased by those who have suffered for the faith they profess with amazing steadfastness. I myself know among others of a certain Judah called 'the faithful' who, in the midst of flames when he was already believed dead, started to sing the hymn which begins 'To Thee, O God, I commit my soul', and so singing, died.[382]

The organisation of the Roman Church, which you so warmly praise, I admit is politic and a source of gain to many, nor would I believe there is any better arranged for deceiving the people and controlling men's minds if it were not for the organisation of the Mahomedan Church, which far surpasses it. For ever since this superstition originated, no schisms have arisen in their Church.[383]

If, therefore, you reckon up your accounts aright, you will see that it is only your third point that is in favour of Christians, namely, that men who were unlearned and of humble condition were able to convert practically the whole world to the Christian faith. But this point

---

his youth Spinoza may have met Da Costa, perhaps shortly before the latter's suicide. See Jean-Pierre Osier, *D'Uriel da Costa à Spinoza* (Paris: Berg International, 1983); and Gabriel Albiac, *La synagogue vide* (Paris: Presses Universitaires de France, 1994), 239-325.

382. Don Lope de Vera y Alarcon ('Judah the Faithful') was, like Uriel da Costa, a convert (or 'revert', since he was born into a crypto-Jewish family) to Judaism. He was burned at the stake on 25 July 1644. An account of his martyrdom is given by Manasseh ben Israel in his *Esperança de Israel* (Amsterdam, 1652).

383. Spinoza is, of course, completely ignorant of the history of Islamic religion.

militates in favour not of the Roman Church, but of all Churches that profess the name of Christ.

But suppose that all the arguments that you offer tell in favour only of the Roman Church. Do you think that by these arguments you can prove with mathematical certainty the authority of that same Church? Since this is far from being so, why do you want me to believe that my demonstrations are inspired by the Prince of wicked spirits, and yours by God? Especially as I see, and your letter clearly shows, that you have become the slave of this Church not so much through love of God as fear of Hell, which is the single cause of superstition.[384] Is this your humility, to put no trust in yourself but in others, who are condemned by a great number of people? Do you take it for arrogance and pride that I resort to reason, and that I give my acceptance to this, the true Word of God, which is in the mind and can never be distorted or corrupted? Away with this destructive superstition, and acknowledge the faculty of reason which God gave you, and cultivate it, unless you would be counted among the beasts. Cease, I say, to give the title of mysteries to your absurd errors, and do not shamefully confuse those things which are unknown to us or not yet discovered with things that are shown to be absurd, as are the fearsome secrets of this church, which you believe to transcend the understanding the more so as they are opposed to right reason.

However, the fundamental principle of the *Tractatus Theologico-Politicus* that Scripture must be explained only through Scripture, which you so wantonly and unreasonably proclaim to be false, is not mere supposition but is categorically proved to be true or sound, particularly in Chapter 7 which also refutes the opinions of its adversaries. See also what is proved towards the end of Chapter 15. If you will pay attention to these things and also examine the histories of the Church (of which I see that you are quite ignorant) so as to realise how false are many Papal traditions, and through what turn of events and with what craft the Pope of Rome finally gained supremacy over the Church six hundred years after the birth of Christ, I have no doubt that you will at last recover your senses. That this may come about is my sincere wish for you. Farewell, etc.

[December 1675].

---

384. This theme is echoed in E5P42Schol.

LETTER 77
To the esteemed B.d.S., from Henry Oldenburg,
with greetings

[Reply to Letter 75]
[Known only from the O.P. The original is lost.]

You hit the mark exactly when you perceive that the reason why I advised against the publication of the doctrine of the fatalistic necessity of all things is my fear lest the practise of virtue may thereby be impeded, and rewards and punishments be made of little account. The points made by you on this subject in your last letter do not as yet appear to solve this problem or to set the human mind at rest. For if in all our actions, both moral and natural, we human beings are in God's power just as clay in the hands of the potter, on what grounds, pray, can any one of us be blamed for acting in this or that way, when it was quite impossible for him to act otherwise? Can we not, each one of us, reply to God, 'Your unbending fate and your irresistible power has compelled us to act in this way, nor could we have acted otherwise. Why, then, and with what right will you deliver us up to such dreadful punishments which could in no way have been avoided, in as much as you control and direct all things through a supreme necessity in accordance with your will and pleasure?' When you say that men are without excuse in the eyes of God for no other reason than that they are in the power of God, I would turn that argument the other way round and would say, I think with more reason, that it is just because they are in the power of God that men are excusable. For everyone has this excuse to hand, 'Ineluctable is your power, O God, and therefore I think I deserve to be excused for not acting otherwise'.

Again, in insisting that miracles and ignorance are equivalents, you seem to confine the power of God and the knowledge of men, even the most intelligent of men, within the same bounds, as if God cannot do or effect anything of which men cannot give an account if they exert their faculties to the full. Furthermore, the history of Christ's passion, death, burial and resurrection seems to be depicted in such vivid and natural colours that I even venture to appeal to your conscience; do you, provided that you are convinced of the truth of the narrative, believe that these things should be taken allegorically rather than literally? The details of this event so lucidly recorded by the Evangelists seem to urge strongly that the narrative should be taken literally.

These are the brief observations I want in turn to make regarding your argument, and I earnestly beg you to forgive them and to answer them with your customary candour of a friend. Mr. Boyle sends his kind regards. The present proceedings of the Royal Society I shall explain on another occasion. Farewell, and keep me in your affection.

Henry Oldenburg.

London, 14 January 1676.

LETTER 78
To the noble and learned Henry Oldenburg, from B.d.S.

[Printed in the O.P. The original is lost,
but a copy made by Leibniz is extant.]

Most noble Sir,

When I said in my previous letter[385] that the reason why we are without excuse is that we are in God's power as clay in the hands of the potter, I meant to be understood in this sense, that no one can accuse God for having given him a weak nature or a feeble character. For just as it would be absurd for a circle to complain that God has not given it the properties of a sphere, or a child suffering from kidney-stone that God has not given it a healthy body, it would be equally absurd for a man of feeble character to complain that God has denied him strength of spirit and true knowledge and love of God, and has given him so weak a nature that he cannot contain or control his desires. In the case of each thing, it is only that which follows necessarily from its given cause that is within its competence. That it is not within the competence of every man's nature that he should be of strong character, and that it is no more within our power to have a healthy body than to have a healthy mind, nobody can deny without flying in the face of both experience and reason.

"But," you urge, "if men sin from the necessity of their nature, they are therefore excusable." You do not explain what conclusion you wish to draw from this. Is it that God cannot be angry with them, or is it that they are worthy of blessedness, that is, the knowledge and love of God? If the former, I entirely agree that God is not angry, and that all things happen in accordance with his will. But I deny that on that account all men ought to be blessed; for men may be excusable, but nevertheless be without blessedness and afflicted in many ways. A horse is excusable for being a horse, and not a man; nevertheless, he needs must be a horse, and not a man. He who goes mad from the bite of a dog is indeed to be excused; still, it is right that he should die of suffocation.

---

385. See Ep75.

Finally, he who cannot control his desires and keep them in check through fear of the law, although he also is to be excused for his weakness, nevertheless cannot enjoy tranquillity of mind and the knowledge and love of God, but of necessity he is lost. I do not think I need here remind you that Scripture, when it says that God is angry with sinners, that he is a judge who takes cognizance of the actions of men, decides, and passes sentence, is speaking in merely human terms according to the accepted beliefs of the multitude; for its aim is not to teach philosophy, nor to make men learned, but to make them obedient.

Again, I fail to see how you come to think that, by equating miracles with ignorance, I am confining God's power and man's knowledge within the same bounds.

The passion, death and burial of Christ I accept literally, but his resurrection I understand in an allegorical sense. I do indeed admit that this is related by the Evangelists with such detail that we cannot deny that the Evangelists themselves believed that the body of Christ rose again and ascended to heaven to sit at God's right hand, and that this could also have been seen by unbelievers if they had been present at the places where Christ appeared to the disciples. Nevertheless, without injury to the teaching of the Gospel, they could have been deceived, as was the case with other prophets, examples of which I gave in my last letter. But Paul, to whom Christ also appeared later, rejoices that he knows Christ not after the flesh, but after the spirit.

I am most grateful to you for the catalogue of the books of the distinguished Mr. Boyle.[386] Lastly, I wait to hear from you, when you have an opportunity, about the present proceedings of the Royal Society. Farewell, most honoured Sir, and believe me yours in all zeal and affection.

The Hague, 7 February 1676.

---

386. Oldenburg published in 1677 a catalogue of Boyle's works in the *Philosophical Transactions* of the Royal Society, Vol. CXXX. He apparently sent Spinoza an advance copy of the catalogue.

LETTER 79
To the esteemed Mr. Benedict de Spinosa,
from Henry Oldenburg

[Not in the O.P. The original is lost, but
a copy, perhaps intended for the printers
of the O.P., has been preserved.]

Many greetings.

In your last letter written to me on 7 February, there seem still some
points open to criticism. You say that man cannot complain that God
has denied him true knowledge of Himself and strength sufficient to
avoid sin, because there belongs to the nature of each thing nothing
other than what necessarily follows from its cause. But I say that
inasmuch as God, the creator of men, has formed them in his own
image, which seems to include in its concept wisdom, goodness and
power, it seems bound to follow that it is more within man's power to
have a healthy mind than a healthy body, seeing that the physical health
of the body depends on mechanical principles, whereas the health of
the mind depends on deliberate choice and purpose. You also say that
men can be excusable, and yet suffer many afflictions. This seems
harsh at first sight, and what you add by way of proof, that a dog who
goes mad from a bite[387] is indeed excusable but is nevertheless rightly
killed, does not appear to settle the matter. For the killing of such a
dog would argue cruelty, were it not necessary for the protection of
other dogs or other animals, or even men, from a maddening bite of
that kind. But if God had endowed men with a healthy mind, as he can
do, no contagion of vices would need to be feared. And indeed it seems
very cruel that God should deliver men up to eternal, or at least dreadful temporary, torments because of sins which they could in no way
have avoided. Moreover, the whole tenor of Holy Scripture seems to
suppose and imply that men can refrain from sin. For it is full of

---

387. In this letter, Oldenburg has misunderstood Spinoza's Latin regarding the mad
dog, and takes 'canis' as nominative rather than genitive. Spinoza has the dog bit-
ing, rather than being bitten.

denunciations and promises, proclamations of rewards and punishments, all of which seem to argue against the necessity of sinning and to imply the possibility of avoiding punishment. To deny this would be to say that the human mind operates no less mechanically than the human body.

Furthermore, your continual assumption that miracles and ignorance are equivalent appears to rest on this foundation, that a creature can and should have complete insight into the Creator's infinite power and wisdom. I am still firmly convinced that this is quite otherwise.

Finally, your assertion that Christ's passion, death and burial is to be taken literally, but his resurrection allegorically, is not supported by any argument that I can see. In the gospels, Christ's resurrection seems to be narrated as literally as the rest. And on this article of the resurrection stands the whole Christian religion and its truth, and with its removal the mission of Christ Jesus and his heavenly teaching collapse. You cannot be unaware how urgently, when he was raised from the dead, Christ laboured to convince his disciples of the truth of the resurrection properly so called. To seek to turn all this into allegory is the same as if one were to set about destroying the entire truth of Gospel history.

These are the few observations which I again wish to bring to your attention, in accordance with my freedom to philosophise. I earnestly beg you to take them in good part.

London, 11 February 1676.

I shall give you a full account of the present studies and investigations of the Royal Society, if God grants me life and health.[388]

---

388. This is in fact the last letter in the extant correspondence between the two men. Oldenburg wrote again to Spinoza in October of 1676, and entrusted the letter to Leibniz for transmission; but the latter never delivered it. In a letter written the day following Spinoza's death, Oldenburg complains of its non-delivery.

LETTER 80
To the acute and learned philosopher, B.d.S.,
from Ehrenfried Walther von Tschirnhaus

[Known only from the O.P. The original is
lost. The last paragraph appears only in
the Dutch edition of the O.P.]

Esteemed Sir,

First, I find it very difficulty to understand how the existence of bodies
having motion and figure can be demonstrated a priori, since there is
nothing of this kind to be found in Extension, taken in the absolute
sense. Secondly, I should like you to inform me in what way one is to
understand the following passage in your letter[389] on the Infinite: 'Yet
they do not draw the conclusion that it is because of the multitude of
parts that such things exceed all number'. For, in fact, in the case of
such infinites all mathematicians always seem to demonstrate that the
number of parts is so great as to exceed any assignable number; and in
the example of the two circles which you adduce you do not seem to
clear up this point, as you had undertaken to do. For there you merely
show that they do not reach this conclusion from the excessive magnitude of the intervening space and 'because we do not know its maximum and minimum', but you do not demonstrate, as you intended,
that they do not reach this conclusion from the multitude of parts.

   Further, I have learned from Mr. Leibniz that the tutor of the Dauphin of France, by name Huet,[390] a man of outstanding learning, is
going to write about the truth of human religion, and to refute your
Tractatus Theologico-Politicus. Farewell.

2 May 1676.

---

389. This is Ep12; see section 3 of our Introduction.
390. Pierre Daniel Huet (1630-1721) was appointed as assistant tutor to the Dauphin
   in 1670. In 1676 he became a priest and was later made bishop (1685). The book
   probably intended is the *Demonstratio evangelica* (1679). Another attack on the
   TTP, *Quaestiones aletnanae de concordia rationis et fidei*, was published in 1690.

LETTER 81
To the most noble and learned Mr. Ehrenfried Walther von Tschirnhaus, from B.d.S.

[Known only from the O.P. The original is lost.]

Most noble Sir,

My statement in my letter concerning the Infinite,[391] that it is not from the multitude of parts that an infinity of parts is inferred, is clear from this consideration: if it were inferred from the multitude of parts, we would not be able to conceive a greater multitude of parts, but their multitude would have to be greater than any given number. This is not true, because in the entire space between the two non-concentric circles we conceive there to be twice the number of parts as in half that space, and yet the number of parts both in the half as well as the whole of this space is greater than any assignable number.[392]

Further, from Extension as conceived by Descartes, to wit, an inert mass, it is not only difficult, as you say, but quite impossible to demonstrate the existence of bodies. For matter at rest, as far as in it lies, will continue to be at rest, and will not be set in motion except by a more powerful external cause.[393] For this reason I have not hesitated on a previous occasion to affirm that Descartes' principles of natural things are of no service, not to say quite wrong.

The Hague, 5 May 1676.

---

391. Ep12; see our Introduction, section 3 for more information.
392. This is another indication of Spinoza's reserving the term 'number' for finite magnitudes: he will speak of 'infinity' but not of an 'infinite number'. The false assumption that multiplying an infinite number by a finite number (here, two) produces an infinity with 'twice the number of parts' was common to seventeenth-century thinkers, and appears also in Newton.
393. Spinoza's conception of extension or matter is, unlike that of Descartes, essentially dynamic. Motion must be imposed on the material universe in Descartes' view by divine 'thrust'. This is because there is no concept of force within Cartesian physics and it must be imported by God. This feature figures heavily in Descartes' explanation of divine concurrence.

LETTER 82
To the acute and learned philosopher B.d.S.,
from Ehrenfried Walther von Tschirnhaus

[Known only from the O.P. The original is lost.]

Most learned Sir,

I should like you to do me the kindness of showing how, from Extension as conceived in your philosophy, the variety of things can be demonstrated a priori. For you mention Descartes' view, by which he maintains that he cannot deduce this variety from Extension in any other way than by supposing that this was an effect produced in Extension by motion started by God. Therefore, in my opinion, it is not from inert matter that he deduces the existence of bodies, unless you discount the supposition of God as mover. For you have not shown how this must necessarily follow a priori from the essence of God, a point whose demonstration Descartes believed to surpass human understanding. Therefore, knowing well that you entertain a different view, I seek from you an answer to this question, unless there is some weighty reason why you have hitherto refrained from making this public. If there had been no need for this – which I do not doubt – you would have given some kind of indication of your meaning. But be quite assured that, whether you speak to me frankly or with reserve, my regard for you will remain unchanged.

However, my particular reasons for making this request are as follows. In mathematics I have always observed that from any thing considered in itself – that is, from the definition of any thing – we are able to deduce at least one property; but if we wish to deduce more properties, we have to relate the thing defined to other things. It is only then, from the combination of the definitions of these things, that new properties emerge. For example, if I consider the circumference of a circle in isolation, I can infer nothing other than that it is everywhere alike or uniform, in respect of which property it differs essentially from all other curves; nor shall I ever be able to deduce any other properties. But if I relate it to other things, such as the radii drawn from the centre, or two intersecting chords, or many other things, I shall in some way be able to deduce more properties. This seems to be at variance to some extent with Proposition 16 of the *Ethics*,[394] almost the most important proposition of the first book of your Treatise. In this proposition it is taken for granted that several properties can be deduced from the given definition of any thing, which seems to me impossible if we do not relate the thing defined to other things. In consequence, I fail to see how from an Attribute considered only by itself, for example, Extension, an infinite variety of bodies can arise. Or if you think that, while this cannot be inferred from a single Attribute considered by itself, it can so be from all taken together, I should like you to instruct me on this point, and how this should be conceived. Farewell, etc.

Paris, 23 June 1676.

---

394. E1P16: "From the necessity of the divine nature there must follow infinite things in infinite ways, that is, everything that can come within the scope of infinite intellect."

LETTER 83
To the most noble and learned Mr. Ehrenfried Walther von Tschirnhaus, from B.d.S.

[Known only from the O.P. The original is lost. The signature appears only in the Dutch edition of the O.P.]

Most noble Sir,

With regard to your question as to whether the variety of things can be demonstrated a priori solely from the conception of Extension, I think I have already made it quite clear that this is impossible. That is why Descartes is wrong in defining matter through Extension; it must necessarily be explicated through an attribute which expresses eternal and infinite essence. But perhaps, if I live long enough,[395] I shall some time discuss this with you more clearly; for as yet I have not had the opportunity to arrange in due order anything on this subject.

As to what you add, that from the definition of any thing, considered in itself, we can deduce only one property, this may hold good in the case of the most simple things, or in the case of mental constructs (*entia rationis*), in which I include figures, but not in the case of real things.[396] Simply from the fact that I define God as an Entity to whose essence existence belongs, I infer several properties of him, such as that he necessarily exists, that he is one alone, immutable, infinite, etc. I could adduce several examples of this kind, which I omit for the present.

Finally, I beg you to enquire whether Mr. Huet's Treatise (the one against the *Tractatus Theologico-Politicus*),[397] of which you previously wrote, has yet been published, and whether you will be able to send me a copy. Also, do you yet know what are the recent discoveries about refraction?[398]

---

395. Spinoza died only seven months after writing this letter.
396. Spinoza was partly indebted to Hobbes in his account of constructive definition. See Martial Gueroult, *Spinoza: Dieu* (*Ethique, 1*) (Paris: Aubier, 1968), 19-48.
397. See our note to Ep80 for more information.
398. This could refer to Newton's discovery in 1670 that a prism refracts white light into colored beams which have various capacities for further refraction; this was communicated in 1672 and discussed for several more years. It could also refer to Erasmus Bartholinus' 1669 publication *Experimenta crystalli islandici disdiaclastici*

And so farewell, most noble Sir, and continue to hold in your affection,

      Yours,
      B.d.S.

The Hague, 15 July 1676.

---

which reported on the double refraction achieved by passing light through a piece of Iceland spar.

LETTER 84
To a friend, concerning the Tractatus Politicus

[Printed in the O.P., but not in the Correspondence. It
appears as a Preface to the *Tractatus Politicus*. The
original is lost, and it is not known to whom it was addressed.]

Dear Friend,

Your welcome letter was delivered to me yesterday. I thank you
most sincerely for the considerable trouble you take on my behalf. I
should not let pass this opportunity, etc., if I were not engaged in a certain matter which I believe to be more important, and which I think
will be more to your liking, namely, in composing a Political Treatise,
which I began some time ago at your suggestion. Of this Treatise six
chapters are already completed. The first is a kind of Introduction to
the work itself; the second deals with natural right; the third with the
right of Sovereign Powers; the fourth with the question of what political
matters are under the control of Sovereign Powers, the fifth with what
is the ultimate and highest aim a Society can contemplate, and the sixth
with the way a monarchy should be organised so as not to degenerate
into tyranny. At present I am engaged on the seventh chapter, in which
I justify methodically all those sections of the preceding sixth chapter
that concern the constitution of a well organised monarchy. Then I
shall pass on to Aristocracy and Democracy, and finally to Laws and
other particular questions concerning Politics.[399]

And so, farewell, etc.

[The Hague, 1676].

---

399. The TP ends with an incomplete chapter XI which was to have begun the
extended discussion of democracy. See the text with notes and commentary by
Sylvain Zac: Spinoza, *Traité politique* (Paris: Vrin, 1968).

Bibliography

Editions of the Correspondence

De Nagelate Schriften van B.d.S. Als Zedekunst, Staatkunde, Verbetering van't Verstant. Amsterdam, publisher not cited, 1677.

B. de S. Opera Posthuma, quorum series post Praefationem exhibetur. Amsterdam, publisher not cited, 1677.

Opera quae supersunt omnia. 4 vols. Leipzig: Bernhardt Tauchnitz, 1844. Carolus Bruder, ed.

Opera quotquot reperta sunt. 4 vols. Hague: Martinus Nijhoff, 1914. J. Van Vloten and J. P. N. Land, Eds.

Opera, im Auftrag der Heidelberger Akademie der Wissenschaften, ed. Carl Gebhardt. 5 vols. Heidelberg: Carl Winter Universitätsverlag, 1925.

Translations of the Correspondence

Oeuvres de Spinoza, Edition Garnier. Charles Appuhn, tr. 2 vols. Paris: Garnier, 1945.

Oeuvres Complètes. Edition Pléiade. R. Caillois, M. Francès, and R. Misrahi, tr. Paris: Gallimard, 1954.

Altwicker, Norbert, ed. *Opera V: Supplementa.* Heidelberg: Carl Winter Universitätsverlag, 1987.

Curley, Edwin, tr. *The Collected Works of Spinoza.* Vol. 1. Princeton: Princeton University Press, 1985. [Ep1-29].

Domínguez, Atilano, tr. *Correspondencia.* Madrid: Alianza Editorial, 1988.

Elwes, R. H. M., tr. *Chief Works.* 2 vols. New York: Dover, 1951. [Selections].

Estop, Juan D. S., tr. *Correspondencia completa.* Madrid: Edición Hiperion, 1988.

Gawlick, G., and Niewohner, F., tr. *Opera – Werke.* 2 vols. Darmstadt: Wissenschaftliche Buchgesellschaft, 1980.

Gebhardt, Carl, ed. *Opera V: Supplementa.* Heidelberg: Carl Winter Universitätsverlag, 1987.

___, tr. *Briefwechsel*. Anhang und Bibliographie von Manfred Walther. Hamburg: Felix Meiner, 1986.

Saisset, Emile, ed. & tr. *Oeuvres de Spinoza*. 3 vols. Paris: Charpentier, 1872.

Shirley, Samuel, tr. *The Ethics and Selected Letters*. Indianapolis: Hackett, 1982. [Selections].

___, tr. *Ethics, Treatise on the Emendation of the Intellect, and Selected Letters*. Indianapolis: Hackett, 1992. [Selections].

Wolf, A., tr. *The Correspondence of Spinoza*. London: George Allen & Unwin, 1928. [Reprinted, London: Frank Cass, 1966].

Reviews and Collections

Chronicon spinozanum, Hagae Comitis, curis Societatis Spinozanae, 5 vols., 1921-1927.

Mededelingen vanwege het Spinozahuis. Vols. 1-58 (1934-1989): Leiden, E. J. Brill. Vols. 59 and later: Delft, Eburon.

Cahiers Spinoza, Paris, Éditions Répliques, since 1977, irregular.

Bulletin de l'Association des Amis de Spinoza (newsletter), Paris, since 1978, irregular.

Bulletin de bibliographie spinoziste, published in *Archives de Philosophie*, since 1979, annual.

Studia Spinozana, since 1985, irregular.

Travaux et documents du Groupe de recherches spinozistes, Presses de l'Université de Paris-Sorbonne, since 1989, irregular.

Guest Lectures and Seminar Papers on Spinozism, Rotterdam, Erasmus Universiteit, since 1986, irregular.

NASS Newsletter, Newsletter of the North American Spinoza Society, three issues annually, since 1992.

NASS Monographs, since 1993, irregular.

Bibliography of Secondary Sources

Adelphe, Louis. "La formation et la diffusion de la politique de Spinoza: Questions et hypothèses fondées sur des documents nouveaux," *Revue de Synthèse Historique* 28 (1914), 253-280.

Adler, Jacob. "Divine Attributes in Spinoza: Intrinsic and Relational," *Philosophy & Theology* 4 (1989), 33-52.

Akkerman, Fokke. "L'édition de Gebhardt de l'*Ethique* de Spinoza et ses sources," *Raison présente* 43 (1977a), 37-51.

___. "Vers une meilleure édition de la correspondance de Spinoza," *Revue internationale de philosophie* 31 (1977), 4-26.

___. *Studies in the Posthumous Works of Spinoza.* Groningen: Krips Repro Meppel, 1980.

___. "J. H. Glazemaker, An Early Translator of Spinoza," *Spinoza's Political and Theological Thought*, ed. C. de Deugd (Amsterdam: North Holland Publishing Co., 1984), 23-29.

___. "Leopold en Spinoza," *Ontroering door det Woord. Over J.H. Leopold*. Ed. P. Everard and H. Hartsuiker. The Gaue: Historische Uitgeverij, 1991a. 13-47.

___. "Etablissement du texte du *Tractatus Theologico-Politicus*," *L'Ecriture sainte au temps de Spinoza et dans le système spinoziste*, ed. Groupe de Recherches Spinozistes (Paris: Presses de l'Université de Paris-Sorbonne, 1992), 91-108.

Albiac, Gabriel. *La sinagoga vacia: Un estudio de las fuentes marranas del espinosismo.* Madrid: Hiperion, 1987.

___. "Epicurisme et saducéisme dans la communauté sépharade d'Amsterdam," *Archives de Philosophie* 57 (1994), 503-512.

___. *La synagogue vide : Les sources marranes du spinozisme.* Tr. Marie-Lucie Copete and Jean-Frédéric Schaub. Paris: Presses Universitaires de France, 1994.

___, and H. G. Hubbeling. "The Preface to Spinoza's Posthumous Works, 1677, and its Author Jarig Jelles (c. 1619/20-1683)," *Lias* 6 (1979), 103-173.

Altkirch, Ernst. *Maledictus und Benedictus.* Leipzig: Felix Meiner, 1924.

Atlas, Samuel. "Solomon Maimon and Spinoza," *Hebrew Union College Annual (Cincinnati)* 30 (1959), 233-285.

Baer, Titzhak. *A History of the Jews in Christian Spain.* Philadelphia: Jewish Publication Society, 1992.

Balan, Bernard, "Spinoza et la théorie de l'identité dans las philosophie de l'esprit" *Spinoza au XXe siècle*, ed. Olivier Bloch (Paris: Presses Universitaires de France, 1993) 307-326.

Balen, Petrus Van, and Van Den Hoven, M. J. ed. *De verbetering der gedachten (1684)*. Baarn: Ambo, 1988.

Balet, Leo. *Rembrandt and Spinoza.* New York: Philosophical Library, 1962.

Balibar, Etienne. *Spinoza et la politique*. Paris: Presses Universitaires de France, 1985.

Balling, Pieter. *Het Licht op den Kandelaar* (1662). Carl Gebhardt, ed. and tr. *Chronicon Spinozanum* 4 (1924-1926).

Barbone, Steven. "Spinoza and Cognitivism: A Critique," *Studia Spinozana* 8 (1992), 227-231.

___. "Virtue and Sociality in Spinoza," *Iyyun* 42 (1993), 383-395.

___. "Putting Order in Order," *Nass Monograph* #2 (Milwaukee: North American Spinoza Society, 1994), 17-22.

___, and Rice, Lee. "Spinoza and the Problem of Suicide," *International Philosophical Quarterly* 34 (1994), 229-241.

Bartuschat, W. "Spinoza in der Philosophie von Leibniz," *Spinozas Ethik und ihre frühe Wirkung*, ed. K. Cramer, W. G. Jacobs, and W. Schmidt-Biggeman (Wolfenbuttel: Herzog August Bibliotek, 1981), 51-66.

Bedjai, Marc. "Métaphysique, éthique et politiques dans l'oeuvre du docteur Franciscus van den Enden (1602-1674)," *Studia Spinozana* 6 (1990), 291-302.

___. "Franciscus van den Enden, maître spirituel de Spinoza," *Revue de l'Histoire des Religions* 207 (1990), 289-311.

___. *Le docteur Franciscus van den Enden, son cercle et l'alchimie dans les Provinces-Unies au XVIIe siècle*. Paris: République des Lettres, 1991.

___. "Métaphysique, éthique et politique dans l'oeuvre du Dr Franciscus van den Enden," *Aries* 12-13 (1991), 116-120.

Belaval, Yvon. "Le *Leibniz et Spinoza* de M. Georges Friedmann," *Revue de Métaphysique et de Morale* 53 (1948), 307-321.

___. "Leibniz lecteur de Spinoza," *Archives de Philosophie* 1983, 531-552.

Beltrán, Miguel. *El "marrano" Spinoza y la racionalidad de los Colegiantes*. Madrid: Cuadernos Salmantinos de Filosofía, 1993.

Benamozegh, Elia. *Ecrits. Première Partie: Spinoza et la Kabbalah*. Haifa: University of Haifa, 1988.

Bennassar, Bartholome. *L'Inquisition espagnole*. Paris: Presses Universitaires de France, 1979.

Bennett, Jonathan. *A Study of Spinoza's Ethics*. Indianapolis: Hackett, 1984.

Berti, Sylvia. "La vie et l'esprit de Spinoza (1719)," *Revista Storica Italiana* 98 (1986), 32-46.

Bertrand, Michèle. *Spinoza et l'imaginaire*. Paris: Presses Universitaires de France, 1983.

Biderman, A. K.-S. "Why was Baruch de Spinoza Excommunicated?" *Sceptics, Millenariums and Jews*, ed. David S. Katz-Jonathan (Leiden: Brill, 1990), 98-141.

Bloch, Olivier. "Damiron et Spinoza," *Spinoza entre Lumières et Romantisme*, ed. J. Bonnamour (Fontenay-aux-Roses: Ecole Normale Supérieure, 1985), 229-232.

___. "Le médecin Gaultier, *Parité de la vie et de la mort*, et Spinoza," *Spinoza au XVIIIe siècle*, ed. O. Bloch. Actes des Journées d'Etudes à la Sorbonne (1987). Paris: Méridiens Klincksieck, 1990. 105-120.

Blom, Hans W. "Lambert van Velthuysen et le naturalisme," *Cahiers Spinoza* 6 (1991), 203-212.

Boros, Gabor. *Heilsfragment Rekonstruktion der Spinozianischen Ethik.* Budapest: Doxa Library, 1990.

Bouillier, Francisque. *Histoire de la philosophie cartésienne.* 3rd ed. Paris: Delagrave, 1868.

Bourel, Dominique. "La réfutation de Spinoza par Christian Wolff," *Spinoza au XVIIIe siècle*, ed. O. Bloch. Actes des Journées d'Etudes à la Sorbonne (1987) (Paris: Méridiens Klincksieck, 1990), 219-224.

Bouveresse, R. "Une lettre de Spinoza," *Revue philosophique de Louvain* 76 (1978), 427-446.

___. *Spinoza et Leibniz: l'idée d'animisme universel.* Paris: Vrin, 1992.

Boyle, Robert. *The Complete Works*, ed. Thomas Birch, introduction by Douglas McKie. 6 vols. Hildesheim: Georg Olms Verlag, 1965-1966. [Photographic reprint of the London edition of 1772.]

Brunschvicq, L. "Spinoza et ses contemporains," *Revue de Métaphysique et de Morale* 13-14 (1906), (13) 673-705; (14) 35-82.

Brykman, Genevieve. *La Judéité de Spinoza.* Paris: Vrin, 1972.

___. "Bayle's Case for Spinoza," *Proceedings of the Aristotelian Society* 88 (1988), 259-270.

Burbage, Frank, and Chouchan, Nathalie. "A propos du rapport Diderot-Spinoza: Spinozisme et matérialisme," *Spinoza au XVIIIe siècle*, ed. O. Bloch. Actes des Journées d'Etudes à la Sorbonne (1987) (Paris: Méridiens Klincksieck, 1990), 169-180.

Calvetti, Carla G. *Benedetto Spinoza di fronte a Leone Ebreo: Problemi etico-religiosi e amor Dei intellectualis.* Milan: CUSL, 1982.

Canone, Eugenio, and Totaro, Giuseppina. "In *Tractatus de intellectus emendatione* di Spinoza. Index locorum," *Lexicon Philosophicum* 5 (1991), 21-127.

Charles-Daubert, F. "Spinoza et les libertins – le *Traité des trois imposteurs* ou *L'esprit de Spinoza*," *Spinoza: Science et Religion*, ed. Renée Bouveresse (Paris: Vrin, 1988), 171-182.

Clair, Pierre. *Libertinage et incrédules*. Paris: CNRS, 1983.

Constans, Lucius A. *De jure ecclesiasticorum*. Amsterdam: Alethopoli, 1665. French reprint with facing translation by V. Butori: *Du droit des ecclésiastiques*. Caen: Centre de philosophie politique et juridique, 1991.

Crescas, Hasdai [Hasdai, Chasdai]. *Or Adonai*. Ferrara: Abraham Usque, 1555.

___. *Or Adonai*, ed. Shelomoh Fisher. Jerusalem: Sifre Ramot, 1988.

Curley, Edwin. "Notes on a Neglected Masterpiece, II: The *Theologico-Political Treatise* as a Prolegomenon to the *Ethics*," *Central Themes in Early Modern Philosophy*, ed. A. J. Cover and Mark Kulstad (Indianapolis: Hackett, 1990), 109-159.

Da Costa, Uriel [Gabriel da Costa, Uriel d'Acosta]. "Où l'on établit les erreurs et les maux qu'entraine le fait de tenir l'âme humaine pour immortelle," tr. J.-P. Osier. *Cahiers Spinoza* 3 (1980), 111-116.

___. *Espejo de una vida humana (Exemplar humanae vitae)*. Madrid: Libros Hiperion, 1984.

d'Allonnes, Myriam Revault. "Spinoza et la 'crise' du théologico-politique," *Le Religieux dans le Politique: Le Genre Humain* (Paris: Seuil, 1991), 69-80.

Daudin, A. "Spinoza et la science expérimentale: sa discussion de l'expérience de Boyle," *Revue de l'Histoire des Sciences* II (1949), 179-190.

Delbos, Victor. "La doctrine spinoziste des attributs de Dieu," *L'Année Philosophique* 23 (1913), 1-17.

Deleuze, Gilles. *Spinoza et le problème de l'expression*. Paris: Editions de Minuit, 1968.

___. *Expressionism in Philosophy: Spinoza*, tr. Martin Joughin. Cambridge, MA: MIT Press, 1990.

Den Uyl, Douglas J. *Power, State and Freedom*. Assen: Van Gorcum, 1983.

___. "Sociality and Social Contract: A Spinozistic Perspective," *Studia Spinozana* 1 (1985), 19-52.

___. "Passion, State and Progress: Spinoza and Mandeville on the Nature of Human Association," *Journal of the History of Philosophy* 25 (1987), 369-395.

___, and Rice, Lee C. "Spinoza and Hume on Individuals," *Reason Papers* 15 (1990), 91-117.

___, and Warner, Stuart D. "Liberalism and Hobbes and Spinoza," *Studia Spinozana* 3 (1987), 261-318.

Deugd, Cornelius de, and Roger Henrard. *Guido van Suchtelen - Niet als Sacretaris Maar als Auteur. De Vereniging det Spinozahuis en haar Secretarissen.* Leiden: Brill, 1990.

De Vet, J. J. V. M. "Was Spinoza de Auteur Van Stelkonstige Reeckening Van den Regenboog en van Reeckening van Kanssen," *Tijdschrift voor filosofie* 45 (1983), 602-639.

Diaz, A. M. Vaz. *Spinoza – Merchant and Autodidact.* Paris: Institut Néerlandais, 1977.

___. *Spinoza and Joosten De Vries.* Delft: Eburon, 1989.

Dilthey, Wilhelm. "Das natürliche System der Geisteswissenschaften in siebzehnten Jahrhundert," *Archiv für Geschichte der Philosophie* 5-6 (1892-93): (5) 480-502; (6) 60-126, 225-256, 347-379, 509-545.

Domínguez, Atilano. "Modos infinitos y entendimiento divino en la metafísica de Spinoza," *Sefarad* 38 (1978), 107-141.

___. "Libertad y democracia en la filosofía política de Spinoza," *Revista de Estudios politicos* 11 (1979), 131-156.

___. "La morale de Spinoza et le salut par la foi," *Revue philosophique de Louvain* 78 (1980), 345-364.

___. "Bibliographie espagnole ey hispanoaméricaine sur Spinoza," *Bulletin de Bibliographie Spinoziste* 6 (1984), 1-8.

___. "Présence et absence de Spinoza en Espagne (1750-1878)," *Spinoza entre Lumières et Romantisme*, ed. J. Bonnamour. Fontenay-aux-Roses: Ecole Normale Supérieure, 1985. 285-302.

___. "Conocimiento y perfección humana en el 'Tratado breve' de Spinoza," *La Etica de Spinoza: Fundamentos y significado*, ed. Atilano Domínguez (Castilla-La Mancha: Ediciones de la Universidad, 1992), 37-52.

___, ed. *La Etica de Spinoza: Fundamentos y significado.* Castilla-La Mancha: Ediciones de la Universidad, 1992.

___. "Apunte bibliográfico sobre Spinoza en Brasil" *Spinoza y España*, ed. Atilano Domínguez (La Mancha: Universidad de Castilla-La Mancha, 1994), 121-122.

___. "España en Spinoza y Spinoza en España." *Spinoza y España*, ed. Atilano Domínguez (La Mancha: Universidad de Castilla-La Mancha, 1994), 9-46.

___. "Presencia de Antonio Pérez en Spinoza." *Spinoza y España*, ed. Atilano Domínguez (La Mancha: Universidad de Castilla-La Mancha, 1994), 165-178.

___. "Relaciones entre Spinoza y España." *Nass Monograph* #2 (Milwaukee: North American Spinoza Society, 1994), 23-27.

___, ed. *Spinoza y España*. La Mancha: Universidad de Castilla-La Mancha, 1994.

Donagan, Alan. *Spinoza*. Chicago: University of Chicago Press, 1988.

Dujovne, Leon. *Spinoza: Su vida, su época, su obra, su influencia*. 4 vols. Buenos Aires: Imprenta López, 1941-1945.

___. "Spinoza y el Judaísmo," *Homenaje a Baruch Spinoza*, ed. Rene Cassin (Buenos Aires: Museo Judío de Buenos Aires, 1976), 77-82.

Dunin-Borkowski, Stanislaus von, S.J. "Nachlese zur ältesten Geschichte des Spinozismus," *Archiv für Geschichte der Philosophie* 24 (1910), 61-98.

___. *Das Lebenswerk Spinozas*. 4 vols. Munster im Westen: Aschendorffschen Verlagsbuchhandlung, 1932-1936.

Dunner, Joseph. *Spinoza and Western Democracy*. New York: Philosophical Library, 1955.

Duukerius, Johannes. *Het leven van Philopater: Vervolg van Philopater: Een spinozistische sleutelroman uit 1691-1697*. Amsterdam: Rodopi, 1991.

Eugenio, Fernández G. "Potentia et Potestas dans les premiers écrits de Spinoza," *Studia Spinozana* 4 (1988), 195-226.

Feld, Edouard. *Spinoza the Jew*. Princeton: Princeton University Press, 1982.

Feldman, Seymour. "Spinoza: A Marrano of Reason?" *Inquiry* 35 (1992), 37-53.

Fix, Andrew C. *Prophecy and Reason: The Dutch Collegiants in the Early Enlightenment*. Princeton: Princeton University Press, 1991.

Francès, Madeleine. *Spinoza dans les pays néerlandais de la seconde moitié du xviie siècle*. 2 vols. Paris: Alcan, 1937.

Franck, I. "Spinoza's Onslaught on Judaism," *Judaism* 28 (1979), 177-193.

Frankena, William. "Spinoza on the Knowledge of Good and Evil," *Philosophia* 7 (1977), 15-44.

Freudenthal, J. *Die Lebensgeschichte Spinoza*. Leipzig: Verlag von Veit, 1899.

___. *Spinoza und die Scholastik*. Leipzig: Verlag von Veit, 1899.

___. *Spinoza, sein Leben und sein Lehre*. 2 vols. Stuttgart: F. Fromanns Verlag, 1904.

Friedman, J. I. "Spinoza's Denial of Free Will in Man and God," *Spinoza's Philosophy of Man*, ed. Jon Wetlesen (Oslo: Universitetsforlaget, 1978), 51-84.

Friedmann, Georges. *Leibniz et Spinoza*, 2nd ed. Paris: Gallimard, 1962.

Furlan, Augusto. "Spinoza: presencia de la tradición en la modernidad," *Sapientia* 47 (1992), 45-64.

Garoux, Alain. *Spinoza: Bibliographie 1971-1977*. Université de Reims: Centre de Philosophie Politique, 1981.

Garrett, Don. "Freedom and the Good in Spinoza's *Ethics*," *Spinoza: Issues and Directions*, ed. Edwin Curley and Pierre-François Moreau (Leiden: E. J. Brill, 1990), 221-238.

___. "Ethics 1P5: Shared Attributes and the Basis of Spinoza's Monism," *Central Themes in Early Modern Philosophy*, ed. A. J. Cover and Mark Kulstad (Indianapolis: Hackett, 1990), 69-107.

Gebhardt, Carl. *Spinoza: Vier Reden*. Heidelberg: Winter, 1927.

___. "Spinoza in unsrer Zeit," *Septimana Spinozana*, ed. Societas Spinozana (The Hague: M. Nijhoff, 1933), 21-27.

___. "Le déchirement de la conscience," *Cahiers Spinoza* 3 (1980), 135-142.

Gehlhaar, Sabine S. *Prophetie und Gesetz bei Jehudah Hallevi, Maimonides, und Spinoza*. Frankfurt am Main: Peter Lang, 1987.

Giancotti, Emilia. *Lexicon Spinozanum*. The Hague: Nijhoff, 1970.

___. "Giovanni Gentile, éditeur et exégète de l'*Ethique*," *Spinoza au XXe Siècle*, ed. Olivier Bloch (Paris: Presses Universitaires de France, 1993), 405-420.

Gouhier, Henri. *L'Anti-humanisme au XVIIe siècle*. Paris: Presses Universitaires de France, 1987.

Grene, Marjorie, and Nails, Debra, eds. *Spinoza and the Sciences*. Dordrecht: Reidel, 1986.

Groupe de Recherches Spinozistes, ed. *Les premiers écrits de Spinoza*, Actes du colloque organisé par le Groupe de recherches spinozistes, *Revue des sciences philosophiques et théologiques* 71 (1987). [Reprinted in *Archives de philosophie* 51 (1988).]

___. *Travaux et documents 1: Lire et traduire Spinoza*. Paris: Presses de l'Université de Paris-Sorbonne, 1989.

___. *Travaux et documents 2: Méthode et métaphysique*. Paris: Presses Universitaires de France, 1989.

Grunder, Karlfriend, and Schmidt-Biggeman, Wilhelm, eds., *Spinoza in der Frühzeit seiner religiösen Wirkung*. Heidelberg: Lambert Schneider, 1984.

Gueroult, Martial. "La lettre de Spinoza sur l'infini," *Revue de Métaphysique et de Morale* 71 (1966), 385-411.

___. *Spinoza I: Dieu*. Paris: Aubier-Montaigne, 1968.

___. *Spinoza II: L'âme*. Hildesheim: Georg Olms Verlag, 1974.

Hall, Marie B. *Robert Boyle on Natural Philosophy*. Bloomington: Indiana University Press, 1965.

Hallett, H. F. *Aeternitas: A Spinozistic Study*. Oxford: Clarendon Press, 1930.

___. *Benedict de Spinoza: The Elements of His Philosophy*. London: Athlone Press, 1957.

___. *Creation, Emanation, and Salvation*. The Hague: Martinus Nijhoff, 1962.

Hampshire, Stuart. "Spinoza's Theory of Human Freedom," *Monist* 55 (1971), 554-566.

Harris, Errol E. *Is There an Esoteric Doctrine in the Tractatus Theologico-Politicus?* Leiden: E. J. Brill, 1978.

___. *The Substance of Spinoza*. Atlantic Highlands, N.J.: Humanities Press, 1995.

Harvey, Warren Z. "A Portrait of Spinoza as a Maimonidean," *Journal of the History of Philosophy* 19 (1981), 151-172.

Haserot, F. S. "Spinoza's Definition of Attribute," *Philosophical Review* 62 (1953), 499-513.

Heimbrock, H. G. *Vom Heil der Seele: Studien zum Verhältnis von Religion und Psychologie bei Baruch Spinoza*. Frankfurt am Main: Peter Lang, 1981.

Herer, Maximilien. *Spinoza*. Jerusalem: Jerusalem Spinoza Institute, 1971.

Hubbeling, H. G. "Aperçu général de la réception de la philosophie de Spinoza en Hollande au XVIIe siècle," *Cahiers Spinoza* 5 (1985), 167-186.

___. *De Studie van het Spinozisme in Nederland sedert de tweede Wereldoorlog*. Leiden: Brill, 1987.

Janet, Paul. "Spinoza et le spinozisme d'après les travaux récens," *Revue des Deux Mondes* 70 (1867), 470-498.

Jelles, Jarig. *Belydenisse des algemeenen en Christelyken geloofs, vervattet in een brief aan N. N., door Jarig Jelles*. Amsterdam: Jan Rieuwertsz, 1684.

Jongeneelen, Gerrit H. "An Unknown Pamphlet of Adriann Koerbagh," *Studia Spinozana* 3 (1987), 405-418.

Kaplan, Yosef. "The Portuguese Jews in Amsterdam," *Studia Rosenthaliana* 15 (1981), 37-51.

___. "On the Relation of Spinoza's Contemporaries in the Portuguese Jewish Community of Amsterdam to Spanish Culture and the Marrano Experience," *Spinoza's Political and Theological Thought*, ed. C. De Deugd (Amsterdam: North-Holland Publishing Co., 1984), 82-94.

___. "Spinoza Scholarship in Israel," *Spinoza's Political and Theological Thought*, ed. C. De Deugd (Amsterdam: North-Holland Publishing Co., 1984), 19-22.

___, ed. *Menasseh ben Israel and his World*. Leiden: E. J. Brill, 1989.

___. *From Christianity to Judaism: The Story of Isaac Orobio de Castro*, tr. R. Loewe. Oxford: Oxford University Press, 1989.

___, and Loewe, Raphael, tr. *From Christianity to Judaism: The Story of Isaac Orobio de Castro*. Oxford: Oxford U.P., 1989.

Kashap, S. Paul. *Spinoza and Moral Freedom*. New York: State University of New York Press, 1987.

Katz, David S., and Jonathan I. Israel, eds. *Jews, Millenarians and Sceptics*. Leiden: E. J. Brill, 1990.

Kerkhoven, Jaap. *Spinoza's Clausules Aangaan de Uitsluiting van Politieke Rechten in Hun Maatschaapelijke Context*. Leiden: Brill, 1991. [Vol. 63 of *Mededelingen vanwege het Spinozahuis*.]

Kingma, J., and Offenberg, A. K. *Bibliography of Spinoza's Works up to 1800*, *Studia Rosenthalia* 11 (1977), 1-32. [Separately printed, Assen: Van Gorcum, 1977.]

Klever, W. N. A. "The Helvetius Affair, or Spinoza and the Philosophers' Stone: A Document on the Background of Letter 40," *Studia Spinozana* 3 (1987), 439-458.

___. "Letters to and from Neercassel about Spinoza and Rieuwertsz," *Studia Spinozana* 4 (1988), 329-340.

___. "Spinoza Interviewed by Willem van Blyenbergh," *Studia Spinozana* 4 (1988), 317-320.

___. "Spinoza and Van den Enden in Borch's Diary in 1661 and 1662," *Studia Spinozana* 5 (1989), 311-326.

___. "Spinoza's Fame in 1667," *Studia Spinozana* 5 (1989), 359-364.

___. "Spinoza's *Hebrew Grammar* Praised by Petrus van Balen," *Studia Spinozana* 5 (1989), 365-368.

___. "Proto-Spinoza Franciscus van den Enden," *Studia Spinozana* 6 (1990), 281-290.

___. "Steno's Statements on Spinoza and Spinozism," *Studia Spinozana* 6 (1990), 303-316.

___. *Zuivere economische wetenschap: Een ontwerp basis von spinozistische beginselen*. Amsterdam: Boom Meppel, 1990.

___. "La clé du nom: Petrus van Gent (et Schuller) à partir d'une correspondance," *Cahiers Spinoza* 6 (1991), 169-202.

___. *Verba et sententiae Spinozae or Lambert van Velthuysen (1662-1685) on Benedictus de Spinoza.* Amsterdam: APA–North Holland, 1991.

___. "La clé du nom: Petrus van Gent (et Schuller) à partie d'une correspondance," *Cahiers Spinoza* 6 (1991), 169-202.

___. "La philosophie politique d'Adrien Koerbagh," *Cahiers Spinoza* 6 (1991), 247-268.

___. "Information on Spinoza and Some of His Acquaintances," *Studia Spinozana* 8 (1992), 297-309.

___. "Qui était l'Homunculus?" *Bulletin de l'Association des Amis de Spinoza* 29 (1993), 24-26.

___. "Blijenbergh's Tussing with Evil and Spinoza's Response," *Tijdschrift voor Filosofie* 55 (1993), 307-329.

Klijnsmit, Anthony J. *Spinoza and Grammatical Tradition.* Leiden: E. J. Brill, 1986.

___. *Spinoza on the Imperfection of Words.* Amsterdam: Stichting Neerlandistiek, 1989.

Kline, George L. "Absolute and Relative Senses of *Liberum* and *Libertas* in Spinoza," *Spinoza nel 350o anniversario della nascita*, ed. Emilia Giancotti (Urbino: Bibliopolis, 1982), 259-280.

Koerbagh, Adriaan, and Koerbagh, Jan. *Een ligt schijende in duystere plaatsen.* Brussels: Vrije Universiteit Brussel, Centrum voor de Studie van de Verlichting, 1974. [Based upon first edition.]

Lagrée, J. "Le thème des deux livres de la nature et l'écriture," *L'Ecriture sainte au temps de Spinoza et dans le système spinoziste*, ed. Groupe de Recherches Spinozistes (Paris: Presses de l'Université de Paris-Sorbonne, 1992), 11-40.

Laplanche, F. "L'érudition chrétienne aux XVIe et XVIIe siècles," *L'Ecriture sainte au temps de Spinoza et dans le système spinoziste*, ed. Groupe de Recherches Spinozistes (Paris: Presses de l'Université de Paris-Sorbonne, 1992), 133-148.

Laux, Henri. "Le Christ et les Ecritures chez Spinoza," *Bulletin de l'Association des Amis de Spinoza* 28 (1992), 1-10.

___. *Imagination et religion chez Spinoza.* Paris: Vrin, 1993.

LeClerc, Jean, and Sina, Mario, eds. *Epistolario, Vol. I: 1679-1689.* Florence: Leo Olschki Editore, 1987.

Leopold, J. H. *Ad Spinozae Opera Posthuma.* The Hague: M. Nijhoff, 1902.

Levi, Z. "The Impact of Jewish Influences on Spinoza's Philosophy," *Spinoza Studies (Haifa)* 1978 (1978), 147-166.

___. "On Some Early Responses to Spinoza's Philosophy in Jewish Thought," *Studia Spinozana* 6 (1990), 251-280.

Lewis, Christopher E. "Baruch Spinoza, A Critic of Robert Boyle: On Matter," *Dialogue* (PST) 27 (1984), 11-22.

Macherey, Pierre. *Hegel ou Spinoza*. Paris: Editions de la Découverte, 1990.

___. *Introduction à l'Ethique de Spinoza: La cinquième partie, les voies de la libération*. Paris: Presses Universitaires de France, 1994.

McKeon, Richard. *The Philosophy of Spinoza*. New York: Longmans, Green, and Co., 1928.

Mark, Thomas C. "The Spinozistic Attributes," *Philosophia* 7 (1977), 55-82.

Matheron, Alexandre. *Individu et communauté chez Spinoza*. Paris: Editions de Minuit, 1969.

___. *Le Christ et le salut des ignorants chez Spinoza*. Paris: Aubier, 1971.

___. "Femmes et serviteurs dans la démocratie spinoziste," *Speculum Spinozanum: 1677-1977*, ed. Siegfried Hessing (London: Routledge and Kegan Paul, 1977), 368-386.

___. "Le *Traité Théologico-Politique* vu par le jeune Marx," *Cahiers Spinoza* 1 (1977), 159-212.

___. "*L'Anomalie sauvage* d'Antonio Negri," *Cahiers Spinoza* 4 (1983), 39-60.

___. "Spinoza et le problématique juridique de Grotius," *Philosophie* 4 (1984), 69-89.

___. "Le droit du plus fort: Hobbes contre Spinoza," *Revue Philosophique* 1985/2 (1985), 149-176.

___. "La fonction théorique de la démocratie chez Spinoza," *Studia Spinozana* 1 (1985), 259-274.

___. *Etudes sur Spinoza: Anthropologie et politique au XVIIe siècle*. Paris: Vrin, 1986.

___. "Les modes de connaissance du *Traité de la réforme de l'entendement* et les genres de connaissance de l'*Ethique*," *Spinoza: Science et Religion*, ed. Renée Bouveresse (Paris: Vrin, 1988), 97-108.

___. "Idée de l'idée et certitude," *Travaux et documents 2: Méthode et métaphysique*, ed. Groupe de recherches spinozistes (Paris: Presses Universitaires de France, 1989), 93-104.

___. "Le problème de l'évolution de Spinoza du *Traité théologico-politique* au *Traité politique*," *Spinoza: Issues and Directions*, ed. Edwin Curley and Pierre-François Moreau (Leiden: E. J. Brill, 1990), 258-270.

___. "Essence, Existence and Power in Ethics I: The Foundations of Proposition 16," *God and Nature: Spinoza's Metaphysics*, ed. Yirmiyahu Yovel (Leiden: E. J. Brill, 1991), 23-34.

___. "Physique et ontologie chez Spinoza: l'énigmatique réponse à Tschirnhaus," *Cahiers Spinoza* 6 (1991), 83-110.

___. "La déduction de la loi divine et les stratégies discursives de Spinoza," *Nature, Croyance, Raison: Mélanges offerts à Sylvain Zac*, ed. P.-F. Moreau, Jacqueline Lagree, and Michele Crampe-Casnabet (St-Cloud: E. N. S. Fontenay, 1992), 53-80.

___. "Le statut ontologique de l'Ecriture sainte," *L'Ecriture sainte au temps de Spinoza et dans le système spinoziste*, ed. Groupe de Recherches Spinozistes (Paris: Presses de l'Université de Paris-Sorbonne, 1992), 109-118.

___. "Ideas of Ideas and Certainty in the *Tractatus de Intellectus Emendatione* and the *Ethics*," *Spinoza on Knowledge and the Human Mind*, ed. Y. Yovel and G. Segal (Leiden: E. J. Brill, 1994), 83-92.

___. "L'indignation et le conatus de l'état spinoziste," *Spinoza: Puissance et ontologie*, ed. Myriam R. D'Allones and Hadi Rizk (Paris: Editions Kimé, 1994), 153-165.

___. "La vie éternelle et le corps selon Spinoza," *Revue Philosophique de la France et de l'Etranger* 1994#1, 27-40.

___, and Moreau, P.-F. "Martial Gueroult et Etienne Gilson lecteurs de Spinoza," *Bulletin de Bibliographie Spinoziste* 1 (1979), 1-7.

Méchoulan, Henry. "Le *herem* à Amsterdam et 'l'excommunication' de Spinoza," *Cahiers Spinoza* 3 (1980), 117-134.

___. "Un regard sur la pensée juive è Amsterdam au temps de Spinoza," *Cahiers Spinoza* 3 (1980), 51-66.

___. "Spinoza et le judaïsme," *Spinoza : Science et Religion*, ed. Renée Bouveresse (Paris: Vrin, 1988), 151-154.

___. *Etre Juif à Amsterdam au temps de Spinoza*. Paris: Albin Michel, 1991.

Meijer, Jaap. *Balans der ballingschap. Bijdragen tot de geschiedenis des Joden in Nederland*. 4 vols. Hemstede: Herman Meijermanslaan, 1989.

Meinsma, K. O. *Spinoza en zijn Kring*. The Hague: Martinus Nijhoff, 1896.

___. *Spinoza und sein Kreis*. Berlin: Karl Schnabel Verlag, 1909.

___. *Spinoza et son cercle*. Traduit du néerlandais par S. Roosenburg. Appendices latins et allemands traduits par J.-P. Osier. Précisions et notes par Henry Méchoulan et Pierre-François Moreau. Paris: Vrin, 1983.

Metzger, H. *Les doctrines chimiques en France du début du XVIIe siècle à la fin du XVIIIe siècle*. Paris: A. Blanchard, 1922.

Meyer, Louis. [Meijer; Ludovicus, Lodewijk, Ludwig]. *De materia, ejusque affectionibus motu, et quiete*. Amsterdam: Francisci Hackii, 1660. Reprinted in *Chronicon Spinozanum* 22 (1922), 187-198. Reprinted with French translation in Renée Bouveresse, *Spinoza et Leibniz: L'idée d'animisme universel* (Paris: Vrin, 1992), 295-312.

___. *De calido nativo, ejusque morbis*. Leiden: Francisci Hackii, 1660.

___. *Philosophia interpres scripturae sanctae*. Amsterdam: Alethopoli, 1666. French translation: *La philosophie l'interprète de l'écriture sainte*, tr. J. Lagrée et P.-F. Moreau. Paris: Intertextes Editeur, 1988.

Mignini, Filippo. "Sur la genèse du *Court Traité*: l'hypothèse d'une dictée originaire est-elle fondée?" *Cahiers Spinoza* 5 (1985), 147-166.

___. "Per una nuova edizione del *Tractatus de Intellectus Emendatione*," *Studia Spinozana* 4 (1988), 15-36.

Moreau, Pierre-François. "Spinoza et le *Jus circa sacra*," *Studia Spinozana* 1 (1985), 335-344.

___, ed. *Les premiers écrits de Spinoza*. Paris: Vrin, 1987.

___. "Les principes de la lecture de l'Ecriture sainte dans le T.T.P.," *L'Ecriture sainte au temps de Spinoza et dans le système spinoziste*, ed. Groupe de Recherches Spinozistes (Paris: Presses de l'Université de Paris-Sorbonne, 1992), 119-132.

___. *Spinoza: L'Expérience et l'éternité*. Paris: Presses Universitaires de France, 1994.

Moutaux, Jacques. "Exotérisme et philosophie: Léo Strauss et l'interprétation du *Traité théologico-politique*," *Spinoza au XXe Siècle*, ed. Olivier Bloch (Paris: Presses Universitaires de France, 1993), 421-444.

Nahon, Gerard. "Amsterdam, métropole occidentale des *Séfarades* au XVIIe siècle," *Cahiers Spinoza* 3 (1980), 15-50.

Negri, Antonio. *L'anomalia selvaggia: Saggio su petere e potenza in Baruch Spinoza*. Rome: Feltrinelli, 1981.

___. *L'anomalie sauvage: puissance et pouvoir chez Spinoza*, tr. F. Matheron. Paris: Vrin, 1982.

___. *The Savage Anomaly: The Power of Spinoza's Metaphysics and Politics*, tr. M. Hardt. Minneapolis: University of Minnesota Press, 1991.

___. *Spinoza subversif: Variations (in)actuelles*, tr. M. Raiola and F. Matheron. Paris: Editions Kimé, 1994.

Niewöhner, Friedrich. "Spinoza und die Pharisäer: Eine begriffsgeschichtliche Miszelle zu einem antisemitischen Slogan," *Studia Spinoza* 1 (1985), 347-358.

Offenberg, A. K. "Jacob Jehuda Leon (1602-1675) and his Model of the Temple," *Jewish-Christian Relations in the Seventeenth Century*, ed. J. van den Berg and E. G. E. van der Wall (Dordrecht: Kluwer, 1988), 95-118.

Oko, Adolph S. *The Spinoza Bibliography*. Boston: G. K. Hall, 1964.

Olschki, Leo S., ed. *Niccolo Stenone, 1638-1686*. Florence: Leo S. Olschki, 1988.

Osier, Jean-Pierre. "Un aspect du judäisme individualiste d'Uriel da Costa," *Cahiers Spinoza* 3 (1980), 101-110.

Paniagua, Juan A. P. "El *Mahasin al-mayalis* de Ibn al-Arif y la *Etica* de Spinoza," *Ciudad de Dios* 22 (1990), 671-681.

Parkinson, G. H. R. "Spinoza on the Power and Freedom of Man," *Monist* 55 (1971), 527-553.

Popkin, Richard. "Spinoza, the Quakers, and the Millenarians," *Manuscrito* 6 (1982), 113-133.

___. *History of Scepticism from Erasmus to Spinoza*. New York: John Wiley, 1983.

___. "Menasseh ben Israel and Isaac La Peyrere II," *Studia Rosenthaliana* 18 (1984), 12-20.

___. "Spinoza and the Conversion of the Jews," *Spinoza's Political and Theological Thought*, ed. C. De Deugd (Amsterdam: North-Holland Publishing Co., 1984), 171-183.

___. "Spinoza's Relations with the Quakers in Amsterdam," *Quaker History* 73 (1984), 14-28.

___. "The First Published Discussion of a Central Theme in Spinoza's Tractatus," *Philosophia* 17 (1987), 101-109.

___. *Isaac La Peyrre (1596-1676), His Life, Work and Influence*. Leiden: E. J. Brill, 1987.

___. "Some Aspects of Jewish-Christian Theological Interchanges in Holland and England 1640-1700," *Jewish-Christian Relations in the Seventeenth Century*, ed. J. van den Berg and E. G. E. van der Wall (Dordrecht: Kluwer, 1988), 3-32.

___. "Spinoza and the *Three Imposters*," *Spinoza: Issues and Directions*, ed. Edwin Curley and Pierre-François Moreau (Leiden: E. J. Brill, 1990), 347-358.

___. "Was Spinoza a Marrano of Reason?" *Philosophia* 20 (1990), 243-246.

___. *The Third Force in Seventeenth Century Thought*. Leiden: Koln, 1992.

Préposiet, Jean. *Spinoza et la liberté des hommes*. Paris: Gallimard, 1967.

___. *Bibliographie spinoziste*. Paris: Belles Lettres, 1973.

Ramond, Charles. *Qualité et quantité dans la philosophie de Spinoza*. Paris: Press Universitaires de France, 1995.

Revah, J. S. *Spinoza et le Dr. Juan de Prado*. Paris: Mouton, 1959.

Rice, Lee C. "Spinoza on Individuation," *Monist* 55 (1971), 640-659. [Reprinted in *Spinoza; Essays in Interpretation*, ed. M. Mandelbaum and E. Freeman (LaSalle: Open Court, 1975), 195-214.]

___. "Spinoza y el spinocismo en el siglo XX," *Homenaje a Baruch Spinoza*, ed. Rene Cassin (Buenos Aires: Museo Judio de Buenos Aires, 1976), 211-214.

___. "Emotion, Appetition, and Conatus in Spinoza," *Revue Internationale de Philosophie* 31 (1977), 101-116.

___. "Servitus in Spinoza: A Programmatic Analysis," *Spinoza's Philosophy of Man*, ed. Jon Wetlesen (Oslo: Universitetsforlaget, 1978), 179-191.

___. "Piety and Philosophical Freedom in Spinoza," *Spinoza's Political and Theological Thought*, ed. C. De Deugd (Amsterdam: North-Holland Publishing Co., 1984), 184-205.

___. "Spinoza, Bennett, and Teleology," *Southern Journal of Philosophy* 23 (1985), 241-254.

___. "Individual and Community in Spinoza's Social Psychology," *Spinoza: Issues and Directions*, ed. Edwin Curley and Pierre-François Moreau (Leiden: E. J. Brill, 1990), 271-285.

___. "Reflexive Ideas in Spinoza," *Journal of the History of Philosophy* 28 (1990), 201-211.

___. "Tanquam Humanae Naturae Exemplar: Spinoza on Human Nature," *Modern Schoolman* 68 (1991), 291-304.

___. "La causalité adéquate chez Spinoza," *Philosophiques* 19 (1992), 45-60.

___. "Autour de l'éthique de Spinoza et de Hume," *La Etica de Spinoza: Fundamentos y significado*, ed. Atilano Dominguez (Castilla-La Mancha: Ediciones de la Universidad, 1992), 99-108.

___. "Mind Eternity in Spinoza," *Iyyun* 41 (1992c), 319-334.

___. "Le nominalisme de Spinoza," *Canadian Journal of Philosophy* 24 (1994), 19-32.

___. "Spinoza's Infinite Extension," *History of European Ideas*, 1995.

Richter, Gustav T. *Spinozas philosophische Terminologie*. Leipzig: Barth, 1913.

Rivaud, Albert. "Documents inédits sur la vie de Spinoza," *Revue de Métaphysique et de Morale* 41 (1934), 253-262.

Roth, Cecil. *Histoire des Marranes*. Paris: Presses Universitaires de France, 1990.

Rothaan, Angelica. "Pontiaan van Hattem: critique ou hérétique," *Cahiers Spinoza* 6 (1991), 213-228.

Sanchez-Estop, Juan D. "Des présages à l'entendement; Notes sur les présages, l'imagination et l'amour dans la lettre à P. Balling," *Studia Spinozana* 4 (1988), 57-74.

Sandius, Christophorus. *Bibliotheca Antitrinitariorum*. Freistadii [Amsterdam]: Apud Johannem Aconium, 1684. Reprinted, Warsaw: Panstwowe Wydawnictswo Naukowe, 1967.

Schmidt-Biggeman, W. "Spinoza, Spinozismus, Geschichtlichkeit. Ein Nach-Wort," in *Spinozas Ethik und ihre frühe Wirkung*, ed. K. Cramer, W. G. Jacobs, and W. Schmidt-Biggemann (Wolfenbuttel: Herzog August Bibliothek, 1981), 117-129.

___. "Spinoza dans le cartésianisme," *L'Ecriture sainte au temps de Spinoza et dans le système spinoziste*, ed. Groupe de Recherches Spinozistes (Paris: Presses de l'Université de Paris-Sorbonne, 1992), 71-90.

Schoffer, I. "The Jews in the Netherlands: The Position of a Minority after Three Centuries," *Studia Rosenthaliana* 15 (1981), 85-100.

Scholem, Gershom. *Sabbatai Sevi: The Mystical Messiah*. Princeton: Princeton University Press, 1973.

___. "Marranisme et sabbatianisme," *Cahiers Spinoza* 3 (1980), 143-146.

Schroder, Winfried. "Das *Symbolum Sapientiae/Cymbalum Mundi* und der *Tractatus Theologico-politicus*," *Studia Spinozana* 7 (1991), 227-239.

Scribano, Maria E. *Da Descartes a Spinoza, percorsi della teologia razionale nel Seicento*. Milan: Franco Angeli, 1988.

Shimizu, Reiko. "Excommunication and the Philosophy of Spinoza," *Inquiry* 23 (1980), 327-348.

Siebrand, H. J. *Spinoza and the Netherlanders*. Assen: Van Gorcum, 1988.

Socinus, Faustus. *De Jesu Christo Servatore*. Rakow, Poland: Typis Alexii Rodecii, 1594.

Sokolow, Nahum. "Der Jude Spinoza," *Spinoza: Dreihundert Jahre Ewigheit*, ed. Siegfried Hessing, 2nd ed. (The Hague: Martinus Nijhoff, 1962), 182-192.

Steenbakkers, P. *Opera minora van Spinoza. Een bespreking an aantekeningen*. Amsterdam: Richard Tummers Boekverkoper, 1988.

___. "La nouvelle édition critique du texte latin de l'*Ethique*," *Travaux et documents 2: Méthode et métaphysique*, ed. Groupe de recherches spinozistes (Paris: Presses Universitaires de France, 1989), 105-120.

___. "Le texte de la cinquième partie de l'*Ethique*," *Revue Philosophique de la France et de l'Etranger* 1994#1, 81-96.

___. *Spinoza's Ethica from manuscript to print: Studies on text, form, and related topics*. Assen: Van Gorcum, 1994.

Strauss, Leo. *Die Religionskritik Spinozas als Grundlage seiner Bibelwissenschaft: Untersuchungen zu Spinozas Theologisch-Politischen Traktat*. Berlin: Akademie-Verlag, 1930.

___. "How to Study Spinoza's *Theologico-Political Treatise*," *Persecution and the Art of Writing*, ed. J. Wilson (Glencoe: Free Press, 1952), 142-201.

Thijssen-Schoute, C. L. *Lodewijk Meyer en diens verhouding tot Descartes en Spinoza*. Leiden: E. J. Brill, 1954.

Tosel, André. *Spinoza ou le crépuscule de la servitude: essai sur le Traité théologico-politique*. Paris: Aubier, 1984.

___. *Du matérialisme de Spinoza*. Paris: Editions Kimé, 1994.

Totaro, Giuseppina. "Perfectio e realitas nell'opera di Spinoza," *Lexicon Philosophicum* 3 (1988), 71-113.

___. "Un manoscritto inedito delle 'Adnotationes' al *Tractatus Theologico-Politicus* di Spinoza," *Studia Spinozana* 5 (1989), 205-224.

___. "Un document inédit sur Spinoza," *Bulletin de l'Association des Amis de Spinoza* 29 (1993), 27.

___, and M. Veneziani. "Indice e Concordanze del *Tractatus theologico-politicus* di Spinoza," *Lexicon Philosophicum* 6 (1993), 51-193.

Trompeter, Lydia. "Spinoza: A Response to de Vries," *Canadian Journal of Philosophy* 11 (1981), 525-538.

Tschirnhaus, Ehrenfried. *Médecine de l'Esprit ou principes généraux de l'art de découvrir*, introduction, translation, notes, and appendices by Jean-Paul Wurtz. Strasbourg: Université de Strasbourg, 1980.

Valk, Th. de. "Spinoza en Vondel," *De Beiaard* 6 (1921), 440-458.

Van Bunge, Wiep. "Johannes Bredenburg and the *Korte Verhandeling*," *Studia Spinozana* 4 (1988), 321-328.

___. *Johannes Bredenburg (1643-1691). Een Rooterdamse Collegiant in de ban van Spinoza.* Rotterdam: Universiteits Erasmus Drukkerij, 1990.

___. "Les premiers pas de Bredenburg vers le spinozisme," *Cahiers Spinoza* 6 (1991), 229-246.

___. "L'Athéisme de Spinoza," *Bulletin de l'Association des Amis de Spinoza* 29 (1993), 1-23.

Van den Berg, J. *Jewish-Christian Relations in the Seventeenth Century.* Dordrecht: Reidel, 1988.

Vandenbossche, Hubert. *Spinozisme en Kritiek bij Koerbagh.* Brussels: Vrije Universiteit Brussel, Centrum voor de Studie van de Verlichting, 1974.

Van den Hoven, M. J. *Petrus van Balen en Spinoza over de verbetering van het verstand.* Leiden: E. J. Brill, 1988.

Van der Linde, Antonius. *Benedictus Spinoza: Bibliografie.* The Hague: Nijhoff, 1871. [reprint, Nieuwkoop: B. de Graaf, 1961.]

Van der Wall, Ernestine G. E. "Petrus Serrarius (1600-1669) et l'interprétation de l'Ecriture," *Cahiers Spinoza* 5 (1985), 187-218.

___. *De mystieke chileast Petrus Serrarius (1600-1669) en zijn wereld.* University of Leiden dissertation, 1987.

___. "The Amsterdam Millenarian Petrus Serrarius (1600-1669) and the Anglo-Dutch Circle of Philo-Judaists," in *Jewish-Christian Relations in the Seventeenth Century*, ed. J. van den Berg and E. G. E. van der Wall (Dordrecht: Kluwer, 1988), 73-94.

Velthuysen, Lambert van. *Opera Omnia.* Rotterdam: 1680.

Von Schmid, J. J. *Coornhert en Spinoza.* Leiden: E. J. Brill, 1957.

Walther, Manfred. "Discours sur la réalité du mal ou l'irritation d'une conscience quotidienne," *La Etica de Spinoza: Fundamentos y significado*, ed. Atilano Domínguez (Castilla-La Mancha: Ediciones de la Universidad, 1992), 213-216.

Werf, Theo van der, Siebrand, Heine, and Westerveen, Coen. *A Spinoza Bibliography 1971-1983.* Leiden: E. J. Brill, 1984.

Wesselius, Jam Wim. "Spinoza's excommunication and related matters," *Studia Rosenthaliana* 1 (1990), 43-63.

Wetlesen, J. *A Spinoza Bibliography: Particularly on the Period 1940-1967.* Oslo: Universitetsforlaget, 1968. [2nd edition arranged as a supplement to Oko's Spinoza bibliography.]

Wilson, Margaret D. "Notes on Modes and Attributes," *Journal of Philosophy* 78 (1981), 584-586.

Winter, E. *E. W. von Tschirnhaus (1651-1708). Ein Leben im Dienste Akademiegedankens.* Berlin: Walther de Gruyter, 1959.

Wolfson, Harry A. "Spinoza's Definition of Substance and Mode," *Chronicon Spinozanum* 1 (1921), 101-112.

___. "Spinoza on the Unity of Substance," *Chronicon Spinozanum* 2 (1922), 92-117.

___. "Spinoza on the Simplicity of Substance," *Chronicon Spinozanum* 3 (1923), 142-178.

___. "Spinoza on the Infinity of Corporeal Substance," *Chronicon Spinozanum* 4 (1924-25), 79-103.

___. *Crescas' Critique of Aristotle*. Cambridge, Mass.: Harvard University Press, 1929.

___. *Spinoza and Religion*. New York: New School for Social Research, 1950.

___. *The Philosophy of Spinoza*. 2 vols. New York: Meridian, 1958. [Reprinted, New York: Schocken, 1969.]

___. "Maimonides on Modes and Universals," *Studies in Rationalism, Judaism and Universalism*, ed. R. Loewe (London: Routledge and Kegan Paul, 1967), 311-322.

___. "Behind the Geometrical Method," *Spinoza*, ed. Marjorie Grene (Garden City: Doubleday, 1973), 3-24.

Wollgast, Siegfried. *Ehrenfried Walter von Tschirnhaus und die deutsche Frühaufklärung*. Berlin: Akademie-Verlag, 1988.

Yakira, E. "Boyle et Spinoza," *Archives de Philosophie* 51 (1988), 107-124.

Yovel, Yirmiyahu. "Marranisme et dissidence: Spinoza et quelques prédécesseurs," *Cahiers Spinoza* 3 (1980), 67-100.

___. *Marrano Patterns in Spinoza*. Jerusalem: Jerusalem Spinoza Institute, 1983.

___. *Spinoza and Other Heretics*. 2 vols. Princeton: Princeton University Press, 1989.

___. *Spinoza et d'autres hérétiques*, tr. E. Beaumatin and J. Lagrée. Paris: Seuil, 1991.

Zac, Sylvain. *Spinoza et l'interprétation de l'Ecriture*. Paris: Presses Universitaires de France, 1965.

___. "Spinoza et l'état des Hébreux," *Speculum Spinozanum: 1677-1977*, ed. S. Hessing (London: Routledge and Kegan Paul, 1977), 543-571.

Zevi, Sabbatai. *The Restauration of the Jewes*. London: R.R., 1665.

___. *God's Love for His People Israel*. London: Printed by A. Maxwell, 1666.

___. *Several New Letters Concerning the Jevves*. London: Printed by A. Maxwel, 1666.

Zweerman, Theo. *L'introduction à la philosophie selon Spinoza: Une analyse structurelle de l'Introduction du Traité de la Réforme de l'Entendement suivie d'un commentaire de ce texte.* Assen: Van Gorcum, 1993.

Index of Persons

Index of Topics